Fabulous to Futile
in Flushing

About the Author

David Russell is an associate editor with the *Queens Chronicle* and also writes for *NY Sports Day*. He is a graduate of St. John's University and a lifelong fan of the Mets.

David covered the 2015 World Series for the *Queens Tribune*. He attended his first Mets game in 1997. The most memorable game he ever went to was the Mets beating the Cardinals 8-7 on August 22, 1999. Mark McGwire hit two homers, but the Mets rallied with a John Olerud grand slam and Mike Piazza solo shot. Edgardo Alfonzo delivered the game-winning single.

Fabulous to Futile in Flushing

A Year-by-Year History of the Mets

By David Russell

SUMMER
GAME
BOOKS

Dedication

For my parents and all the men who put on the Mets uniform.

Acknowledgments and Sources

This book wouldn't have happened without Walt Friedman and Summer Game Books, who contributed to the sidebars and other features of the book and took all of the information and helped organize it into an easy-to-read format. Thanks also to Jason D. Antos for providing some classic photographs.

Numeous resources were used to compile details of the Mets history. Baseball-Reference.com was the source of much of the statistical information, and each season's narrative was sourced from the online archives of the *New York Post, New York Daily News, The New York Times, Sports Illustrated*, ESPN, UPI, and other publications.

Table of Contents

About the Quizzes   ix

Mets All-Time Trivia   1

1960s Trivia   5
Mets History, 1962–1969   7

1970s Trivia   49
Mets History, 1970–1979   51

1980s Trivia   97
Mets History, 1980–1989   99

1990s Trivia   151
Mets History, 1990–1999   153

2000s Trivia   208
Mets History, 2000–2009   210

2010s Trivia   275
Mets History, 2010–2019   277

Mets Quiz Answers   339

About the Quizzes

Fabulous to Futile in Flushing contains 7 challenging trivia quizzes. Six of these focus on each decade of the Mets' existence—1960s, 1970s, 1980s, 1990s, 2000s, 2010s. These precede the section for each decade. Answers to these questions come from a player or event in the associated decade.

There is also a quiz covering more general Mets topics, the answers to which could come from any time period of their history. That quiz appears immediately after this introduction. Answers to all the quizzes appear at the back of the book, and often provide additional information about the subjects of the questions.

Each quiz has between 15 and 19 questions; there are 115 questions in all. If you're interested in testing your Mets baseball knowledge in earnest, you should take each decade's quiz BEFORE you read the section, because the answers to some of the questions will be revealed in the text.

And although the questions are challenging, they all come from general information about the Mets—their players, managers, important games—so it would not be difficult to search up the answers on the Internet or in some other reference if you were so inclined. If that is the case, you might as well just flip to the back of the book and consider it additional, often very interesting, information.

But for those of you who want to measure your knowledge about the Mets, and/or enjoy trivia quizzes, each question has been given a points value between 6 and 12. Most are worth 8 or 10. Points values are mentioned at the end of each question and the total possible points for each quiz is also listed.

The total possible points for all the quizzes is 1000 points. Bonus points totaling 80 can also be earned for a few "extra credit" and particularly challenging questions. So in actuality, the highest total possible points is 1080, but 1000 is still considered a perfect score.

The fact is anything even in the neighborhood of 1000 would be quite extraordinary. Here's a scale to measure your performance.

900-1000 – There's a place for you in the Mets organization—or there should be.

800-899 – Expert. You bleed Mets orange and blue.

750-799 – Excellent. Your devotion is clear.

700-749 – Very fine. You'd be tough to beat in a bar bet.

650-699 – Traveling in rarefied air; you know your stuff.

600-649 – Damn good. A solid member of the Mets fandom family.

500-599 – Take a bow. Job well done.

400-499 – Pretty good. You're part of Mets Nation.

300-399 – Probably a more casual fan, or one who doesn't get caught up in a lot of details.

200-299 – Consider the quizzes a learning experience.

000-199 – Thanks for playing. Parting gifts are not included.

Quiz #1: Mets All-Time Trivia

1. Which Mets batter holds the all-time team record for both outs made and grounded into double plays? **[8 points]**

2. Who holds the Mets record for grand slams for a batter? **[8 points]**

3. Who holds Mets single-season record for batting average among hitters who qualified for the batting title? **[8 points]**

4. Name the four men to have managed both the Mets and the Yankees. **[3 points each]**

5. Who is the only player to collect his 500th home run while playing for the Mets? **[8 points]**

6. True or false: No Mets pitcher ever pitched 300 or more innings in a season? **[6 points]**

7. Who holds the Mets all-time record for games played at catcher? **[8 points]**

8. Name the only Mets pitcher to hurl a 1-hitter in a postseason game. **[8 bonus points]**

9. Which Mets pitcher threw back-to-back one-hitters? **[10 points]**

10. Who was the first Mets player to homer in an All-Star game? **[12 points]**

11. Who was the first Mets manager to lead the team to consecutive postseason appearances? **[8 points]**

12. Name the top 4 career home run hitters for the Mets (including only home runs hit for the Mets). **[2 points each; 4 bonus points for ranking them correctly]**

13. Who is the only Mets player to drive in more than 100 runs 3 straight seasons? **[10 points]**

14. Who holds the Mets single-season record for strikeouts for a pitcher? **[10 points]**

15. Which Mets player drove in at least one run in 15 consecutive games? **[8 points]**

16. Who holds the Mets single-season record for wins by a reliever? **[10 points]**

17. Who is the only pitcher to win 20 games for both the Mets and Yankees? **[8 points]**

18. Including Wild Card games, in how many of the Mets' 58 seasons have they made the postseason, and among those, how many times have they reached the World Series? **[10 points for post-season, 2 bonus points for correct number of World Series]**

QUIZ 1: TOTAL POINTS – 152; BONUS POINTS – 14

Fabulous to Futile in Flushing

Quiz #2: 1960s

1. (1962) Who hit the first regular season home run in Mets history? **[10 points]**

2. Who was the first Mets player to hit 3 HR in a game? **[12 points]**

3. How old was Ed Kranepool when he had his first major league at bat? **[8 points]**

4. What particular skill did Casey Stengel attribute to catcher Choo Choo Coleman? **[8 bonus points]**

5. (1962) Name the player who eventually had a long career as coach and manager who went 4-for-52 for the 1962 Mets before being traded. **[10 points]**

6. (1963) Ron Hunt hit a solid .272 in 1963 and finished second in the NL Rookie of the Year voting. Who won the award? **[8 points]**

7. (1963) Name the pitcher who hurled 4 of the Mets' 5 shutouts in 1963. **[12 points]**

8. (1960s) Name the slick-fielding shortstop who spent 13 years with two other NL teams before being traded to the Mets and manned that position for the last 3 seasons of his career. He played in nearly 2100 games in his career. **[10 points]**

9. (1960s) Jack Fisher lost a total of 74 games in his 4 seasons with the Mets (1964-1967), twice leading the league in that category. But Fisher is perhaps most famous for allowing two historically significant home runs (both before his time with the Mets). What are they? **[6 points for each]**

10. (1960s) Name the first Mets player to start in an All-Star game. **[10 points]**

11. (1960s) Greg Goossen, about whom Casey Stengel said "He's 20 and in 10 years he has a chance to be 30," had a second career after baseball that could be considered more glamorous than being a major leaguer. What was it? **[8 bonus points]**

12. (1966) When the Mets finally escaped last place and finished 9th in 1966, what team did they beat out? **[6 points]**

13. (1960s) What team signed Tom Seaver illegally and had the contract with him voided, making Seaver eligible again? **[8 points]**

14. (1968) As a 24-year-old rookie, this righter went only 4-7 in 12 starts, but had a very impressive ERA of 2.28. He went on to pitch 5 more seasons for New York, twice achieving double-figures in wins. **[12 points]**

15. (1969) The Mets were 6-6 against Cincinnati in 1969 and had a winning record against every other team in the league (including 11-1 vs San Diego) except one. Name that team and the Mets' record against them. **[8 points]**

16. Who was the only person in uniform for the Mets in both 1969 and 1986? **[8 points]**

QUIZ 2: TOTAL POINTS – 134; BONUS POINTS – 16

1962

OPENING DAY LINEUP

Richie Ashburn, CF
Felix Mantilla, SS
Charlie Neal, 2B
Frank Thomas, LF
Gus Bell, RF
Gil Hodges, 1B
Don Zimmer, 3B
Hobie Landrith, C
Roger Craig, P

	W	L	GB	Pos
	40	120	60.5	10th
RS/G	RA/G	Manager		
3.86	5.93	Casey Stengel		

Brand-New Mets Amaze and Amuse

The Moves

The Brooklyn Dodgers and New York Giants left for California after the 1957 season, leaving the city devoid of National League baseball. Mayor Robert Wagner set up a committee to find a replacement team. One man on the committee was lawyer William A. Shea.

Shea's friend George McLaughlin was head of the Brooklyn Trust Company, the Dodgers' old bank. McLaughlin put Shea in touch with Branch Rickey, the former general manager and part-owner of the Dodgers, who had helped break the color barrier and oversaw an NL dynasty.

They worked on creating the Continental League, which would field teams in eight cities. And Major League Baseball would be investigated for antitrust issues if the league was rejected. An agreement was made for the Continental League to disband with the National and American leagues adding two teams apiece. There would be National League baseball in New York.

The club was owned by Joan Whitney Payson, Dorothy Killian and Dwight Davis Jr. Payson would buy out the other two and make M. Donald Grant her main decision maker. When the Giants voted to move out West, one vote against the move was made by Grant, representing Payson.

Members of the press voted on the team name, with the choices narrowed down from a list of hundreds of the public's suggestions. Mets edged out Skyliners, though Payson's preference was Meadowlarks.

🄫 He Was a Met?

Gene Woodling was a solid hitter for the Yankees and then several other AL teams. Casey Stengel was glad to draft him in the Expansion Draft, and Woodling performed well as a backup outfielder, putting up a slash line of .274/.353/.405, and then retiring after the season.

Charles Hurth, a minor league executive and Rickey's son-in-law, had been named general manager but Grant believed the job needed major league experience. Enter George Weiss, who had been GM of the Yankees from 1947 through 1960 and had been head of the team's player development system before that. Then he hired Casey Stengel to manage the Mets. Stengel had won 10 pennants and seven World Series titles in 12 seasons with the Yankees before being forced into retirement, along with Weiss, after losing the 1960 World Series to the Pittsburgh Pirates. "It's a great honor for me to be joining the Knickerbockers," Stengel said.

On October 10, 1961, the expansion draft was held for the Mets and Houston Colt .45s. "I figured the lists of players would be bad, but they're worse than I thought they would be," Houston GM Paul Richards said.

San Francisco catcher Hobie Landrith was the first pick of the Mets. "If you don't have a catcher you're gonna have a lot of passed balls," Stengel said. Gil Hodges, the beloved Dodger, returned to New York. The Mets drafted Gus Bell, a four-time All-Star outfielder with the Reds. Former Dodger Don Zimmer, a 1961 All-Star with the Cubs, was selected. And starter Roger Craig, who helped the Dodgers win two World Series, joined the Mets. Richie Ashburn, a five-time All-Star with the Phillies, was taken from the Cubs. Charlie Neal, a Gold Glove winner and All-Star, was acquired from the Dodgers. Weiss acquired slugger Frank Thomas from the Braves for a player to be named later.

The Situation

 Final Resting Ground

Clem Labine had pitched decently in 1961 for the Pirates after a long career with the Dodgers. Stengel knew him well from all those Subway Series, but after only 3 appearances in April, Labine was released.

"I didn't know it at the time, but I knew later that if we had put that group together a few years earlier, it would have been a hell of a club," Al Jackson said in 2012. "We got them a little too late." Craig thought the team might be able to play .500 ball.

Evans Killeen, a pitcher who appeared in a few games with the Athletics in 1959, impressed Stengel during the spring but reached into his shaving bag and cut his right thumb. He never appeared in a regular season game with the Mets. It was up to Stengel to sell the team to the fans and the media, who mostly enjoyed his stories, even if they weren't always coherent.

In April, there was a parade for the team down Broadway and Shea had a message for the fans. "It still sticks in my craw," Ashburn said 30 years later. "Before we had played a single home game, Shea told the fans, 'Be patient with us until we can bring some real ballplayers in here.' And the players – we were standing right there! I mean, he was probably right, but he didn't have to say it."

The Season

The first game in Mets history was on April 11 in St. Louis. Sherman Jones was going to be the first starter but when he attempted to light a match, it flew off the cover and struck him in the eye. Sidelined, Craig would instead receive the first start. He gave up two runs in the first inning. Bell had the first hit, a second inning single off Larry Jackson. The Mets tied the game in the third but Craig quickly gave up three runs. Hodges homered in the fourth and Neal hit one in the fifth to make it 5-4 but the Cardinals pulled away for an 11-4 win. None of the Mets three relievers – Bob Moorhead, Herb Moford and Clem Labine – would last the summer.

Casey Stengel was the driving force behind the Mets going from sadly inept to lovable losers. He happily took the spotlight from his struggling players and his legend was further cemented. In 1964, the last-place Mets outdrew AL champ Yankees (who were in a tight, season-long pennant race) by well over 400,000 fans. (Photo Courtesy Jason D. Antos)

Two nights later, the Mets lost their first home game at the Polo Grounds. Jones gave up two runs in five innings in the 4-3 loss to the Pirates though Thomas hit a homer in the sixth. The Mets would lose the first nine games, even dropping an 11-inning game to Houston. The Colt .45s actually won their first three games, sweeping the Cubs.

Bill Mazeroski's RBI triple beat the Mets to send New York to 0-9, with Jones losing three games. On April 24, Jay Hook took the mound against the 10-0 Pirates and pitched a complete game, giving up one run on five hits. The Mets hit Tom Sturdivant and Diomedes Olivo early, taking a 6-0 lead in the second and came away with a 9-1 win.

Three more losses followed and then the team won consecutive games for the first time, scoring eight runs two straight days against the Phillies. The Phillies avoided a sweep, hammering Jones to end the month.

Bell was sent to the Braves to complete the Thomas trade. Zimmer, who had suffered through an 0-for-34 slump, was traded to the Reds. The Mets made a

FABULOUS: RICHIE ASHBURN

Amidst the epic incompetence of the '62 Mets, Ashburn, in his final big league season, put up fine numbers. He hit .306 with an OBA of .424 in nearly 500 plate appearances, and also drilled 7 of his 29 career home runs.

deal with the Orioles for Marv Throneberry, who would become the poster child of the 1962 Mets.

The team won nine of 12 in mid-May to improve to 12-19 and eighth place. The exciting Mets won four games in their final at-bat. Then the team lost 17 in a row. The Dodgers and Giants returned to New York and swept the Mets. In the first Dodgers game at the Polo Grounds, the Mets hit Sandy Koufax for six runs and 13 hits only to lose 13-6. On June 8, the Mets beat the Cubs 4-3 with Craig Anderson retiring Ron Santo with two on and two outs in

FUTILE: CRAIG ANDERSON

Craig Anderson was a versatile pitcher in 1962, starting 14 games, finishing 20, and saving 4. But Anderson's results were spotty; he finished 3-17 with an ERA of 5.35. His overall W-L record for the Mets was 3-20.

TOP BATTERS

Pos	Name	G	AB	H	BA	HR	RBI	RS	SB	OPS
1B	Marv Throneberry	116	357	87	.244	16	49	29	1	.732
3B	Felix Mantilla	141	466	128	.275	11	59	54	3	.729
LF	Frank Thomas	156	571	152	.266	34	94	69	2	.824
OF	Richie Ashburn	135	389	119	.306	7	28	60	12	.817

TOP PITCHERS

Pos	Name	G	GS	W	L	SV	ERA	IP	SO	BB
SP	Roger Craig	42	33	10	24	3	4.51	233.1	118	70
SP	Al Jackson	36	33	8	20	0	4.40	231.1	118	78
SP	Jay Hook	37	34	8	19	0	4.84	213.2	113	71
RP	Ken MacKenzie	42	1	5	4	1	4.95	80.0	51	34

the ninth for the first win since May 20.

On June 17, Chicago's Lou Brock homered to center at the Polo Grounds. In the bottom of the first, Throneberry drove in two runs with a triple. Ernie Banks called for the ball and stepped on first as Throneberry was called out for not touching the bag. When Stengel came out to argue, first base coach Cookie Lavagetto said, "Forget it, Casey. He missed second too." With the bases empty, Neal followed with a home run. The Mets would lose by one. In the second game of the doubleheader, Throneberry made an error on the first play of the game and the Mets lost on Santo's homer in the ninth.

New York kept losing and the month ended with Koufax pitching a no-hitter. He struck out the side on nine pitches in the first and fanned 13 in the game. The Mets went 6-23 in July, falling 50 games under .500. The pitching staff gave up at least 10 runs seven times in the month. The team was eliminated in the first week of August. The Mets lost 13 straight during the month. The 100th loss of the season came in Philadelphia on August 29.

On September 20, the Mets blew a ninth inning lead to Houston and lost in 12 innings for the 115th loss, tying the 1935 Braves for the NL record. Six days later, the Mets set the record for losses in a season as a 6-3 defeat to the Braves marked No. 118. Even Bob Uecker had an RBI single for Milwaukee in the eighth.

The Mets did have one last, rare triumph. Bob Miller, the righty, not the lefty, was 0-12 on the season. No pitcher had ever gone 0-13. Miller pitched a complete game to edge the Cubs 2-1. The next day, the Mets lost 5-1 for the 120th loss. Joe Pignatano hit into a triple play in the final at-bat of his career.

In typical 1962 Mets fashion, the team fell even further in the standings after the season was over. The Giants took two of three from the Dodgers in a dramatic playoff, meaning New York finished 60.5 games out of first instead of 60.

Top 5 Highlights

1 In the 10th game, the Mets pick up their first win. Jay Hook goes the distance and drives in two runs with a second inning single. Hook gives up one run on five hits in the 9-1 win.

2 Down to the final out, Hobie Landrith hits a two-run homer in the bottom of the ninth off Warren Spahn to beat the Braves 3-2 in the first game of a May 12 doubleheader.

3 Gil Hodges homers off Hank Fischer in the bottom of the ninth of the second game to give the Mets an 8-7 win. Craig Anderson wins both games of the twinbill to improve to 3-1. He would finish 3-17.

4 Landrith draws a bases loaded walk in the bottom of the 13th to beat the Cubs 6-5 on May 13. The Mets were down 4-3 with two outs in the ninth when Gus Bell tied the game with a single. Down 5-4 with two outs in the 10th, Charlie Neal tied the game with a single.

5 Al Jackson pitches a one-hit shutout in a 2-0 win over Houston on June 22. Joey Amalfitano's single with one out in the first is the lone hit. Richie Ashburn homers off Turk Farrell to lead off the Mets' first.

1963

	W	L	GB	Pos
	51	111	48.0	10th

RS/G	RA/G	Manager	
3.09	5.93	Casey Stengel	

OPENING DAY LINEUP

Larry Burright, 2B
Choo-Choo Coleman, C
Ed Kranepool, RF
Duke Snider, CF
Frank Thomas, LF
Tim Harkness, 1B
Charlie Neal, 3B
Al Moran, SS
Roger Craig, P

Duke Joins Collection of True Bums

The Moves

New York made a few changes to the roster after losing 120 games. Ron Hunt and Carl Willey were purchased from the Braves. The Mets sent Felix Mantilla to the Red Sox for pitcher Tracy Stallard, and infielders Pumpsie Green and Al Moran. Stallard had given up Roger Maris' record breaking 61st home run of the 1961 season.

And the Mets added some Dodgers. They purchased catcher Norm Sherry and prospect infielder-outfielder Dick Smith. On December 1, the Mets traded right-handed Bob Miller to the Dodgers for first baseman Tim Harkness and middle infielder Larry Burright. Then on April 1, the Mets purchased New York icon Duke Snider for $40,000.

The 36-year-old "Duke of Flatbush" was going from a Dodger team that was three outs away from winning the 1962 pennant to a team that would lose over 100 games. But he had advice for Burright. "Duke said, 'don't let it get you down. You just stay with me because I played in Brooklyn and I'll take you everywhere', which he did," Burright said in an interview for the book. "He was a good old boy, Duke Snider. He was one of my buddies."

Burright had been the Los Angeles second baseman in the first game when the Dodgers came back to New York to play the Mets in 1062. And he had a good attitude going into 1963. "You go to spring training and try to have a good spring training and say when our season starts give it hell and do the best you can," Burright said. "A lot of clubs had a little more talent-wise than we had but we had some good players."

Unfortunately, most of the good players had seen better days. The Mets home had also seen better days and 1963 was the last season at the Polo Grounds before the team moved to Shea Stadium. "I didn't mind playing in the Polo Grounds," Burright said. "The playing field I liked. It was a good playing field except they had the short porch in right, but left-handed hitters liked that."

The Situation

As *Sports Illustrated* described it, "While other teams were trading good ballplayers with abandon, Weiss dealt only in fringe players. This was a policy reminiscent of the days when he was with the Yankees, where he always held four to a flush. But with the Mets, where it is a question of drawing to an inside straight, Weiss's standpat attitude is confusing."

The burden would be on a trio of pitchers: "No 'big three' is as valuable to any team as Roger Craig, Al Jackson and Jay Hook are to the Mets. Last year they accounted for 26 of the 40 Met victories – 65% of them, a figure no three pitchers on any other team could manage."

SI proclaimed the day before the season began, "There is a more youthful look to the Mets, but youth is not enough. George Weiss seems incapable of preventing New York from being the worst team in the major leagues again."

Marv Throneberry didn't join the Mets until May of 1962 in a trade with Baltimore. Marvelous Marv belted 16 home runs, including several walk-off winners. But his horrendous fielding and comical baserunning made him the poster boy for the struggling Mets. The following year, Throneberry was 2-for-14 on when he was sent to the minors and he never made it back the bigs. (Photo Courtesy Jason D. Antos)

Burright roomed with another first-year Met. "I roomed with Tracy Stallard. We stayed at the Loews Midtown Motor Inn which was like a block and a half away where the old Madison Square Garden and train station were," Burright said. "We just walked a block and a half and got on the subways and went to the ballpark. I didn't travel around because, to me, being in New York, I figured you could get lost on the subway real easy."

The Season

The Mets began the season 0-8 with four shutout losses. Frank Thomas was hitting .105 and infielder-outfielder Cliff Cook was hitting .118. At least Snider

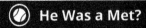

He Was a Met?

Brooklyn legend Duke Snider, who belted 40 or more home runs 5 years in a row, played decently in his one season with the Mets, though his bad knees made fielding and baserunning a challenge. Snider achieved career milestones of 400 HR and 2000 hits while on the Mets

picked up his 2,000th career hit, a single off Cincinnati's Jim Maloney. Snider did look odd wearing number 11 as Charlie Neal didn't give up 4.

Another 0-9 start looked likely but Ron Hunt's two-run double in the bottom of the ninth off Milwaukee's Claude Raymond gave the Mets a 5-4 win. New York would actually sweep Milwaukee four straight. Jim Hickman and Ron Hunt were off to good starts but they were the only ones.

 Final Resting Ground

Elijah "Pumpsie" Green was most famous for breaking the Boston Red Sox color line in 1959. In 1963, Green appeared in 17 games at 3B for the the Amazins, batting .278 with an OBA of .409, but a bad back prevented him from continuing to play in the majors. Green's brother Cornell was a 5-time All Pro cornerback for the Dallas Cowboys in the 1960s and 70s.

Craig won his last two starts in April. He wouldn't win another until August. The Mets did have some fun. There was a five-game winning streak in May, including a sweep of the Phillies, with the Mets as high as sixth place. Ed Kranepool's RBI double off Philadelphia's Jack Baldschun in the bottom of the ninth gave New York a win on May 8. The next day, pinch-runner Al Jackson scored the winning run when Johnny Klippstein uncorked a wild pitch to finish off a three-run ninth. And there was a wild 13-12 win over the Reds at the Polo Grounds. The Mets scored 100 runs in May, the only month they did so.

Gil Hodges was sent to Washington to become the manager of the Senators but he would return several years later. Jimmy Piersall, who had been portrayed by Anthony Perkins in "Fear Strikes Out" joined the Mets. He would be released after hitting .194 in 40 games though he did hit his 100th career homer and celebrated by facing backwards as he ran around the bases.

A seven-game losing streak in May included a four-game sweep at the hands of the Dodgers. A frustrating doubleheader saw Sandy Koufax beat Craig 1-0 and then Frank Howard hit a two-run homer off Ken MacKenzie in the bottom of the 13th to beat the Mets 4-2.

As they did in May, the Mets won 11 games in June. Hickman's homer in the bottom of the 10th on June 2 off Roy Face gave the Mets a doubleheader sweep over the Pirates. Snider hit his 400th career homer on June 14 off Reds pitcher Bob Purkey in a 10-3 win. The Mets won again the next day but then lost their next 22 road games.

From late June though late July the team lost 27 of 30. One of the rare wins came when Joe Hicks hit a two-run homer off San Francisco's Don Larsen. At least the Mets had a flair for the dramatic. No one was more tortured than Craig, who dropped to 2-20 after 18 consecutive losses.

FUTILE: NORM SHERRY

Norm Sherry put up a slash line of .136/.205/.184 serving as backup catcher to Choo Choo Coleman. Luckily for Sherry, OPS+ hadn't been invented yet because his was 13, meaning his offensive production was 87% below average.

In a July start, he switched from number 38 to 36 to change his luck. He lost and went back to 38. A 2-1 loss to the Braves on August 4 tied him for the NL record with Boston's Cliff Curtis, who had done it in 1910. Philadelphia A's hurler Jack Nabors had lost 19 in a row in 1916, the MLB record. On August 9, Craig switched to number 13 and picked up a win when Hickman hit a grand slam in the bottom of the ninth. Craig then won two more decisions in a row.

Ed Kranepool spent nearly two months in the minors after being demoted in early July with a .190 average. There was a mini-controversy when he took batting practice with Stengel advising him to hit to the opposite field but Snider asked Kranepool why he was doing that. "Duke, mind your own business. You're not doing too good yourself," Kranepool said. He later explained that he was following the manager's orders but some of the writers had heard his comment to the beloved Snider and wrote about it.

At least Snider got his number 4 after Neal was traded with Sammy Taylor to the Reds for catcher Jesse Gonder at the beginning of July. Gonder would hit .302 in 42 games.

The Mets went 9-19 in both August and September. Willey's six-hit shutout over the Cubs on August 24 gave the team its 41st win of the season, passing the 1962 total. And Cleon Jones made his MLB debut on September 14, playing in six games late in the season.

> ## FABULOUS: CARL WILLEY
>
> *Willey was a solid starter for the '63 Mets, posting a record of 9-14, with an ERA of 3.10. In 183 IP he allowed only 149 hits. Willey saw limited action for the Mets the next two years and won only one game.*

The Mets staggered to the finish line, losing 14 of the final 16 games and finishing with 111 losses. On September 18, the Phillies won the final MLB

TOP BATTERS

Pos	Name	G	AB	H	BA	HR	RBI	RS	SB	OPS
2B	Ron Hunt	143	533	145	.272	10	42	64	5	.730
LF	Frank Thomas	126	420	109	.260	15	60	34	0	.709
CF	Jim Hickman	146	494	113	.229	17	51	53	0	.690
RF	Duke Snider	129	354	86	.243	14	45	44	0	.746

TOP PITCHERS

Pos	Name	G	GS	W	L	SV	ERA	IP	SO	BB
SP	Roger Craig	46	31	5	22	2	3.78	236.0	108	58
SP	Al Jackson	37	34	13	17	1	3.96	227.0	142	84
SP	Carlton Willey	30	28	9	14	0	3.10	183.0	101	69
RP	Larry Bearnarth	58	2	3	8	4	3.42	126.1	48	47

game at the Polo Grounds 5-1. Only 1,752 fans came to see Chris Short go the distance against the Mets.

Top 5 Highlights

1 Ron Hunt's two-run double off Milwaukee's Claude Raymond give the Mets a 5-4 win on April 19. Choo-Choo Coleman singled and Jim Hickman doubled off Frank Funk earlier in the inning. The Braves took a 4-3 lead in the top of the ninth when Eddie Mathews walked with the bases loaded.

2 Duke Snider's three-run homer off Diomedes Olivo in the bottom of the ninth gives the Mets a 3-2 win over the Cardinals on June 7. St. Louis starter Ron Taylor took a two-hit shutout into the ninth. With one out, Frank Thomas singled and Ron Hunt drew a walk. The lefty Olivo came in to pitch to Snider. A passed ball moved the runners up before Snider's liner ended the game.

3 Down to their final out, Tim Harkness' 14th inning grand slam gives the Mets an 8-6 win over the Cubs on June 26. Billy Williams hit an inside-the-park home run in the top of the inning to give Chicago a 6-4 lead. But Harkness' shot off Jim Brewer gave the Mets the win.

4 Carl Willey becomes the first Mets pitcher to hit a grand slam off Houston's Ken Johnson in a 14-5 win on July 15. Willey's shot gives the Mets a 5-2 in the second inning. The win snapped a 15-game losing streak and was the first win since Harkness' grand slam beat the Cubs.

5 Jim Hickman's grand slam off Chicago's Lindy McDaniel gives the Mets a 7-3 win over the Cubs on August 9 and snaps Roger Craig's 18-game losing streak. Al Moran's double off Paul Toth put runners on second and third with two outs. McDaniel intentionally walked Tim Harkness, who was pinch-hitting for Craig. Hickman then won the game with a shot to left.

1964

OPENING DAY LINEUP

Dick Smith, 1B
Amado Samuel, 2B
Ron Hunt, 3B
Frank Thomas, LF
Jim Hickman, CF
Hawk Taylor, C
Joe Christopher, RF
Al Moran, SS
Al Jackson, P

	W	L	GB	Pos
	53	109	40.0	10th
RS/G	RA/G		Manager	
3.51	4.79		Casey Stengel	

Shea Hello to Queens!

The Moves

The biggest move for the Mets was the one they made to Queens and state-of-the-art Shea Stadium. "Anybody can come out and see us, women, men and children, because we got 50 bathrooms all over the place," Casey Stengel said. As the giant scoreboard flashed: "Isn't this the most beautiful stadium in the world."

There was still the issue of improving the team that would actually play at Shea Stadium. The team picked up pitcher Jack Fisher in a special draft for New York and Houston, the league's way of apologizing for the poor rosters they had been given two years earlier. Workhorse Roger Craig was traded to the Cardinals for former All-Star outfielder George Altman and pitcher Bill Wakefield. Craig would help St. Louis win the World Series. Neither Altman nor Wakefield would be a Met in 1965.

Duke Snider was sold to the Giants as the legend wanted to return to the West coast.

The Situation

Low expectations again. "If some of the young hard-throwing Met pitchers come through and if the hitters score more runs than the butter-fingered fielders allow, the Mets have a fighting chance for ninth. Or, as Stengel would say, 29th." (SI 4/13/64)

Carl Willey was lost for the first two months of the season when a liner from Detroit's Gates Brown broke his jaw.

⚾ He Was a Met?

George Altman's career took him from the Negro Leagues, to the Cubs (where he made 2 All Star teams), to Japan, where he hit more than 200 career homers. Altman also played one season for the Mets, but he struggled, batting only .230 with 9 home runs in over 400 at bats.

The Season

The Mets were improving. In 1962, they lost their first nine games. In 1963, the first eight. This year, the Mets won their fifth game, with Al Jackson tossing a shutout to beat the Pirates.

After two losses in Philadelphia, the Mets played their first game at Shea on April 17. Willie Stargell hit the stadium's first homer, a second inning shot off Fisher. New York led 3-1 but the Pirates rallied and Bill Mazeroski's ninth inning single off Ed Bauta gave Pittsburgh a 4-3 win.

The Mets called Shea Stadium home for 45 seasons. But while it made a splash in the National League when it opened in 1964, but it was in sorry shape by the time it closed. (Photo Courtesy Jason D. Antos)

The team traded for White Sox third baseman Charley Smith. The ongoing search for an answer at the hot corner continued, as the team would use 10 players at third during the season. Hunt had opened the season at third with new shortstop Amado Samuel going to second and Al Moran at short.

Through almost two weeks the Mets were in ninth place. Then they dropped to 10th and stayed there. A loss on May 4 in Milwaukee ended with Hunt crashing into catcher Ed Bailey in a 2-1 loss. A brawl ensued with Braves shortstop Denis Menke throwing Stengel off of him. One week into May the team was 3-16. There would be the occasional win. A Joe Christopher game-winning single in the bottom of the ninth to beat the Cardinals. A 12-4 win over the Braves at Shea with the Mets pounding Warren Spahn. And a

FABULOUS: JOE CHRISTOPHER

Christopher had a career year in 1964, batting an even .300 and belting 16 home runs. He led the team in RS with 78 and RBI with 76, as well as hits and total bases.

FUTILE: WAYNE GRAHAM

Wayne Graham got into 20 games for the 1964 Mets, but managed only 3 hits in 33 at bats. Coupled with his 4-for-22 the year before for the Phillies, Graham completed his major league career with a lifetime BA of .127 and zero RBI.

19-run outburst at Wrigley Field in a laugher over the Cubs.

The Mets traded struggling Jay Hook to the Braves for veteran shortstop Roy McMillan. The team added veteran pitcher Tom Sturdivant, though he would be gone by the end of June. New York also purchased pitcher Frank Lary from the Tigers.

On the final day of the month, the Mets dropped a doubleheader to the Giants. The second game lasted 23 innings and took seven hours and 23 minutes. The Mets turned a triple play, Willie Mays played shortstop, and Gaylord Perry pitched 10 innings of shutout relief. And the Mets lost when Galen Cisco, in his ninth inning of relief, gave up two runs in the 23rd inning.

Three weeks later, on Father's Day, Philadelphia's Jim Bunning pitched a perfect game against the Mets, fanning John Stephenson to end it. The Mets also lost game two of the doubleheader, exploding for two runs on three hits. Hunt was batting .322 and Joe Christopher was at .289 but many other players were struggling.

Shea Stadium did host the All-Star Game, which saw Ron Hunt become the first Met to start in the Midsummer Classic. The NL pulled out a 7-4 win in the ninth with Philadelphia's Johnny Callison hitting a three-run homer off Boston's Dick Radatz. Callison was actually wearing Hunt's helmet when he hit the homer.

Third base was still a work in progress for the Mets. Smith would commit 31 errors while seeing time at third, short and left. In late July, the team traded first baseman Tim Harkness and his .282 average to the Reds for infielder Bobby Klaus. Harkness had been injured for two months and Ed Kranepool was now planted at first base. Harkness took aim at Casey Stengel, who was suddenly coming under fire during a third losing season. "Casey has been a great man for baseball as far as publicity is concerned, but the game has passed him by," Harkness said. "Some players he likes and some he doesn't like. The players feel it and it isn't too inspiring when the manager goes to sleep on the bench during a game."

Jackie Robinson said Stengel was "too critical of his players and falls asleep on the bench." Though most media members liked Stengel, Howard Cosell often criticized the 73-year-old.

The Giants came to town in early August with the Mets 40 games under .500. The Associated Press reported that Stengel would be done as manager after the season. "They feel the club after three years of existence, all in the National League basement, has reached a stage in its young life where it must be developed on the field, as well as at the box office. And they agree, too, that a younger man is needed for the job – a man closer to the age of the Mets

TOP BATTERS										
Pos	Name	G	AB	H	BA	HR	RBI	RS	SB	OPS
2B	Ron Hunt	127	475	144	.303	6	42	59	6	.763
3B	Charley Smith	127	443	106	.239	20	58	44	2	.676
CF	Jim Hickman	139	409	105	.257	11	57	48	0	.696
RF	Joe Christopher	154	543	163	.300	16	76	78	6	.826

TOP PITCHERS										
Pos	Name	G	GS	W	L	SV	ERA	IP	SO	BB
SP	Jack Fisher	40	34	10	17	0	4.23	227.2	115	56
SP	Tracy Stallard	36	34	10	20	0	3.79	225.2	118	73
SP	Al Jackson	40	31	11	16	1	4.26	213.1	112	60
RP	Bill Wakefield	62	4	3	5	2	3.61	119.2	61	61

players."

Stengel was still in charge for the time being though the Mets kept losing. At least Bunning didn't pitch another perfect game against them. On August 9, in his first start against the Mets since his perfect game, he retired the first 14 batters before Joe Christopher's bunt single provided the first baserunner with two outs in the fifth.

The team was getting younger. Frank Thomas was traded to the Phillies in exchange for infielder Wayne Graham and pitcher Gary Kroll. Graham, who was plugged in at third, would have three hits in 20 games though he would eventually become a Hall of Fame college coach. Lary was traded to Milwaukee for minor league pitcher Dennis Ribant, who made his MLB debut the next day.

The Mets played a week of inspired baseball, winning seven of eight. Ribant picked up his first win with a four-hit shutout over the Pirates with Charley Smith hitting two homers. Jim Hickman hit a grand slam in a 4-2 win against Pittsburgh. New York was 12-12 with two games remaining in August but couldn't pull off the first non-losing month in franchise history as the team dropped two straight to the Cubs.

The team went 7-21 and took an eight-game losing streak into the final series of the season in St. Louis as the Cardinals fought for the pennant. In the first game, Jackson beat Bob Gibson 1-0. The next day, the Mets exploded for 15 runs with Tom Parsons picking up the win with 5.1 innings of relief. Heading into the final day, the Cardinals and Reds were tied for first place with the collapsing Phillies one game behind them. The Mets took a 3-2 lead in the fifth inning but Gibson returned to pitch four innings of relief and the Cardinals got to Cisco, Willard Hunter and Dennis Ribant. But the Mets had nearly thrown the playoff race into chaos, nearly causing a three-way tie.

A franchise record was set with 53 wins. There was improvement. New records were set for team batting average (.246) as well as hits and doubles. Mets pitchers threw 10 shutouts and only allowed 130 homers. Mets fielders committed 167 errors, getting under the horrific 200 mark.

While the Yankees won a fifth straight American League pennant, the Mets outdrew the Yankees, with more than 1.7 million fans coming to see the team at Shea Stadium.

Top 5 Highlights

1 Al Jackson pitches a six-hit shutout in a 6-0 win over the Pirates on April 19, the first Mets win at Shea Stadium. Rod Kanehl and Ron Hunt deliver two-run singles off Bob Veale in the bottom of the fourth.

2 The Mets pound out 19 runs on 23 hits in a 19-1 win on May 26 at Wrigley. Dick Smith becomes the first Met with five hits in a game.

3 Galen Cisco pitches a four-hit shutout and the Mets batter Joe Moeller in an 8-0 win over the Dodgers on June 5. The Dodgers had taken 35 of 39 games from the Mets coming into the Friday night game. Ed Kranepool and Charley Smith homer off Moeller.

4 Jesse Gonder's single in the bottom of the 12th gives the Mets a 6-5 win on June 9. The Cubs took a 5-4 lead in the top of the inning but the Mets rally with Amado Samuel's RBI single off Lindy McDaniel tying the game.

5 Charley Smith's single off Chicago's Don Elston in the bottom of the ninth gives the Mets a 5-4 win and a doubleheader sweep over the Cubs on August 23. Ed Kranepool's 10th inning single off Lee Gregory gave the Mets a game one win.

1965

	W	L	GB	Pos
	50	112	47.0	10th
RS/G	RA/G		Manager	
3.06	4.64		Casey Stengel	

Yogi and Warren and Another 100+ Losses

The Moves

Yogi Berra joined the Mets coaching staff with the possibility of being a pinch-hitter after the Yankees fired him as manager despite leading them to Game 7 of the World Series. Chris Cannizzaro switched to number five so Berra could wear number eight. Berra said he was "glad to be with an up-and-coming young club, like the Mets."

Then Warren Spahn was brought in as a pitcher and pitching coach. Spahn, who had 356 wins with the Braves, spoke of his goal to win 20 games and spoke of trying to eventually get to 400. "It may look as if Warren Spahn is decrepit and wants to hang on," he said. "That is what I want to destroy. I have an ego, too. I will knock myself out trying to beat out young guys to show that I can pitch on this team." He won 23 games in 1963 – the 13th time he won 20 games in his career – but was coming off a 6-13 season in 1964 in which he put up a 5.29 ERA. He also wasn't happy with being moved to the bullpen.

Spahn had said he didn't think a man could be both pitcher and pitching coach when Whitey Ford did it for Berra's Yankees the year before but clarified he could be a pitching coach as a teacher but not in terms of making all the schedules as well.

Bing Devine, who helped build the 1964 world champion Cardinals, joined the organization as assistant general manager and successor to George Weiss. Also joining him was Eddie Stanky, heading player development. In December,

🔘 He Was a Met?

Warren Spahn broke into the big leagues in 1942 with the Boston Braves and was managed by Casey Stengel. He won 356 games with the Braves despite not winning one before the age of 25. He went 4-12 with a 4.36 ERA with the Mets before the Giants acquired him. It was his final season in the majors.

the Mets sent Elio Chacon and Tracy Stallard to the Cardinals in return for Johnny Lewis and Gordie Richardson.

The Mets sent George Altman to the Cubs for Billy Cowan. In 1964, Cowan struck out 128 times, second most in the NL, and committed a league-high 11 errors in centerfield. The team also acquired Frank Lary from the Braves. Lary had developed a reputation as a "Yankee Killer" against Stengel's Yankees, having gone 13-1 against them from 1957 to 1959, including seven wins in 1958.

Spahn and Berra

Warren Spahn joined the Mets for 1965 and pitched decently, though his record was 4-12 when he was released in July. Spahn joined fellow 40+ year-old and fellow all-time great Yogi Berra as a marquis battery well past its prime. When Berra was asked if he and Spahn were the oldest pitcher-catcher combo in baseball history, he replied "We may not be the oldest, but we're the ugliest."

The Situation

Ron Swoboda and Cleon Jones both made the Opening Day roster. Young southpaw Tug McGraw also made the trip up north. Also on the roster was outfielder Danny Napoleon, who hit .351 in 1964 at Single-A Auburn. Charley Smith and Bobby Klaus looked to platoon at the never-ending question mark of third base.

"There's a new feeling around the Mets," said Larry Bearnarth. "Last year there was optimism, but it was all talk. This year we all feel it."

Sports Illustrated noted that perhaps 1965 could be the year the Mets escaped the cellar: "The Mets will go on filling Shea Stadium – especially when the battery of Spahn and Berra is announced – and if Spahn pitches back to his form the Mets may nudge the Astros out of ninth place."

The Season

The Mets played nearly .500 ball for two weeks, sitting at 6-7 after Spahn pitched a complete game in San Francisco. New York took three of four from the Giants, including an 11-inning win and a 7-6 victory with Napoleon delivering a three-run triple in the ninth.

And Berra joined the active roster though he would only play four games. His three-strikeout game on May 9 against the Braves was only the second of his career. Lindsey Nelson also made history as he broadcast the Mets' April 28 game at the Astrodome from a gondola hanging over second base.

Swoboda was off to a hot start and looked like the first great homegrown talent. After a two-homer, four RBI performance on May 8, the outfielder was hitting .320 with seven homers. Unfortunately, the team had a six-game losing streak from late April to early May and another six-game slide late in the month. And in June the team lost 20 of 23. Ed Kranepool got off to a blazing start and was batting .341 in early June but a 31-at-bat hitless streak cooled him off.

Spahn lost eight decisions in a row and the Giants picked him up on waivers for $1. Al Jackson was off to a rough start, sporting a 5.82 ERA in mid-June. Ron Hunt was lost for several months with a separated shoulder, courtesy of a collision with St. Louis' Phil Gagliano. Chuck Hiller was acquired and filled in both outfield and infield spots. Lary was traded to the White Sox for Jimmie Schaffer though his 1-3 record was more a factor of low run support.

The abysmal Mets rolled off a 10-game losing streak in mid-July. A 5-1 loss to the Phillies on July 24 dropped the team to 31-64. That night, Stengel fell and broke his hip at Toots Shor's. Wes Westrum, who became pitching coach following Spahn's departure, took over as

FUTILE: TOM PARSONS

Tom Parsons was ineffective in numerous pitching roles for the '65 Mets staff, starting 11 games and relieving in 24 others. Parsons allowed a dizzying 17 home runs in 90.2 IP on his way to finishing the season with a record of 1-10.

Final Resting Ground

Yogi Berra joined the Mets as player-coach after managing the Yankees in 1964, but took the field in only 4 games. His final appearance came on May 9th, when he caught the whole game in a home loss to Milwaukee. Berra fanned 3 times and made an error, which may have contributed to his decision to hang 'em up.

TOP BATTERS

Pos	Name	G	AB	H	BA	HR	RBI	RS	SB	OPS
1B	Ed Kranepool	153	525	133	.253	10	53	44	1	.675
3B	Charley Smith	135	499	122	.244	16	62	49	2	.666
LF	Ron Swoboda	135	399	91	.228	19	50	52	2	.714
RF	Johnny Lewis	148	477	117	.245	15	45	64	4	.715

TOP PITCHERS

Pos	Name	G	GS	W	L	SV	ERA	IP	SO	BB
SP	Jack Fisher	43	36	8	24	1	3.94	253.2	116	68
SP	Al Jackson	37	31	8	20	1	4.34	205.1	120	61
SP	Warren Spahn	20	19	4	12	0	4.36	126.0	56	35
RP	Tug McGraw	37	9	2	7	1	3.32	97.2	57	48

FABULOUS: JOHNNY LEWIS

This was a tough one, as it was a very rough year for the Mets. Lewis cranked 15 homers and scored 64 runs in his one full season in the majors. His 59 bases on balls and .331 OBA led the team.

interim manager. The team began August with 11 straight losses. The team did take seven of nine from the Cardinals, Dodgers and Giants late in the month.

Stengel announced his retirement at the start of September. His number 37 was retired on September 2. The team reached the 50-win mark on September 28, when Hunt singled off Pittsburgh's Roy Face in the bottom of the 12th to give the Mets a 1-0 win.

Top 5 Highlights

1 Spahn pitches a complete game against the Dodgers as the Mets hold on for a 3-2 win on April 20. Leading 3-0 heading into the bottom of the ninth, LA scores twice and puts runners on the corners with nobody out. Stengel opts to leave Spahn in and he works out of the jam.

2 Jim Maloney pitches 10 no-hit innings against the Mets but Johnny Lewis homers leading off the 11th and Larry Bearnarth pitches a scoreless bottom of the 11th as the Mets stun the Reds 1-0 at Crosley Field on June 14.

3 The Mets finally beat Sandy Koufax on August 26 at Shea, breaking the legendary lefty's 13-0 mark against them. New York scores three runs (two earned) in seven innings against Koufax. McGraw only gives up two runs in 7.2 innings. Joe Christopher and Ron Swoboda hit back-to-back homers in the eighth off Johnny Podres and Jack Fisher records the final four outs in the 5-2 triumph.

4 Jim Hickman becomes the first Met to homer three times in one game with all three coming off St. Louis southpaw Ray Sadecki in New York's 6-3 win on September 3.

5 Dick Selma makes his Shea Stadium debut by striking out a team-record 13 batters and pitching 10 shutout innings in New York's 1-0 win over the Braves on September 12. Charley Smith singles off Bob Sadowski in the bottom of the 10th to win it.

1966

	W	L	GB	Pos
	66	95	28.5	9th

RS/G	RA/G	Manager		
3.65	4.73	Wes Westrum		

Out of the Cellar and Into 9th Place

The Moves

The Mets acquired Jerry Grote from Houston for Tom Parsons. Grote was raw, defensive-first catcher who hit .181 in 100 games in 1964 before spending 1965 in the minors. But he would win the starting job in spring training over Greg Goosen and turn into one of the most important players for the team over the next decade.

Then New York pulled off a trade with the Cardinals for 1964 MVP Ken Boyer, stunning St. Louis fans. Boyer was an All-Star in seven seasons and a five-time Gold Glove winner. The Mets sent Al Jackson and Charley Smith to the Cardinals. Though Boyer's productivity slipped in 1965, it was still extremely unpopular with Cardinals fans.

Dick Stuart gave the Mets a power bat, when they acquired him from the Phillies for Bobby Klaus, Wayne Graham and Jimmie Schaffer. Stuart hit 220 home runs since 1958 and led the AL in RBI in 1963. But his shoddy fielding earned him the nickname "Dr. Strangeglove."

Other acquisitions included right-hander Jack Hamilton from the Tigers, outfielder Al Luplow from the Indians and outfielder Joe Christopher from the Red Sox.

The Situation

Wes Westrum remained as manager and set a goal of 70 wins in spring training. *Sports Illustrated* declared, "The Mets may be the most improved team in the

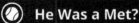

He Was a Met?

Dick Stuart had 3 seasons with more than 110 RBI, but managed only 13 with the Mets, along with 4 HR. He was popular enough that he had a pregame show, "Stump Stuart," during which fans would ask him trivia questions.

majors. Keep in mind, though, they have to improve 15 full games before they can catch even the ninth-place Astros."

The Season

After losing on Opening Day, the Mets took two in a row from the Braves and were 2-1, above .500 for the first time in team history. The team then lost five straight and wouldn't get back to .500, losing four different games in May that would've brought them even. Boyer was hitting .395 at the end of April and Cleon Jones was at .345.

A major problem in May was Tug McGraw, who was shelled in all four of his starts during the month and out for three months with elbow problems. Also scuffling was Rob Gardner, who lost six straight decisions from mid-May through the end of June. It was Gardner, Dave Eilers and Larry Bearnarth who combined to give up 17 runs in a 17-1 loss in Atlanta on June 16.

George Weiss achieved great success as director of minor leagues and then General Manager of the New York Yankees, as his Hall of Fame plaque attests. Weiss's "genius" disappeared upon joining the Mets (as did Casey Stengel's), but he did have the wisdom to hire old colleague Stengel as the team's first manager, which altered the team's, and baseball's, history for the much, much better.

Final Resting Ground

Bob Friend spent 15 seasons with the Pirates before being traded to the Yankees in the winter of 1965. Part way through 1966, the Mets purchased Friend from the Yankees, and the veteran starter picked up 5 wins and then retired. Friend collected 197 wins in his career and had a very good ERA of 3.58 in over 3600 career IP.

Temporarily forgoing the youth movement in order to escape finishing last place, the Mets acquired Don Shaw and Bob Friend. Shaw had led the AL in winning percentage in 1959 and finished third in the Cy Young voting with the pennant-winning White Sox. By 1966, he seemed done, struggling with the Giants but the veteran won his first four starts with the Mets, including three complete games.

The offense was lackluster and would finish last in runs scored and first in strikeouts. Stuart was let go after batting .218 with four home runs in 31 games. Ron Swoboda's batting average was under .200 in late July. Ron Hunt was a bright spot as the lone Met All-Star was hitting .293 at the break.

July began with the Mets losing 12-0. Hunt singled to lead off and Woody Fryman set down the next 27 Mets. But the Mets would play better, going 18-14 in July for the first winning month in team history. The team lost seven straight, getting swept in Pittsburgh and at home by the Dodgers, but then responded by winning seven straight. The Mets took five of six to end the month.

Ed Kranepool's breakout was to thank for the surge as his batting average went from .205 at the end of June to .244 to the end of July. Hamilton, who moved to the bullpen after struggling as a starter, saved seven games in July. Friend won three straight

FABULOUS: DENNIS RIBANT

Ribant went 11-9 for the '66 Mets, collecting one-sixth of the team's wins, and making him their first starter ever to finish the season with a winning record. Ribant collected 10 CG in 26 starts, had a solid ERA of 3.20, and even collected 3 saves. He was dealt that off season and won 13 more games in his career.

FUTILE: TUG MCGRAW

McGraw was ill-suited in a starter's role, going 2-9 with an ERA of 5.29. 12 of his 15 appearances were starts. The next year he was 0-3/7.79 in four starts before being moved to the bullpen and becoming one of the National League's top relievers for more than a decade.

TOP BATTERS

Pos	Name	G	AB	H	BA	HR	RBI	RS	SB	OPS
1B	Ed Kranepool	146	464	118	.254	16	57	51	1	.715
2B	Ron Hunt	132	479	138	.288	3	33	63	8	.711
3B	Ken Boyer	136	496	132	.266	14	61	62	4	.719
CF	Cleon Jones	139	495	136	.275	8	57	74	16	.689

TOP PITCHERS

Pos	Name	G	GS	W	L	SV	ERA	IP	SO	BB
SP	Jack Fisher	38	33	11	14	0	3.68	230.0	127	54
SP	Dennis Ribant	39	26	11	9	3	3.20	188.1	84	40
SP	Bob Shaw	26	25	11	10	0	3.92	167.2	104	42
CL	Jack Hamilton	57	13	6	13	13	3.93	148.2	93	88

starts, including a shutout of the Dodgers in LA. Dennis Ribant also won three straight starts late in the month.

The Mets came back to earth with an 11-21 August and an 8-17 September, then losing a pair of games in October. There were signs of optimism. The 66 wins set a new franchise record. Thanks to the 103-loss Cubs, the Mets finished in ninth place for the first time. And though they were susceptible to blowouts, going 10-33 in games decided by five or more runs, the Mets were 25-24 in one-run games.

Top 5 Highlights

1 Ron Swoboda draws a bases loaded walk in the bottom of the ninth to give the Mets a 5-4 win over the Braves on April 17 as New York is over .500 for the first time in franchise history. The next time they will be over .500 is April 10, 1969.

2 The Mets beat the Giants 11-4 on May 14 and collect 17 hits, all singles. Hunt, Jones and Stephenson deliver three hits apiece.

3 Swoboda hits a three-run homer in the ninth off Bill Henry to give the Mets an 8-6 win over the Giants on August 4. Juan Marichal retired the first 17 Mets until Dennis Ribant singled with two outs in the sixth – Westrum let him hit for himself down 3-0. Trailing 6-1 in the bottom of the eighth, Stephenson hit a two-run homer and Larry Elliott delivered an RBI single. Boyer led off the ninth with a homer to make it 6-5.

4 The Mets knock out Sandy Koufax in the third inning of a 10-4 New York win on August 30. The lefty gives up six runs (five earned) on four hits and three walks in two innings. Bob Friend pitches 7.2 innings in relief of Tug McGraw.

5 Jack Fisher pitches a shutout and Ron Hunt wins it in the bottom of the ninth for a 1-0 victory over the Astros on September 30. Houston's Larry Dierker pitches eight perfect innings until Bressoud doubles leading off the ninth. He moved to third on a wild pitch and scored on a single from Hunt, pinch-hitting for Danny Napoleon.

1967

	W	L	GB	Pos
	61	101	40.5	10th

RS/G	RA/G	Manager
3.07	4.15	Wes Westrum Salty Parker

OPENING DAY LINEUP

Don Bosch, CF
Cleon Jones, RF
Ken Boyer, 3B
Tommy Davis, LF
Ron Swoboda, 1B
Jerry Buchek, 2B
Jerry Grote, C
Bud Harrelson, SS
Don Cardwell, P

Seaver Terrific but Mets Lose 101

The Moves

George Weiss retired and former Cardinals general manager Bing Devine was brought in to replace him. He sent Ron Hunt and Jim Hickman to the Dodgers for Tommy Davis, the outfielder who had won two batting titles and once led the league in RBI.

Dennis Ribant and Gary Kolb were sent to the Pirates for right-hander Don Cardwell and centerfielder of the future Don Bosch. New York acquired Houston reliever Ron Taylor, who had helped the Cardinals win the 1964 World Series. Before the start of the season, Ed Bressoud and Danny Napoleon were sent to St. Louis for second baseman Jerry Buchek, who would be one of the better Mets hitters in 1967.

The Situation

Tom Seaver was ready for the majors. The Braves signed the USC pitcher after the collegiate season had begun in 1966, invalidating the contract. But he wasn't eligible for college play either. There would be a lottery for any teams matching Atlanta's $50,000 offer. The Mets, Phillies and Indians entered. The Mets' name was picked out of a hat. Seaver went 12-12 with a 3.13 ERA in Triple-A Jacksonville in 1966.

Also making his debut in April would be Jerry Koosman. He had been pitching on a US Army service team in Fort Bliss. His catcher was John Luchesi, whose

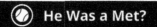

He Was a Met?

After a sparkling 1966 season at various minor league levels, the Mets hoped Joe Moock would solve their perennial problems at 3B. Moock had driven in 130 runs in 181 games (!), but for the Mets in 1967 he was a quiet 9-for-40 in 13 games and never played in the majors again.

Tom Seaver made his debut in 1967 and the days of the Mets as Lovable Losers was over. The righthander changed the attitude of the club on the field and in the clubhouse. The Franchise would lead the Mets to two pennants and a World Series title. Tom Terrific won three Cy Young awards and is the Mets all-time leader in wins, ERA, innings pitched, strikeouts, games started, complete games, and shutouts.

father happened to be a Shea Stadium usher. Word was passed along about the young southpaw and the Mets signed Koosman.

Still, *Sports Illustrated* predicted the Mets would have trouble holding onto ninth place, though a big year from Davis could make a difference.

The Season

After Cardwell lost on Opening Day, Seaver made his debut on April 13. He gave up two runs on six hits in 5.1 innings, getting a no-decision in New York's 3-2 win. The Mets lost three straight but then won three straight, including Seaver's first career win. The 4-4 mark would be the last time the Mets were at .500 in 1967.

They finished April 6-11. Ken Boyer was hitting .189. Bosch was at .146. Cleon Jones was hitting .100. Bud Harrelson committed nine errors in the month. Koosman made his debut the day after Seaver, in a relief outing in Philadelphia.

Final Resting Ground

Ralph Terry, four years removed from his 23-win season with the Yankees (plus 2 more in the World Series), was purchased by the Mets from the KC Athletics late in 1966. He appeared in 11 games for the Amazins that year, and two more in April 1967, before his career ended at the young age of 31.

Any hope of hanging around the race ended in May with a five-game losing streak in the middle of the month as well as a six-game stretch from late May to early June. Jack Hamilton hit a grand slam off former Met Al Jackson but the New York still lost on May 20 on 11-9. The team did add veteran third baseman Ed Charles from the Kansas City A's.

The team struggled through an 11-18 June. Hamilton was traded to the California Angels for pitcher Nick Willhite. In his first start as a Met, Willhite gave up five runs in two innings in a game the Cubs would eventually win 18-10 with the teams combining for 11 homers. Trader Bing was wheeling and dealing. Johnny Stephenson and Rob Gardner were sent to the

FABULOUS: TOMMY DAVIS

Two-time batting champ Tommy Davis spent one year with the Mets, and it was a productive one. Davis hit .302 with 174 hits and a team-leading 73 RBI. That winter, Davis was part of deal with the White Sox that brought Tommy Agee to the team.

Cubs for pitcher Bob Hendley. Al Luplow was sold to the Pirates. Hal Reniff was acquired from the Yankees. Wes Westrum was looking for any production as the team would use 54 players during the season, including 20 starting pitchers. It took until June 24 for Jones to get to a .200 batting average. Jerry Grote's average was at .200 at the end of June.

There were some positives. The Mets beat Juan Marichal on July 4. The 8-7 win was the first victory over the ace who had been 19-0 against the Mets. Five days later, New York trailed Atlanta 4-3 with two outs in the ninth when Westrum pinch-hit for Harrelson, who was 4-for-4. Buchek delivered a game-tying homer and the Mets went on to win in the 10th.

And there was Seaver, who made the All-Star team with an 8-5 record 2.70 ERA. In a marathon game, Seaver recorded the final three outs in the National League's 2-1 15 inning win.

Devine continued to move pieces. Chuck Hiller was traded to the Phillies for Phil Linz and his infamous harmonica. Jack Lamabe was sent to St. Louis for

TOP BATTERS

Pos	Name	G	AB	H	BA	HR	RBI	RS	SB	OPS
1B	Ed Kranepool	141	469	126	.269	10	54	37	0	.694
SS	Bud Harrelson	151	540	137	.254	1	28	59	12	.621
LF	Tommy Davis	154	577	174	.302	16	73	72	9	.782
RF	Ron Swaboda	134	449	126	.281	13	53	47	3	.759

TOP PITCHERS

Pos	Name	G	GS	W	L	SV	ERA	IP	SO	BB
SP	Tom Seaver	35	34	16	13	0	2.76	251.0	170	78
SP	Jack Fisher	39	30	9	18	0	4.70	220.1	117	64
SP	Don Cardwell	26	16	5	9	0	3.57	118.1	71	39
CL	Ron Taylor	50	0	4	6	8	2.34	73.0	46	23

FUTILE: DON BOSCH

Don Bosch made the least of his playing time as backup CF for the '67 Mets, collecting only 13 hits in 93 AB. He had no doubles or homers, finishing with a .140 BA and OPS+ of 1. Bosch played for 2 more seasons, batting .171 and .179 in a total of 223 AB, finishing his career at .164.

Al Jackson. Boyer, his disappointing .235 average, and Sandy Alomar were sent to the White Sox for J.C. Martin. Hawk Taylor was traded to the Angels. Cal Koonce came from the Cubs.

On the field, the losses were racking up. On July 27, Grote was ejected for arguing. Outfielder Tommie Reynolds was pressed into emergency catching duty and surrendered a passed ball to end a 7-6 11-inning loss in Los Angeles. Westrum fined the hot-headed catcher $100.

Seaver had some hiccups in the second half, including a start in Houston in which the Astros knocked him out in the first inning, but he won four straight starts in September.

Westrum, not given reassurance he would be back in 1968, resigned with 11 games remaining. Salty Parker finished the season, going 4-7.

Top 5 Highlights

1 Tom Seaver earns his first win, giving up one run on eight hits over 7.1 innings in a 6-1 victory over the Cubs on April 20. Don Shaw records the final five outs.

2 The Mets take both games of a June 6 doubleheader in Pittsburgh in 10 innings. Ron Swoboda homers off Roy Face in the top of the 10th in the nightcap to put the Mets ahead for good.

3 New York scores eight runs (five earned) on 14 hits against Juan Marichal on July 4. Big blows include an Ed Charles homer, Tommy Davis two-run double and Ron Swoboda two-run single. An 8-3 lead was cut to 8-7 but Hal Reniff got Willie Mays to ground into a double play in the ninth and Jim Ray Hart grounded out to end it.

4 After Tony Perez homers off Catfish Hunter in the top of the 15th, Tom Seaver enters his first All-Star Game. Tony Conigliaro flies out to left, Carl Yastrzemski draws a walk, Bill Freehan flies out to center and Ken Berry strikes out to end the 2-1 game.

5 With the Mets holding onto a 3-1 lead on August 1 in Houston, Don Shaw enters in the bottom of the fifth with the bases loaded and nobody out. Shaw strikes out Rusty Staub, Eddie Mathews and Bob Aspromonte to escape the jam and then finishes off the final four innings.

1968

	W	L	GB	Pos
	73	89	24.0	9th

RS/G	RA/G	Manager	
2.92	3.08	Gil Hodges	

Pitching and Gil Push Mets

The Moves

It's not easy for a perennial laughingstock coming off a 101-loss season to add credibility, but Gil Hodges was returning to New York as manager. He had slowly improved Washington into a sixth place team in 1967 and Johnny Murphy was able to swing a deal with Senators general manager – and former Yankees teammate – George Selkirk, for him.

The Mets sent Bill Denehy and $100,000 for the old Dodgers hero. It would turn out to be arguably the greatest deal in team history.

Bing Devine left the Mets to return to the Cardinals organization but not before acquiring Art Shamsky from the Reds for Bob Johnson. Murphy completed a trade initiated by Devine, acquiring Tommie Agee and Al Weis from the White Sox for Tommy Davis and Jack Fisher. Agee was 1966 Rookie of the Year with the White Sox (despite playing parts of four seasons with Cleveland and Chicago) and won a Gold Glove. The 1967 season was the second straight All-Star campaign for the centerfielder but second-half struggles saw him finish with a .234 batting average. Still, Hodges was impressed enough by what he saw up close in the Junior Circuit to tell Murphy to make the deal. And Weis, who hit .239 in his White Sox career would turn out to be a clutch hitter for the Mets.

⚾ He Was a Met?

Phil Linz would be another forgotten slap-hitting (96 RBI in 1317 career at-bats) SS and utility man were it not for his harmonica playing on the Yankees' bus after they had been swept by the White Sox. Linz finished his 7-year career playing 2B in about half the Mets' games in 1968.

The Situation

Sports Illustrated spoke highly of the Mets new centerfielder, writing, "At 25 Agee is potentially the most exciting player the Mets have ever had. He has tailored himself in the image of Mays and can gallop over the outfield as well as any player. Although he will strike out a lot, Agee can run the bases and hit home runs."

However, spring training started with Agee getting beaned from a Bob Gibson fastball. The team was about to see some serious offensive struggles in what would be known as "The Year of the Pitcher."

Though the team went 9-18 in spring training, the team was making fewer fundamental mistakes.

Gil Hodges

Hodges managed the Washington Senators from 1963-1967. The Mets brought him to New York that winter in a trade (!) for prospect Bill Denehey and $100,000. Hodges brought credibility to the Mets though his experience, dignity, and long history in Brooklyn. Thanks to Hodges and strong young pitchers, the Mets improved to 73 wins. The most in their history. The stage was set for the 100-win "Miracle Mets" of 1969. After managing the Mets the next two seasons, Hodges died of a heart attack in April 1972, after playing golf with friends from his Brooklyn and Washington days, at the young age of 47.

The Season

The Mets opener was postponed for Martin Luther King Jr.'s funeral and the team lost its lone game in San Francisco to begin the season. Jerry Koosman's complete game four-hit shutout in Los Angeles evened the Mets record at 1-1.

On April 15 in Houston, the Mets lost 1-0 in 24 innings. The six-hour, six-minute affair ended with Al Weis' error at short. Tommie Agee and Ron Swoboda each went hitless in 10 at-bats in the three and four spots in the order. Koosman pitched a complete game shutout in the home opener against the Giants. The 3-3 record would be the last time the Mets were at .500 in 1968.

 Final Resting Ground

Before becoming a longtime pitching coach with several organizations, including the Yankees, Billy Connors pitched in 15 games over two seasons with the Mets. He went 0-1 in 1968, his final season in the majors. Connors would stay in the organization as a minor league pitcher and then minor league coach.

New York lost a pair of 11-inning games and a 16-inning marathon in May but also beat the Pirates in a 17-inning victory. Nolan Ryan took some attention away from Seaver and Koosman with a 14-strikeout performance on May 14 against the Reds.

A four-game sweep at the hands of the Cardinals in early June put the Mets at 20-27 but the team came back with four straight wins, including another complete game shutout by Koosman, who was 9-2 with a 1.43 after beating the Cubs on June 4.

FABULOUS: JERRY KOOSMAN

The Kooz had one of the great rookie seasons among pitchers, with 19 wins, 17 CG, and 7 shutouts. His ERA was 2.08 in 263 IP. Koosman lost out on the Rookie of the Year award to Johnny Bench.

There was no game June 8 after the Mets chose not to play in the wake of Robert Kennedy's assassination. New York left San Francisco 24-29 and only scored six runs in a three-game series with the Dodgers but won all three. Another complete game by Koosman against the Giants at Shea improved the team to 28-29.

The team flirted with .500, sitting at 35-36 on June 27 but the team lost five of six. Koosman's complete game shutout on July 12 improved the team to 41-44 before a six-game losing streak ended any hope of getting back to .500.

In a pitching-dominated All-Star Game – a 1-0 NL win – Seaver pitched two shutout innings, including a seventh-inning strikeout of Mickey Mantle. Koosman earned a one-out save by striking out Carl Yastrzemski to end the game.

A fight at the Astrodome made for the the most exciting action in a low-scoring August. Doug Rader knocked out third baseman Kevin Collins with an elbow to the jaw on a pop-up slide. A brawl ensued with Cardwell punching Rader in the face. Perhaps the conservative Cardwell was still high-strung after snatching love beads off Ron Swoboda on the team plane several days earlier.

TOP BATTERS

Pos	Name	G	AB	H	BA	HR	RBI	RS	SB	OPS
C	Jerry Grote	124	404	114	.282	3	31	29	1	.706
3B	Ed Charles	117	369	102	.276	15	53	41	5	.761
LF	Cleon Jones	147	509	151	.297	14	55	63	23	.793
RF	Ron Swoboda	132	450	109	.242	11	59	46	8	.699

TOP PITCHERS

Pos	Name	G	GS	W	L	SV	ERA	IP	SO	BB
SP	Tom Seaver	36	35	16	12	1	2.20	278.0	205	48
SP	Jerry Koosman	35	34	19	12	0	2.08	263.2	178	69
SP	Dick Selma	33	23	9	10	0	2.75	170.1	117	54
RP	Cal Koonce	55	2	6	4	11	2.42	96.2	50	32

FUTILE: TOMMIE AGEE

Agee showed no indication of the stud he was to become in his first year with the Mets, batting only .217 with 5 HR, 17 RBI, and 30 RS in 368 at bats. He also drew only 15 BB, while striking out 107 times.

In one ten-game stretch in August, the Mets lost 1-0, 2-1, 5-0, 3-1 in 12 innings, 1-0, 5-2 and 1-0 in 17 innings. The offense was nonexistent but Agee saw his average creep up over .200 for the first time in late September. And the team hit the 70-win mark for the first time.

Gil Hodges wasn't around to see the last few games after suffering a minor heart attack in Atlanta during the season's final week. The team did win its final road game of the season to finish with a 41-40 road record. New York finished 73-89, one game ahead of the Astros for ninth place.

Top 5 Highlights

1. In the home opener, the Giants load the bases with nobody out in the first against Jerry Koosman but the southpaw strikes out Willie Mays, gets Jim Ray Hart on a pop-up and strikes out Jack Hiatt to get out of the jam. Koosman would pitch a complete game shutout and the Mets beat defending NL Cy Young winner Mike McComick 3-0.

2. Nolan Ryan sets a team mark by striking out 14 Reds in a 3-2 win on May 14.

3. Tom Seaver strikes out Mickey Mantle, in his final season, in the All-Star Game. Koosman strikes out Carl Yastrzemski to finish off the 1-0 NL win.

4. Jim McAndrew earns his first career win with a complete game shutout on August 26 in St. Louis. A Cleon Jones sac fly against Steve Carlton in the eighth was all the support McAndrew would need in the 1-0 win as Roger Maris flied out to end the game.

5. Koosman ties the NL rookie record with his seventh shutout in a 2-0 win over the Pirates on September 13. It's the 67th win of the season for New York, a new franchise record.

1969

	W	L	GB	Pos
	100	62	8.0 GA	1st

RS/G	RA/G	Manager	
3.90	3.34	Gil Hodges	

OPENING DAY LINEUP

Tommie Agee, CF
Rod Gaspar, RF
Ken Boswell, 2B
Cleon Jones, LF
Ed Charles, 3B
Ed Kranepool, 1B
Jerry Grote, C
Bud Harrelson, SS
Tom Seaver, P

It's a Miracle! Mets Win It All

The Moves

The only notable acquisition was Wayne Garrett, a Rule V Draft pick from the Braves. There was some good news for Mets hitters. The mounds were lowered after pitching dominated 1968. Atlanta was shopping Joe Torre and the Mets were interested. "We're not going to give him up for a bunch of donkeys," Braves executive vice president Paul Richards said. Reportedly, Ed Kranepool, Amos Otis and Bobby Heise were the players turned down. Atlanta wanted Jerry Grote, Nolan Ryan and Otis. Instead, Torre went to the defending NL champion Cardinals.

The Situation

At worst, the Mets would finish sixth. Expansion led to realignment and the Mets were in the newly formed National League East division. The new Montreal Expos were in the division, so the Mets looked like they could finish at least fifth. An Art Shamsky injury opened the door for Rod Gaspar, who had a strong spring. Otis also made the team. Gary Gentry impressed and would be the third starter. Cleon Jones was shifted to first, lighting a fire under Kranepool.

Could the Mets finally finish over .500? Gil Hodges predicted 85 wins for his club. Grote had a good feeling in the spring. "We're a young team. We're just coming," the catcher said. "We all played together last year and we're together

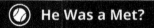

He Was a Met?

Amos Otis played 19 games with the Mets in 1967 before returning in 1969 but he hit a mere .151 in 48 games. He was traded to the Royals where he would become one of the best hitters of the 1970s, making five All-Star teams, winning three Gold Gloves, and finishing in the top 10 of the MVP voting four times.

again this year. When you play together a few years, you get to know each other and things improve. Yes sir, there's a different feeling on the team this year. There's more togetherness. There's more pride. We're a close-knit team."

Las Vegas had the Mets as 100-to-1 odds to win the World Series.

Fans at Shea Stadium celebrate after the Mets stun the Orioles to win the 1969 World Series. (Photo Courtesy Jason D. Antos)

The Season

It looked like the makings of another losing season. The expansion Expos beat the Mets 11-10 on Opening Day. New York made three errors and Seaver gave up four runs (two earned) in five innings. The team trailed 11-6 entering the ninth but scored four times and put two runners on before Gaspar went down on strikes to end the game.

New York won the next game, with Tug McGraw giving up one run in 6.1 innings of relief. The Mets improved to 2-1 with a 4-2 win in the rubber game. Tommie Agee homered twice, including a blast to left off Larry Jaster that made it to the upper deck, the only such shot in the 45-year history of Shea Stadium. Gentry made his MLB debut and pitched into the ninth with Cal Koonce recording the final out, getting Don Bosch on a fly out with the bases loaded.

Off to a hot start, the Cubs came to Shea and took three straight before Jones hit a three-run home run off Rich Nye in the bottom of the ninth to give the Mets a 3-0 win after Jim McAndrew and McGraw combined to blank Chicago. The Mets finished April 9-11, 5.5 games out of first. Jones was off to a blazing .410 start, hitting safely in 17 of 20 games. Ron Swoboda was batting .320. Kranepool was batting .310 and hit his first two home runs off Mudcat Grant in a 2-0 win over the Expos on April 29, while Ryan pitched 4.2 innings of shutout relief for the win.

 Final Resting Ground

Al Jackson is well known for being probably the Mets' best starter in their early years, but it's less well remembered that Jackson returned to the Mets for part of the 1968 and then 1969 seasons, the latter was the last of his career.

Koosman was gone for several weeks with shoulder pain. The Mets did take a doubleheader at Wrigley from the Cubs on May 4. Seaver and McGraw both pitched complete games, each giving up two runs on nine hits. Ryan would miss a month with a groin injury. The Mets beat the Reds in a wild 10-9 victory on May 16, with Cal Koonce pitching the final three innings for the win. The offense kept it going the next day in an 11-3 win with Jones hitting his seventh home run. When Seaver pitched a three-hit shutout against the Braves on May 21, the 18-18 Mets were at .500. Seaver had six of the 18 wins and an ERA of 1.96. He told the reporters he wasn't excited. "What's so good about .500? That's only mediocre. We didn't come into this season to play .500. Let Rod Kanehl and Marvelous Marv laugh about the Mets."

A .500 record looked good after the Mets lost their next five. McGraw failed to make it out of the third in a 15-3 loss to Atlanta and was moved to the bullpen. The team went to Houston and lost three straight to the Astros. New York struck out 31 times in three games. "They all looked like wooden soldiers," Hodges said. The Mets returned home for an eight-game homestand and lost the first game to the expansion Padres to drop to 18-23.

FABULOUS: ART SHAMSKY

Art Shamsky is one of the unsung stars of the 1969 Mets, batting .300 with 14 HR and 47 RBI in a half-season's worth of at bats. Shamsky also went 7-for-13 in the NLCS.

But then the Mets showed 1969 was different, winning 11 games in a row. The streak began with a 1-0 squeaker over the Padres, won on Bud Harrelson's 11th inning single after Koosman fanned 15 batters in 10 innings. The team then swept the Giants. New York came back from a 3-1 deficit in the eighth of the first win, Ed Charles hit a three-run homer off Gaylord Perry in the second win and Swoboda drew a bases loaded walk to finish off the sweep.

Then the Mets took care of another West coast for, sweeping the Dodgers. Koosman and Seaver won the first two games, with Kranepool hitting two homers in the second win. Suddenly the Mets were in second place. The Dodgers must have been happy to see Jack DiLauro make his first career start in the final game but the lefty, who made three relief appearances under his belt, threw 10 shutout innings. In the top of the 15th, the Dodgers put runners on the corners with one out for Willie Davis. Al Weis, playing second base, darted to his left for the grounder that was deflected by Ron Taylor, leapt to the right for the carom, came up with the ball and threw the runner out at home. Hodges later said the double reverse and throw was one of the best plays he had ever seen. In the bottom of the frame, Garrett singled to center and Davis misplayed the ball, allowing Harrelson to score with the winning run.

The Mets went to San Diego and swept the Padres, then beat the Giants on June 10 to improve to 29-23. The team was hot even if the offense was not. Kranepool was hitting .261, Grote .231 and Swoboda was down to .224. Shamsky was batting .289 but not playing full-time. Harrelson was hitting

FUTILE: WAYNE GARRETT

Rookie Garrett managed only 1 HR and 39 RBI in 400 Abs; He slashed .218/.290/.268. He hit well in the NLCS, but then started only one game in the World Series as the Mets went with veteran Ed Charles instead.

.244. On June 15, the team sent Steve Renko, Kevin Collins, Bill Carden and Dave Colon to the Expos for slugging first baseman Donn Clendenon. The veteran hit 28 home runs with the Pirates in 1966. He led the league with 163 strikeouts in 1968 and was selected by the Expos in the expansion draft. He was traded to the Astros in January 1969 but refused to report. Clendenon was batting .240 with four home runs and 14 RBI in 38 games at the time of the trade. The Mets picked up both a presence in the lineup and in the clubhouse.

Seven wins in eight games improved the Mets to 38-28. The stretch included doubleheader sweeps over the Cardinals and Phillies. Gaspar threw out Lou Brock at the plate in the eighth inning to preserve a 1-0 win over St. Louis. McAndrew pitched eight shutout innings in a win over Philadelphia. But then the team lost four straight. The Mets took three of five in St. Louis, then swept the Pirates, exploding for 28 runs in three games. In the finale, the Mets erased a 6-1 deficit with Clendenon hitting a three-run homer, his first as a Met, in an 8-7 win.

Leading the Mets by 4.5 games, the Cubs came to town for the most anticipated series since the Mets' inception. In the first game, Ferguson Jenkins took a one-hitter and a 3-1 lead into the bottom of the ninth, having only allowed a Kranepool home run. Ken Boswell led off the inning with a fly ball to center. Cubs centerfielder Don Young saw the ball fall in front of him after initially breaking back and a hustling Boswell had a double. With one out, Clendenon drove Young to the track in left-center. Young dropped the ball before crashing into the wall, putting runners on second and third. Jones followed with a double to left, tying the game at three. Shamsky was intentionally walked and Garrett grounded out, putting runners on second and third. Kranepool singled to left, giving the Mets a thrilling 4-3 win. It was the best win in team history. The Cubs clubhouse was not as celebratory. "My 3-year-old could have caught those balls," manager Leo Durocher said. Star third baseman Ron Santo was also critical. "He was just thinking about himself," Santo said. "He had a bad day at the plate, so he's got his head down. He's worrying about his batting average, not the team." Angry Young quickly dressing, and as he left the clubhouse Santo added, "He can keep going out of sight for all I care."

The next night, Seaver pitched the game of his life. The Mets provided the offense with three runs in the first two innings and Jones homered in the seventh. Tom Terrific went through the Chicago lineup easily, pitching eight perfect innings and striking out 11. Randy Hundley led off the ninth with a bunt attempt but Seaver threw him out. Jimmy Qualls came to the plate, playing in center instead of Young. Qualls singled to left-center, breaking up the historic bid. But the Mets had arrived as contenders.

TOP BATTERS										
Pos	Name	G	AB	H	BA	HR	RBI	RS	SB	OPS
LF	Cleon Jones	137	483	164	.340	12	75	92	16	.904
CF	Tommie Agee	149	565	153	.271	26	76	97	12	.806
RF	Ron Swoboda	109	327	77	.235	9	52	38	1	.687
RF	Art Shamsky	100	303	91	.300	14	47	42	1	.863

TOP PITCHERS										
Pos	Name	G	GS	W	L	SV	ERA	IP	SO	BB
SP	Tom Seaver	36	35	25	7	0	2.21	273.1	208	82
SP	Jerry Koosman	32	32	17	9	0	2.28	241.0	180	68
SP	Gary Gentry	35	35	13	12	0	3.43	233.2	154	81
CL	Ron Taylor	59	0	9	4	13	2.72	76.0	42	24
RP	Tug McGraw	42	4	9	3	12	2.24	100.1	92	47

New York couldn't complete the sweep, playing a sloppy game in a 6-2 loss. "Those were the real Mets," Durocher said. After the Mets took two of three from the Expos, the team traveled to Chicago to take on the Cubs again.

The Cubs took the first game 1-0 with Bill Hands outdueling Seaver. Santo leaped and clicked his heels when it was over, much to the chagrin of coach Joe Pignatano. The two carried over the issue to batting practice the next day. Hodges and Santo exchanged lineup cards. "You remind me of someone. You remind me of Tug McGraw," Hodges said. "When he was young and immature and nervous, he used to jump up and down. He doesn't do it anymore." Weis hit a three-run homer off Dick Selma, his first of the season, in a 5-4 win. The next day Weis hit another homer and Koonce picked up the win with five innings of shutout relief. On July 20, the day of the moon landing, Bobby Pfeil was an unlikely hero. With two outs and Swoboda on third, Pfeil laid down a bunt with the third baseman back and the Mets had a 4-3 win in Montreal.

The Mets stumbled through early August, including a sweep at the hands of the pesky Astros, and Chicago's division lead increased to 10 games over the 62-51 Mets. Back home, the Mets were limited to 11 runs in the next five games but won all five. Seaver, McAndrew, Koosman and Don Cardwell pitched gems to sweep the Padres. On August 19, Gentry blanked the Giants for 10 innings. McGraw pitched four more, with Jones making a catch against wall to prevent an extra-base hit from Willie McCovey, as Hodges used a four-man outfield in the at-bat. Juan Marichal struck out 13 Mets and was still pitching in the 14th when Agee hit his 21st home run of the season to win it for the Mets. The next night, McAndrew tossed a two-hit shutout in a 6-0 win over the Giants. The Mets lost in 11 innings the next day but then won six in a row, including a Grote game-winning double scoring Clendenon to beat the Dodgers.

It looked like McCovey beat the Mets on August 30. With Bob Burda on first in a tie game in the ninth, McCovey took a McGraw pitch and drove it down the line in left. Gaspar had been playing in the gap as part of a shift. Gaspar threw a rocket to Grote at the plate to nail Burda. A stunned Grote flipped the ball toward the mound, not realizing there were only two outs. A heads-up Clendenon picked up the ball and threw out McCovey at third, completing a 7-2-3-5 double play. Clendenon homered in the top of the 10th to win it.

The Cubs came to Queens on September 8 with the lead down to 2.5 games. Chicago had lost four straight coming into the two-game series. Hands nearly beaned Agee. Koosman retaliated by drilling Santo in the arm. In Agee's next at-bat, he hit a two-run homer. With the game tied in the bottom of the sixth, Agee doubled and then scored on Garrett's single to right, just beating the throw home, though Hundley put up an argument. Koosman went the distance, striking out 13. The next night, the Mets won 7-1, with Seaver pitching a complete game. Clendenon and Shamsky homered and the Shea fans taunted Durocher. In the top of the fourth inning, a black cat ran on the field and stared in the Cubs dugout. It would become a symbol for the struggles Chicago had late in the season.

On September 10, the Mets moved into first. McAndrew and Mike Wegener both gave up two runs in 11 innings. With two outs in the bottom of the 12th, Jones singled and Gaspar walked. Boswell then singled off Bill Stoneman, giving the Mets a 3-2 win. Combined with Chicago's loss to the Phillies earlier, the Mets were at the top of the division. It was the first time all season the Cubs weren't in first.

Ryan beat the Expos to finish a doubleheader sweep and then Gentry beat Montreal. In Pittsburgh, the Mets won a doubleheader over the Pirates. Koosman and Cardwell both drove in the only run in each of their 1-0 victories. On September 15, Steve Carlton set a nine-inning record with 19 strikeouts but the Mets won 4-3 with Swoboda hitting a pair of two-run homers. Koosman and Seaver then pitched consecutive shutouts in Montreal.

The offense fizzled against the Pirates, scoring two runs in three games, including being no-hit by Bob Moose. The Mets swept a doubleheader from the Pirates and welcomed the Cardinals to town. On September 22, in a game rescheduled from St. Louis the previous week, giving the Mets an 82nd home date, Seaver notched his 23rd victory of the season. The next night, Harrelson's single in the 11th off Bob Gibson beat St. Louis.

The team had clinched at least a tie of the NL East. September 24 was the final home game of the regular season and the team wasted no time jumping on Carlton with Clendenon hitting a three-run homer and Charles hitting a two-run homer in the first. Clendenon hit another homer in the fifth. Gentry was in control, taking a shutout into the ninth. The game ended with Torre grounding into a 6-4-3 double play. The Mets were number one. Ralph Kiner asked Hodges to compare the title with the ones he won as a player. "I would have to say this was the biggest thrill of all of them because these boys have been coming on and how lightly-regarded at the opening of the season" the team was.

After the 6-0 win, the Mets went to Philadelphia and swept three games without giving up a run. The team won game number 100 in Chicago on October 1. They went 38-11 from August 13 to the end of the season.

Top 5 Highlights

1 Tom Seaver pitches his "Imperfect Game," retiring the first 25 Cubs before Jimmy Qualls singles in New York's 4-0 win on July 9 to draw closer to Chicago.

2 The Mets turn a 7-2-3-5 double play in the bottom of the ninth against the Giants on August 30. Rod Gaspar throws out Bob Burda at the plate to preserve the tie. Jerry Grote rolls the ball to the mound and Donn Clendenon picks it up and throws out Willie McCovey at third. Clendenon homers in the 10th.

3 Jerry Koosman drills Ron Santo in the arm, defending his teammates after Tommie Agee was nearly beaned. The Mets win 3-2 on September 8 and Koosman fans 13 Cubs.

4 Ken Boswell's 12th inning single scores Cleon Jones and puts the Mets in first place on September 10. The Mets wouldn't relinquish the lead.

5 Gary Gentry pitches a shutout against the Cardinals as the Mets clinch the division. Lindsey Nelson's famous call: "Ground ball to short, this could be it – there's one, there's two – the game is over, and the Mets are the champions. At 9:07 on September 24, the Mets have won the championship of the Eastern Division of the National League."

1969 NLCS

The first ever National League Championship Series saw the Mets take on the 93-win Braves, who won the NL West by three games over the Giants. The first two games were in Atlanta and a pitching duel was expected in the opener with Seaver facing Phil Niekro. The Mets took a 2-0 in the second, with Grote delivering an RBI single and Boswell scoring on a passed ball. In the bottom of the second, Rico Carty doubled, advanced to third on a Boswell error and scored on sacrifice fly. In the bottom of the third, the Braves used three straight doubles to take a 3-2 lead.

Harrelson's two-run triple in the fourth gave the Mets a 4-3 lead but a Tony Gonzalez homer tied it in the fifth. In the seventh, Hank Aaron put the Braves ahead with a home run. In the eighth, Garrett led off with a double and scored the tying run when Jones singled. With runners on the corners and one out, Kranepool hit one to Cepeda at first. Cepeda's throw home was wide and Jones scored to make it 6-5. With the bases loaded and two outs, Martin, pinch-hitting for Seaver, delivered a single and combined with an error, all three runners scored. Taylor's two innings of scoreless relief preserved the 9-5 win.

New York's offense, full of left handers in Hodges' platoon, exploded again in the second game. The Mets jumped all over Ron Reed, Paul Doyle and Milt Pappas, taking a 9-1 lead in the fifth. Agee and Boswell homered. New York seemed to have the game in hand with an eight-run lead and Koosman on the mound but with two outs in the fifth the Braves scored five times. Taylor entered and pitched 1.1 innings to keep it a three-run game. With two outs in the top of the seventh a two-run homer by Jones made it 11-6. McGraw pitched three scoreless innings to wrap it up.

The series shifted to Shea but Aaron hit another home run, giving the Braves a 2-0 lead in the first. In the third, Gonzalez singled and Aaron doubled, putting runners on second and third with nobody out for Carty. Carty just missed a home run down the line and Hodges came out to pull Gentry in the middle of the at-bat. Ryan entered and fanned Carty. After intentionally walking Cepeda, Ryan struck out Boyer and got Bob Didier on a pop-up. Agee homered off Pat Jarvis in the bottom of the inning to make it 2-1.

In the fourth, Boswell's two-run homer into the Mets bullpen to give New York a 3-2 lead. In the top of the fifth, Cepeda's two-run homer made it 4-3 Braves. In the bottom of the frame, Ryan led off with a single and Garrett's two-run shot to right giving the Mets the lead again. Three batters later, Boswell singled off George Stone to score Jones and make it 6-4. In the sixth, Agee singled off Cecil Upshaw to extend the lead to 7-4.

Atlanta brought the tying run to the plate in the eighth but Felipe Alou lined out to short. Ryan pitched a 1-2-3 ninth with Gonzalez grounding out to third to end it. The Mets were National League champions and they did it scoring 27 runs in three games. Shamsky hit .538. Jones hit .429 with a homer. Garrett hit .385 with a home run. Agee hit .357 with two home runs. Boswell hit .333 with two home runs. The New York bullpen allowed two runs in 13.1 innings.

1969 World Series

The Mets were given no chance by many pundits against the 109-win Baltimore Orioles. Frank Robinson and Boog Powell each hit more than 30 home runs and drove in more than 100 runs. They had Brooks Robinson and his vacuum at the hot corner. Mike Cuellar, Dave McNally and Jim Palmer combined to win more than 60 games.

Baltimore looked as good as advertised when Don Buford led off with a home run off Seaver. A less-than-stellar Seaver struggled in the fourth, giving up three runs, including an RBI single from Cuellar. In the seventh the Mets put together a threat. Weis' sacrifice fly put the Mets on the board and Gaspar came to the plate with two on and two outs. Gaspar hit a slow grounder to third and Brooks Robinson made a highlight-reel throw to nail him. The Mets got the tying run to the plate in the ninth but Shamsky grounded out to second to end the 4-1 loss.

In the second game, Koosman and McNally matched zeroes for three innings before Clendenon homered to right leading off the fourth. Koosman pitched six no-hit innings. Paul Blair led off the bottom of the seventh with a single. With two outs, Blair stole second and then Brooks Robinson singled to center, tying the game. The game was still tied in the ninth when Charles singled with two outs. Grote followed with a single of his own to put runners on the corners. Weis came to the plate with Koosman on deck but Orioles manager Earl Weaver made the decision to have McNally go after Weis. Weis delivered an RBI single. Koosman grounded out to end the inning.

Koosman retired the first two batters in the bottom of the ninth. Frank Robinson and Powell drew walks, bringing up Brooks Robinson. Hodges took Koosman out and Taylor came in. Robinson worked the count to 3-2 and then hit a chopper to third. Charles made a move to the third base bag, then decided to throw to first. Clendenon picked the throw out of the dirt and the series was even.

The series moved to Shea and Agee started the offense with a long homer to center off Palmer. The Mets added three more runs and the O's were kept at bay in part by Tommie Agee's first of two great catches.

In the seventh, Gentry walked three straight batters. Ryan came in and gave up a liner to center and again Agee saved the day with a diving catch. Another bases-loaded rally for Baltimore ended with an out and the Mets had a 5-0 victory.

Seaver and Cuellar met again in the fourth game. Clendenon homered into the Baltimore bullpen in the second to give the Mets a 1-0 lead. Weaver was ejected by home plate umpire Shag Crawford for arguing balls and strikes in the top of the third. The Orioles put two runners on with nobody out and had runners on the corners with one out for Blair, who popped up a bunt that Seaver let fall before throwing to first. Frank Robinson popped up to Clendenon to end the inning. Seaver didn't allow another hit until the ninth. Holding onto a 1-0 lead, Frank Robinson and Powell singled to put runners on the corners.

Brooks Robinson hit a liner to right. Swoboda, who had often been replaced by Gaspar for defensive purposes earlier in the season, made a full-body dive and made the catch. Robinson scored to tie the game, but without Swoboda's stunning catch, the Orioles likely would have taken the lead. Hendricks came to the plate and nearly hit a homer to right, landing just foul. Then he flied out to right with Swoboda making a routine catch.

Seaver was still on the mound in the 10th when the Orioles put two runners on with one out. Buford flied out deep to right and Blair struck out. In the bottom of the inning, Grote hit a fly ball to left. Buford went back before coming in and saw the ball fall in front of him as a hustling Grote went into second with a double. Gaspar went in as a pinch-runner and Weis was intentionally walked. Martin pinch-hit for Seaver and Weaver went to lefty Pete Richert. Martin laid down a bunt. Richert picked the ball up and his throw to first hit Martin and rolled away as Gaspar scored the winning run. The Orioles complained that Martin ran inside the baseline but no umpire ruled interference. The Mets had a 3-1 series lead.

One more win meant the title but a loss would send the series back to Baltimore. In the third, Mark Belanger singled, bringing up McNally, who hit a two-run homer. Frank Robinson's homer later in the inning made it 3-0. Robinson's next at-bat was in the top of the sixth. He appeared to be hit by a pitch but home plate umpire Lou DiMuro said it hit the bat first. Robinson struck out. In the bottom of the inning, it looked like Jones was hit by a pitch but DiMuro ruled it hit the bat first. Hodges came out of the dugout with a ball containing shoe polish and DiMuro awarded Jones first base, much to the chagrin of Weaver and the Orioles. Clendenon followed with a homer to cut it to 3-2.

Even decades later, there is still debate about the shoe polish ball. Koosman said Hodges asked him to swipe the ball against his foot. Gaspar said he turned around and saw the manager reaching into a bag of balls and pulled one out with the scuff mark. Either way, Hodges had convinced the umpire Jones was hit. In the seventh, Weis homered to tie the game. It was the first homer he hit at Shea Stadium. He had only hit six home runs in his career but one of them, five years earlier, had come off McNally.

In the bottom of the eighth, Jones doubled off the wall to start the inning. With one out, Swoboda doubled down the line in left before Buford could make a running catch. Jones scored the go-ahead run. With two outs, Grote hit a grounder to first. Powell's flip to Eddie Watt covering first was off the mark and Swoboda came around to extend the lead to 5-3. All the O's could manage in the ninth was a lead-off walk to Frank Robinson and the Mets were champions in five games.

"This is the summit," Charles said. "We're No. 1 in the world and you just can't get any bigger than this." Clendenon was named MVP with his three home runs. Weis hit .455 in the series. Koosman gave up four runs in 17.2 innings.

The team spent most of the decade as laughingstocks and finished it on top.

"Some people still might not believe in us but then, some people still think the world is flat," Jones said.

Quiz #3: 1970s

1. (1970) This Bronx native was part of the Mets' never-ending parade of third basemen, coming to the team from the American League in 1970 in what is considered one of their worst trades ever. He played for the Mets for one season, managing 22 SB and an OBA of .373, but off-the-field troubles contributed to his departure, and he was out of baseball for good the next season. **[10 points]**

2. (1970) Name the 5 pitchers who spent time with the 1970 Mets who won 20 games in a season at least once in their career. Hint: One pitched in only 3 games that season, and he is known as one of the worst hitters in major league history. **[3 points each up to 4, 4 bonus points for 5th]**

3. (1971) This reliever was nothing short of fantastic in 1971, posting an ERA of 1.70 and chalking up 11 wins in 110 innings pitched. **[6 points]**

4. (1972) Name the Mets player who led the team in OBA among players with more than 200 plate appearances. **[8 points]**

5. (1973) Name the pitcher who walked the only 2 batters he faced in his major league debut, one of whom scored. It was his only appearance of the season, giving him an ERA of "infinity," but he later became a long-time pitching coach for the Mets and other major league teams. **[10 points]**

6. (1973) Who started in CF for the Mets in Games 2-7 of the 1973 World Series, ahead of Willie Mays who had started Game 1? **[10 points]**

7. (1974) Name the Mets outfielder with a humorous nickname whose brief career ended after a season with 89 plate appearances, a .158 BA, and only 1 RBI. **[8 points]**

8. (1975) This right-hander's sole season in the major leagues was not a successful one as he went 5-13 in 23 starts. He was even worse at the plate, going 0-for-41 in his career with one walk. **[8 bonus points]**

9. (1976) Name the Mets manager who guided them to a solid 86-76 record in 1976 but who was fired and replaced by Joe Torre after a 15-30 start in 1977. **[8 points]**

10. (1970s) Who was the first Mets player to drive in 100 runs in a season? **[8 points]**

11. (1976) After many years as a top-line starter in the American League, this veteran won 8 games in 30 starts at age 35, with a solid ERA of 3.22. **[10 points]**

12. (1976-1977) What rare statistical feat did Jerry Koosman accomplish over the 1976 and 1977 seasons? **[12 points]**

13. (1977) This player became the first Met since 1974 to reach double figures in SB (John Milner 10) when he blew past the mark with 33, though his 21 CS negated any positive value from his thievery. **[10 points]**

14. (1977) This right-hander, who pitched all but 2 games of his career with the Mets, led the NL in ERA (2.43), managing a 9-6 W-L record for a team that finished 30 games under .500. **[8 points]**

15. (1978) This outfielder and sometime infielder, who also played 2+ seasons with the Yankees, drew 71 walks against only 38 strikeouts, but was caught stealing on 11 of 13 attempts for the season. **[12 points]**

16. This hurler made his major league debut in 1979, making 18 appearances, including 9 starts. He went on to win a Cy Young Award for another team and became a feared opponent against the powerhouse Mets of the mid-1980s. **[8 points]**

QUIZ 3: TOTAL POINTS – 140; BONUS POINTS – 12

1970

	W	L	GB	Pos
	83	79	6.0	3rd

RS/G	RA/G	Manager	
4.29	3.89	Gil Hodges	

Agee Shines, but Miracle Is Missing

The Moves

Less than two weeks after the World Series, the Mets released Ed Charles. In early December, the team filled its right-handed third base void with Joe Foy, who hit .262 with 71 RBI in 1969 with the Royals. The trade cost the Mets Amos Otis, who would turn into a five-time All-Star in Kansas City and one of the best players of the decade. Also in the trade was Bob Johnson, who pitched two games for the 1969 Mets and would go on to help the Pirates win the 1971 championship.

The team also acquired southpaw Ray Sadecki and outfielder Dave Marshall from the Giants for Jim Gosger and Bob Heise. Though Sadecki was no longer the pitcher who won 20 games for the 1964 Cardinals, he would help the Mets down the stretch in 1973.

The Situation

In January, general manager Johnny Murphy died of a heart attack. Bob Scheffing, who had been director of player development, took over.

Most of the 1969 team was back with Mike Jorgensen, who had a cup of coffee in 1968, the only rookie to make the team out of spring training. Whitey Herzog said Jorgensen was as good defensively at first base as anyone in the game, including Wes Parker.

 ## He Was a Met?

After a strong 7 seasons in the AL, including a Cy Young Award in 1964 when he posted an ERA of 1.65 with 11 shutouts (!), Dean Chance was washed up when pitched in 3 games for the Mets in 1970.

The Season

The defending champions finally won an Opening Day game, beating the Pirates 5-3 in 11 innings at Forbes Field. Seaver pitched a complete game over the Phillies on April 17 and Ryan followed it up the next night with a complete game shutout of his own. Denny Doyle's leadoff single was the only hit off Ryan, who struck out 15 Phillies, including 14 over the first six innings.

Ryan's club record for strikeouts didn't last long as Seaver fanned 19 Padres on April 22. He struck out the final 10 batters to finish off a 2-1 win.

Donn Clendenon (far right) celebrating with teammates after their World Series victory. Clendenon drove in 97 runs in 1970. (Photo Courtesy Jason D. Antos)

An inconsistent offense had the Mets hovering around .500 but still in the thick of things in a mediocre NL East. In mid-May, Gentry and Seaver tossed consecutive complete game one-hit shutouts. Koosman followed with a complete game four-hit shutout on May 16 though it would be his last win until June 25 as he was sidelined with an elbow injury. Sadecki won four straight starts.

The Mets began June with five straight losses, the last a 10-2 thumping in Cincinnati. The offense was in a funk with Agee hitting .241, Swoboda .240, Jones .213. Kranepool would be demoted to Triple-A with a .118 average. Cal Koonce was sold to the Red Sox.

A Jim McAndrew shutout on June 8

Final Resting Ground

Bronx native Joe Foy showed great promise in his first few years in the majors, including as 3B for the Impossible Dream 1967 Red Sox. But Foy was haunted by personal problems, and by the time he landed with the Mets in 1970, his skills were fading fast. Foy played in 99 games in 1970, but was then dropped by New York. Fourty-one games later, his career was over at age 28.

in Houston got the Mets rolling and the team finished the month winning 15 of its last 20 and had a two game lead in the division. The highlight was a five game sweep of the Cubs at Wrigley Field during which the Mets scored 44 runs. Ken Singleton made his debut in the series and would provide the Mets with a solid bat until the final weeks of the season.

Don Cardwell was sold to the Braves after sporting a 6.48 ERA in 16 appearances. But by the end of the month, a 55-46 record was good enough for first place. Jones was up to .247, Agee was at .284 and Harrelson was batting .265. Clendenon was batting .316 at the end of the month.

Even a 13-18 August didn't eliminate the team from a pennant race in which they were 1.5 games out of first entering the final month. Seeking pitching help, the team traded Gaspar to the Padres for Ron Herbel. One problem was Seaver. The man who had won six straight starts in June and July was scuffling. He lost four consecutive starts in late August.

The Mets were tied for first place after a 9-5 win in Montreal on September 14. But then the team lost four straight to drop 3.5 back. Koosman beat the Pirates in Game 1 of a September 20 doubleheader, but Seaver failed to make it out of the sixth inning in the nightcap, giving up five runs in 5.1 innings in his most important start of the

FUTILE: ED KRANEPOOL

Fighting for playing time with Donn Clendenon, Art Shamsky and Mike Jorgensen, Kranepool struggled mightily and was sent down to the minors in June with a .118 average. He was batting .108 at the end of August and finished at .170. But the original Met would become adept at pinch-hitting, giving the Mets an option off the bench during the decade.

TOP BATTERS

Pos	Name	G	AB	H	BA	HR	RBI	RS	SB	OPS
CF	Tommie Agee	153	636	182	.286	24	75	107	31	.812
LF	Cleon Jones	134	506	140	.277	10	63	71	12	.769
1B	Donn Clendenon	121	396	114	.288	22	97	65	4	.863
IF	Wayne Garrett	114	366	93	.254	12	45	74	5	.811

TOP PITCHERS

Pos	Name	G	GS	W	L	SV	ERA	IP	SO	BB
SP	Tom Seaver	37	36	18	12	0	2.82	290.2	283	83
SP	Jerry Koosman	30	29	12	7	0	3.14	212.0	118	71
SP	Jim McAndrew	32	27	10	14	2	3.56	184.1	111	38
SP	Nolan Ryan	27	19	7	11	1	3.42	131.2	125	97
CL	Ron Taylor	57	0	5	4	13	3.93	66.1	28	16

FABULOUS: TOMMIE AGEE

Tommie Agee followed up his excellent 1969 campaign by hitting .286 with 24 home runs, 75 RBI, and a career-high 107 RS. Agee also stole 31 bases. In June, he hit .364 with 11 homers and 30 RBI.

season. New York rallied to tie it, but Pittsburgh scored four in the 10th off Tug McGraw and recently acquired Dean Chance to win 9-5.

The team took a pair of games in Philadelphia and traveled to Pittsburgh trailing by 2.5 games with 7 remaining. There was no miracle as a Pirates sweep clinched the division. The Mets finished the season splitting four games in Chicago to finish 83-79, six games out of first. The last two losses gave the Cubs second place.

Top 5 Highlights

1 Clendenon delivers a two-run single off Pittsburgh's Joe Gibbon in the 11th inning to give the Mets a 5-3 win over the Pirates for the first Opening Day win in team history.

2 Ryan strikes out 15 Phillies in an April 18 win. Denny Doyle's leadoff single was the only hit off Ryan.

3 April 22 was the first Earth Day and the day Seaver is presented with his 1969 Cy Young award. And The Franchise fans 19 Padres in a 2-1 win. Al Ferrara, who homered in the second inning, strikes out to end the sixth, the first of 10 consecutive strikeouts for Seaver.

4 Dave Marshall, in his first at-bat against the Giants after being acquired by the Mets, hits a grand slam off Gaylord Perry in the first inning of their April 28 meeting. The grand slam gave New York a 5-0 first inning lead and they would hold on to win 5-2.

5 Gentry takes a no-hitter two outs into the eighth inning before Ernie Banks singles. The right-hander finishes with a complete game one-hit shutout and even delivers an RBI single in the 4-0 win on May 13.

1971

	W	L	GB	Pos
	83	79	14.0	3rdT

RS/G	RA/G	Manager
3.81	5.85	Gil Hodges

OPENING DAY LINEUP

Tommie Agee, CF
Bud Harrelson, SS
Cleon Jones, LF
Art Shamsky, RF
Donn Clendenon, 1B
Ken Boswell, 2B
Bob Aspromonte, 3B
Jerry Grote, C
Tom Seaver, P

Tom Is Terrific – Bats Are Quiet

The Moves

Frank Robinson in a Mets uniform? The Orioles shopped the superstar around in the winter but the Mets deemed the asking price too high. "Two years ago the price was Tom Seaver and Jerry Koosman and we would not want him at that price," general manager Bob Scheffing said. "Now they are willing to take Gary Gentry and Nolan Ryan. They could have one, but not both."

The future Hall of Fame outfielder wasn't acquired but the Mets did pick up third baseman Bob Aspromonte, the last active player who had been on the Brooklyn Dodgers. Aspromonte only hit .213 in 1970 with the Braves but Wayne Garrett was looking at spending several months in the National Guard and the team didn't want to go to spring training with rookies Tim Foli and Ted Martinez at third base. The Mets sent right-hander Ron Herbel to Atlanta in return.

Ed Kranepool believed he was going to be moved as he was unhappy with the Gil Hodges platoon system and also realized Donn Clendenon, Art Shamsky, Mike Jorgensen and John Milner were all looking for work at first base. The Krane wanted consistent at-bats, though Tom Seaver asked, "He's been to bat nearly 3,000 times in the majors. That's not a chance?"

If there was anyone unhappier than Kranepool it was Ron Swoboda. The vocal outfielder wasn't shy in his criticism of all things Mets, even Seaver and Hodges. Swoboda, who was the Mets all-time home run leader with 69, was traded to the Expos at the end of March for Don Hahn, who had played parts of two seasons and had not yet hit a homer.

 He Was a Met?

Tim Foli had a cup of coffee in 1970 as a 19-year-old for the Mets, then played regularly in 1971 before embarking on a long career as a back-up middle infielder with Expos and four other teams, including a return to the Mets in 1978.

The Situation

Hodges said the 1971 team was "stronger" than the 1969 champions because they had matured. *Sports Illustrated* also wrote that it was "now or never" for Ryan and Gentry to perform.

The Season

After a 7-7 start, the Mets won five in a row to end April. The team was in first place with a 2.5 game lead on May 15 before a five-game losing streak knocked them out of the division lead. It

The Ryan Express Departs

The Mets grew tired of waiting for Nolan Ryan to reach his potential, so they traded him to the Angels for Jim Fregosi. Fregosi was only 29 at the time of the trade and had made the AL All-Star team 6 times. But his productivity with the Angels had fallen off a cliff the previous season, going from 22 HR and 82 RBI in 1970 to 5 HR and 33 RBI in 1971. Fregosi had two disappointing seasons before being shipped out, while Ryan, who was 29-38 as a Met, became an eight-time All-Star and pitched seven no-hitters.

was Seaver and Ryan leading the way early on. At the end of May, Seaver was 6-2 with a 2.11 ERA. Ryan was a revelation, going 6-1 with a 1.08 ERA. In a May 29 doubleheader sweep of the Padres, Seaver struck out 10 in a 5-1 win, followed by Ryan striking out 16 in a 2-1 triumph.

The Mets went 18-11 in June, putting them at 45-29 and only two games out of first. Then the season went off the rails. The team lost 11 of 12 to begin July, including a homestand during which the Mets were shut out twice and held to one run three times. Jerry Koosman only made two starts during the month as he dealt with an elbow injury. Ryan was suddenly ineffective.

Things became so desperate that on July 11 in Cincinnati, Hodges called on Seaver to hold a 3-2 lead in the eighth inning in the final game before the All-Star break. Tony Perez greeted Seaver by hitting a three-run homer.

The offense was the main culprit. Cleon Jones led the team with 32 RBI at the All-Star break. Clendenon was gathering dust on the bench as a revitalized Kranepool who was over .300 during the season and at .283 at the break. Kranepool was moved to the outfield so Clendenon and his bat could get in the lineup.

FABULOUS: TOM SEAVER

The Franchise had career bests in ERA (1.76) CG (21), K (289), K/9ip (9.1), and WHIP (.946). Poor run support limited him to "only" 20 wins, and he was beaten out for the Cy Young Award by Ferguson Jenkins, who won 24.

A 12-17 August put them at .500 at the end of August though a 17-13 September ensured a third straight winning season. And Seaver was perhaps better than ever, finishing the season with a 1.76 ERA and 20

TOP BATTERS

Pos	Name	G	AB	H	BA	HR	RBI	RS	SB	OPS
1B	Ed Kranepool	122	421	118	.280	14	58	61	0	.786
SS	Bud Harrelson	142	547	138	.252	0	32	55	28	.622
LF	Cleon Jones	136	505	161	.319	14	69	63	6	.856
CF	Tommie Agee	113	425	121	.285	14	50	58	28	.790

TOP PITCHERS

Pos	Name	G	GS	W	L	SV	ERA	IP	SO	BB
SP	Tom Seaver	36	35	20	10	0	1.76	286.1	289	61
SP	Gary Gentry	32	31	12	11	0	3.23	203.1	155	82
SP	Nolan Ryan	30	26	10	14	0	3.97	152.0	137	116
CL	Danny Frisella	53	0	8	5	12	1.99	90.2	93	30
RP	Tug McGraw	51	1	11	4	8	1.70	111.0	109	41

Final Resting Ground

Bob Aspromonte had one at bat as an 18-year-old for the Brooklyn Dodgers. He went on to have a solid career at 3B, mainly for the Astros, before wrapping up his career with the Mets in 1971, batting .225 with 5 home runs in 104 games.

wins. The other bright spot was the lefty-righty bullpen combo of Tug McGraw and Danny Frisella, who both finished with ERAs under 2.00.

Top 5 Highlights

1 Jerry Grote beats the Reds on April 11 with a home run to lead off the bottom of the 11th off Wayne Granger to give the Mets a 1-0 win.

2 On June 2 in San Francisco, Charlie Williams comes out of the bullpen to pitch five shutout innings and keep the Giants at bay as the Mets rally for five runs against Juan Marichal and a 5-2 win.

3 Cleon Jones hits the 1,000th home run in Mets history on June 25 off Ken Forsch in a 7-6 win over the Astros at Shea.

4 The Mets pound out 21 hits in a 20-6 win in Atlanta on August 7. Ken Boswell's grand slam off Mike McQueen made it 10-1 in the second inning.

5 Seaver struck out 289 batters, breaking the record for National League right-handers. The record would stand until Houston's J.R. Richard fanned 303 batters in 1978.

1972

	W	L	GB	Pos
	83	73	13.5	3rd

RS/G	RA/G	Manager
3.38	3.71	Yogi Berra

A Leader Lost in Somber Season

The Moves

Miracle Met Art Shamsky was gone, traded to St. Louis after the 1971 season, along with Rich Folkers and Jim Bibby, in exchange for Jim Beachump and pitchers Harry Parker and Chuck Taylor. The Mets sold Ron Taylor to the Expos, though he would be released before pitching in Montreal and instead wound up on the Padres. Bob Aspromonte was released, as was Donn Clendenon.

To solve the everlasting third base problem, the Mets acquired Jim Fregosi, a six-time All-Star with the Angels. The Mets gave up four players, including Nolan Ryan.

"You hate to give up on an arm like Ryan's," Gil Hodges said. "He could put things together overnight, but he hasn't done it for us and the Angels wanted him. I would not hesitate making a trade for somebody who might help us right now, and Fregosi is such a guy."

Bob Scheffing said he didn't quit on Ryan: "But we've had three full years and, although he's a hell of a prospect, he hasn't done it for us. How long can you wait? I can't rate him in the same category with Tom Seaver, Jerry Koosman or Gary Gentry." Ryan would go on to win 329 games, pitch seven no-hitters and strikeout 5,714 batters. Fregosi would not solve the hot corner issue for the Mets.

🎾 He Was a Met?

Before becoming one of the most respected pitching coaches in the league and being a member on the staff of the 2017 Astros, Brent Strom went 0-3 with a 6.82 ERA in 11 appearances with the Mets. After five starts he was moved to the bullpen where he didn't fare much better.

The Situation

The end of the platoon? Hodges said in his 10th season as a big league manager that "our lineup this season will be the most 'set' that I've ever had. Except for first base, we conceivably could play the same lineup most days." Fregosi would break his thumb fielding a grounder hit by Hodges during an infield drill but would be good to go by Opening Day, which was pushed back because of a players' strike.

On April 2, Hodges collapsed after playing golf with his coaches. He was dead of a heart attack, two days shy of his 48th birthday.

"Say Hey" Kid Comes to Shea

New York fan favorite Willie Mays returned to the city in May 1972. Joan Payson had tried almost a decade earlier to bring her favorite Giant back where he started his career. In his first game with the Mets, Mays's homer was the difference in a win against the Giants. Mays performed decently in 1972, and contributed to the team with his leadership and expertise. Both were in even greater evidence the following year During the Mets' push for the postseason up to their Game 7 loss in the World Series. Overall, Mays hit 14 home runs as a Met, giving him 660 in his career.

Four days later, Yogi Berra was named manager. The team also announced Rusty Staub had been acquired from the Expos for Ken Singleton, Tim Foli and Mike Jorgensen. Staub was an All-Star each of the previous five seasons and hit .311 in 162 games in 1971. "We're not traders by nature," M. Donald Grant said. "We like to train our own young men. But you've got to give something to get something. We need a man who can knock in runs."

The Season

A seven-game win streak in April and a team-record tying 11-game win streak in May propelled the Mets to a 25-7 start and a six-game lead in the NL East with Seaver off to a 7-1 start, despite not completing games as he previously done. And the team acquired Willie Mays for pitcher Charlie Williams as the Giants hero returned to New York. Joan Payson had dreamed of bringing the "Say Hey Kid" to Queens for a decade and has accomplished it. Jim Beachump switched to number 5 so Mays could wear number 24. Mays homered in his first game as a Met, a fifth inning solo shot against the Giants.

A two-game sweep of the Phillies put the Mets at 30-11 after June 1. This was despite Jerry Koosman being moved to the bullpen after three lousy starts to begin the season. He would rejoin the rotation on June 10. Jon Matlack began the season 6-0 with a 1.95

FABULOUS: TUG MCGRAW

Tug McGraw made his first All-Star team, pitching to a 1.70 ERA in 106 IP with 27 saves. The lefty had an ERA of 0.80 at Shea.

FUTILE: JIM FREGOSI

After being acquired for Nolan Ryan, Jim Fregosi was batting over .300 in May but struggled throughout the summer. He hit finished with a .232 average along with only 32 RBI and 31 RS in 340 at bats. Ryan, meanwhile, won 19 games, struck out 329, and had an ERA of 2.28.

ERA, culminating with a complete game shutout against the Phillies.

Then injuries depleted the Mets offense. Staub, who was hitting .325 at the end of May, was hit on the hand by a pitch. He fought through it but he left the lineup on June 18. He returned on July 18 for one game and wasn't seen again until September 18. John Milner's hot bat forced Cleon Jones to move to first base, where he was injured in a collision with Joe Morgan.

Gary Gentry went 0-4 in June as his ERA ballooned from 2.47 to 4.06. Infielder Teddy Martinez moved around the outfield as the injuries piled up.

The team began July tied for first place and finished it seven games out. New York's anemic offense was shut out three times and held to one run on six occasions. The Mets staggered to the finish line and were as few as four games over .500 (74-70) on September 22 before winning nine of its final 12 games.

Montreal's Bill Stoneman no-hit the Mets on October 2, the fifth no-hitter thrown against the team in 11 seasons.

They finished 83-73 despite being outscored by 50 runs.

TOP BATTERS

Pos	Name	G	AB	H	BA	HR	RBI	RS	SB	OPS
3B	Jim Fregosi	101	340	79	.232	5	32	31	0	.655
LF	John Milner	117	362	86	.238	17	38	52	2	.762
CF	Tommie Agee	114	422	96	.227	13	47	52	8	.692
RF	Rusty Staub	66	239	70	.293	9	38	32	0	.824
CF	Willie Mays	69	195	52	.267	8	19	27	1	.848

TOP PITCHERS

Pos	Name	G	GS	W	L	SV	ERA	IP	SO	BB
SP	Tom Seaver	35	35	21	12	0	2.92	262.0	249	77
SP	Jon Matlack	34	32	15	10	0	2.32	244.0	169	71
SP	Jerry Koosman	34	24	11	12	1	4.14	163.0	147	52
SP	Jim McAndrew	28	23	11	8	1	2.80	160.2	81	38
CL	Tug McGraw	54	0	8	6	27	1.70	106.0	92	40

Top 5 Highlights

1 Seaver and McGraw combine to shutout the defending-champion Pirates on Opening Day. Seaver pitches six shutout innings and McGraw retires all nine batters he faces in the 4-0 win. Kranepool connects for a two-run homer off Dock Ellis in the sixth.

2 Buzz Capra pitches eight shutout innings against the Giants and delivers a second inning RBI single off Juan Marichal in New York's 1-0 win on May 13. McGraw strikes out the side in the ninth for the save.

3 In his first game as a Met, Mays hits a fifth inning home run off Don Carrithers, the deciding run in New York's 5-4 win on May 14. The other four Mets runs scored on Staub's first inning grand slam.

4 The Franchise took a no-hitter into the ninth inning in Game 1 of a July 4 doubleheader against the Padres but this time it was Leron Lee playing the part of Jimmy Qualls, as Lee singled with one out in the ninth. Still, Seaver finished with a complete game one-hit shutout, striking out 11 and walking four in the 2-0 win.

5 Matlack shuts out Pittsburgh on September 18 and then tosses another complete game five days later in a 5-3 win against the Phillies.

1973

	W	L	GB	Pos
	82	79	1.5 GA	1st
RS/G	RA/G		Manager	
3.78	3.65		Yogi Berra	

Worst to First: Mets Rally to Win Pennant

The Moves

The Mets sent Gary Gentry and Danny Frisella to the Braves for second baseman Felix Millan and southpaw pitcher George Stone. Millan was a three-time All-Star though Stone struggled in 1972, pitching to a 5.51 ERA.

Tommie Agee was traded to the Astros for two prospects, Rich Chiles and Buddy Harris. "I guess you'd have to say we were dissatisfied with Agee's playing," an honest Bob Scheffing said.

The Situation

Pittsburgh had won three straight division titles but Roberto Clemente tragically died in a plane crash on New Year's Eve. It looked like an open division full of flawed teams.

There was an issue between two legends. Willie Mays left training camp for two days for an unauthorized trip home and was fined by Yogi Berra. "I told him he was fined for two things – leaving the club without permission and missing the workout Saturday," Berra said. "He seemed down and said he was sorry. It was my decision."

Mays admitted he made a mistake, saying his wife would get lonely. "I didn't think I'd have to tell them every time I cross the street," Mays said. "The only other time I was fined was with the Giants about a dozen years ago by Bill

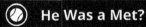

He Was a Met?

Acquired from Houston for Tommie Agee, Rich Chiles batted .120 in eight games in April, his only action with the Mets. He made it back to the majors for a cup of coffee with the Astros in 1976 and then played two seasons with the Twins.

Rigney – for not running out a pop fly that the wind blew back in. But I got the money back."

Was the iconic Mays, beloved by Joan Payson, bigger than the team? Tug McGraw said the outfielder was appreciated, not resented. But another Met joked that the $1,000 fine broke down to "$100 for going and $900 for coming back."

The Season

Mets Lose Battle but Win War

With the Reds frustrated in Game 3 of the NLCS, Pete Rose and Bud Harrelson fought at second base after Rose tried to break up a double play. Rose got the best of the much smaller Harrelson, but the scene symbolized the tough, underdog spirit of the team, who shocked the Big Red Machine in 5 games. It was an intense brawl, but later Rose and Harrelson became friends as Phillies teammates in 1979, and Harrelson later managed Pete Rose Jr. on the Long Island Ducks.

The Mets jumped out of the gate winning the first four games, with two-game sweeps against the Phillies and Cardinals. The team would lose eight of the next 14 with the offense struggling mightily. The Mets were shut out four times and held to one run in two others. The Mets dropped to 10-8 in a 2-0 loss to the Braves on April 27, which lasted one hour and 36 minutes. New York's batting averages were ghastly. Harrelson was hitting .182, Staub .164, Millan .162 and Mays .069.

John Milner was batting .327 with five homers and 13 RBI in 16 games, but pulled his hamstring stretching for a ball at first in a win at Houston and was gone for three weeks. Cleon Jones hit two homers on Opening Day but was hurt in Chicago and was out for three weeks.

Two wins to end April, including a 1-0 Koosman shutout over the Braves, had the Mets tied for first at the end of the month. But the Mets lost five straight to begin May. The offense picked up a bit but the pitching gave up 44 runs in the five games. Mays hurt his shoulder making a throw on his 42nd birthday in a 14-8 loss to the Astros and was gone for a month.

On May 8, Jon Matlack was pitching with a 3-1 lead in the seventh with the bases loaded, two outs and Marty Perez at the plate. Perez hit a liner, beaning Matlack and rolling into the Mets dugout for a game-tying two-run double. Matlack had a hairline fracture of his skull but would return to pitch 11 days later. Meanwhile, Phil Hennigan came in and gave up a three-run homer to Davey Johnson.

Three days later, Pirates pitcher Ramon Hernandez hit Staub to begin the seventh. Staub was removed but X-rays revealed no cracks. Jerry Grote wasn't as lucky. He was drilled three batters later and his arm was fractured, keeping him out two months. Berra was trying everything in center: Mays, Chiles, rookie George Theodore, Jones, utility man Ted Martinez and Jim Gosger.

Final Resting Ground

Willie Mays is perhaps the most famous of the Mets's end-of-career guys. His struggles in the World Series are well known, though he did hit .300 (3-for-10) in the postseason. Mays' last career home run came off hard-throwing Don Gullet on August 17th in a 2-1 loss to the Reds.

Millan was out nearly two weeks with a twisted ankle and then took a ground ball to the groin. The Mets lost six of seven, with the one win a 19-inning marathon in Los Angeles. The team lost six of eight to begin June with the floundering offense shutout four times. The team also lost a 10-inning game on June 5 in Cincinnati. Duffy Dyer delivered a bases clearing triple in the top of the inning off Don Gullett to give the Mets a 5-2 lead. In the bottom of the 10th, McGraw walked two batters with a single and wild pitch mixed in. With the lead 5-3, Berra took him out for Hennigan. Johnny Bench greeted him with a three-run homer to end the game.

Seaver was 7-3 with a 1.74 ERA and had a 16-strikeout performance in San Francisco but the rest of the rotation wasn't sharp. Koosman lost five straight decisions after a 5-0 start. Matlack was 2-8 with a 4.63 ERA. Jim McAndrew had a 5.30 ERA.

In late June, the Mets fell to last place, losing 10 of 13. The Pirates won two games in their final at-bat in a series in Pittsburgh. On June 25, Matlack took a 2-0 lead into the ninth against the Cubs but was taken out after a single and walk began the inning. McGraw gave up a game-tying double and then an RBI single in a 3-2 loss. The Mets were one out from beating the Cubs on June 29 when Gene Hiser homered off Buzz Capra. McGraw gave up a game-ending single to Jose Cardenal in the 10th. On July 1, the Mets led the Cubs 5-3 in the ninth. Hennigan gave up consecutive singles and McGraw came in. With two outs, Randy Hundley hit a three-run homer. The team went to Montreal and lost the next night in the 10th inning when Boots Day homered off Capra.

There was no heartbreak on July 3, only embarrassment. The Mets lost 19-8. McAndrew gave up six runs (five earned) in 4.1 innings. McGraw gave up seven runs on four hits and walked four in 1.1 innings. Hennigan gave up six runs in two innings. Things were looking up the next day as Seaver took a 5-0 lead into the bottom of the eighth. The Expos scored four times and then Ron Woods hit a three-run home run off Capra.

As Berra observed during the horrible stretch, "if you ain't got a bullpen, you ain't got nothin'."

The Mets were trailing 4-3 to the Braves on July 7 when Ralph Garr hit a fly ball. Don Hahn and George Theodore crashed into each other in a scary collision. Both were down. Garr had an inside-the-park home run. Theodore wouldn't play again until September 20. New York did score four times in the eighth, with a two-run single from Mays and two-run double from Wayne Garrett to take a 7-6 lead. But McGraw struggled in the ninth, giving up the tying run and leaving with the bases loaded. Harry Parker allowed two of the inherited runners to score and the Mets had lost another late lead. McGraw was 0-4 with a 6.20 ERA. Hennigan wouldn't pitch again in the majors. The Mets sold Jim Fregosi to the Rangers as the team cut ties with the infielder who was batting .245.

McGraw made his first start of the year on July 17. He gave up seven runs (six earned) on 10 hits in six innings. The Mets trailed 7-1 going into the ninth but improbably scored seven runs and escaped with an 8-7 stunner. Still, the Mets lost the final four of the month and were in last place with a 44-57 record.

FABULOUS: FELIX MILLAN

Felix Millan batted .290 with 185 hits and 83 RS in his first season with the Mets. Millan's famous bat control was in evidence as he fanned just 22 times in 699 plate appearances.

Berra was coming under fire. Mays questioned the manager after being asked to bunt twice in a game. Mays popped up both times. "I think I sacrificed only 10 times in my career and never twice in one game," Mays said. Donald Grant said Berra wouldn't be fired "unless public opinion demands it."

That wasn't a rousing endorsement. The *New York Post* had a poll with pictures of Berra, Grant and Scheffing, asking readers who should be fired. Scheffing received the most votes, Grant the second most. Also of note was a July visit to the clubhouse from Grant. Grant told the team they had to believe. McGraw started screaming "Ya Gotta Believe." Whether he was mocking the executive or was inspired by a motivational speaker he had seen earlier in the day who told him he had to believe, the slogan would turn into a rallying cry.

The Mets were inconsistent. Four wins to begin August. Three straight losses. Three straight wins. There was a 13-inning loss in San Francisco and a 10-inning loss at Shea to the Reds. On August 20, Berra left Seaver in for 12 innings against the Reds. Cincinnati won with five runs in the 16th.

Slowly, things turned around. The Mets won consecutive games with Milner delivering game-ending hits in two straight games to beat the Dodgers. Two days later, Millan's RBI single off Juan Marichal beat the Giants in the bottom of the 10th. Koosman pitched 10 shutouts innings in the 1-0 win.

Seaver was a tough-luck loser on August 30, giving up a 10th inning single to Jose Cruz in a 1-0 loss at St. Louis. Seaver was 15-8 with a 1.71 ERA. At 61-71, the Mets were in last place. But incredibly, they were only 6.5 games out of first. The 68-65 Cardinals were the only team in the NL East with a winning record.

On August 31, the Cardinals jumped on Ray Sadecki for three runs in the first. The Mets came back to tie it and five straight singles in the 10th scored three runs. McGraw gave up a run but saved the game. The Mets moved out of last place.

The Mets won four straight with McGraw even driving in two runs with a 15th inning single in Montreal. Berra was milking Seaver, letting his ace go 11 innings in a win against the Phillies on September 13, with McGraw saving the

FUTILE: DUFFY DYER

Duffy Dyer was a strong defensive catcher in his years with the Mets, which was particularly important in 1973 when it's hard to imagine he could have been any less productive. In 189 at bats over 70 games, Dyer drove in a total of 9 runs and scored an equally paltry 9.

game in the 12th. The Mets hadn't been at .500 since May but were in a pennant chase

Berra would go with a four-man rotation of Seaver, Koosman, Matlack and Stone. Stone was 8-3 with a 2.96 ERA through August and would be a key contributor down the stretch.

After a 4-3 win over the Cubs on September 16, the 73-76 fourth place Mets were 2.5 games out of first. The Mets had five games with the first-place Pirates. Pittsburgh jumped on Seaver 10-3 in the opener in Pittsburgh. On September 18, the Mets trailed 4-1 heading into the ninth but New York rallied. Millan tripled in two runs. Ron Hodges tied the game with a single. Hahn singled in two runs to make it 6-4. The Pirates scored once in the bottom of the ninth and loaded the bases for Manny Sanguillen. Capra got him to fly out to left to end the game. Then the teams moved to Shea for three games.

The Mets won 7-3 with Stone winning his fifth start in a row to improve to 12-3. Jones put the game away with a three-run homer in the bottom of the eighth. Jones was a large part of the pennant race, driving in 17 runs in his final 14 games. Garrett hit six homers and drove in 17 runs in September.

TOP BATTERS

Pos	Name	G	AB	H	BA	HR	RBI	RS	SB	OPS
1B	John Milner	129	451	108	.239	23	72	69	1	.762
2B	Felix Millan	153	638	185	.290	3	37	82	2	.685
3B	Wayne Garrett	140	504	129	.256	16	58	76	6	.751
LF	Cleon Jones	92	339	88	.260	11	48	48	1	.710
RF	Rusty Staub	152	585	163	.279	15	76	77	1	.781

TOP PITCHERS

Pos	Name	G	GS	W	L	SV	ERA	IP	SO	BB
SP	Tom Seaver	36	36	19	10	0	2.08	290.0	251	64
SP	Jerry Koosman	35	35	14	15	0	2.84	263.0	156	76
SP	Jon Matlack	34	34	14	16	0	3.20	242.0	205	99
SP	George Stone	27	20	12	3	1	2.80	148.0	77	31
CL	Tug McGraw	60	2	5	6	25	3.87	118.2	81	55

On September 20, the Mets trailed 3-2 and were one out away from losing when Dyer doubled to left, scoring Ken Boswell. In the top of the 13th, Dave Augustine came to the plate with Richie Zisk on first. Augustine hit Sadecki's pitch deep to left and it looked like it would be a home run. Instead the ball bounced off the top of the wall and to Jones, who fired it to Harrelson, who threw home to Hodges, who put the tag on Zisk. In the bottom of the inning, Hodges singled to win the game.

The Mets moved into first the next night, with Seaver going the distance and Milner, Garrett and Staub homering in a 10-2 win. Then the Mets took a pair of games from the Cardinals, including a 2-0 win with Matlack tossing a four-hit shutout and Garrett hitting a two-run homer. On September 25, the Mets won again, beating the Expos 2-1 to improve to 80-77, 1.5 in front. The night was also special because Mays, who hadn't been played since September 9 and announced his retirement, was honored. "I look at the kids over here, the way they're playing, the way they're fighting for themselves, and it tells me one thing: 'Willie, say goodbye to America.'" The Mets lost the home finale to the Expos.

In Chicago, the Mets lost 1-0 in the first game of a September 30 doubleheader. But the Mets jumped on Ferguson Jenkins in the second game with Koosman going the distance in a 9-2 win.

On October 1, the Mets had a chance to clinch the division or finish .500, which would've meant a tie with the Cardinals. New York took a 5-0 lead but the Cubs scored twice off Seaver in the fifth. With a 6-2 lead, Seaver gave up a two-run homer to Rick Monday in the seventh. McGraw, who had been terrific in September, entered and retired the first six batters he faced. Ken Rudolph led off the bottom of the ninth with a single and Dave Rosello went down on strikes, bringing up pinch-hitter Glenn Beckert. With Rudolph going, Beckert hit a soft pop-up to first. Milner made the easy catch and went to first for a division-clinching double play. When the umpires determined the field was too wet to play another game, the Mets celebrated.

"It's been a long year," Berra said. "I was on 14 Yankee teams that won, but this has to be a big thrill because we had to jump over five clubs to do it. We were 12 games back and hurt."

Top 5 Highlights

1 Tom Seaver and Tug McGraw combine for an Opening Day shutout and Cleon Jones homers twice off Steve Carlton in a win over the Phillies. Seaver pitches into the eighth and McGraw retires the final four batters.

2 The Mets score seven runs in the top of the ninth to beat the Braves 8-7 on July 17. Rusty Staub and John Milner hit two-run homers to cut the lead to 7-5 and knock Carl Morton from the game. Adrian Devine enters and gets Ron Hodges on a grounder for the second out of the inning. Don Hahn singles to center, Ed Kranepool walks and Jim Beachump singles to make it 7-6. Then Willie Mays delivers a pinch-hit two-run single off Tom House to make it 8-7. Harry Parker pitches a 1-2-3 bottom of the ninth.

③ Milner's single off Pete Richert in the bottom of the ninth gives the Mets a 4-3 win over the Dodgers on August 22. Felix Millan tied the game with a two-out single off Jim Brewer. It was the second straight winning hit for Milner, after he beat Don Sutton and the Dodgers the day before.

④ The Mets turn a 7-6-2 double play against the Pirates after Dave Augustine's 13th inning fly ball hits the top of the wall and comes back to Jones, who begins a relay. Ron Hodges makes the tag and then singles in the winning run in the bottom of the inning as the team inches closer to first place.

⑤ Milner turns an unassisted double play on a Glenn Beckert pop-up as the Mets clinch the NL East with a 6-4 win over the Cubs at Wrigley Field.

1973 NLCS

New York's unlikely division title earned them a date with the 99-win Cincinnati Reds, who were on a mission after losing Game 7 of the World Series in 1972. The Mets would have been a distant fourth in the NL West but instead found themselves in a best-of-five with Seaver starting the opener.

With two outs in the second, Seaver helped his own cause with an RBI double off Jack Billingham. It looked like it might hold up as Seaver pitched seven shutout innings, striking out 11. Pete Rose, the NL MVP, hit a homer to tie the game. In the top of the ninth, Staub walked but Pedro Borbon retired the next three Mets. In the bottom of the ninth, Johnny Bench homered with one out to end the game. Seaver, who fanned 13 Reds, was a 2-1 loser.

It was two lefties, Matlack and Don Gullett, dueling in the second game. Staub broke a scoreless tie with a fourth inning solo shot. Matlack was going through the Big Red Machine. He walked two batters in the fifth but struck out pinch-hitter Phil Gagliano. It was 1-0 entering the ninth when the Mets busted out for four runs on five hits against Tom Hall and Borbon. Jones had an RBI single, Grote's single drove in a pair and Harrelson delivered an RBI single. Matlack set down Joe Morgan, Tony Perez and Bench in the ninth. Matlack only gave up two hits in the 5-0 win, both to Andy Kosco.

Commenting on the game, Harrelson joked the Reds "looked like me hitting."

In Game 3, Staub homered off Ross Grimsley in the first and then hit a three-run shot off Tom Hall in the second to give the Mets a 6-0 lead. The Reds scored twice in the third but the Mets got one back with Koosman's RBI single. The Mets scored twice more off Dave Tomlin in the fourth to make it 9-2.

With one out in the fifth, Rose singled. Morgan hit into an inning-ending 3-6-3 double play to end the inning. Rose and Harrelson got into a fight at second base, leading to a bench-clearing brawl. The bullpens also rushed out, with Borbon punching Capra. When Rose went out to left for the bottom of the fifth, fans threw objects at him. The Reds came off the field and a group of Mets, including Seaver, Mays, Berra, Jones and Staub calmed the fans down for fear of a forfeit. With the drama over, Koosman pitched a complete game.

Stone got the Game 4 start against Fred Norman. Millan broke a scoreless tie in the bottom of the third with an RBI single. Stone took a shutout into the seventh but Perez homered to tie the game. Gullett and McGraw traded zeroes out of the bullpen. With runners on the corners and two outs in the top of the 11th, Staub made a running catch and crashed into the wall to rob Dan Driessen of an extra-base hit. Clay Carroll pitched a scoreless 10th and 11th for the Reds. With one out in the top of the 12th, Rose homered off Parker to give the Reds a 2-1 lead. Rose only hit five home runs during the season and now had two critical homers in the NLCS. Borbon retired the Mets in order to end it.

It was Seaver against Billingham in the deciding Game 5. Staub was out with an injured shoulder so Jones started in right with Kranepool in left. With the bases loaded and out in the first, Kranepool singled in two runs. The Reds cut the lead in half in the third. Cincinnati tied the game in the fifth with a Perez single.

In the bottom of the fifth, Jones came to the plate with runners on the corners and nobody out. Jones doubled off Billingham to give the Mets a 3-2 lead. Gullett came in and walked Milner, loading the bases. Then Berra sent Mays up as a pinch-hitter for Kranepool and Sparky Anderson called on Carroll. Mays hit a slow chopper to the left side and the legend had himself an infield single. Hahn drove in a run with a force-out and Harrelson singled in a run. In the sixth, Jones' RBI single made it 7-2.

Seaver was still on the mound with a 7-2 lead in the ninth but the crowd was impatient and stormed the dugouts, leading to a delay. The Reds loaded the bases and McGraw came in to record the final two outs. Morgan popped up to short. Driessen grounded out to Milner, who flipped to a covering McGraw. McGraw avoided a stampede of fans and made it to the clubhouse.

"I'm just ashamed," Anderson said about the fans. "I'm ashamed that I live in this country. I'm not too sure New York is in this country."

The Mets, in last place on August 30, were National League champions. "We coulda folded," Kranepool said. "We coulda packed our bags and gone home. We didn't because we were professionals. We have pride. We wanted the money and the prestige."

1973 World Series

It was the defending champion Oakland Athletics the Mets would face. There was almost a sequel with the Orioles but the A's took a deciding Game 5 of the ALCS. Of note, the Mets would deny Oakland's request to allow second baseman Manny Trillo on the roster. League rules stated a player had to be on the roster on August 31 but when Bill North sprained his ankle, the A's looked to add Trillo. The Orioles had approved him. The Mets didn't.

With the opening game in a scoreless tie in the bottom of the third, Oakland pitcher Ken Holtzman doubled to keep the inning going. Bert Campaneris hit a grounder to second but Millan had it go through his legs, scoring Holtzman. Campaneris stole second and scored on Joe Rudi's single. A Milner RBI single in the fourth cut the lead to 2-1 but there was no more scoring. Rollie Fingers pitched 3.1 innings of shutout relief and Darold Knowles recorded the final two outs.

The A's scored twice off Koosman in the first inning of Game 2. Jones homered off Vida Blue in the second, Oakland got it right back and then Garrett homered in the third. The Mets chased Blue in the sixth and Horacio Pina walked Grote to load the bases with one out. Hahn's infield single tied the game and Harrelson's single gave the Mets a 4-3 lead. With Knowles in, pinch-hitter Beachump hit one which Knowles fielded but his throw home was off the mark and two runs scored. Reggie Jackson's RBI double off McGraw in the seventh cut the lead to 6-4 but the Mets still led going into the ninth.

Deron Johnson doubled to begin the ninth, but McGraw retired the next two batters. Sal Bando walked and Jackson singled, making it 6-5. Gene Tenace singled to tie the game though McGraw retired Jesus Alou to send the game to extra innings. In the top of the 10th, the Mets put runners on the corners with one out for Millan. Millan hit a fly ball to left. Harrelson attempted to score the go-ahead run but was thrown out at the plate. Ray Fosse's tag appeared to miss Harrelson, who didn't slide, but home plate umpire Augie Donatelli called the runner out, leading to shocked, angry reactions from the Mets.

In the 12th, the Mets broke through. With two on and two outs, Mays singled to center off Fingers to give New York a 7-6 lead. Jones singled to left, loading the bases. Paul Lindblad came in for Oakland. Milner hit a ground ball to second, which Mike Andrews booted, allowing McGraw to score. Then Grote hit one to Andrews, whose throw to first was off the mark, allowing another run to score. The Mets had a 10-6 lead but McGraw had pitched six innings and was trying for a seventh. A triple and walk began the bottom of the 12th and Stone came in. Alou singled to right, making it 10-7 and bringing up the tying run. Fosse hit into a force and Andrews walked to load the bases. Vic Davalillo popped up to second and Campaneris grounded out to end the four hour, 13 minute game, which saw Oakland commit five errors.

As the series moved to Queens, Oakland owner Charlie Finley forced Andrews to sign an affidavit saying he was injured, making him ineligible for the rest of the series. The team was outraged and commissioner Bowie Kuhn would reinstate the infielder.

Garrett led off with a homer off Catfish Hunter and the Mets scored another first-inning run on a wild pitch. Seaver pitched five shutout innings before Tenace's two-out RBI double in the sixth put the A's on the board. In the eighth, Campaneris singled, stole second and scored on Rudi's single. The game became a battle of bullpens and Campaneris' 11th inning single off Parker scored Ted Kubiak to give the A's a 3-2 lead. The Mets put a runner in scoring position in the bottom of the inning but Fingers retired Staub and Jones to end the game.

The Mets won an easy Game 4. Staub hit a three-run homer off Holtzman in the first. The Mets would chase the lefty after he recorded only one out. Staub singled in two more runs in the fourth to make it 6-1. The score would hold up with Matlack giving up one run on three hits in eight innings. Sadecki loaded the bases in the ninth before striking out Campaneris.

In Game 5, Milner's RBI single off Blue gave the Mets a lead in the second and Hahn added an RBI triple in the sixth. In the top of the seventh, Koosman walked Tenace and allowed a one-out double to Fosse, putting the tying runs in scoring position. McGraw came in and walked Johnson, loading the bases. Pinch-hitter Angel Mangual popped up to short and Campaneris struck out looking to end the inning. In the eighth, McGraw walked two batters put Alou lined out to end the inning. McGraw set down the side in order in the ninth, striking out Billy Conigliaro to end the game.

Who to start? Stone or Seaver? Seaver lobbied to start, wanting to pitch the clincher. Berra went with Seaver.

Jackson had an RBI double off Seaver in the first and another in the third. Hunter pitched seven shutout innings. In the eighth, Boswell's one-out single ended Hunter's day and Knowles came in. Back-to-back singles from Garrett and Millan made it 2-1 with runners on the corners. Staub came up, but Knowles struck him out. Fingers came in and Jones flied out to center. Oakland added an insurance run in the eighth against McGraw and Fingers closed out the 3-1 game.

Matlack and Holtzman matched zeroes until the bottom of the third in Game 7. Campaneris and Jackson both hit two-run home runs. Rudi's RBI single off Sadecki in the fifth made it 5-0. Staub's RBI double in the sixth got the Mets on the board.

The Mets trailed 5-1 entering the ninth. There were two on and two out for Kranepool. A grounder could've ended the series but Deron Johnson's error gave the Mets another chance. With the lead down to 5-2, Knowles, who appeared in every game, came in to pitch to Garrett. Representing the tying run, Garrett popped up to short to end the series.

Drinking a beer in the clubhouse, Harrelson said "It sure doesn't taste like champagne."

1974

	W	L	GB	Pos
	71	91	17.0	5th
RS/G	RA/G		Manager	
3.53	3.99		Yogi Berra	

Wheels Fall Off in Worst Season Since '67

The Moves

It was a quiet offseason for the Mets, who chose to focus on the fact that they were the NL champions and not a team a little over .500 that won the division with an 82-79 record. Jim McAndrew was traded to the Padres and Buzz Capra was sold to the Braves.

There were trades they didn't make for outfield help. Houston offered Jimmy Wynn for George Stone and Craig Swan. Instead, the Astros sent Wynn to the Dodgers. Houston got a southpaw pitcher in Claude Osteen and the Dodgers would win the pennant with Wynn contributing 32 homers and 108 RBI.

Jon Matlack going to Baltimore for Merv Rettenmund didn't happen. Neither did Matlack going to San Francisco for Dave Kingman. The team was content with Cleon Jones, Don Hahn and Rusty Staub starting in the outfield, with George Theodore and Dave Schneck fighting for time, with Benny Ayala looming in the minors.

The Situation

The other five teams in the division made major deals while the Mets virtually stood pat. But if they could stay healthy and the rotation was as good as usual, why couldn't they keep winning? And the Mets figured Tug McGraw wouldn't struggle as he did for five months in 1973.

He Was a Met?

Jack Aker had a successful 10-year career as a reliever, mainly with the Athletics and Yankees, before coming over to the Mets in June. He pitched pretty well over the last few months, but the 24 games turned out to be the last of his career.

The Season

New York started the season in Philadelphia with a new uniform as the "New York" wordmark was gone in favor of "Mets." The magic of 1973 was quickly erased on Opening Day when Mike Schmidt hit a two-run homer in the bottom of the ninth off McGraw to stun the Mets and give the Phillies a 5-4 win. The Mets played terribly out of the gate, starting 3-11, including a seven-game losing streak.

The most alarming situation was with Seaver and his 6.12 ERA through four starts. On April 21, the Pirates pounded him for six runs on 12 hits in five innings. He won his first game five days later with a four-hit shutout of the Giants. Then when he pitched 12 innings of three-hit ball in Los Angeles, the offense wasted it, losing 2-1 in 14 innings.

McGraw was off to a dreadful start, giving up at least one run in each of his first six appearances. He was 0-3 with an ERA of 9.00 at the end of May. Seaver was mediocre, though he mixed in another shutout and finished the month at 2-5 with a 3.89 ERA.

Hahn was hitting .328 through May and part-time Ed Kranepool was at .348. Matlack was outstanding, but Stone couldn't recapture the magic from the season before and saw his ERA reach five. Somehow the 20-28 Mets were only five games out of first at the heading into June.

Any dreams of another run ended with a 10-16 June. The offense was faltering. Even Staub was

Joan Whitney Payson was the first woman to own a professional team in North America who did not inherit it. Payson was an active and popular president of the team from 1962 to 1975 when she passed away, handing down ownership to her heirs, who sold their interest in the team in 1980. Payson was well liked and highly respected in the organization and around baseball. Players to a man said she was a kind, caring person, who despite her enormous wealth, had no airs or pretensions.

Final Resting Ground

Bob Miller had a long, distinguished career as a major league reliever, appearing in nearly 700 games for 10 teams over 17 seasons. Miller was on the inaugural 1962 Mets, limping to a 1-12 record, which he followed up with a 10-8 for the world champion Dodgers the next season. He finished up his career with the 1974 Mets, appearing in 58 games and posting a respectable ERA of 3.58.

FABULOUS: JON MATLACK

Though he finished 13-15, Jon Matlack tossed a league-leading seven shutouts and completed 14 of 34 starts, pitching to a 2.41 ERA.

hitting .257 at the end of June. Jones was hitting .270, but Schneck was at .217 and would force Yogi Berra to forgo platooning in centerfield and give Hahn more playing time. The Mets lost seven of eight in the middle of the month, including a stretch of scoring three runs in four games.

Harry Parker was moved to the rotation, where he lost four straight decisions (two 1-0 defeats followed by a pair of starts where he failed to make it out of the second inning). Stone struggled in three of his four June starts. The 30-44 Mets were in dead last. To add insult to injury, Capra went 6-0 with the Braves during the month.

Jerry Grote and Matlack were selected to the All-Star Game but it was also notable as the first time in Seaver's eight-year career that he wasn't. Seaver won his first three starts of the month but the Pirates again pounded him in an ugly 8-3 Pittsburgh win, during which both teams committed three errors in the nearly three and a half hour contest. The Mets did go 15-12 in July, the team's only winning month of 1974.

The team continued to struggle as Berra was often criticized. As the joke went, the difference between Berra and Gil Hodges was six innings: In the third, Hodges was thinking about what he'd do in the sixth. In the sixth, Yogi was thinking about what he should have done in the third.

Seemingly lifeless at 53-70 on August 24, the Mets won 10 of 11. McGraw was moved to the rotation and won a pair of starts, including a shutout of

TOP BATTERS

Pos	Name	G	AB	H	BA	HR	RBI	RS	SB	OPS
1B	John Milner	137	507	128	.252	20	63	70	10	.745
2B	Felix Millan	136	518	139	.268	1	33	50	5	.628
3B	Wayne Garrett	151	522	117	.224	13	53	55	4	.674
LF	Cleon Jones	124	461	130	.282	13	60	62	3	.763
RF	Rusty Staub	151	561	145	.258	19	78	65	2	.754

TOP PITCHERS

Pos	Name	G	GS	W	L	SV	ERA	IP	SO	BB
SP	Jon Matlack	34	34	13	15	0	2.41	265.1	195	76
SP	Jerry Koosman	35	35	15	11	0	3.36	265.0	188	85
SP	Tom Seaver	32	32	11	11	0	3.20	236.0	201	75
RP	Bob Apodaca	35	8	6	6	3	3.50	103.0	54	42
RP-SP	Ray Sadecki	34	10	8	8	0	3.41	103.0	46	35

the Braves. But the Mets couldn't cut into the insurmountable lead. New York was one out away from winning on September 11 when Ken Reitz hit a two-run homer off Koosman to tie the game. A lot of time would have been saved as St. Louis would win in the 25th inning when Bake McBride scored from first on Hank Webb's pickoff attempt. Wayne Garrett went hitless in 10 at-bats in the seven hour, four minute game.

FUTILE: DAVE SCHNECK

Dave Schneck, whose greatest claim to fame may have been his funny last name, had a career year in 1974, belting 5 home runs and driving in 25 in...254 at bats. Four of Schneck's 5 home runs came in April. His .205 average is the only time he broke the Mendoza Line in his career, which ended after the 1974 season.

The Mets would lose 20 of 28 to end the season and Bob Scheffing was done as general manager. The team was done in by close games, going 17-36 in one run games and 4-16 in extra inning games.

Top 5 Highlights

1 John Milner hits a two-run homer off Larry Hardy in the bottom of the 10th to give the Mets a 6-4 win over the Padres on May 5. New York tied the game with a Ken Boswell single in the ninth.

2 Ed Kranepool collects his 1,000th career hit with an eighth inning single off Chicago's Steve Stone at Wrigley Field on May 12.

3 Jon Matlack pitches a one-hit shutout in a 4-0 win over the Cardinals on June 29. Opposing pitcher John Curtis singled in the third.

4 Harry Parker goes the distance in a 3-1 win over the Dodgers on August 12. Parker strikes out Steve Yeager with two on and two out to end the game.

5 In his first at-bat in the majors, Benny Ayala hits a second inning homer off Houston's Tom Griffin in a 4-2 win over the Astros on August 27. Ayala is the first Met to homer in his first MLB at-bat.

1975

OPENING DAY LINEUP

Gene Clines, LF
Felix Millan, 2B
John Milner, 1B
Joe Torre, 3B
Dave Kingman, RF
Jerry Grote, C
Del Unser, CF
Bud Harrelson, SS
Tom Seaver, P

	W	L	GB	Pos
	82	80	10.5	3rdT
RS/G	RA/G		Manager	
3.99	3.86		Yogi Berra Roy McMillan	

Seaver Cys, Staub Delivers, Yogi fired

The Moves

"Everybody's for sale except for the front three," Yogi Berra said. Seaver, Koosman and Matlack were untouchable, but the roster would be revamped after a 91-loss season. New general manager Joe McDonald explained, "The Untouchables was the name of a TV series."

The Mets acquired nine-time All-Star Joe Torre from St. Louis for Ray Sadecki as the Cardinals looked to make room for young prospect Keith Hernandez.

Gene Clines was acquired from Pittsburgh. Clines had some trouble with playing time on a talented Pirates team but he had hit .334 on the 1972 division champions. He only hit .225 in 1974, but stole 14 bases in 16 attempts and was expected to add some speed to the plodding Mets. Ken Boswell was sent to Houston in exchange for outfielder Bob Gallagher, who hit .172 the previous season.

In early December, the Mets sent Tug McGraw, Don Hahn and Dave Schneck to the Phillies for centerfielder Del Unser, southpaw reliever Mac Scarce and catching prospect John Stearns. Though McGraw struggled for most of the previous two seasons, minus the final six weeks of 1973, the trade would turn out to be a big win for the Phillies.

The team sent Ted Martinez to the Cardinals for minor league outfielder Mike Vail and shortstop Jack Heidemann, who would serve as Bud Harrelson's backup.

At the end of February, the Mets paid nearly $150,000 to the Giants for Dave Kingman who hit 77 home runs since coming to the majors in July 1971. He

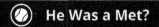

He Was a Met?

The 1974 season was the last for both Felipe and Matty Alou but the Mets picked up the third brother Jesus for the 1975 season. Used primarily as a pinch-hitter, he batted .265 in 62 games.

was a career .224 hitter with plenty of strikeouts, but the Mets hoped the power would more than make up for it.

The Situation

The acquisitions were impressive on paper though it raised the question of where everybody would play and when. After Kingman was acquired, Cleon Jones said, "Maybe the Mets think I need help, but I don't." There was also the question of the rotation: who would be making the other 60 or so starts when Seaver, Koosman and Matlack weren't on the mound? It was rookie Randy Tate who would be a fourth starter during the season.

Rusty Staub, Professional Hitter

Rusty Staub had his best Mets season in 1975, belting 19 home runs and driving in 105. Staub was consistently the best hitter on the Mets in his first stint with the team, and he truly excelled in the 1973 postseason when he hit 3 home runs in the LCS against the Reds, and batting .423 with 11 hits to lead all hitters in the World Series. Staub was traded after the 1975 season, shocking both him and Mets fans, but came back in 1981 and playing through 1985, serving mostly as pinch hitter. Staub tied major league records in 1983 with 8 consecutive pinch hits and 25 RBIs on pinch hits. He finished his career with 499 2B, 292 HR, 2716 hits.

The Season

Opening Day was a success as Kingman homered and Torre won it with a hit in the bottom of the ninth, but the Mets would lose their next five games. Looking for more bullpen help the team traded Scarce, who appeared in one game, to the Reds for Tom Hall, who had playoff experience with the Twins and Reds.

The Mets won seven straight in late April, capped off by a Seaver complete game at Wrigley Field as the ace improved to 3-2 with a 1.80 ERA. The streaky Mets lost six straight in early May, then won five straight. Mike Phillips was acquired from the Giants to backup an injury-plagued Harrelson. Only two games out of first at the end of May despite a 21-19 record, Staub was leading the way with a .304 average and Seaver was 7-4 with a pair of complete game victories to end his month.

Meanwhile, the Mets were dealing with off-field issues. Cleon Jones,

FABULOUS: BOB APODACA

The future long-time pitching coach had the best season of his 5-year career, appearing in 46 games and logging 84.2 IP. Apodaca had a microscopic ERA of 1.49 and led the Mets with 13 saves.

FUTILE: RANDY TATE

In his only season as a major leaguer, 22-year-old Randy Tate made 23 starts for the Mets but struggled with a 5-13 record. He was even worse at the plate, going hitless in 41 at bats, 22 of which were strikeouts. On August 4th, Tate took a no-hitter into the 8th inning against the Expos but allowed 4 runs and lost.

who stayed in Florida to rehab an injury, was arrested in early May and charged with indecent exposure after being found sleeping nude in a station wagon. Also in the vehicle was a woman whom was not his wife. When Jones returned to New York, M. Donald Grant had Jones read an apology at a press conference with his wife at his side.

George Stone returned to the rotation for the first time since the previous summer and beat the Padres. Gary Gentry, who was released by Atlanta, had been signed in May but was let go after one start in the minors as the injury-plagued righty saw his pro career end. At 32-25 on June 17, a pair of extra-inning losses in Montreal began a seven-game skid that saw the team fall back to .500, with the Mets being shutout in three straight games.

By mid-July, frustration was mounting. Though the Mets were a little over .500, they had fallen 10.5 games out of first. On July 18, Jones pinch-hit for Kranepool but refused to take the field in what would become a 4-3 loss to the Braves. Yogi Berra told the organization either he or Jones would have to go.

After being unable to trade Jones, the team released the franchise leader in hits, home runs and RBI. Jones had been relegated to the bench and Kingman hitting 13 home runs in July made Jones expendable. Berra didn't last much

TOP BATTERS

Pos	Name	G	AB	H	BA	HR	RBI	RS	SB	OPS
1B	Ed Kranepool	106	325	105	.323	4	43	42	1	.779
2B	Felix Millan	162	676	191	.283	1	56	81	1	.677
LF	Dave Kingman	134	502	116	.231	36	88	65	7	.778
CF	Del Unser	147	531	156	.294	10	53	65	4	.729
RF	Rusty Staub	155	574	162	.282	19	105	93	2	.818

TOP PITCHERS

Pos	Name	G	GS	W	L	SV	ERA	IP	SO	BB
SP	Tom Seaver	36	36	22	9	0	2.38	280.1	243	88
SP	Jerry Koosman	36	34	14	13	2	3.42	239.2	173	98
SP	Jon Matlack	33	32	16	12	0	3.38	228.2	154	58
SP	Hank Webb	29	15	7	6	0	4.07	115.0	38	62
CL	Bob Apodaca	46	0	3	4	13	1.49	84.2	45	28

longer. The 56-50 Mets welcomed the Expos to Shea and lost the first three games of the series. Randy Tate took a no-hitter into the eighth inning and gave up four runs in a 4-3 loss. A pair of 7-0 losses followed and Berra was canned.

Grant said it was a decision that had been thought about for some time. Jon Matlack said, "It was obvious that things were being wasted. They were being wasted either because we weren't playing up to our capabilities or he wasn't managing up to his."

One unnamed player said, "We won the pennant in 1973 in spite of his moves on the field. And this year the club had some rough stretches." The quiet Roy McMillan was named Berra's replacement.

The inconsistent Mets were no-hit by San Francisco's Ed Halicki on August 24 but win their next five. On September 1, Seaver pitched a complete game shutout against the Pirates. It was his 20th win of the season and his seventh inning strikeout of Manny Sanguillen made the right-hander the first pitcher to strike out 200 batters in eight straight seasons. Mike Vail hit his first home run in the win. The outfielder was called up to the majors in mid-August and provided a spark with a 23-game hitting streak.

New York was only four games out of first after the win but would get no closer. The next night Koosman failed to make it out of the fourth inning and in the rubber game, Jerry Reuss outpitched Matlack. Matlack had won five starts in a row but would go 0-4 in September.

The team lost two of three in St. Louis and were swept in Montreal as the season unraveled. The Mets managed to finish the season over .500, with a 5-4 win over the Phillies on the final day of the season. Seaver won his 22nd game with Skip Lockwood picking up a four-inning save.

Top 5 Highlights

1 Joe Torre's ninth inning single off Steve Carlton scores Felix Millan and gives the Mets an Opening Day win.

2 Jerry Koosman notches his 100th career win with a 5-1 triumph over the Cardinals on June 24 at Shea. Koosman gives up one run on five hits in the complete game victory.

3 Down 3-2 with two outs in the ninth inning, Jerry Grote hits a two-run homer off former batterymate Tug McGraw to give the Mets a stunning 4-3 win in Philadelphia on July 4.

4 Tom Seaver strikes out 200 batters for the eighth consecutive season, fanning Manny Sanguillen in a win against Pittsburgh on September 1.

5 Dave Kingman sets the team record with his 35th home run of the season with a two-run shot off Chicago's Darold Knowles in the bottom of the ninth to give the Mets a 7-5 win on September 18.

1976

	W	L	GB	Pos
	86	76	15.0	3rd
RS/G	RA/G		Manager	
3.80	3.32		Joe Frazier	

Kooz and Matlack's 38 Wins Not Enough

The Moves

Joe Frazier, not the heavyweight champion but a part-time major leaguer who won five pennants in 10 years as a minor league manager, was the new skipper.

M. Donald Grant acknowledged the team almost called up Frazier to replace Berra, but left him in the minors because Tidewater was going for the pennant. McMillan would have kept the job if the team had played better in the final weeks of the season. Joe Torre was also mentioned for the manager's job and even discussed the Tidewater opening briefly but decided to keep playing.

The team traded Rusty Staub, coming off the first 100-RBI season in team history, to the Tigers for veteran southpaw Mickey Lolich, who had amassed 207 wins and 2,679 strikeouts in Detroit. Lolich, who initially vetoed the trade before the Mets convinced him to come to New York, had been the hero of the 1968 World Series, winning three games. Staub was one year away from being able to veto a trade and the Mets believed they had a replacement in Mike Vail anyway.

Vail was injured playing basketball in the offseason and would never again show the spark of his 23-game hitting streak late in 1975.

He Was a Met?

World Series hero and iron man extraordinaire Mickey Lolich had enough left in the tank to give the Mets 192 IP with an ERA of 3.22. Tough luck and a mediocre offense kept his win total down to 8. After missing 1977, Lolich played his last 2 seasons as part of the SD Padres' bullpen.

The Situation

It was now the world of free agency and Tom Seaver signed a $225,000 deal, much to the chagrin of Mets management. The team discussed a trade that would've sent Seaver to the Dodgers for Don Sutton, which also might have included Bill Russell and Joe Ferguson. Instead, Seaver stayed and the Mets looked to have a formidable rotation with him, Koosman, Matlack and Lolich.

An early sighting of Mr. Met, who first appeared on the field when the Mets moved into Shea Stadium in 1964. Mr. Mets faded away gradually through the 1970s, and in 1976 began a 20-year absence from the team. (Photo courtesy Jason D. Antos)

The Season

A seven-game winning streak to end April had the Mets in first place. Seaver and Matlack were both 3-0 at the end of the month and John Milner was batting .488 to lead the offense. Torre's decision to continue playing paid off as the veteran was hitting .393 through mid-May.

Lolich's complete game on May 8 against the Padres improved the Mets to 18-9 but the team dropped 22 of the next 30. Combined with the Phillies hot tear, the NL East was already getting out of reach. One of the bright spots was Koosman, who went 5-0 in May but then lost five straight starts. Lolich suffered through a six-start stretch during which the Mets gave him six runs of support.

Kingman was crushing the ball, including three home runs and eight RBI in an 11-0 win over the Dodgers. He had 27 home runs at the end of June. With 32 home runs in mid-July, he injured his thumb

 Final Resting Ground

Ken Sanders was perhaps the top reliever in baseball in 1971, winning 7, saving 31 and posting an ERA of 1.91 in 83 appearances and 136.1 IP! Sanders pitched well for the Mets in 1975 (2.30) and 1976 (2.70), but they sold him to the Royals in late 1976, after which he pitched in only 3 more games in his career.

FUTILE: ROY STAIGER

Another man who was not the answer for the Mets at the hot corner, Steiger batted .220 and was decidedly unproductive, hitting 2 home runs and collecting only 26 RBI and 23 RS in 304 at bats. He would be traded to the Yankees after the 1977 season and his career ended soon thereafter.

diving for a ball and wouldn't hit another homer until September. He was one of three Mets All-Stars along with Seaver and Matlack.

The Mets won 10 straight from late June to early July, including a 43-run outburst in five games. But they only gained two games in the standings and were still 12.5 out.

In July the team sent Wayne Garrett and Del Unser to the Expos for outfielders Pepe Mangual and Jim

TOP BATTERS

Pos	Name	G	AB	H	BA	HR	RBI	RS	SB	OPS
1B	Ed Kranepool	123	415	121	.292	10	49	47	1	.754
2B	Felix Millan	139	531	150	.282	1	35	55	2	.684
LF	John Milner	127	443	120	.271	15	78	56	0	.809
RF	Dave Kingman	123	474	113	.238	37	86	70	7	.793

TOP PITCHERS

Pos	Name	G	GS	W	L	SV	ERA	IP	SO	BB
SP	Tom Seaver	35	34	14	11	0	2.59	271.0	235	77
SP	Jon Matlack	35	35	17	10	0	2.95	262.0	153	57
SP	Jerry Koosman	34	32	21	10	0	2.69	247.1	200	66
SP	Mickey Lolich	31	30	8	13	0	3.22	192.2	120	52
CL	Skip Lockwood	56	0	10	7	19	2.67	94.1	108	34

Dwyer. Both Mets were batting under .230. Unser blamed his lousy season on being hit by a pitch in April and not sitting out a week.

The Mets won 20 games in September. John Stearns gave the Mets some hope for the future with a solid September and Lee Mazzilli hit a pair of home runs. Though the Mets lost their final five games, the 86 wins were the second-most in team history.

Top 5 Highlights

1 Dave Kingman ties a team record with three home runs in a June 4 win against the Dodgers. Kingman hits a two-run shot off Burt Hooton in the fourth, a three-run homer off Hooton in the fifth and a three-run blast off Al Downing in the seventh. Seaver pitched a complete-game, three-hitter in New York's 11-0 win.

2 Kingman homers off Charlie Hough in the bottom of the 14th to give the Mets a 1-0 win on June 17. Craig Swan pitched 10 shutout innings and Skip Lockwood pitched four more. Don Sutton pitched nine shutout innings for LA.

3 Mike Phillips hits for the cycle in a 7-4 win on June 25 against the Cubs at Wrigley. The shortstop doubles off Ray Burris in the third, triples off Burris in the fifth, homers off Burris in the seventh and singles off Mike Garman in the eighth.

4 Jerry Koosman wins his 20th game of the season with a 4-1 triumph over the Cardinals on September 16. The southpaw gives up one run on four hits and fans 13 batters. A Keith Hernandez homer in the eighth accounted for the only St. Louis run. Koosman struck out the side in the ninth to finish it off.

5 Lee Mazzilli stuns the Pirates with a two-run, two-out home run in the bottom of the ninth off Kent Tekulve to give the Mets a 5-4 win on September 20.

1977

OPENING DAY LINEUP

Lee Mazzilli, CF
Felix Millan, 2B
John Milner, LF
Dave Kingman, RF
Ed Kranepool, 1B
John Stearns, C
Roy Staiger, 3B
Bud Harrelson, SS
Tom Seaver, P

	W	L	GB	Pos
	64	98	37.0	6th

RS/G	RA/G	Manager
3.62	4.09	Joe Frazier Joe Torre

Midnight Massacre and "The Franchise" Is Gone

The Moves

There were no major moves but the news was the extensions that didn't happen. Tom Seaver and Dave Kingman were not pleased with management. Kingman wanted a six-year deal and more than Seaver's $225,000 per year. In the new world of free agency, Kingman said the Mets were "treating you like in the Dark Ages."

General manager Joe McDonald said Kingman's request was more than double was what offered. There were no signings. The Mets went into the season with a disgruntled slugger and unhappy ace. Mickey Lolich announced his retirement.

The Situation

"We'll do better this year if Roy Staiger and Lee Mazzilli can do the job and if Kingman stays healthy and if John Milner can play the way he is capable of playing," Joe Frazier said.

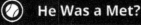

He Was a Met?

Doc Medich was plucked off waivers by the Mets at the end of the 1977 season. He lost his one start, though he pitched well. Medich had some of the best seasons of his career at Shea Stadium as a member of the Yankees in the mid-1970s. He would sign with the Rangers after the season.

The Season

Frazier jumbled the lineup a lot – 14 different ones in the first 20 games as he looked for a spark – but the Mets were 9-9 and three games out on May 1. Seaver went 4-0 with a 1.52 ERA and a pair of shutouts in April. Nino Espinosa won two of his first three starts, including a complete game win over the Cubs. The team added Lenny Randle, acquiring him from the Rangers after the third baseman punched manager Frank Lucchesi during batting practice. In his first game with the Mets, Randle collected three hits and scored twice, taking over the position as Staiger struggled at the plate.

The "Midnight Massacre"

June 15, 1977: A date etched in the minds of Mets fans. Tom Seaver traded for four Reds and Dave Kingman sent to San Diego. After months of battling with the front office, Seaver was sent to Cincinnati, an unthinkable happening. The team would become irrelevant for several years. Seaver, meanwhile, went 14-3 for the Reds over the remainder of the season to finish at 21-6. He followed that up with a no-hitter for the Reds and 6 seasons with double-figure wins in what was one of the greatest careers among right-handed pitchers in the history of the major leagues.

Things fell apart in May as the team lost 12 of 14. Kingman took himself out of a lineup in LA. "If he doesn't want to play, the hell with him," Matlack said. Matlack asked to be traded. He was annoyed after a 10-0 loss in San Francisco, which was stopped in the seventh inning in bad weather. "They never should have played after the third inning. The umpire just had some sand thrown on the pitcher's mound. That didn't help. What would you rather pitch on – mud or a beach? And the manager never complained until after the game."

Frazier was losing respect. There were the constant lineup changes. And a game against the Padres in which Staiger and John Stearns unknowingly batted out of order. Seaver went 0-3 in May and saw his ERA rise nearly two runs. When pitching coach Rube Walker was sent out to talk to Seaver by Frazier, the ace said, "Tell him leave me alone."

Koosman was 2-4 despite an ERA under 2.50. "Working without any runs is starting to get to me after 10 years." Seaver called Grant a "maniac" for emphasizing the importance of the Mayor's Trophy Game against the Yankees.

"He's trying to force me to trade him," Grant said. "I'm going to think about it."

The Mets swept the Giants but then lost nine of 10. Frazier was fired and Torre was promoted as player-manager, though his playing days would end shortly thereafter. "I don't

 Final Resting Ground

Joe Torre became manager of the Mets on May 31, 1977, 15 days before the Midnight Massacre sent The Franchise to the Reds. Two days after the trade, Torre put himself up as a pinch hitter, flying to right for the final appearance for his career.

FABULOUS: LENNY RANDLE

Lenny Randle was a bright spot in a dark season, batting .304 with an OBA of .383, stealing 33 bases, and leading the team with 78 runs scored. Randle also played five positions.

know how it will work, managing my own former teammates," Torre said. "Maybe some of the excuses won't work now. But May is a little early for a team to quit."

New York responded by winning seven of Torre's first eight games, capped off by a Seaver shutout against the Reds as trade rumors swirled. Seaver won his next start on June 12 in Houston to improve to 7-3 with a 3.00 ERA.

The drama of Seaver and Grant played out in the tabloids, specifically through Dick Young of the Daily News. Young's son-in-law worked for the Mets in communications and Young often took Grant's side in the ongoing battle. It seemed as if Seaver was placated after he went over Grant's head to Lorinda de Roulet and worked out a deal for a raise. On the morning of June 15, a specific passage from Grant incensed Seaver: "Nolan Ryan is getting more money than Tom Seaver and that galls Tom because Nancy Seaver and Ruth Ryan are very friendly and Tom Seaver long has treated Ryan like a little brother." Seaver demanded to be traded.

In what came to be known as the Midnight Massacre, Seaver was traded to the Reds for pitcher Pat Zachry, infielder Doug Flynn and minor league outfielders Steve Henderson and Dan Norman. The Mets also traded Kingman, who was batting .209 with nine homers and 28 RBI in 58 games to the Padres for Bobby Valentine and pitcher Paul Siebert. The Mets also sent Mike Phillips to the Cardinals for outfielder Joel Youngblood.

"This has to be one of the biggest steals since the Babe Ruth trade," Dodgers second baseman Davey Lopes said. "A trade is supposed to help both teams. But I don't think the Mets are as good a club as they were before. I can't see how they improved their team one iota."

The Mets lost six in a row in late June and nine in a row in early July. One of the few bright spots was Henderson, who was worked into the lineup and proved to be one of the few bright spots in the summer, finishing as runner up to Andre Dawson in the Rookie of the Yearr voting. Randle kept his consistent bat going. Flynn got a chance to play after Bud Harrelson injured himself diving back to first base. Then Flynn moved to second after Felix Millan broke his collarbone, courtesy of a bodyslam from Pittsburgh's Ed Ott. Ott had slid hard into second and Millan punched him.

FUTILE: DOUG FLYNN

Doug Flynn's offense in 1977 was horrendous even by Mets middle infielder standards. Flynn's slash line was .191/.220/.220, good for an OPS+ of 22, with 14 RBI and 14 RS in 282 at bats.

New York lost 21 of 26 to end August. At the end of the month, Jerry Grote was traded to the Dodgers for a pair of minor leaguers. Grote, who batted .270 in 42 games, had threatened retirement after 1976 before returning.

On August 21, more than 46,000 fans came out to Shea to see Seaver battle Koosman. Seaver pitched a complete game, winning 5-1 and even doubled and scored. Koosman went 0-7 in August. In September, he lost twice more and joined the 20-loss club one season after winning 20.

TOP BATTERS

Pos	Name	G	AB	H	BA	HR	RBI	RS	SB	OPS
C	John Stearns	139	431	108	.251	12	55	52	9	.767
3B	Lenny Randle	136	513	156	.304	5	27	78	33	.787
LF	Steve Henderson	99	350	104	.297	12	65	67	6	.852
CF	Lee Mazzilli	159	537	134	.250	6	46	66	22	.679
OF	Bruce Boisclair	127	307	90	.293	4	44	41	6	.766

TOP PITCHERS

Pos	Name	G	GS	W	L	SV	ERA	IP	SO	BB
SP	Jerry Koosman	32	32	8	20	0	3.49	226.2	192	81
SP	Nino Espinosa	32	29	10	13	0	3.42	200.0	105	55
SP	Craig Swan	26	24	9	10	0	4.23	146.2	71	56
SP	Pat Zachry	19	19	7	6	0	3.76	119.2	63	48
CL	Skip Lockwood	63	0	4	8	20	3.38	104.0	84	31

Top 5 Highlights

1 Tom Seaver pitches another one-hitter against the Cubs in a 6-0 win at Shea on April 17. Steve Ontiveros singles to right with one out in the fifth for the lone Chicago hit.

2 Steve Henderson hits a three-run homer in the bottom of the 11th off Atlanta's Don Collins to give the Mets a 5-2 win over the Braves on June 21. Ed Kranepool tied the game in the bottom of the ninth with a homer off Andy Messersmith.

3 Lenny Randle's two-run homer in the bottom of the 17th off Montreal's Will McEnaney gives the Mets a marathon 7-5 win on July 9. Steve Henderson tied the game in the bottom of the 11th with a homer off Joe Kerrigan.

4 Lee Mazzilli's 14th inning single off Los Angeles pitcher Mike Garman gives the Mets a 4-3 win on August 3 as New York takes two of three from the eventual National League champs Down 3-1 with two outs in the ninth, Mike Vail delivered an RBI single and Doug Flynn worked a bases loaded walk to tie it.

5 Nino Espinosa pitches a three-hit shutout and delivers an RBI single in the fifth inning off Steve Carlton in a 1-0 win over the Phillies on September 14.

1978

	W	L	GB	Pos
	66	96	24.0	6th

RS/G	RA/G	Manager
3.75	4.26	Joe Torre

Irrelevant Mets Flop at Empty Shea

The Moves

The Mets signed their first free agents, former Milwaukee starter Tom Hausman and Baltimore outfielder Elliott Maddox. Tim Foli was back in Queens, purchased from the Giants. He was expected to have the inside track to be the starting shortstop. Foli also brought with him a temper. "I guess we should just take him out and shoot him," Joe Torre joked. "It's a risk, but it's a good risk for me and a good gamble for the club. He'll just have to harness his temper."

Foli's bat was better than Harrelson's. A brutally honest Joe McDonald said, "With Buddy, Doug Flynn and the pitcher at the bottom of the batting order, you have three outs."

Then came a four-team trade that saw Jon Matlack and John Milner sent away to Texas and Pittsburgh, respectively. New York received Willie Montanez, who hit 20 home runs for the Braves in an All-Star 1977 season, Tom Grieve, who hit 20 homers for the Rangers in 1976 and veteran outfielder Ken Henderson. The trade also saw Bert Blyleven go to the Pirates and Al Oliver go to the Rangers.

Bud Harrelson, feeling unwanted and wanting to play for a contender, was traded to the Phillies.

The Situation

After years of trying to recapture the pennant, it was rebuilding time. "We saw what we were doing with Seaver and Matlack, and we knew we had to add some

 He Was a Met?

Tom Grieve spent one season with the Mets as a backup outfielder. Despite being on the team the whole season, Grieve collected only 101 at bats. He retired from baseball soon thereafter, embarking on a long career as general manager and then announcer for the Texas Rangers.

Jerry Koosman (with Pearl Bailey who had sung the National Anthem before Game 5), was a very good pitcher for a very long time. He twice won 20+ games, and won 14 games for the Phillies age 41. Koosman finished his career with 222 wins and more than 3800 career IP. With a better supporting cast over the years, a much higher win total and Hall of Fame consideration are likely. (Photo Courtesy Jason D. Antos)

offense," Torre said. "Seaver is the best in the business, and Matlack is a fine pitcher. But we are building."

Jerry Koosman noted the increased presence in the lineup. "When I see all those new guys, I get kind of excited," he said. "I think we're two runs a game better."

Sports Illustrated wrote, "New York could be the most improved team in the league, without showing it in the standings."

The Season

The Mets started 3-0 and were in first place on April 22. A number of late-inning wins saw the Mets at 9-6. But then they lost six straight, not to see .500 for the rest of the season. Pat Zachry was off to a hot start, going 3-0 with a 1.85 ERA.

New York played tight games in May, splitting six walk-offs. The team was only three games out of first on May 23. Other than Lee Mazzilli, the offense wasn't hitting. Foli was at .190 through May. Joel Youngblood, Steve Henderson and Willie Montanez had identical .259 averages and John Stearns was at .252. Montanez did have a strong May, hitting .313 with six homers and 28 RBI.

Though under .500, the Mets remained scrappy. They took two of three from the Dodgers in early June. The Mets pulled to within three games under .500 with a 3-2 win over the Giants on June 9. But the team lost 15 of the next 20, including four walk-offs.

FABULOUS: CRAIG SWAN

Swan snuck his way onto the NL leader board, pacing the senior circuit with an ERA of 2.43. His stat line was strange, with only 15 decisions in 29 appearances (28 starts), but logging 207.1 innings.

Dale Murray had been acquired from the Reds on May 19 for Ken Henderson. In his first appearance as a Met he allowed five runs in the 11th inning against the Phillies and got the loss. On June 12, he surrendered a game-ending hit in the bottom of the ninth to San Diego's Fernando Gonzalez. On June 16, San Francisco's Jack Clark ended the game with a three-run blast off Murray. And two days later, Rob Andrews delivered a winning hit in the bottom of the 10th off Murray.

Butch Metzger, who was acquired from St. Louis in early April, didn't provide much relief. Metzger and Murray combined to allow six runs in the bottom of the fifth of a June 26 loss at Wrigley. Two days later, the Cubs pulled off a game-ending squeeze against Metzger.

FUTILE: MIKE BRUHERT

Mike Bruhert, one-time son-in-law of Gil Hodges, went 4-11 with a 4.78 ERA in his one season in the majors. The right-hander from Queens did pitch a four-hit shutout against the Phillies in September 17.

Zachry started the year 10-3, including a two-hit shutout of the Phillies on July 4. He lost his next three starts and then was removed in the seventh inning of his July 24 start against the Reds. Frustrated, he went to kick a batting helmet on a dugout step, missed and hit the cement. He fractured his foot and would be lost for the rest of the season.

The Mets staggered through the rest of the year. Their 66-96 record included 27-35 in one-run games. The only drama was if Swan would win the ERA crown, which he held on to with a sterling 2.43 mark.

TOP BATTERS

Pos	Name	G	AB	H	BA	HR	RBI	RS	SB	OPS
1B	Willie Montanez	159	609	156	.256	17	96	66	9	.712
LF	Steve Henderson	157	587	156	.266	10	65	83	13	.732
CF	Lee Mazzilli	148	542	148	.273	16	61	78	20	.785
RF	Ellio Maddox	119	389	100	.257	2	39	43	2	.699
OF	Bruce Boisclair	127	307	90	.293	4	44	41	6	.766

TOP PITCHERS

Pos	Name	G	GS	W	L	SV	ERA	IP	SO	BB
SP	Craig Swan	29	28	9	6	0	2.43	207.1	125	58
SP	Nino Espinosa	32	32	11	15	0	4.73	203.2	76	75
SP	Pat Zachry	21	21	10	6	0	3.33	138.0	78	60
CL	Skip Lockwood	57	0	7	13	15	3.57	90.2	73	31
RP	Dale Murray	53	0	8	5	5	3.65	86.1	37	36

Top 5 Highlights

1 An Opening Day crowd of 11,736 watches Jerry Koosman pitch a complete game victory over the Expos. Kooz allows one run on eight hits in the 3-1 win.

2 On April 8, the Mets trail 5-2 in the eighth when Lee Mazilli hits a two-run homer to cut the lead to 5-4. With two outs in the ninth, Ed Kranepool smacks a two-run homer off Stan Bahnsen to give the Mets a 6-5 win.

3 Pat Zachry pitches a complete game to give the Mets a 3-2 win over the Dodgers on June 7 and take two of three from the defending and eventual NL champions.

4 Lee Mazzilli homers from both sides of the plate in New York's 8-5 win in Los Angeles on September 3. Mazzilli leads off the game with a shot off Tommy John and goes deep in the seventh against Charlie Hough.

5 Craig Swan gives up one run in seven innings in New York's 3-1 win against the Cardinals on September 26. Swan became the first Met to lead the league in ERA since Tom Seaver in 1973.

1979

OPENING DAY LINEUP

Lee Mazzilli, CF
Kelvin Chapman, 2B
Richie Hebner, 3B
John Stearns, C
Willie Montanez, 1B
Steve Henderson, LF
Elliott Maddox, RF
Doug Flynn, SS
Craig Swan, P

	W	L	GB	Pos
	63	99	35.0	6th
RS/G	RA/G		Manager	
3.66	4.36		Joe Torre	

At Least They Didn't Lose 100

The Moves

M. Donald Grant was out as Chairman of the Board and Lorinda de Roulet – the daughter of late owner Joan Payson – was in charge. She had officially been president for three years but was now calling the shots.

Jerry Koosman was traded to the Twins for Jesse Orosco. Only Ed Kranepool remained from the glory days. Even Lindsey Nelson left, taking an announcing job with the San Francisco Giants.

The team traded Tom Grieve to St. Louis for southpaw pitcher Pete Falcone, who had above-five ERAs in 1977 and 1978.

In late March, the team acquired power-hitting third baseman Richie Hebner from the Phillies for Nino Espinosa. Hebner had been a contributor to Pirates playoff teams and the Phillies NL East champions in 1977 and 1978. Philadelphia's signing of Pete Rose made Hebner the odd man out.

The Phillies originally asked for Pat Zachry or Craig Swan, but eventually took Espinosa.

Joe McDonald added, "I don't particularly like to trade a starting pitcher. But we need a productive third baseman. We've been looking for a long time. We'll miss Nino, but you don't get anything unless you give something. We had to get the bat. It gives us [a] more formidable lineup."

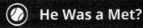

He Was a Met?

Richie Hebner played one season with the Mets in his solid 18-year career, performing well in 1979, batting .268 with 79 RBI. But Hebner was unhappy throughout his time in New York so that winter they dealt him to the Tigers, receiving an over-the-hill Jerry Morales and Phil Mankowski.

Booth Trio Breakup

In 1979, Lindsey Nelson left the Mets' booth to became an announcer for the San Francisco Giants. It brought an end to the 17-season run working with Bob Murphy and Ralph Kiner. Famous for wearing garish suit jackets, Nelson was also a national voice, calling the Cotton Bowl for more than a quarter-century. In 1985, when Tom Seaver won his 300th game at Yankee Stadium, Nelson called the bottom of the ninth for WPIX.

The Hebner trade meant he would play third, Lenny Randle was released, Joel Youngblood, who had been working at third, was sent back to the outfield. Dan Norman, one of few possible power bats, was sent down to the minors to begin the season.

The Situation

McDonald said the Mets were "one year older and one year better." But as *Sports Illustrated* wrote, "It is going to take more than such platitudes for the Mets to escape the cellar."

The Season

New York started 2-0, scoring 19 runs at Wrigley Field. Any hope of contending quickly vanished as the team lost eight of nine. Hebner went 4-5 with a homer, two doubles, four RBI and two runs scored on Opening Day but went 1 for his next 21. The Mets sent Tim Foli to Pittsburgh. He was spending time on the bench with Doug Flynn and Kelvin Chapman playing up the middle. New York acquired Frank Taveras, who had stolen 118 bases the previous two seasons.

The Mets were 8-10 at the end of April and lost eight of nine to begin May. Torre had Hebner bat cleanup for the first time on May 10. The team responded by losing 14-1. Mazzilli was hitting but wasn't getting much protection.

A 9-4 loss to the Cardinals on May 19 dropped the team to 11-23. Despite its struggles, the team split its next 72 games and were 12 games under .500 (47-59) on August 5.

 Final Resting Ground

A former All-Star and World Series champion, Dock Ellis, was acquired in June. Ellis went 3-7 (6.04) before closing out his career with 3 games with the Pirates in September. His best game as a Met came in Montreal when he gave up two runs in six innings and picked up the win in Game 1 of an August 5 doubleheader.

Craig Swan pitched a complete game on June 4 to beat the Reds 6-2, despite a Tom Seaver home run. Pat Zachry, Skip Lockwood and Neil Allen were injured, so the team added Dock Ellis and Andy Hassler in mid-June.

The Mets took two straight from Atlanta in mid-June but the final game of the series was suspended in the eighth inning because of a predetermined curfew allowing the Mets to catch a 7:30 p.m. flight to

Houston. New York won when the game reconvened in late August.

Falcone, the Brooklyn native, won his first game on June 25, tossing a five-hit shutout against the Pirates. His next win came on July 28 despite Dave Kingman hitting three homers for the Cubs.

On August 2, the Mets acquired Jose Cardenal from the Phillies between games of a doubleheader. The nightcap was overshadowed by the news of Thurman Munson's death, as the somber news was announced on the scoreboard during the first inning.

The Mets took two straight from Montreal, but lost 20 of the next 25. Willie Montanez was traded to the Rangers for Mike Jorgensen and Ed Lynch. The first baseman was hitting .236 with five homers. The final straw may have been when he committed an error against the Cardinals, swiping at the ball with an uppercut swing of his mitt.

September saw another dreadful stretch with 14 losses in 15 games – including being swept in doubleheaders on four consecutive days – to finish a 9-39 stretch.

FUTILE: FRANK TAVERAS

Frank Taveras epitomized the no-hit middle infielder that the Mets invariably had in the lineup in the 1970s. Despite exceeding 500 at bats in a season 5 times in his career, Taveras never totaled more than 38 RBI, including 1979 when he had 725 plate appearances and drove in only 33 runs.

FABULOUS: SKIP LOCKWOOD

Lockwood pitched quite well in his 5 seasons with the Mets, with 1979 being the final one. He had 3 seasons averaging 59 appearances and 96 IP out of the bullpen. In 1979, though limited to 27 games, he had a sparkling ERA of 1.49, the same ERA he posted in 1975, his first year with the team.

New York was 57-99 but the team won its final six games to avoid 100 losses.

TOP BATTERS										
Pos	Name	G	AB	H	BA	HR	RBI	RS	SB	OPS
C	John Stearns	155	538	131	.243	9	66	58	15	.667
3B	Richie Hebner	136	473	127	.268	10	79	54	3	.747
CF	Lee Mazzilli	158	597	181	.303	15	79	78	34	.844
RF	Joel Youngblood	158	590	162	.275	16	60	90	18	.782

TOP PITCHERS										
Pos	Name	G	GS	W	L	SV	ERA	IP	SO	BB
SP	Craig Swan	35	35	14	13	0	3.29	251.1	145	57
SP	Pete Falcone	33	31	6	14	0	4.16	184.0	113	76
SP	Kevin Kobel	30	27	6	8	0	3.51	161.2	67	46
CL	Skip Lockwood	27	0	2	5	9	1.49	42.1	42	14
RP	Neil Allen	50	5	6	10	8	3.55	99.0	65	47

Top 5 Highlights

1 The Mets score 10 runs on Opening Day. They take a 10-3 lead into the bottom of the ninth. Dwight Bernard gives up three runs before Joe Torre calls on Jesse Orosco in his MLB debut. Orosco gets Bill Bucker on a fly out to end the game.

2 Mike Scott wins his first career start giving up one earned run (three runs) in five innings in a 10-3 win on April 24 against Vida Blue and the Giants.

3 Trailing 5-2 heading into the bottom of the sixth, the Mets explode for a team-record 10 runs in an inning on June 12. The inning is capped off by Doug Flynn's inside-the-park three-run home run.

4 Lee Mazzilli ties the All-Star in Seattle game with an eighth inning home run off Jim Kern. With two outs in the ninth, he draws a go-ahead bases loaded walk against defending Cy Young winner Ron Guidry and the NL holds on for a 7-6 win.

5 The Mets win game number 63 and avoid 100 losses on the final day of the season. With two outs in the ninth, Elliott Maddox singles off Mark Littell to score Alex Trevino with the go-ahead run and Maddox scores on an error. Jeff Reardon pitches a 1-2-3 inning to close it out. The game was the last for Ed Kranepool, who delivered a pinch-hit double in the seventh, as well as Lou Brock.

Quiz #4: 1980s

1. (1980s) After many years in Pittsburgh, this infielder put together 3 remarkably unproductive seasons for the Mets, hitting just one home run and driving in 69 runs in 1480 at bats. **[10 points]**

2. (1980s) Name the first Mets rookie to hit over .300 (minimum 350 AB). **[8 points]**

3. Name the 3 pitchers on the 1981 Mets staff who won the Cy Young Award sometime in their career. **[10 points for 2, 5 bonus points for all 3]**

4. This Mets sometime slugger led the NL in home runs in 1982 for the second time of his career. **[6 points]**

5. (1982) This backup catcher appeared in only 17 games in his only season with the Mets, and appeared in only 358 in a 9-year career. But he went on to be very successful manager who is considered a candidate for the Hall of Fame. **[10 points]**

6. (1983) This pitcher led the Mets staff with 13 wins and posted a microscopic ERA of 1.47 in 110 IP. **[8 points]**

7. (1980s) What team did George Bamberger manage before and after his 1+ year stint with the Mets? **[6 points]**

8. Whom did Davey Johnson replace as Mets manager to start the 1984 season? **[8 points]**

9. (1983) Which Mets pitcher led NL pitchers in losses with 17? **[10 points]**

10. (1984) He broke in with the Mets at age 22, appearing in 5 games, 3 of which as a starter. Two years later he pitched against them in one of the most important innings in their history. **[8 points]**

11. (1985) Who served as the other half of the 2B platoon in 1985, but his anemic bat (0 HR, 7 RBI in 144 AB) was his ticket out of major league baseball after that season? **[10 points]**

12. Name the pitcher who was the winner in 3 of the 4 Mets victories in the 1986 NLCS against the Astros. **[8 points]**

13. This Red Sox led all players in hits and BA in the 1986 WS, but he also made the last out of the series, fanning against Jesse Orosco. **[8 points]**

14. (1986) Which Mets pitcher started 3 games in the 1986 World Series, finishing 1-1 with a 1.53 ERA in 17.2 IP? **[6 points]**

15. Who led the Mets in RBI in the 1986 World Series, totaling 4 more than the next best batter? **[10 points]**

16. This Mets' first round draft pick appeared in 8 games at catcher for the 1986 Mets, pounding out 9 hits in 19 at bats, including 4 doubles and a home run. He never again appeared in a major league game but became a major league manager, skippering for 11 seasons. **[8 bonus points]**

17. (1980s) Who was the first Mets player to hit at least 30 HR and have 100 or more RBI in a season? **[8 points]**

18. This Mets reliever went an incredible 18-3 over the 1987 and 1988 seasons, mixing in 12 starts. But the next season he was traded, and he won only 13 more games in his career. **[10 points]**

19. Name the Mets player who was a perfect 21 for 21 in SB for the Mets in 1988 after going 14-for-15 the year before? **[8 points]**

QUIZ #4; TOTAL POINTS – 152; BONUS POINTS – 13

1980

	W	L	GB	Pos
	67	95	24.0	5th
RS/G	RA/G		Manager	
3.77	4.33		Joe Torre	

OPENING DAY LINEUP

Frank Taveras, SS
Elliott Maddox, 3B
Lee Mazzilli, 1B
Steve Henderson, LF
Mike Jorgensen, RF
John Stearns, C
Jerry Morales, CF
Doug Flynn, 2B
Craig Swan, P

The Magic Is Back...Until August

The Moves

Ownership of the Mets changed hands in January, as Doubleday & Co. bought the company for more than $21 million, a shocking figure for a losing team with sagging attendance. Nelson Doubleday was the new chairman. Long Island-based real estate investor Fred Wilpon was the new president.

Doubleday received a call from former Orioles owner Jerold C. Hoffberger, who recommended the Mets hire Frank Cashen as general manager. "I can't tell you how long it's going to take to win a pennant," Cashen said when he was introduced. "I think we're going to win a pennant. If I didn't really feel that way I wouldn't have taken the job in the first place."

Before the new leadership was in place, Richie Hebner was traded to the Tigers for Jerry Morales and Phil Mankowski. Dwight Bernard was sent to the Brewers for Mark Bomback. But as new ownership was sought, the moves stopped. The Angels thought they had a deal done to acquire Craig Swan and one other Met – reportedly Ron Hodges or Elliott Maddox – for Willie Aikens and Dickie Thon, before Linda de Roulet vetoed the move.

"I thought it over and I decided to leave the team in place as much as possible in fairness to the new owners," she said. "We don't think it would be fair to the new owner to trade a pitcher of his quality."

He Was a Met?

Claudell Washington passed through New York on his way from the Chicago White Sox to the Atlanta Braves. He played well in 79 games, but was signed by the Braves that winter, where he played for 5 seasons.

The Situation

"The Magic Is Back," at least according to the new advertising slogan. Despite new leadership and even new-look seats at Shea, the Mets were still expected to finish at the bottom of the standings. The team did show it was no longer the M. Donald Grant era as Swan was signed to a five-year, three-million dollar deal.

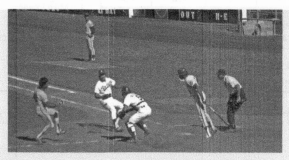

Lee Mazzilli (approaching home) was a fan favorite during the dark days at Shea. The Brooklyn product was one of the rare offensive threats in the lineup. He was traded after 1981 but returned in 1986 and delivered clutch pinch-hits in Games 6 and 7 of the World Series.

The Season

The Mets beat the Cubs 5-2 on Opening Day, but lost 14 of its first 20. There was a six-error game in a loss to the Expos. They blew a 9-1 lead on April 19th, including a go-ahead grand slam to Dave Kingman and were pummeled 14-8 in game they had led 8-3. There were some bright spots, such as Mark Bomback beating the Phillies twice in late April.

On May 6, the Mets erased a 7-0 lead but lost 12-10 in 14 innings. Another extra-inning loss followed the next night. Cincinnati pounded New York 15-4 on May 13 with Ray Knight hitting two homers in one inning as the Mets dropped to 9-18.

New York squandered a four-run ninth inning lead on May 14 but a Jerry Morales single scored John Stearns in the top of the 10th and the Mets won 7-6. An unlikely winning stretch of baseball followed during the summer. A 13-win May included a sweep of the Braves with Elliott Maddox delivering the winning single in the second game.

The Mets won eight of 10 in June, including four by walk-off. There

 Final Resting Ground

Jose Cardenal first appeared in the majors in 1963 and the Mets were his 8th team when they picked him up in the summer of 1979. Though he struggled for New York, he ended his long career in 1980 on an up note, batting .340 in limited playing time for AL champion Royals after the Mets dropped him, and batting 10 times in the World Series.

was also a bench-clearing brawl after Pat Zachry drilled Ron Cey after surrendering back-to-back home runs. Cashen made his first notable addition, acquiring outfielder Claudell Washington from the White Sox. But the 27-28 Mets couldn't get back to .500 as the team lost seven straight, with the cardiac kids losing three by walk-off.

FUTILE: JOHN PACELLA

As a starter, Pacella went 3-4 with a 5.49 ERA in 15 games, though he did defeat Steve Carlton 4-3 on June 27th. A hard thrower, he would often lose his cap on the mound.

But the Mets battled back in more ways than one. There was another brawl, this time on July 4 against the Expos, with Stearns charging out of the dugout at Montreal pitcher Bill Gullickson, who had beaned Mike Jorgensen. Stearns would be named to the All-Star team, hitting .291 at the break. And Lee Mazzilli was a large part of the burst. He had one RBI in April but put together an 18-game hitting streak from June to July. Mazzilli hit 11 home runs from July 1 through July 20.

The fans were back, with 51,097 coming to Shea on July 5 to see the Mets beat the Expos and draw to within 3.5 games of first. The team even made it back to .500, with John Pacella and Jeff Reardon combining to shutout the Braves on July 17 to bring the record to 43-43.

The team kept flirting with .500 and returned to Shea in mid-August with a 56-57 mark, having gone 47-39 since May 13. The Mets could pull ahead of the Phillies for third place, but Philadelphia swept a five-game series. The Mets would win 11 games over the season's final six weeks, losing 38 of 49, including a 13-game losing streak. Despite an exciting summer, the team still lost 95 times.

FABULOUS: LEE MAZZILLI

Mazzilli had his third consecutive solid season for the Mets, driving in 76 runs and scoring 82. He also drew 82 walks and stole a career-high 41 bases.

TOP BATTERS										
Pos	Name	G	AB	H	BA	HR	RBI	RS	SB	OPS
1B	Lee Mazzilli	152	578	162	.280	16	76	82	41	.801
SS	Frank Taveras	141	562	157	.279	0	25	65	32	.635
LF	Steve Henderson	143	513	149	.290	8	58	75	23	.770
RF	Joel Youngblood	146	514	142	.276	8	69	58	14	.721
RF	Claud. Washingtn	79	284	78	.275	10	42	38	17	.788

Pos	Name	G	GS	W	L	SV	ERA	IP	SO	BB
TOP PITCHERS										
SP	Pat Zachry	28	26	6	10	0	3.01	164.2	88	58
SP	Mark Bomback	36	25	10	8	0	4.09	162.2	68	49
SP	Pete Falcone	37	23	7	10	1	4.52	157.1	109	58
CL	Neil Allen	59	0	7	10	22	3.70	97.1	79	40
RP	Jeff Reardon	61	0	8	7	6	2.61	110.1	101	47

Top 5 Highlights

1 Joel Youngblood robs Larry Biittner of a seventh-inning home run and the Mets beat the Cubs 5-2 on Opening Day.

2 Mike Jorgensen hits a grand slam in the bottom of the 10th off Rick Sutcliffe to give the Mets a 6-2 win on June 11. Steve Garvey had tied the game in the ninth with a homer off Craig Swan.

3 Steve Henderson hits a three-run homer off Allen Ripley on June 14 to give the Mets a 7-6 win on fireworks night at Shea. New York trailed 6-0 and 6-2 heading into the ninth. Down to their final out, Mazzilli singled, Taveras walked, Washington singled and Henderson connected for an opposite-field shot.

4 Claudell Washington hits three homers in a 9-6 win at Dodger Stadium on June 22. He hits a two-run homer off Dave Goltz in the first, a two-run shot off Goltz in the fifth and a solo shot off Charlie Hough in the seventh.

5 Mookie Wilson and Wally Backman make their MLB debuts on September 2 in Los Angeles. Backman collects his first hit with an RBI single in the second against Dave Goltz.

1981

	W	L	GB	Pos
	41	62	18.5	5th
RS/G	RA/G		Manager	
3.38	4.19		Joe Torre	

Unlikely Playoff Push in Split Season

The Moves

After being quiet in his first year as general manager, Frank Cashen brought in some notable names. Randy Jones, the 1976 NL Cy Young winner, was acquired from the Padres with John Pacella and Jose Moreno going to San Diego. Jones was 5-13 with a 3.91 ERA in 1980.

Rusty Staub returned to Queens, signing a three-year, $1 million contract. Staub hit .300 in 109 games with the Rangers in 1980. He was only 453 hits away from 3,000 and considered a candidate for first base and right field.

The team also brought back Dave Kingman, as Steve Henderson was sent to the Cubs. Kingman led the league with 48 homers in 1979 but only hit 18 in 81 games in 1980 as he was sidelined by a shoulder injury. "Dave Kingman is a quality home run hitter that we have been missing since we traded him," Torre said.

Other moves included trading Roy Lee Jackson to the Blue Jays for infielder Bob Bailor and signing infielder Mike Cubbage from the Twins. Somewhat surprisingly, the team released Elliott Maddox.

"At least I won't have to put up with the negativism," Maddox said. "Every year, the Mets said there was no room for me, no position. Then the season would start and I'd play a great deal."

He Was a Met?

Record-setting reliever Mike Marshall, he of 106 G, 15 W, and 208.1 IP in 1974, had a very memorable career, though his stint with the Mets is all but forgotten. The Amazins' were Marshall's 9th and final team he played for.

The Original Joe Torre

The strike-interrupted 1981 season marked Joe Torre's last as manager of the Mets. Torre, who ultimately was elected to the baseball Hall of Fame as a manager, was more deserving of the honor for his ballplaying. As a player, Torre accumulated more than 57 WAR, 9 All-Star berths, an MVP, and a lifetime batting average of .297. He was very successful as Yankees' manager, twice named manager of the year. But for the Mets—who during his reign suffered from a serious lack of talent and the Curse of the Midnight Massacre—he had an overall winning percentage of .405, never exceeding .419 in any of his 5 seasons.

The Situation

The team signed Doug Flynn and Pat Zachry to extensions. John Stearns was more of a third baseman than catcher after years of wear and tear. The pitching staff had question marks. If only they could suit up new coach Bob Gibson, who Torre brought in to adjust the attitudes of the pitchers on the staff.

"Rube Walker obviously has a good track record as a pitching coach and he can tell you how to pitch. Bob Gibson can tell you how to win," Torre said.

Even with some blasts from the pasts, the Mets were expected to be near the bottom of the division with the Cubs.

The Season

The Mets started 3-1 but lost 10 of the next 11. Tim Leary, who had already been labeled "the next Tom Seaver," had to leave his MLB debut after two innings. Leary, who made the team over Cashen's objections, was done after two innings and would miss the rest of the season and all of 1982. Later in the month, Swan was sidelined when Ron Hodges hit him with a throw while attempting to throw out Tim Raines stealing second base.

There were problems all over the place. Through 20 games, Lee Mazzilli was batting .162. Frank Taveras, who made 25 errors the season before,

 Final Resting Ground

Dyar Miller was a pretty good reliever in the AL before landing with the Mets in 1980. He followed up a 31-appearance 1.93 ERA 1980 season with 23 appearances in strike-shortened 1981. But after the season he was released, never to play in the majors again.

committed seven in April. Hubie Brooks committed an error on three consecutive plays in a loss to the Dodgers. In mid-May, Jones was 0-5 with a 4.88 ERA. The team lost eight straight to drop to 8-24. The meager offense scored three runs in the final four games of the slide. Doug Flynn was hitting .300 on Memorial Day, but would see his batting average drop more than 60 points over the next two-and-a-half weeks. Only Brooks, Staub and Joel

Youngblood were giving the team signs of life on offense, other than the occasional Kingman blast.

Wilson became the primary centerfielder and Mazzilli moved to left. Kingman moved from left to first. Staub began to see diminished time, working mainly as a pinch-hitter. The team acquired Montreal outfielder Ellis Valentine for Jeff Reardon and Dan Norman. Valentine was a former All-Star and Gold Glove winner but was only hitting .211 with three homers at the time of the trade and he was on the DL with a pulled hamstring. Valentine would become the primary right fielder.

FABULOUS: JOEL YOUNGBLOOD

Joel Youngblood collected only 143 at bats in strike-shortened 1981, but he made the most of them, batting .350 with 25 RBI. Youngblood appeared in only 43 games for the Mets but was their representative at that season's All Star Game.

On June 11, Tom Seaver pitched a complete game as the Mets lost to the Reds 5-2 at Shea. The defeat dropped the Mets to 17-34 and 15 games out of first. Then the players went on strike. There had been issues between players and owners over free agency and compensation. There would be no games for about two months until the All-Star Game on August 9. The decision was made to have a split season with the winners of each half facing off in a five-game divisional playoff.

All of a sudden the Mets were 0-0. Yet, misfortune seemed to follow the team. The team played exhibition games in Toronto before the regular season resumed and lost three pitchers to injury. Swan's rotator cuff bothered him.

TOP BATTERS

Pos	Name	G	AB	H	BA	HR	RBI	RS	SB	OPS
1B	Dave Kingman	100	353	78	.221	22	59	40	6	.782
3B	Hubie Brooks	98	358	110	.307	4	38	34	9	.756
CF	Mookie Wilson	92	328	89	.271	3	14	49	24	.689
1B	Rusty Staub	70	161	51	.317	5	21	9	1	.864
RF	Joel Youngblood	43	143	50	.350	4	25	16	2	.929

TOP PITCHERS

Pos	Name	G	GS	W	L	SV	ERA	IP	SO	BB
SP	Pat Zachry	24	24	7	14	0	4.14	139.0	76	56
SP	Mike Scott	23	23	5	10	0	3.90	136.0	54	34
SP	Ed Lynch	17	13	4	5	0	2.91	80.1	27	21
CL	Neil Allen	43	0	7	6	18	2.97	66.2	50	26
RP	Pete Falcone	35	9	5	3	1	2.55	95.1	56	36

He would only pitch once more in 1981, in a meaningless October game. Jones hurt his ankle on the mound. He would only pitch twice, each time in September. Tom Hausman, who had a 2.18 ERA in 20 appearances, would miss the rest of the season with a bone chip in his right elbow. And a knee injury would cost Joel Youngblood his season in the first week back.

In the first game after the strike, the Mets beat the Cubs in 13 innings, with both teams scoring three times in the 11th and once in the 12th before the Mets scored twice to win 7-5. New York won six of eight and were in first place. On August 18, Kingman hit a pair of homers while Ed Lynch and Neil Allen combined to pitch the team's first shutout since Opening Day. It was Allen who saved seven games in an 18-game stretch. Kingman's batting average went up by more than 20 points as he felt better with Valentine batting behind him though he would dramatically drop off.

The team lost three straight and Torre changed the lineup for August 22 with Kingman moving to left, Staub at first and Alex Trevino behind the plate. Trailing 4-1 in the eighth, Kingman hit a go-ahead grand slam and the Mets went on to win 7-4.

Three days later, the Mets beat the Astros 2-1. New York got past Nolan Ryan and into the Houston bullpen with Mookie Wilson homering off Joe Sambito in the bottom of the eighth to put the Mets in a virtual tie for first with St. Louis.

It looked like the Mets hit a wall when they lost 12 of 17, including a sweep in St. Louis. But the Mets returned the favor, sweeping the Cardinals, pulling to within 2.5 games of first with two weeks left to play. In the finale, the Mets trailed 5-0 before coming back to tie the game. The Cardinals took the lead in the ninth on a Wilson error but with the Mets down to their final out, Wilson hit a two-run homer off Bruce Sutter. It was the first sweep since June 1980 for the Mets and it was the kids who were responsible. Wilson was the hero and Brooks had his first four-hit game in the majors and hit .500 during the week.

The Mets beat the Pirates on a 13th inning wild pitch the following night as the team remained 2.5 out of first, though only 7,429 fans showed up. Then the run ended with five straight losses. Ron Hodges and Dyar Miller were suspended for three days without pay for violating a club rule by patronizing the bar of a hotel that the players are based. "I guess a clean record doesn't count," Hodges said. "I've never been involved in this kind of thing before. The more I think about it, the madder I get."

The Expos clinched the second-season division title in the second to last game of the season at Shea, with Reardon recording the final out.

FUTILE: ELLIS VALENTINE

Valentine came to the Mets in a trade with Montreal after injury and drug problems, plus a fractured jaw from a hit by pitch, had rendered him a shadow of his former All-Star self. The price was high (Jeff Reardon), and Valentine batted only .205 with 5 home runs in 169 at bats.

New York went 24-28 in the second half, finishing 5.5 games out of first but the 41-62 overall record wasn't good enough for Torre to save his job. Cashen had been thinking about the move since June and said he thought the team had the material to play .500 ball. It was also the end for the coaching staff, including Rube Walker and Joe Pignatano, who had arrived with Gil Hodges. Mazzilli said, "when three key guys like me and Dave Kingman and Ellis Valentine are hitting .220, you can't blame Joe."

Despite being in contention in the final two weeks – thanks to the split season – the team finished last in runs and second-to-last in doubles and strikeouts. The pitching staff led the league in homers allowed.

Top 5 Highlights

1 Dave Kingman homers for the fourth consecutive game in the Mets' 6-1 win over the Cubs on May 29. Kingman hits a three-run shot in the bottom of the fifth off Randy Martz.

2 Dave Kingman hits a go-ahead grand slam in the top of the eighth off Cincinnati's Frank Pastore to give the Mets a 5-4 lead on August 22. Neil Allen strands the bases loaded in the bottom of the inning and the Mets tack on two more runs to win 7-4.

3 Down to their final out, Mookie Wilson's two-run homer off Bruce Sutter on September 20 beats the Cardinals 7-6 and brings the Mets to within 2.5 games of first. The Mets pound out 22 hits in the dramatic win.

4 John Stearns scores on a Mark Lee wild pitch in the bottom of the 13th to beat the Pirates 4-3 on September 21. Pittsburgh tied the game in the ninth with two runs off Allen but the Mets won to remain 2.5 games back.

5 Pete Falcone pitches a four-hit shutout and goes two-for-four with a homer and three RBI in a 7-0 laugher over the Phillies on September 29. Falcone hits a solo shot off Mark Davis in the third and delivers a two-run single off Warren Brusstar in the sixth. No Phillie reaches second base against Falcone.

1982

	W	L	GB	Pos
	65	97	27.0	6th
RS/G	**RA/G**	**Manager**		
3.76	4.46	George Bamberger		

Bamberger's Hamburgers Fry for 97 Losses

The Moves

George Bamberger was the new manager. Bambi had been Baltimore's pitching coach when Cashen ran the team and had recently improved the Brewers before stepping down as skipper for health reasons. Bamberger warned against high expectations for a team that had the fourth-worst record in the NL in 1981.

"I don't know the Mets' exact record last season but you must get to .500 first," he said. "Then you go from there. We are going to have to be fundamental-wise and win the one-run games."

A light appeared in the dark days of Shea, as the Mets added George Foster in a February trade with the Reds. The 1977 NL MVP, Foster had wanted a five-year deal, and the unwilling Reds sent him to the Big Apple. The Mets signed Foster to a five-year, $10 million deal.

The Mets had traded Doug Flynn to the Rangers for three-time All-Star reliever Jim Kern. Kern would never pitch for the Mets, as he went sent to the Reds along with Alex Trevino and Greg Harris in the Foster deal. Frank Taveras was traded to the Expos for Steve Ratzer, who would spend 1982 in the minors and never play for the Mets.

 He Was a Met?/Final Resting Ground

Randy Jones is best known as the soft-tossing lefty who won 20 games twice for the San Diego Padres, including a 22-14 with 25 complete games in 1976. Jones played his last two years with the Mets, bouncing back from a 1-8 record for the Mets in 1981 by going 7-10. Jones had a losing record in all six seasons after his Cy Young Award-winning season.

Mazzilli was traded to the Rangers for Ron Darling and Walt Terrell. The Mets had been looking for pitching, while Ellis Valentine and Joel Youngblood won outfield playing time.

The Situation

Cashen believed the Foster deal put the Mets ahead of schedule to be a contender.

"We're tired of finishing fifth or sixth," Cashen said. "We have enough talent to be a contender, and any year you're a contender you can win."

The lineup now included Foster, Dave Kingman and Ellis Valentine and Bamberger was expected to work on some reclamation projects on the pitching staff, including Randy Jones who went 1-8 with an ERA nearing five in 1981.

The One-and-Only Dave Kingman

Dave "Kong" Kingman was both fabulous and futile for the Mets, hitting home runs at a high frequency, many of them prodigious, but also striking out a lot and being a serious liability in the field. 1982 was a prime example as Kingman led the National League in home runs with 37, but somehow managed to get only 10 other extra-base hits; he had 99 RBI, but batted .204. That season, Kingman played first base, where he committed 18 errors. Kingman had an abrasive personality and has the distinction of playing for a team in all 4 divisions in one season (1977—Mets, Padres, Angels, Yankees). In his final major league season in 1986 at age 37, he belted 35 homers, but he found no takers for his services for the 1987 season.

The Season

New York jumped out to a 5-2 start, with Jones defeating Steve Carlton on Opening Day and again in the Mets home opener. The Mets were 10-10 after April but a 17-11 May to put the team at 27-21 and in second place, 3.5 games behind St. Louis. The team won five series in a row.

John Stearns had a 15-game hitting streak and was hitting .327 at the end of May. Mookie Wilson was hitting just under .300 at the end of the month. Jones was off to a 6-2 start, capped off by a shutout in Houston on May 23. Charlie Puleo was moved from the bullpen to the rotation and went 3-0 in May, including a shutout over the Padres. The team was rolling despite a slow start from Foster. The pitching staff had walked 110 batters in the first 28 games but only issued 41 in the next 19. Neil Allen closed 13 games.

FABULOUS: MOOKIE WILSON

Mookie Wilson achieved career highs in games played (159), at bats (639), hits (178), and stolen bases (58); he also scored 90 runs as the Mets' primary lead-off man.

TOP BATTERS

Pos	Name	G	AB	H	BA	HR	RBI	RS	SB	OPS
1B	Dave Kingman	149	535	109	.204	37	99	80	4	.717
LF	George Foster	151	550	136	.247	13	70	64	1	.676
CF	Mookie Wilson	159	639	178	.279	5	55	90	58	.683
RF	Ellis Valentine	111	337	97	.288	8	48	33	1	.701
IF	Bob Bailor	110	376	104	.277	0	31	44	20	.633

TOP PITCHERS

Pos	Name	G	GS	W	L	SV	ERA	IP	SO	BB
SP	Charlie Puleo	36	24	9	9	1	4.47	171.0	98	90
SP	Pete Falcone	40	23	8	10	2	3.84	171.0	101	71
SP	Craig Swan	37	21	11	7	1	3.35	166.1	67	37
CL	Neil Allen	50	0	3	7	19	3.06	64.2	59	30
RP	Jesse Orosco	54	2	4	10	4	2.72	109.1	89	40

They even beat the struggling Yankees in the Mayors Trophy Game in the Bronx. "The game may not have meant anything but it was the most meaningful game I've ever played in," Stearns said. "We've been the second dog in this town too long."

Kingman had 14 home runs. Tom Veryzer was hitting .375 through May. Bob Bailor was at .353 and Wally Backman was at .314.

Veryzer was injured on June 1 and lost for the season when Claudell Washington broke his fibula trying to break up a double play. The Mets went 9-18 in June, scoring 85 runs. Jones went 0-4. In his June 1 start he was pulled after failing to record an out. In his June 22 start against the Expos, he walked the first four batters and was removed.

FUTILE: MIKE SCOTT

Mike Scott went 7-13 with a 5.14 ERA in 37 appearances. He was 14-27 in four seasons with the Mets but would win 110 games and a Cy Young with the Astros.

The team lost eight of nine late in the month. Falcone lost three straight starts, including a 1-0 loss in Philadelphia when he walked in the winning run in the bottom of the ninth. Craig Swan moved from the bullpen to the rotation. Scuffling Mike Scott went from the rotation to the bullpen. Pete Falcone eventually went from the rotation to the bullpen.

Craig Swan and third base coach Frank Howard got into an altercation after the Mets returned to Shea an hour late from St. Louis with the pitcher grousing about flying commercial. The team would lose eight of the next nine.

The Mets were 38-39 heading into July 4 but lost seven straight. They would suffer another five game losing streak toward the end of the month. Foster had 45 RBI at the end of July. Kingman was hitting .215. Ellis Valentine, who was splitting time in right with Joel Youngblood, said the Mets could offer him "all the money in the world" and he wouldn't re-sign as a free agent, adding "This is the worst organization in baseball."

New York finished August on a 15-game losing streak to drop to 50-80. It was the second-longest streak in team history. The Mets would finish 65-97, 27 games out of first.

Top 5 Highlights

1 After Opening Day is snowed out twice, the Mets defeat Steve Carlton and the Phillies 7-2. Foster drives in two with a double in his first at-bat. Jones gives up one run on four hits in six innings to pick up the win.

2 On April 10 in Chicago, Zachry takes a no-hitter two outs into the eighth inning until Bob Molinaro singles to break it up. New York holds on for a 9-5 win.

3 The Mets turn a triple play for the first time since 1966 at Wrigley Field on August 3. With runners on first and second, Larry Bowa loops a pitch to short left where Bob Bailor makes a running catch, turns and throws to second for the second out. Wally Backman fires it to Dave Kingman at first to complete the trifecta.

4 Joel Youngblood delivers a two-run single off Ferguson Jenkins in the third inning of New York's 7-4 win at Wrigley. Youngblood was traded during the game and joined the Expos later that night. Youngblood entered the game and singled off Carlton.

5 Ron Hodges delivers the lone Mets grand slam of the season with a ninth inning shot off Pirates lefty Grant Jackson on September 8 as the Mets win a rare laugher, 9-1.

1983

	W	L	GB	Pos
	68	94	22.0	6th
RS/G	RA/G		Manager	
3.55	4.20		George Bamberger Frank Howard	

Strawberry and Hernandez Bring Hope

The Moves

Tom Seaver returned to Queens, as the Mets brought back The Franchise in a December trade with the Reds. The Mets sent Charlie Puleo along with minor leaguers Lloyd McClendon and Jason Felice to Cincinnati.

It was a sign that the dark days at Shea were ending. Seaver had helped the Reds win the NL West in 1979 and finished second in the Cy Young voting in 1981. However, Seaver had gone 5-13 with a 5.50 ERA in 1982.

The Mets had traded away Mike Scott, who had gone 7-13 with a 5.14 ERA in 1982, to the Astros for Danny Heep a few days earlier. Heep led the Pacific Coast League in batting in 1980.

Pat Zachry, who had been acquired in the Midnight Massacre in 1977, was traded to the Dodgers for Jorge Orta. Later in the offseason, Orta was traded to Toronto.

They also acquired Mike Torrez from Boston. Torrez, 36, was expected to buy some time, along with Seaver, as the pitching prospects worked their way up the system. Torrez had also won 20 games in 1975 for the Orioles, when George Bamberger was the pitching coach.

Several days before the season began the Mets traded Tom Veryzer, who led the team with a .429 batting average and 11 RBI in spring training, to the Cubs for a pair of minor league pitchers who never pitched for New York. Darryl Strawberry had a strong spring but would begin the year in Tidewater.

He Was a Met?

Before settling into a 10-year career with the Cardinals, Jose Oquendo broke in at age 19 with the Mets. Despite collecting only 8 extra-base hits and 17 RBI on the season, Oquendo appeared in 120 games and came to bat more than 350 times. He was traded to the Cardinals for two players who never made it to the major leagues.

The Situation

Low expectations. Again. Strawberry said he could "play in New York right now." *Sports Illustrated* raised the question, but can anyone else?

The Season

A large Shea Stadium crowd cheered returning hero Tom Seaver as he walked in from the bullpen on Opening Day and proceeded to blank the Phillies for six innings. The offensive hero was Mike Howard, who delivered a go-ahead RBI single off Steve Carlton in the bottom of the seventh and then never played in the majors again. When the Mets followed it up with another win over the eventual National League champions, Bamberger's squad was 2-0.

The acquisition of Keith Hernandez in June of 1983 was a key turning point in the history of the franchise. For the Mets, Hernandez put up a string of remarkably consistent and productive years at the plate, played all-world at first base, and was a team leader.

Then the team lost 10 of 12. Neil Allen struggled, losing three games out of the bullpen. The Mets wouldn't sniff .500 for the rest of the season.

With the team off to a 6-15 start, Darryl Strawberry was called up and made his debut on May 6. He hit his first career home run on May 16 in Pittsburgh off Lee Tunnell. The team won four straight in mid-May though eight losses in nine games from late May to early June would finish off any hope the team might've had.

After a 14-inning loss at Dodger Stadium dropped the team to 16-30, Bamberger resigned, saying "I probably suffered enough." Frank Howard took over.

Neil Allen's was struggling. He had an ERA of 9.31 at the end of April and failed to show for a game against the Braves. Worried about alcohol problems, it was stress-related issues causing Allen problems. Bamberger moved him to the rotation, where he won two games including a complete game six-hit shutout against the Dodgers. But after two losses, he was sent back to the bullpen where his inconsistent pitching continued.

 Final Resting Ground

Mike Howard was the Opening Day hero, driving in Dave Kingman with a single off Steve Carlton to give the Mets a 1-0 lead. Howard never played in the majors again. He was sent down to the minors, where he remained for the rest of the season. Howard batted .182 in parts of three seasons with the Mets.

FABULOUS: JESSE OROSCO

Jesse Orosco had one of the greatest seasons ever for a Mets reliever, winning 13 games and saving another 17, and posting an incredible ERA of 1.47 in 110 IP!

On June 15, Allen was sent with Rick Ownbey to the Cardinals for Keith Hernandez. The acquisition of the 1979 NL MVP and best fielding first baseman in the game is now celebrated as a move that turned around the franchise, but Hernandez wept when he learned he had been traded from the defending champions to a perennial cellar dweller. He even asked his agent if he had enough money to retire rather than play for the Mets.

Nine losses in 10 games put the team at 30-52 on July 9. The Mets fell 30 games under .500 after a 4-1 loss to the Cubs made them 62-92. The team won six of eight to finish 68-94. The season ended with a two-run, two-out double from Rusty Staub in the bottom of the ninth to give the Mets a 5-4 win over the Expos.

And another piece of the championship puzzle fell into place as Ron Darling made his MLB debut on September 6 against the Phillies.

The Mets finished 22 games out of first place, but would be a lot closer in 1984.

FUTILE: CRAIG SWAN

Craig Swan's career took a serious dive from which it would never recover, as he finished 2-8 with a 5.51 ERA. He had a 5.93 ERA at Shea. Swan pitched in only 12 more games before retiring.

TOP BATTERS

Pos	Name	G	AB	H	BA	HR	RBI	RS	SB	OPS
1B	Keith Hernandez	95	320	98	.306	9	37	43	8	.858
LF	George Foster	157	601	145	.241	28	90	74	1	.708
CF	Mookie Wilson	152	638	176	.276	7	51	91	54	.666
RF	Darryl Strawberry	122	420	108	.257	26	74	63	19	.848

TOP PITCHERS

Pos	Name	G	GS	W	L	SV	ERA	IP	SO	BB
SP	Tom Seaver	34	34	9	14	0	3.55	231.0	135	86
SP	Mike Torrez	39	34	10	17	0	4.37	222.1	94	113
SP	Ed Lynch	30	27	10	10	0	4.28	174.2	44	41
CL	Jesse Orosco	62	0	13	7	17	1.47	110.0	84	38
RP	Doug Sisk	67	0	5	4	11	2.24	104.1	33	59

Top 5 Highlights

1 Tom Terrific returns, striking out Pete Rose to begin the game and pitching six shutout innings on Opening Day.

2 Darryl Strawberry makes his debut on May 6 against the Reds, scores a run and draws two walks. Dave Kingman ties the game with a two-out home run in the bottom of the ninth and Hubie Brooks ties the game with a two-out home run in the bottom of the 10th. George Foster's three-run home run in the bottom of the 13th gives the Mets a 7-4 win.

3 Rusty Staub delivers his eighth consecutive pinch-hit with a ninth inning single off Philadelphia's Ron Reed on June 26, tying the record set by Dave Philley of the 1958 hillies.

4 Walt Terrell becomes the first pitcher in team history to homer twice in a game, with two shots off Ferguson Jenkins at Wrigley Field on August 6.

5 Mike Fitzgerald homers off Philadelphia's Tony Ghelfi in his first MLB at-bat on September 13. The Mets would go on to win 5-1.

1984

	W	L	GB	Pos
	90	72	6.5	2nd
RS/G	RA/G		Manager	
4.02	4.17		Davey Johnson	

Brilliant Dr. K Is Not Enough

The Moves

After George Bamberger hadn't been successful as manager, Frank Cashen turned to someone else from his Baltimore days: Davey Johnson.

Johnson had been managing the Mets Triple-A club and certainly didn't lack for confidence. As he said at his introductory press conference, "I would like to thank Frank Cashen for being smart enough to hire me."

It looked like Seaver would be the unofficial pitching coach until the Mets left him unprotected in the free-agency compensation pool and the White Sox took him. Cashen took the blame, saying it was his mistake for not protecting The Franchise. The team protected a number of minor leaguers as well as Craig Swan, who had won two games in 1983.

Cashen did make a move that would eventually help the team win the title in 1986, dealing Bob Bailor and Carlos Diaz to the Dodgers for Sid Fernandez and Ross Jones. Fernandez had been named Texas League Pitcher of the Year and had made two appearances with the Dodgers at the end of the season.

The Mets also signed shortstop Rafael Santana, who had been released by the Cardinals, and veteran pitcher Dick Tidrow. After months of failed trade talks, the team released Dave Kingman. The slugger only hit 13 home runs in 1983 but would hit 100 over the next three seasons in Oakland.

The team did sign Jerry Martin, who had spent 81 days in federal prison during the offseason on cocaine charges. He played 13 games for the Royals in 1983

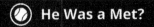

He Was a Met?

Dick Tidrow is well remembered as a solid pitcher for the Indians, Cubs, and especially the Yankees. His career with the Mets was less distinguished, and included 25 hits and 16 runs alloed in 15.2 IP over 11 games. On May 8, he was released and his big-league career was over.

before chipping a bone in his hand and also had to deal with a suspension from Bowie Kuhn for the 1984 season, which was shortened after appeal.

The Situation

"There are more young players than I've ever seen in any camp," Ron Hodges said. "They're young and enthusiastic. Are we entering an era of transition? We'd better be. We can't afford to finish in last place every year."

Plenty of jobs were up for grabs. Would the catcher be Hodges, Junior Ortiz, or Clint Hurdle or Tucker Ashford, two infielders trying to convert, or Mike Fitzgerald, who had homered in his first career at-bat in 1983? John Gibbons had a strong spring and looked to be on his way to making the team until he fractured his cheekbone late in spring training when the Phillies Joe Lefebvre slid into home.

Would Brian Giles and Jose Oquendo be playing up the middle or would it be Wally Backman and Ron Gardenhire?

"Right now, Hernandez is my first baseman, Hubie Brooks is my third baseman, George Foster is the left fielder, Mookie Wilson is the center fielder and Strawberry is the right fielder," Johnson said. "But only two pitchers have set roles: Jesse Orosco and Doug Sisk in the bullpen. I don't know what roles the others will fill."

Johnson, who *Sports Illustrated* said had the "unenviable task" of improving the Mets, looked for bats, saying, "The only team that has three gloves in the batting order is a last-place team."

The roster began to fall in place, including Tucker Ashford being traded to the Royals for pitcher Tom Edens after Kansas City star third baseman George Brett tore ligaments in his knee. And while Seaver wasn't around, the Mets would have Dwight Gooden, who had struck out 300 batters in 191 innings at Single-A Lynchburg the year before.

The Season

After nine straight Opening Day wins, the Reds throttled Mike Torrez in the first game of the season.

Johnson a New Breed of Manager

After the Mets finished their seventh losing season in a row in 1983, Frank Cashen hired Davey Johnson as the new skipper. Johnson, who was Baltimore's second baseman when Cashen ran the Orioles, was one of the first managers to make use of computers. Johnson would become the winningest manager in team history, and his overall winning percentage (including stints with 4 other teams) of .562 ranks in the top 25 all time among all major league managers.

 Final Resting Ground

Mike Torrez had a career of ups and downs, and the end of it was definitely one of the downs. Torrez went 10-17 for the Mets in 1983 and then 1-5 to start 1984. After his release, he pitched in only 2 more games (for Oakland), allowing 7 runs in 2.1 IP.

FABULOUS: KEITH HERNANDEZ

Keith Hernandez put up the first of 4 consecutive excellent seasons for the Mets, drilling 15 HR, driving in 94, and drawing 97 BB, for an OBA of .409. He also won the 7th of his 11 Gold Glove Awards.

Torrez, who had asked for a trade before the season began, was a veteran on a staff that included youngsters Gooden, Ron Darling and Walt Terrell. The Mets would win their next six games, marking the best first week in team history. Gooden won his MLB debut in Houston on April 7 and the next night the Mets finished off their first sweep at the Astrodome in 18 years.

During the early part of the season the Mets would mix close, exciting wins with blowout losses, including giving up 31 runs in three games against the Astros and Reds in May. The Mets responded by releasing Tidrow (9.19 ERA) and Craig Swan (8.20).

On the bright side, Gooden was striking out batters at a record pace, including fanning 11 Dodgers in a complete game shutout against Fernando Valenzuela on May 11 to put the Mets in first place. And Keith Hernandez was leading the offense, hitting .327 as of May 11.

The Mets acquired starting pitcher Bruce Berenyi from the Reds in the middle of June. Berenyi, who led the league in losses in 1982, was 3-7 with an ERA of 6 but pitched well for the Mets during the final two and a half months. One week later, the Mets released Torrez. The right-hander had started the season 0-5 before winning his first game of the season on June 9, despite giving up five runs in six innings against the Expos. He made one relief appearance before being let go.

The team became contenders during two winning streaks: sitting at 23-23, the Mets took 11 of the next 13 to move into first place. Then, with a record of 38-33, the Mets began July winning 12 of their first 13, including a five-game sweep of the Reds.

Ed Lynch became a solid fifth starter, filling in for Tim Leary, though he would be sent back to the bullpen after struggling in four starts. Darling may have

FUTILE: JERRY MARTIN

Another Final Resting Ground candidate for the 1984 Mets, outfielder Jerry Martin ended a fairly solid big-league career with a whimper, not a bang. Martin's slash line of .154/.206/.264 worked out to an OPS+ of 32, numbers that spelled the end.

been overshadowed by Gooden but he won seven straight starts from early June through mid-July, including two complete game shutouts. Meanwhile, Jesse Orosco and Doug Sisk slammed the door on teams in the late innings.

It was the first time the Mets were in first place at the All-Star break and the first time they had four representatives in the midsummer classic with Strawberry, Gooden, Hernandez and Orosco.

TOP BATTERS

Pos	Name	G	AB	H	BA	HR	RBI	RS	SB	OPS
1B	Keith Hernandez	154	550	171	.311	15	94	83	2	.859
3B	Hubie Brooks	153	561	159	.283	16	73	61	6	.758
LF	George Foster	146	553	149	.269	24	86	67	2	.754
CF	Mookie Wilson	154	587	162	.276	10	54	88	46	.717
RF	Darryl Strawberry	147	522	131	.251	26	97	75	27	.810

TOP PITCHERS

Pos	Name	G	GS	W	L	SV	ERA	IP	SO	BB
SP	Dwight Gooden	31	31	17	9	0	2.60	218.0	276	73
SP	Walt Terrell	33	33	11	12	0	3.52	215.0	114	80
SP	Ron Darling	33	33	12	9	0	3.81	205.2	136	104
CL	Jesse Orosco	60	0	10	6	31	2.59	87.0	85	34
RP	Ed Lynch	40	13	9	8	2	4.50	124.0	62	24

The winning continued after the break and the Mets took three straight in late July against the Cardinals at Shea, including two straight extra-inning wins. A win over the Cubs on July 27 put the Mets 4.5 in first place but Chicago would take the next three and the Mets would begin a seven-game losing streak.

And early in August, the Cubs took four straight at Wrigley to go up by 4.5 themselves in a series that included a bench clearing brawl after Lynch threw at Keith Moreland. The main difference makers for Chicago were Cy Young winner Rick Sutcliffe, who would finish the season 16-1 with a 2.69 ERA after being acquired from Cleveland in June, and Ryne Sandberg who would lead the league in runs, triples and earn a Gold Glove on his way to earning MVP.

The Mets did get as close as 1.5 back after beating the Giants 2-0 on August 17 but then lost seven of nine to fall 5.5 back. Looking for an offensive spark, the team acquired Ray Knight in late August for three minor leaguers. Knight would play third base and Hubie Brooks was moved to short.

By the time the Cubs came into Shea on September 7, Chicago led the division by seven games. Gooden pitched a complete game one-hitter but Sutcliffe beat the Mets next night. Gooden was the story of September, striking out 16 in consecutive starts against the Pirates and Phillies. He set a rookie strikeout record with 276, passing Herb Score's 245.

Finishing with 90 wins despite being outscored by 24 runs during the season, the Mets finished 6.5 games behind the Cubs.

Top 5 Highlights

1 Dwight Gooden makes his Major League debut at the Astrodome. Doctor K picked up the win, giving up one run on three hits over five innings, striking out five and walking two.

2 Strawberry Sunday is held on April 29 as the rightfielder was given his 1983 Rookie of the Year trophy and fans were given strawberry sundaes. Strawberry singled, doubled and walked against Jerry Koosman in a 6-2 win.

3 Keith Hernandez delivers a 10th inning game winning single off Neil Allen to give the Mets a 9-8 victory, putting the Mets 20 games over .500 and 3.5 games up in first place.

4 Kelvin Chapman takes Mark Davis deep for the Mets' lone grand slam of the year in the sixth inning of New York's 11-6 win over the Giants on August 26.

5 Dwight Gooden pitches a complete game, one-hit shutout in a 10-0 win over the Cubs on September 7. Keith Moreland's infield single to start the fifth was the only Chicago hit.

1985

OPENING DAY LINEUP

Wally Backman, 2B
Mookie Wilson, CF
Keith Hernandez, 1B
Gary Carter, C
Darryl Strawberry, RF
George Foster, LF
Howard Johnson, 3B
Rafael Santana, SS
Dwight Gooden, P

	W	L	GB	Pos
	98	64	3.0	2nd
RS/G	RA/G		Manager	
4.29	3.51		Davey Johnson	

The Kid, Cy Doc and a Pennant Race

The Moves

The Mets acquired Gary Carter from the Expos for Hubie Brooks, Mike Fitzgerald, Herm Winningham and Floyd Youmans.

At his introductory press conference, Carter mentioned that he had saved his right ring finger for a World Series ring. Carter was a seven-time All-Star. In 1984, he had hit 27 home runs and tied for the league lead with 106 RBI. He was also a three-time Gold Glove winner, who was now being called upon to nurture a young pitching staff.

A few days before the Carter deal, the Mets sent Walt Terrell to the Tigers for Howard Johnson. Ray Knight had undergone surgery, and Johnson was brought in to play third base in case Knight's recovery didn't go according to plan. After winning the 1984 World Series, Detroit needed another starter after Milt Wilcox underwent surgery and Terrell was the odd man out on a staff that included Gooden and Darling. Bringing in Johnson allowed Brooks to be dealt to Montreal.

The Situation

The Mets had improved although the question was if they were now better than the Cubs, who had re-signed pitchers Rick Sutcliffe, Dennis Eckersley and Steve Trout. They also acquired lefty reliever Ray Fontenot from the

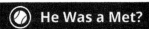

He Was a Met?

Billy Beane, the reovlutionary "Moneyball" GM for the A's, was a can't miss, first-round pick of the Mets, initially ranked ahead of Darryl Strawberry in the depth charts. But Beane struggled for 5 years, was traded several times, until he landed in Oakland's front office. The rest is history.

Although Dwight Gooden never again pitched to the historic level of 1985, he did put up a record of 91-40 from 1986-1991, including 18- and 19-win seasons. (Photo Courtesy Jason D. Antos)

Yankees. And Shawon Dunston, the number one overall pick in the 1982 draft, was going to debut at shortstop. *Sports Illustrated* predicted that the Cubs would edge out the Mets to win the division and then beat the Padres to win the pennant. In "If At First: A Season With The Mets", Keith Hernandez wrote, "For the record right now (and I won't erase this in October): I cautiously pick the Cubs in our division, because they beat us last year and improved over the winter. But we improved too. But we have to prove it."

The Season

Carter made himself a fan favorite immediately. On a freezing Opening Day, Carter hit a 10th inning homer off Neil Allen to give the Mets a 6-5 win. It would be the Cardinals, not the Cubs, battling the Mets for the division crown.

The Mets started 5-0, with four wins by one run and three coming in the last at-bat. The team started 8-1 but lost four of five, including two of three in St. Louis. Bruce Berenyi, the third starter, was lost for the season to a torn rotator cuff.

 Final Resting Ground

The Mets picked up Larry Bowa to be back-up shortstop after his release by the Cubs in August. Bowa collected 2 hits in 19 ABs in the final 14 games of his career, and made 2 errors in 34 innings at shortstop. Bowa chose to retire and begin a managerial career rather than continuing with the Mets in 1986.

On April 28, the Mets won in 18-innings over the Pirates. Rusty Staub flipped between right and left field as Davey Johnson hoped the veteran would avoid having anything hit to him but Le Grand Orange made a running catch in right in what would be his final appearance in the field.

With Mookie Wilson and George Foster battling injuries, Lenny Dykstra was called up and homered in his second at-bat. One downer was Doug Sisk, who was becoming the whipping boy of fans. He allowed at least two runs in five appearances of a seven-game stretch and was sent to the minors for nearly three weeks. Rookie Roger McDowell filled the void in the bullpen, tossing more than 20 straight scoreless innings after a pair of unimpressive starts.

Gooden improved to 5-1 with a 1.31 ERA with a three-hit shutout over the Phillies, striking out 13. The Mets won six straight in early May. Darryl Strawberry, who had been slumping with a .215 and hadn't driven in a run in two weeks,

FABULOUS: DOC GOODEN

Dwight Gooden put together one of the great seasons for a modern-day pitcher compiling a record of 24-4 with an ERA of 1.53. It was a season of total dominance, but as an example of how times have changed, Gooden struck out "only" 268 batters in 276.2 IP, fewer than one per inning.

injured his thumb on May 11 while making a catching catch. He tore a ligament and wouldn't return to the lineup until June 28. The team would only hit .219 in May.

June was a disaster, as the team went 11-18 even with Danny Heep filling in admirably for Strawberry. The Mets lost 10 of 12 and the Cardinals took three of four at Shea. On June 11, the Phillies took a 16-0 lead through two innings. Though the Mets scored seven straight runs, Philly went on to win 26-7, with Tom Gorman, Calvin Schiraldi and Joe Sambito giving up all the runs. Schiraldi would soon be sent to the minors and would only reappear for one September game. The Mets bounced back with five straight wins, including a four-game sweep of the Cubs at Shea. Gooden improved to 10-3 with a 1-0 shutout win and then beat the Cubs again in his next start, again going the distance. But then the Mets lost six straight to drop to 38-35. At the end of the month, Foster was hitting .237. Howard Johnson was hitting .186, which was still better than Ray Knight's .171 mark. Most shocking was the .251 average of Keith Hernandez.

The offense broke out in July, though Wilson would be gone for two months with torn cartilage. On Independence Day, the Mets outlasted the Braves 16-13 in 19 innings with Hernandez hitting for the cycle. Hernandez would raise his batting average 40 points in July. The team scored 11 runs on July 9 in Cincinnati and 10 more in Houston on July 13. The Mets never scored more than 14 runs in a home game and then did it two days in a row against the Braves, winning 16-4 and 15-10. Strawberry hit two homers with seven RBI in the July 20 game. On July 27, the Mets capitalized on five Astros errors to score 16 unearned runs in a 16-4

FUTILE: RAY KNIGHT

Ray Knight's 1986 postseason heroics let Mets fans forget his poor 1985 season, in which he batted .218 and managed only 13 BB and 22 RS in nearly 300 plate appearances.

victory. Gooden went 5-0 during the month, including two shutouts. Darling also made the All-Star team, starting the season 9-2 with a 2.52 ERA.

New York won nine straight in August and moved into first place. Strawberry hit three home runs in a 7-2 win at Wrigley on August 5. Gooden won two straight starts against the Cubs. On August 4, Tom Seaver won his 300th career game at Yankee Stadium as a member of the White Sox. Gooden beat the Cubs 4-1. Rookie right-hander Rick Aguilera won three straight starts, pitching into the eighth twice. Wally Backman was having an impressive year, leaving Kelvin Chapman in the dust at second base, and raising his average as high as .308. Terry Leach pitched a three-hit shutout against the Giants on August 22. Even when Gooden had to settle for a no-decision in a shaky start against the Phillies, the Mets won 10-7, scoring six early runs off Jerry Koosman – in his second to last MLB appearance – and scoring three runs late off Don Carman. Gooden fanned 16 Giants in his next start, a shutout win. Gooden became the youngest 20-game winner with his August 25 victory over the Padres. The Mets entered September two games behind the Cardinals.

The month opened with Hernandez hitting a two-run ninth inning homer to beat the Giants 4-3. Hernandez's travel schedule would be busy as he had to testify about cocaine use in baseball and admitted to using "massive amounts of cocaine" late in the 1980 season. When the team returned to New York, the fans at Shea gave him a standing ovation.

Meanwhile, Carter hit three homers in New York's September 3 win in San Diego and then hit two more the following day. In Los Angeles, Gooden dueled with Fernando Valenzuela. In June, the two hooked up and the Mets scored three in the ninth to win 4-1. The pitchers were even better this time. Gooden pitched nine shutout innings. Valenzuela pitched 11. In the top of the 13th, Strawberry delivered a two-run double and in the bottom half of the frame, Jesse Orosco got Bill Madlock on a pop-up to first with the bases loaded to end the game.

The Mets had gone 7-3 on their West Coast trip and were tied in the standings when the Cardinals came to town for three games. In the first game, Hernandez delivered an RBI single in the bottom of the first to tie the game and, a few batters later, Howard Johnson drilled a grand slam off Danny Cox to give the Mets a 5-1 lead. The Mets held on for a 5-4 win.

Gooden and John Tudor dueled the next night. Gooden pitched nine shutout innings but Cesar Cedeno homered off Orosco in the 10th and Tudor pitched a shutout, his third straight. In the rubber game, New York jumped out to a 6-0 lead through two innings but the Cardinals cut the lead to 6-5 and Willie McGee tied it in the ninth with a homer off Orosco. But in the bottom of the ninth, Hernandez singled off Ken Dayley, scoring Wilson and putting the Mets back in first place.

Unfazed by losing the series to the Mets, the Cardinals won seven straight and 14 of 15 to go up by four games. The Mets went 9-6 in the same time, including losing two of three to the pitiful Pirates at Shea. Carter and Gooden were keeping the Mets alive. Carter hit 13 home runs in September with 34 RBI. Gooden improved to 5-0 with five complete games against the Cubs.

TOP BATTERS

Pos	Name	G	AB	H	BA	HR	RBI	RS	SB	OPS
C	Gary Carter	149	555	156	.281	32	100	83	1	.853
1B	Keith Hernandez	158	593	183	.309	10	91	87	3	.814
LF	George Foster	129	452	119	.263	21	77	57	0	.792
RF	Darryl Strawberry	111	393	109	.277	29	79	78	26	.947

TOP PITCHERS

Pos	Name	G	GS	W	L	SV	ERA	IP	SO	BB
SP	Dwight Gooden	35	35	24	4	0	1.53	276.2	268	69
SP	Ron Darling	36	35	16	6	0	2.90	248.0	167	114
SP	Ed Lynch	31	29	10	8	0	3.44	191.0	65	27
SP	Sid Fernandez	26	26	9	9	0	2.80	170.1	180	80
CL	Roger McDowell	62	2	6	5	17	2.83	127.1	70	37

The Mets went to St. Louis to begin October, three games out of first with six to play and virtually needing a sweep to stay alive. For the first game, Cardinals manager Whitey Herzog moved up Tudor to pitch against Darling instead of Gooden. After starting 1-7, Tudor had won 19 of 20 decisions with 10 shutouts since early June. And he pitched 10 shutout innings against the Mets but Darling, who hadn't lost since August 14, pitched nine shutout innings. In the 11th, Strawberry blasted a homer off the clock behind the bleachers in right-center off Dayley and the Mets had a 1-0 win.

Gooden took a 5-1 lead into the ninth and retired the first two batters, seemingly cruising toward victory number 24. Four straight Cardinals reached and Tom Herr came up as the potential winning run but lined out to second.

It was Aguilera, who won three straight starts, and Cox pitching in the final game of the series. A Mets win would tie them for first. Hernandez gave the Mets a 1-0 lead with a first inning single, but New York could've had more. The bases were loaded with one out but Foster grounded into a force out and Johnson was retired for the final out. Aguilera gave up four runs in six innings and the Mets trailed 4-2 heading into the eighth. A Johnson single scored Strawberry to cut it to 4-3 in the eighth. With two outs in the ninth, Hernandez singled off Ricky Horton, his fifth hit of the game. But Carter flied out against Jeff Lahti and the Mets were down two games with three to play.

The Mets beat the Expos on October 4 but St. Louis' win over the Cubs put the Mets on the brink. The next day, St. Louis won again, clinching the division. When the score flashed on the scoreboard in the eighth, the fans gave the Mets a standing ovation.

Foster added," We achieved a great deal in 1985. But not enough. We should have been head and shoulders above the Cardinals. They got more consistency out of their talent, and that was the difference."

Top 5 Highlights

1 Gary Carter hits a 10th inning homer off Neil Allen in his first game as a Met. St. Louis came back from a 5-2 deficit with Doug Sisk walking Jack Clark with the bases loaded and two outs in the ninth.

2 Clint Hurdle's liner to first goes through the legs of Pirates first baseman Jason Thompson in the 18th inning to score Mookie Wilson and give the Mets a 5-4 win on April 28. Darryl Strawberry hit a grand slam off Mike Bielecki in the first but the Mets wouldn't get another hit until the 12th. Pittsburgh loaded the bases in the ninth with nobody out but couldn't score. With two outs, Orosco bounced a pitch that got away from Carter but the catcher recovered and threw to a covering Orosco, who tagged Rafael Belliard out at the plate. Staub played the field and made a running catch off a Rick Rhoden fly ball to right to end the top of the 18th. Tom Gorman pitches seven innings of shutout relief for the win.

3 On a rainy July 4 in Atlanta, the Mets win 16-13 in 19 innings. New York takes a 7-4 lead into the bottom of the eighth but Dale Murphy's three-run double off Doug Sisk puts the Braves up 8-7. Lenny Dykstra ties the game in the ninth with an RBI single off Bruce Sutter. Keith Hernandez singles in the 12th to complete the cycle. Howard Johnson hits a two-run homer off Terry Forster in the 13th to give the Mets a 10-8 lead but with two outs in the bottom of the inning, Terry Harper hits a two-run homer off Gorman. Strawberry and Davey Johnson are ejected for arguing in the 17th inning. A Dykstra sacrifice fly puts the Mets up 11-10 in the 18th. The last chance for Atlanta was pitcher Rick Camp, a career .060 hitter. Down to his final strike, Camp homers off Gorman. The Mets score five in the 19th off Camp but then the Braves cut it to 16-13. Camp again comes up as the tying run but strikes out against Ron Darling to end the game at nearly 4 a.m.

4 At 20 years, nine months and nine days old, Dwight Gooden becomes the youngest 20-game winner with a 9-3 victory over the Padres on August 25. It wasn't a typical Gooden start as he gave up two earned runs in six innings but the Mets offense picked him up. Roger McDowell retired nine of 10 batters he faced in relief to finish it off.

5 Strawberry's 11th inning homer off Ken Dayley strikes the clock at Busch Stadium on October 1, as the Mets would win a critical 1-0 game. John Tudor pitched 10 shutout innings as he looked to tie Sandy Koufax's record for lefties with 11 shutouts in a season but Ron Darling and Jesse Orosco combined to blank the Cards.

1986

	W	L	GB	Pos
	108	54	21.5 GA	1st
RS/G	RA/G		Manager	
4.83	3.57		Davey Johnson	

Mets Juggernaut Rolls to a WS Crown

The Moves

The Mets picked up Bobby Ojeda in a deal that sent Calvin Schiraldi, John Christensen and Wes Gardner to the Red Sox. Ojeda was 44-39 with the Red Sox but the Mets believed he would be better away from the Green Monster at Fenway Park. Ojeda was to be the fifth starter, with the Mets noting that he wasn't comfortable in a relief role with the Red Sox.

Tim Teufel was acquired from the Twins, as the Mets had been unhappy with right-handed production at second and third base. Teufel hit .262 with 14 home runs in 1984 and .260 with 10 homers in 1985. Wally Backman hit .122 against lefties in 1985. The Mets also believed Teufel's defense would improve away from the artificial turf of the Metrodome.

The Situation

Dwight Gooden had the team holding its breath on two occasions. First, there was an ankle injury in January that he suffered during a workout. Several days before the start of the season, Gooden called Davey Johnson to alert him that he and a friend had been in a car accident. Doctor K wasn't hurt but gave the impression that his friend was. Thinking Gooden was too distraught to be with the team, he let the pitcher throw in Tampa but upon finding out that the friend wasn't hurt, fined Gooden.

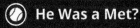

🏐 He Was a Met?

John Gibbons played in eight games, batting .474, including a four-hit game against the Phillies. Gibbons went on to manage the Blue Jays for 11 seasons, reaching the the ALCS in 2015 and 2016.

Roger McDowell: Unsung Hero

Roger McDowell and Jesse Orosco made up a tremendous bullpen duo in 1986. McDowell won 14 games and saved 22 out of the bullpen, even picking up some MVP votes. His finest moment came in Game 6 of the NLCS, when he pitched five shutout innings against and Astros team that had defeated him 3 times during the season. McDowell was also a relentless practical joker who helped calm the waters of a volatile clubhouse. McDowell's trade in June of 1989 along with Lenny Dykstra for Juan Samuel is cited as a critical turning point downward for the franchise—the end of the mid-80s dynasty that never was.

It wasn't all good news as **Mookie** Wilson was injured while working on running drills in spring training and was lost for the first month of the season when a ball hit him and shattered his eyeglasses. Lenny Dykstra would take over in center for the time being.

Sports Illustrated ranked the Mets No. 1 in the league. "This is a simple game when you've got great pitching," Davey Johnson said.

The Season

No drastic changes were necessary. After a 2-3 start, the Mets tied a team-record with 11 straight wins. The team spent virtually the entire season in first place. Ray Knight struggled in 1985 but was off to a hot start. Down 4-2 in the eighth against the Pirates on April 21, Johnson let him hit against right-hander Cecilio Guante and Knight responded by tying the game with a homer. The Mets scored twice in the bottom of the ninth to win 6-5.

The Mets also delivered an early knockout blow to the Cardinals with a four-game sweep in St. Louis. Howard Johnson tied the first game with a two-run homer in the ninth off Todd Worrell and George Foster delivered a go-ahead single in the 10th. Gooden pitched a five-hit shutout the next night and Knight hit two homers, giving him six in the first 12 games. A dramatic 4-6-3 double play from Backman to Rafael Santana to Keith Hernandez let the Mets hold on for a 4-3 win and Ojeda pitched a complete game in the finale. "I could see the frustration on their faces," Hernandez said. "You can see the way they look as they make a right turn and head back toward the dugout."

 Final Resting Ground

George Foster was released in early August of 1986, depriving him of the chance to be on a championship team. It was the end of a largely unsuccessful stint with the Mets. Foster was picked up by the White Sox and appeared in 15 games before calling it a career.

After a loss on May 1, the Mets won seven straight, making it 18 wins in 19 games. The Mets added a six-game winning streak late in the month. Darling tossed a complete game against the Dodgers, striking out 12 to improve to 6-0. Ojeda started 5-0 with a 1.49 ERA. Fernandez won his first four starts and was 5-1 through May. Gooden started 5-0 with a 1.04 ERA, though he would look a bit human for the rest of the season as the strikeouts would decrease and he wouldn't pitch a shutout after May 6.

The offense was clicking as well. Hernandez was batting .347 in early June. Backman was batting .352. Knight was hitting .324. Rookie Kevin Mitchell was batting over .300 and played six different positions. Foster hit seven home runs in May, then hit two more on June 2 against the Padres.

FABULOUS: BOB OJEDA

In his first season as a Met, Bobby Ojeda went 18-5, with a sparkling ERA of 2.57, and leading the league in winning percentage. The lefty finished fourth in the Cy Young voting, even higher than Gooden. He added a win in both the NLCS and World Series, pitching to a combined ERA of 2.33 in 4 starts.

The brash team was becoming the most-hated in the league. On May 27, Foster hit a grand slam of Dodgers righty Tom Niedenfuer. The pitcher then drilled Knight, leading to a benches clearing brawl. Less than two weeks later, the Mets were in Pittsburgh when the Mets accused Rick Rhoden of doctoring the ball. A ball was taken out of play and Rhoden fanned Gary Carter to end the inning. As the Pirates came off the field, Rhoden exchanged words with Mets first-base coach and former teammate Bill Robinson. A brawl ensued.

New York's lead kept growing. Ojeda and Fernandez both started 12-2. Darling would start 11-3. Gooden would throw a complete game against Nolan Ryan and the Astros on July 4 to go 10-3. The Mets were swept at Shea Stadium by the Reds and then took it out on the Braves, winning four straight heading into the All-Star break. On July 11, Carter hit a three-run homer in the first off David Palmer. In the second, he hit a grand slam off Palmer. Palmer's next pitch drilled Darryl Strawberry and the Mets' third bench-clearing brawl ensued. The Mets took a 59-25 record into the break with Gooden, Carter, Strawberry, Hernandez and Fernandez representing the team at the All-Star Game in Houston.

The team stayed in Houston but lost three of four to the Astros. Darling, Teufel, Ojeda and Rick Aguilera were arrested after an altercation with two off-duty police officers outside a bar. The Mets then went to Cincinnati where the fighting was back on the field. Knight threw a punch at Reds pinch-runner Eric Davis after a steal of third was followed by Davis coming up and bumping Knight. The team's fourth brawl of 1986 ensued. Carter had to play third base with Roger McDowell and Jesse Orosco flipping between

FUTILE: GEORGE FOSTER

George Foster's painful years with the Mets came to a painful end in August of 1986 when he was released as the Mets streaked toward their second championship. Foster was batting .227 with 13 HR when he was let go.

TOP BATTERS

Pos	Name	G	AB	H	BA	HR	RBI	RS	SB	OPS
C	Gary Carter	132	490	125	.255	24	105	81	1	.776
1B	Keith Hernandez	149	551	171	.310	13	83	94	2	.859
3B	Ray Knight	137	486	145	.298	11	76	51	2	.775
CF	Lenny Dykstra	147	431	127	.295	8	45	77	31	.822
RF	Darryl Strawberry	136	475	123	.259	27	93	76	28	.865

TOP PITCHERS

Pos	Name	G	GS	W	L	SV	ERA	IP	SO	BB
SP	Dwight Gooden	33	33	17	6	0	2.84	250.0	200	80
SP	Ron Darling	34	34	15	6	0	2.81	237.0	184	81
SP	Bob Ojeda	32	30	18	5	0	2.57	217.1	148	52
SP	Sid Fernandez	32	31	16	6	1	3.52	204.1	200	91
CL	Roger McDowell	75	0	14	9	22	3.02	128.0	65	42

right field and the mound. Orosco caught a Tony Perez liner in the bottom of the 13th and the Mets won the next inning.

Foster did not come out of the dugout during the brawl. He was becoming a part-time player as his batting average sank to .227. "I'm not saying it's a racial thing," Foster said. "But that seems to be the case in sports these days. When a ball club can, they replace a George Foster or a Mookie Wilson with a more popular white player. I think the Mets would rather promote a Gary Carter or a Keith Hernandez to the fans so parents who want to can point to them as role models for their children, rather than a Darryl Strawberry or a Dwight Gooden or a George Foster." Both Foster and Johnson both said "The comments probably were the straw that broke the camel's back" in leading to Foster's release. General manager Frank Cashen pointed out Foster was 2-28 with 10 strikeouts in his last 12 games.

Lee Mazzilli returned to Queens as a part-time player. He tied a game in the ninth with a homer against the Cardinals. Carter had to miss two weeks on the DL with a partial tear of the outer ligament in his left thumb he suffered while playing first base. Though he was only hitting .243, his 19 home runs and a league-leading 87 RBI, along with his handling of the pitching staff, put him on the short list of MVP contenders and the two weeks gone would hurt his chances. "He's got to wear that equipment on a hot day," Davey Johnson said, touting Carter's MVP chances in early August. "He's got to handle pitchers. He's got to block the plate. Catcher is the most critical position in baseball, no doubt about it." Strawberry struggled after the All-Star break and went hitless at Shea in August. He hit .298 in the first half and .214 in the second. He finished the season batting .227 at home and the fans began to get on the star outfielder.

After batting .176 in August, Strawberry would hit .259 with eight homers and 20 RBI in his last 26 games. Carter batted .299 with five home runs and 18 RBI over the final month. The team kept rolling and clinched the division with two-and-a-half weeks remaining in the season. The team set a record with its 101st win en route to a 108-54 season.

Top 5 Highlights

1 Howard Johnson's two-run homer in the top of ninth off Todd Worrell ties the game at four on April 24. George Foster's RBI single in the 10th scores Wally Backman and Roger McDowell pitches a scoreless bottom of the 10th to close out the 5-4 win.

2 Tim Teufel's grand slam in the bottom of the 10th off Tom Hume gives the Mets an 8-4 win over the Phillies on June 10. Down 4-3 in the eighth, Gary Carter tied the game with a homer off Steve Bedrosian.

3 Ray Knight, who struck out four times earlier in the game, hits a homer in the bottom of the 10th off Frank DiPino to beat the Astros 6-5 on July 3. The Mets trailed 5-3 in the 10th but Strawberry tied the game with a two-run homer, his second of the game. Ed Hearn also hit a home run in the win.

4 Howard Johnson's 14th inning home run off Cincinnati's Ted Power puts the Mets ahead 6-3 in a win over the Reds on July 22. The Mets were down to their final out in the ninth when Dave Parker dropped a Keith Hernandez fly ball, allowing two runs to score and the game was tied. After a 10th inning brawl, Carter had to move to third base, with Jesse Orosco and Roger McDowell flipping between right field and pitching. In the 12th, with two on and nobody out, Reds pitcher Carl Willis bunted. Hernandez came in, threw to Carter at third, who threw to Teufel covering first for a 3-5-4 double play. The Mets won the five-hour game in 14 innings.

5 Dwight Gooden pitches a complete game and the Mets clinch the NL East with a 4-2 win over the Cubs on September 17. Dave Magadan makes his first career start and the first baseman delivers three hits, including two run-scoring singles.

1986 NLCS

The Mets would take on the 96-win Astros in the NLCS. Houston had Cy Young winner Mike Scott who won 18 games, had a 2.22 ERA and struck out 306 batters. His improvement was credited to learning the split-fingered baseball, though it was widely speculated that scuffing the ball was the reason for his nastiness on the mound.

Scott struck out 14 in a five-hit shutout in Game 1. Glenn Davis homered off Dwight Gooden in the second inning for the lone Houston run. With Strawberry on third and two outs in the ninth, Knight struck out.

Nolan Ryan blanked the Mets for three innings the next night until Carter's RBI double made it 1-0 in the fourth. Strawberry followed with a sacrifice fly. The Mets scored three in the fifth, on a Backman RBI single and Hernandez two-run triple. Ojeda went the distance, giving up one run on 10 hits in a 5-1 win, tying the series. His play of the game came in the second inning with runners on the corners. Alan Ashby hit a tapper that Ojeda fielded and the pitcher tagged Kevin Bass out at the plate.

At Shea the Astros jumped on Darling, with two in the first and two in the second. Bill Doran's homer made it 4-0 and 17-game winner Bob Knepper blanked the Mets for five innings. Mitchell and Hernandez started the bottom of the sixth with singles and Carter's grounder to short went under the glove of Craig Reynolds to make it 4-1. Strawberry hit the next pitch into the stands to tie the game. Houston took the lead back in the seventh with help from a Knight throwing error. New York trailed 5-4 when Backman led off the bottom of the ninth with a bunt single. Two batters later, Dykstra homered off Dave Smith into the Mets bullpen for a 6-5 win.

Scott dominated the Mets again to even the series at two games apiece. Alan Ashby and Dickie Thon homered off Fernandez in the 3-1 Astros win.

After a day of rain, Gooden and Ryan dueled in Game 5. The Mets caught a break in the second when Reynolds hit into an inning-ending 4-6-3 double play with runners on the corners though it appeared he beat the throw to first. Houston took the lead in the fifth but Strawberry tied it with a homer in the bottom of the inning, after Ryan retired the first 13 Mets. Ryan gave up one run on two hits in nine innings. Gooden gave up one run in 10. With one out in the bottom of the 12th, Backman singled on a liner off the shortstop. A Charlie Kerfeld pickoff throw got away and Backman went to second. Hernandez was walked intentionally, bringing up Carter. The catcher was 1-21 in the series. In Game 3, he hit one back to Kerfeld, who fielded it behind his back and showed the ball to Carter as he ran to first. On a 3-2 pitch, Carter hit one back up the middle. Kerfeld couldn't field it this time. Backman scored on the single to center.

A loss in Game 6 would mean having to face Scott in a seventh game. Houston jumped on Ojeda for three runs in the first inning. It could've been four when Hal Lanier put on a squeeze play but Ashby couldn't get a bunt down on an outside Ojeda pitch and Bass was caught stealing home. It didn't look like it would matter as Knepper took a two-hit shutout into the ninth. Dykstra led off with a triple and Wilson followed with a single. Two batters later, Hernandez doubled, cutting the lead to 3-2 and knocking out Knepper. Smith entered and walked Carter and Strawberry, loading the bases. Knight's sacrifice fly tied the game. McDowell, who was 0-3 with a 4.15 ERA in six regular season games against the Astros, pitched five shutout innings. In the 14th, Backman's single to right scored Strawberry to make it 4-3. Two outs away from the pennant, Billy Hatcher's fly ball off Orosco hit the pole in left to tie the game. In the 16th, the Mets scored three times. Knight's single scored Strawberry and the Mets scored twice more. The Mets had a 7-4 lead but Orosco was tired. It was 7-5 with two on and two outs when Davis, the runner-up for NL MVP, came to the plate. Orosco kept him in the park, but Davis singled to cut the lead to 7-6. Bass came to the plate with the tying and winning runs on base. Throwing nothing but sliders, Orosco went to 3-2 and then got Bass to swing and miss. The Mets had won the pennant.

Orosco was the winning pitcher in three games. Scott, with his 0.50 ERA, was named series MVP. The Mets won the NLCS despite batting .189 in six games. "I feel as if I've been paroled and pardoned," Davey Johnson said. "We got one run in 18 innings off him, and I literally would have had no bullpen left for tomorrow."

How could the World Series top that?

1986 World Series

The Mets would host the Boston Red Sox, who had trailed 3-1 in the ALCS and were down to their final out in Game 5 against the California Angels. Again, the Mets fell behind 1-0 with a 1-0 loss. Bruce Hurst pitched eight shutout innings and Calvin Schiraldi pitched a scoreless ninth. Darling was the tough-luck loser. With Jim Rice on second with one out in the seventh, Rich Gedman hit a grounder to second but it went through the legs of Teufel, allowing Rice to score.

Gooden matched up with Roger Clemens, the AL Cy Young and MVP in Game 2. The Red Sox scored three times in the third, and the Mets answered back with two. But Dave Henderson homered to start the fourth and Dwight Evans' two-run homer in the fifth gave Boston a 6-2 lead. Clemens failed to make it through the fifth but it didn't matter as Boston pounded out nine runs on 18 hits in a 9-3 win.

Dykstra led the third game off with a home run off Oil Can Boyd. The Mets would score four in the first, with help from a botched rundown. Heep's single drove in two runs. Ojeda was in command, giving up one run in seven innings against his former team. Carter singled in two runs and Knight added an RBI double in the Mets' 7-1 triumph.

Darling loaded the bases in the first inning of Game 4 but got Evans to ground out. In the top of the fourth, Carter broke a scoreless tie with a two-run homer off Al Nipper over the Green Monster. Two batters later, Knight's single made it 3-0. In the top of the seventh, Dykstra hit a Steve Crawford pitch deep to right. Evans almost robbed a home run but had the ball pop out of his glove and the Mets had a 5-0 lead. An inning later, Carter hit another home run. Darling pitched seven innings of shutout ball. The Mets bullpen held on for a 6-2 win.

Gooden struggled again in Game 5, giving up four runs in four innings. Fernandez kept the Mets in it. Hurst blanked the Mets until Teufel homered in the eighth. Down 4-1 in the ninth, Wilson doubled and Santana singled, making it 4-2. Dykstra struck out to end it. The Red Sox were one win away from taking the World Series and they had Clemens on the mound for Game 6.

Boston took an early 2-0 lead as Evans doubled home a run in the first and Marty Barrett singled in a run in the second. Clemens took a no-hitter into the fifth. Strawberry walked, stole second and scored on a Knight single. Wilson followed with a single to right and Knight went to third when Evans booted the ball. Heep pinch-hit and grounded into a double play, tying the game. In the seventh, with Barrett on second and one out, Knight made a wild throw on a Rice grounder, putting runners on the corners. Evans grounded one to Backman, who flipped to short but Rice, who was attempting a steal, beat the throw. Evans was out at first but the Red Sox led 3-2. Gedman followed with a single to left but Wilson threw out Rice at the plate to keep it a one-run game.

Clemens was gone, a source of debate for years with the manager saying the pitcher asked out with a blister and the pitcher denying it. Mazzilli led off with a single. Dykstra followed with a bunt that Schiraldi threw in the ground to second, putting two on with none out. After a bunt and an intentional walk, Carter worked the count to 3-0 and then flied out to left, tying the game at three. Strawberry flied out to end the inning and was double-switched out of the game, with Mazzilli staying in the game and Aguilera coming in to pitch.

Dave Henderson's tenth-inning homer off Aguilera gave Boston a 4-3 lead. Barrett added an RBI single to make it 5-3. In the bottom of the 10th, Backman and Hernandez flied out. Carter singled to left. Mitchell pinch-hit and singled to center. Knight fell behind 0-2 before delivering a single to right-center, cutting the lead to 5-4 and putting runners on the corners. Bob Stanley entered. Wilson battled and on a 2-2 pitch, Stanley threw a wild pitch which went off Gedman's glove and to the backstop, tying the game. Wilson grounded a 3-2 pitch to first. The ball went through the legs of Buckner, who was still on the field instead of usual defensive replacement Dave Stapleton, and Knight scored the winning run.

Game 7 was delayed a day by rain, allowing the Red Sox to come back with Hurst. In the top of the second, Evans and Gedman hit back-to-back home runs. A Boggs RBI single made it 3-0. Darling failed to make it out of the fourth. Fernandez entered and kept the Mets in the game with 2.1 shutout innings. Hurst was looking for his third win of the series and blanked the Mets on one hit for five innings. In the sixth, Mazzilli and Wilson singled. Teufel followed with a walk to load the bases. Hernandez delivered a two-run single to left-center. Carter hit one to right, that Evans couldn't catch. Evans threw Hernandez out at second but Backman, pinch-running, scored the tying run.

The Mets made it 6-3, but Boston fought back in the eighth as an Evans double scored two runs and put the tying run on with nobody out. Orosco entered, getting Gedman to line out to second, striking out Henderson and getting Baylor to ground out to short. In the eighth, Strawberry hit a homer off Nipper. He took his time around the bases and would be drilled in spring training the next time he faced Boston. Orosco added an RBI single to extend the lead to 8-5. When Orosco struck out Barrett to end the game, the Mets were World Champions. Knight was named series MVP.

1987

	W	L	GB	Pos
	92	70	3.0	2nd

RS/G	RA/G	Manager	
5.08	4.31	Davey Johnson	

OPENING DAY LINEUP

Mookie Wilson, CF
Tim Teufel, 2B
Keith Hernandez, 1B
Gary Carter, C
Darryl Strawberry, RF
Kevin McReynolds, LF
Howard Johnson, 3B
Rafael Santana, SS
Bob Ojeda, P

Injuries Undermine Repeat Efforts

The Moves

Kevin Mitchell played six positions, hit 12 homers and was part of the Game 6 rally, but was traded to the Padres along with Stan Jefferson and minor leaguer Shawn Abner for power hitting outfielder Kevin McReynolds along with Gene Walter and Adam Ging. Basically, the trade was Mitchell for McReynolds, who hit .288 with 26 homers and 96 RBI in 1986.

Ray Knight was gone, signing with the Orioles after Knight and the Mets couldn't get close during contract negotiations.

Cashen pulled off a heist, acquiring young right-hander David Cone from the Royals for backup catcher Ed Hearn and right-hander Rick Anderson.

The Situation

Dwight Gooden was having a nightmarish offseason, beginning with missing the ticker tape parade for the World Series champions. His engagement was called off in November when it was found out that he had a child with another woman. He was arrested by Tampa police in mid-December, along with a few others, including his nephew Gary Sheffield. One officer was kicked in the head, another kicked in the groin, and Gooden was beaten to the ground with nightsticks and flashlights before being handcuffed and shackled.

He Was a Met?

The Mets picked up long-time Pirate John Candalaria for the September pennant race. The Candy Man did not pitch particularly well in his 3 starts (5.84 ERA), but he collected 2 wins, and that winter he signed with the crosstown rival Yankees.

In late March, Gooden took a drug test that found traces of cocaine. He would miss the first two months of the season while in rehab. Barry Lyons who won the backup catcher spot, making Hearn expendable, and John Gibbons, were sent to Tidewater. Roger McDowell was sidelined for the first two months after hernia surgery.

The Decimation of a Pitching Staff

How badly were the Mets depleted in 1987? The team signed Tom Seaver to see what the 42-year-old had left. Not much as it turned out and The Franchise retired after Barry Lyons knocked him around in a simulated game. Dwight Gooden missed two months for a drug suspension. Bobby Ojeda made seven starts. David Cone broke his finger trying to bunt. Sid Fernandez missed three weeks after the All-Star break with a knee injury. And Ron Darling missed the final three weeks with a thumb injury.

The Season

The Mets jumped out to a 3-0 start with Bobby Ojeda getting the Opening Day start, and win. Darryl Strawberry hit a three-run homer in the first, which held up in the 3-2 win over Pittsburgh. Then he homered in the next two games. New York swept the Phillies in Philadelphia to improve to 6-2.

But then the Mets went to St. Louis and were swept by the Cardinals. In the middle game, the Mets blew a 5-0 lead in the fourth, a 7-6 lead in the ninth and an 8-7 lead in the 10th. The game ended with Tom Herr hitting a grand slam off Jesse Orosco. Then the Cardinals took two of three at Shea the next week.

Ojeda had to undergo surgery on his left elbow in May and would be gone for four months. Rick Aguilera also battled elbow pain and was out for three months. Cone started the season in the bullpen before being moved to the rotation, where he initially struggled before improving. The turning point was an exhibition game against the Red Sox on May 7, with Cone pitching seven innings of three-hit ball in a 2-0 win. In his next start, he got his first major league win with a complete game victory over the Reds and followed it up with eight strong innings against the Giants for another. But in late May, he suffered a broken finger on his pitching hand when trying to lay down a bunt against Atlee Hammaker. Sid Fernandez even missed a pair of starts after he hurt his knee sliding into third base on a triple in the bottom of the fourth of a game against the Giants. He pitched a scoreless fifth but had to leave when his knee buckled as he was winding up to pitch to Mark Wasinger to start the sixth, bringing an end to his no-hit bid.

The Mets were 19-22 and 7.5 games out of first before winning

 Final Resting Ground

No, not that Bob Gibson. This one had four mediocre seasons with the Milwaukee Brewers before joining the Mets. He appeared in one game, pitching a shutout inning and fanning 2, in what would be the last appearance of his career.

five straight. A struggling Gary Carter was batting .228 at the end of May. Fortunately, Strawberry hit 10 homers in May. On May 27, the day Cone was injured, Strawberry and Carter hit back-to-back ninth inning home runs to give the Mets a 4-3 win.

Gooden made a triumphant return on June 5, giving up one run on four hits in 6.2 innings in a 5-1 win over the Pirates. Mookie Wilson and Lenny Dykstra stole the show with a collision in the outfield on a Sid Bream liner, caught by Wilson.

With all the injuries – plus a healthy Ron Darling who hadn't won a game since late April – the team signed Tom Seaver on June 6. He had not pitched since September 19 of the previous season with the Red Sox but an injury kept him out of the postseason.

Seaver made a start with Tidewater and gave up seven runs (six earned) on eight hits and was removed without retiring anyone in the third inning. Two unimpressive simulated games against the Mets later, he decided to call it quits. While the hero of 1969 was done, the current ace was back in form as Gooden went 5-1 in June, with two complete games and a 2.12 ERA.

FUTILE: JESSE OROSCO

In his final season as a Met, Orosco was 3-9 with a 4.44 ERA. He gave up a grand slam to Tommy Herr in St. Louis on April 18 to end a 10-inning game. On May 2, he gave up a 10th inning grand slam to Montreal's Tim Raines. He only managed to pitch for another 16 seasons in the majors.

Gooden got plenty of support on June 10 when the Mets won 13-2. A slumping Keith Hernandez had shaved his moustache and hit two homers that day at Wrigley Field. Hernandez made the All-Star team with a .287 average at the break. Fernandez also made the team on the strength of a 9-3 start and 2.82 ERA. Carter made the team with 11 homers, despite a .236 average.

Though the Mets went 16-12 in June, there was high-stress around the team. There was a deflating loss on June 8, when Barry Lyons was picked off second by Chicago catcher Jody Davis to end the top of the ninth as Lee Smith was issuing an intentional walk to Mookie Wilson. Manny Trillo homered off Doug Sisk in the bottom of the inning to end it. Darling hadn't won since April 22, when he took a no-hitter into the eighth against the Phillies on June 28. He lost the no-hitter and the bullpen lost the game 5-4. Darling's ERA was over five in early July.

Terry Leach was moved from the bullpen to the rotation and went 3-0 in June. An inconsistent John Mitchell was also in the rotation and tossed a complete game victory over the Phillies on June 19. The Mets took two of three from St. Louis but the loss was an 8-7, 11-inning defeat after the Mets blew a 7-3 lead. Jesse Orosco blew the lead in the ninth and lost in the 11th. His ERA was 5.45 at the end of June and he said he would seek a trade if his inconsistent use didn't increase.

Another problem was Strawberry. Sure he was on his way to an All-Star campaign. But he had been fined $1,500 in the spring for missing a pair of workouts and fined $250 more for arriving late for batting practice in Chicago in June. He didn't play in the two wins against the Cardinals, asking out of the lineup because he wasn't feeling well. His teammates were not sympathetic. "What he did, he let his manager down, he let his coaches down and, most importantly, he let his teammates down," Lee Mazzilli said. Wally Backman added, "From the stuff I heard in the trainer's room, he should have been out there. Nobody in the world I know of gets sick 25 times a year. There's only so much you can take."

Strawberry's response: "They rip me and they can't even hold my jock." Of Backman specifically he added, "I'll bust him in the face, that little redneck."

The moody outfielder hit 21 home runs by the All-Star break. "Where would this team be without me? So I miss a couple of games. These guys are asses," Strawberry said. "When I'm gone from here, they'll wonder why I left."

Davey Johnson blamed the media for much of the internal drama and said he would no longer speak with them though he relented. "It's ludicrous, ridiculous, unbelievable," he said. One player threw food at a writer. Another dropped a firecracker at the feet of a group of reporters interviewing Leach.

Wilson held an impromptu press conference demanding a trade to get more playing time in the outfield. "I feel I'd be doing myself a great injustice by not speaking out," he said. "Everybody thinks [that if] everything is peachy in Metsville, good old Mookie isn't going to rock the boat."

Dykstra, who was platooning with Wilson in center, was also unhappy. "I don't even know when I'm playing anymore," he said. "I'm rusting away. I have no chance to put up any kind of numbers. I come to the park prepared to play, and then I'm not in there. I don't know what's going on. They've got to trade someone soon."

TOP BATTERS										
Pos	Name	G	AB	H	BA	HR	RBI	RS	SB	OPS
C	Gary Carter	139	523	123	.235	20	83	55	0	.682
1B	Keith Hernandez	154	587	170	.290	18	89	87	0	.813
3B	Howard Johnson	157	554	147	.265	36	99	93	32	.868
LF	Kevin McReynolds	151	590	163	.276	29	95	86	14	.813
RF	Darryl Strawberry	154	532	151	.284	39	104	108	36	.981

TOP PITCHERS									
Pos	Name	G	GS	W	L	SV	ERA	IP	SO	BB
SP	Ron Darling	32	32	12	8	0	4.29	207.2	167	96
SP	Dwight Gooden	25	25	15	7	0	3.21	179.2	148	53
SP	Sid Fernandez	28	27	12	8	0	3.81	156.0	134	67
CL	Roger McDowell	56	0	7	5	25	4.16	88.2	32	28
RP	Terry Leach	44	12	11	1	0	3.22	131.1	61	29

The Mets fell to 10.5 games out of first on July 9 when Houston's Bill Doran hit a ninth inning homer off lefty Randy Myers. But the team took the next three heading into the All-Star break. And shortly after the break, Strawberry replaced Carter as the cleanup hitter. Suddenly the Mets were on fire, taking 19 of 25, including three straight in St. Louis. Howard Johnson hit 10 homers in July, giving him 25 on the year. His two-run shot off St. Louis' Pat Perry in the top of the 10th gave the Mets the win on July 29 and he hit another against the Cardinals the following day. Cardinals manager Whitey Herzog accused Johnson of using a corked bat.

After going two-and-a-half months without a win, Darling won eight of nine starts. His complete game on August 7 gave the Mets seven straight wins to begin the month as the team was only 3.5 games out of first. New York lost six of eight but turned the momentum around with a 23-10 at Wrigley. Strawberry had four hits, scoring five runs and driving in five more, including a three-run homer.

FABULOUS: KEVIN MCREYNOLDS

McReynolds was solid in his first year with the Mets, with 29 HR and 95 RBI. Three similar seasons followed, making him a reliablly productive offensive player, though there was some criticism of his low-intensity style of play.

Johnson and Strawberry both hit their 30th home runs of the season on August 19 against the Giants. San Francisco manager Roger Craig asked for Johnson's bat to be removed and it was sent to the league office where it was cleared. "When a man hits a ball 480 feet, I have to take a precaution," Craig said. "I knew HoJo well when I with Detroit. He really hit that ball, and I don't recall him hitting them that far in Detroit." Houston's Hal Lanier and Montreal's Buck Rodgers also made allegations.

The Mets started September hot and were only 1.5 game out of first after beating the Phillies on September 9. Aguilera was back, winning his first four starts. He would win six straight before losing.

A crowd of 51,795 came to Shea on September 11 to see the Mets take on the first-place Cardinals, who had lost six of eight and were missing slugging first baseman Jack Clark. The Mets jumped out to a 3-0 first inning lead off John Tudor, who had missed three-and-a-half months of the season when Barry Lyons slid in the dugout during an April game and broke Tudor's leg. Darling took a no-hitter into the sixth before Vince Coleman broke it up with a bunt single. He pitched into the seventh but had broken his thumb diving for the bunt and would miss the rest of the season.

The Mets had a 4-1 lead and were one out away from moving to within a half-game of first. Willie McGee's single off McDowell to make it 4-2. Then Terry Pendleton homered to center, tying the game and silencing Shea. The Cardinals scored twice off Orosco in the 10th and the Mets went down in order against Ken Dayley. The next night, Gooden gave up five runs in the first and the Mets went down quietly in an 8-1 loss.

New York avoided a sweep the following night then won three more to cut the lead back to 1.5. Frustratingly, the Mets couldn't get closer despite the Cardinals leaving the door open. The Mets went to Pittsburgh for three games with the last place Pirates but dropped two of three. The Mets blew an 8-5 lead in the opening game in a 10-9 loss. In the rubber game, the Mets led 6-2 in the sixth, 7-6 in the eighth and 8-7 in the 12th but lost a 14-inning heartbreaker. Davey Johnson had been ejected in the seventh inning. "Angry? I'm tired. These games have worn me down, and the players, too. Every one was a nail-biter," he said.

Still, the Mets weren't dead yet. After a 1-0 win in Philadelphia on September 28, with recent acquisition John Candelaria picking up the win, the Mets were two games back with two more remaining in Philly before traveling to St. Louis for the final three games. But Don Carman pitched a one-hit shutout, with Wilson the only batter to reach on an infield single in the fourth as the Mets lost 3-0. The following night, Luis Aguayo's 10th inning homer off Orosco gave the Phillies a 4-3 win.

The Mets needed the Expos to beat the Cardinals on October 1 to stay alive but the Cardinals clinched the division with an 8-2 win, rendering the final three games meaningless. New York took two of three, but it was too little, too late. During the final weekend, Cashen announced the 1988 season would be Johnson's final as manager.

Top 5 Highlights

1 The Mets hold off a ninth inning rally and beat the Pirates 3-2 on Opening Day. Strawberry hits a three-run homer in the first off Bob Patterson for all the Mets scoring. With the bases loaded and one out in the ninth, Orosco gets Johnny Ray on a pop-up to second and Bobby Bonilla grounds out to second to end it.

2 Gooden returns to Shea with a 5-1 win over the Pirates on June 5. Gooden gives up one run on four hits in 6.2 innings, walking four and striking out five. Orosco pitches the final 2.1 innings for the save.

3 Leach tosses a two-hit shutout against the Reds on July 2 to improve to 7-0. Dykstra homers in New York's 5-0 win.

4 The Mets win a 23-10 slugfest at Wrigley on August 16. Strawberry, Dykstra and Johnson all homer. New York scores in every inning except the second and ninth. Greg Maddux gives up seven run in 3.2 innings. Chicago reliever Drew Hall gives up 10 runs on 10 hits in 1.2 innings.

5 Hernandez collects his 2,000th career hit in the bottom of the eighth of a 12-4 win against the Cubs on September 15. Facing Jay Baller, Hernandez hits one between third and short that Shawon Dunston makes a diving play on but can't throw to first in time.

1988

	W	L	GB	Pos
	100	60	15 GA	1st
RS/G	RA/G		Manager	
4.39	3.33		Davey Johnson	

100 Wins, a Division Title, and Heartbreak

The Moves

It was a quiet offseason for Frank Cashen. Doug Sisk was sent to the Orioles. Rafael Santana went across town to the Yankees with Phil Lombardi and Darren Reed coming to Queens. The team did acquire Mackey Sasser from the Pirates for Randy Milligan. Jesse Orosco went to the Dodgers.

The Situation

The Mets were a runaway choice to win the division, especially with Cardinals slugger Jack Clark leaving for the Yankees.

In *Sports Illustrated*, Steve Wulf wrote, "Barring a rash of major injuries like pulled jaw muscles, you can pretty much count on meeting the Mets in the National League Championship Series."

Darryl Strawberry caused a splash with an Esquire magazine story in which he said the team would've been better off with Herzog as manager, saying Keith Hernandez was distracted by his divorce and that Gary Carter "quit" on the team. "I just wish he had included me," Tim Teufel said.

The Season

The Mets hit six Opening Day homers in a win against the Expos, including two apiece from Strawberry and Kevin McReynolds. The team was 2-3 then

 He Was a Met?

Southpaw reliever Bob McClure played 14 of his 698 games in the majors with the Mets. Signed in July, McClure went 1-0 with a 4.09 ERA for the division champions. He allowed no runs in 12 of 14 appearances.

went 13-3 to end the month. Strawberry was hitting .361 with six homers and 10 RBI in the month. Carter was batting .333 with seven home runs and 15 RBI through April. McReynolds was hitting .318 with three home runs and nine RBI.

After a four-hit shutout of the Reds on May 1, Gooden was 6-0 with a 2.25 ERA. Rick Aguilera went on the DL with a sore elbow. David Cone, who was 2-0 with a 3.63 ERA out of the bullpen in April, was given a start against Atlanta on May 3. Cone responded by pitching a shutout. Strawberry hit his eighth home run and Lee Mazzilli even collected his first two hits of the season as the team moved into first place for good. Cone was in the rotation to stay.

An injured Aguilera would only pitch in 11 games with a 6.93 ERA but the pitching staff was so deep

No Met has ever been MVP, but in 1988 Darryl Strawberry had the strongest case among position players. He led the league with 39 home runs (next best was 30), had 101 RBI and 101 RS, while Kirk Gibson, who won the award, had 25 HR, 76 RBI, and didn't make the All-Star team.

it didn't matter. Cone would go 5-0 in May. Down to the last out, Strawberry hit a two-run homer off Cincinnati closer John Franco to beat the Reds on May 6. Gooden pitched a four-hit shutout in Los Angeles on May 21 to improve to 8-0. It was the team's ninth shutout in 40 games.

On the final day of May, Gooden took a 2-1 lead into the ninth against the Dodgers but Kirk Gibson tied the game with a homer. LA took the lead against Gooden in the 10th and took a 4-2 lead but the Mets tied it in the bottom of the inning and won on Kevin Elster's homer in the 11th. The Mets were 34-15, 4.5 games in first and ready to run away with the division. The spark for the month was Hernandez, who took his batting average from .158 on April 23 to .318 on May 27.

The Mets won a pair of 13-inning games against the Cubs in early June. But on June 6, Hernandez hurt his hamstring and went on the DL for the first time in his career. The Mets lost five straight games with Hernandez watching from the dugout.

The first baseman returned on June 22 and went 1-4 in a win against the

FUTILE: LEE MAZZILLI

Lee Mazzilli's career was sputtering to an end in 1988, when in 68 games and 116 at bats, Mazzilli collected only 17 hits for a batting average of .147 with no home runs and only 12 RBI.

Pirates. The next day, he singled in the first against Greg Maddux but aggravated the hamstring injury. He wouldn't play again until August 5.

Sid Fernandez outdueled Nolan Ryan on July 3, tossing a two-hit shutout as the Mets improved to 52-29 and went up 7.5 games in the division. The Pirates were making sure the Mets didn't run away with the East, winning nine straight games. New York's lead was cut to 1.5 games.

Tom Seaver was honored on July 24, as his number 41 was retired before a game against the Braves. But the Mets lost a second straight game to the Braves. With the Mets leading the Pirates by two games, Pittsburgh came to Shea for a four-game series and the Mets took three of four.

After losing two of three to the Cubs, the Mets went to Pittsburgh for four games. Hernandez was back in the lineup. Again, the Mets took three of four. Darling beat the Pirates again in the opener and Hernandez homered.

On August 11 at Wrigley Field, Carter hit the 300th home run of his career. It was the first home run for Carter since May 16. In the same game, McReynolds hit a grand slam to give the Mets the lead with two outs in the ninth. It was the 17th homer for the left fielder who offered protection behind Strawberry and would also lead the league in assists. Backman and Lenny Dykstra both had averages around .300.

FABULOUS: DARRYL STRAWBERRY

Darryl Strawberry led the league with 39 home runs and drove in 101 runs. He also stole 29 bases. He batted .300 with 9 hits and 6 RBI in the NLCS.

A four-game losing streak in late August dropped the Mets to 71-52 and the lead was down to 3.5 games. The Mets went to LA for a showdown with the first-place Dodgers and won three straight, giving up three runs in the series. Gooden pitched a complete game for his 15th victory. Cone went 7.2 innings to improve to 13-3. To finish the sweep, the Mets beat Orel Hershiser in a 2-1 game. Then the Mets took two of three from the Giants and two of three from the Padres to take a 7.5 game lead into September.

Infielder Gregg Jefferies was called up in late August. The highly-touted prospect was going to pinch-hit and be a weapon on the bench in the playoffs. But he hit his way into the starting lineup, batting .462 with five homers in his first 13 games. He played both second and third base in September. Dave Magadan, who was hitting .278 through August, noted "we did get this far without him."

The Mets were on fire, running away with the division on the strength of a 29-8 finish. Five of the eight losses were by one run. Darling pitched a five-hit shutout against the Dodgers and Gooden beat them the next day. The unsung star of the season was Randy Myers, who became the new closer and converted 26 of 29 save opportunities.

A win over the Phillies on September 21 clinched at least a tie for the division but Bobby Ojeda, who had pitched two shutouts in his previous four starts and had an ERA below three, was done for the season. He needed surgery after he nearly

TOP BATTERS										
Pos	Name	G	AB	H	BA	HR	RBI	RS	SB	OPS
3B	Howard Johnson	148	495	114	.230	24	68	85	23	.765
LF	Kevin McReynolds	147	552	159	.288	27	99	82	21	.832
CF	Lenny Dykstra	126	429	116	.270	8	33	57	30	.706
RF	Darryl Strawberry	153	543	146	.269	39	101	101	29	.911
CF	Mookie Wilson	112	378	112	.296	8	41	61	15	.776

TOP PITCHERS										
Pos	Name	G	GS	W	L	SV	ERA	IP	SO	BB
SP	Dwight Gooden	34	34	18	9	0	3.19	248.1	175	57
SP	Ron Darling	34	34	17	9	0	3.25	240.2	161	60
SP	David Cone	35	28	20	3	0	2.22	231.1	213	80
SP	Sid Fernandez	31	31	12	10	0	3.03	187.0	189	70
CL	Randy Myers	55	0	7	3	26	1.72	68.0	69	17

severed the upper third of his left index finger with an electric hedge clipper in a gardening accident. The next night, Darling went the distance, beating the Phillies and clinching the NL East for the second time in three seasons.

"To all our critics, we're still No. 1," Strawberry said. "This is a lot sweeter than '86 because we know we earned it this year. We had to work."

The Mets swept the Cardinals to end the season. Cone won his 20th game of the year. Strawberry hit two homers on the final day, tying the team-record of 39 he set the year before. His also reached the 100-RBI mark.

Top 5 Highlights

1 Darryl Strawberry's seventh inning blast off Montreal's Randy St. Claire hits the roof at Olympic Stadium. The Mets hit six homers in 10-6 on Opening Day. Strawberry and Kevin McReynolds homer twice with Kevin Elster and Lenny Dykstra also going deep.

2 Dwight Gooden pitches seven no-hit innings and then homers in the bottom of the seventh off Chicago's Bill Landrum. Damon Berryhill singles to begin the eighth and Gooden has to settle for an 11-3 win on June 5.

3 Gary Carter hits a home run off Al Nipper at Wrigley Field on August 11, the 300th of his career. The milestone came after the catcher had a power outage for the summer. Trailing 6-5 with two outs in the ninth, McReynolds hits a grand slam off Goose Gossage and the Mets win 9-6.

4 Ron Darling strikes out Lance Parrish to beat the Phillies 3-1 and clinch the NL East on September 22. It's the fourth division title for the Mets and the second in three seasons.

5 With two on and two outs in the ninth, David Cone gets Rod Booker on a ground out to second to preserve a 4-2 win over the Cardinals on September 30. It's Cone's 20th win of the season and he delivered an RBI single in the sixth. The right-hander is greeted by former president Richard Nixon in the dugout.

1988 NLCS

The only thing standing between the Mets and the World Series was the Dodgers, a team that the Mets went 10-1 against during the regular season and outscored 49-18. But LA had Orel Hershiser, who pitched a record 59 consecutive shutout innings to end the season. Still, the Mets entered the series as heavy favorites.

In the bottom of the first inning of the first game, Mike Marshall, who led LA with 82 RBI, delivered an RBI single off Gooden. In the seventh, Alfredo Griffin added an RBI single for an insurance run. Hershiser took a shutout into the ninth. Jefferies led off with a single and scored on a Strawberry double. Jay Howell was called on to get the final two outs. McReynolds walked but Johnson struck out. Carter fell behind 0-2 before hitting a sinking liner to center. John Shelby dove but couldn't make the catch, scoring Strawberry. The ball got away enough for McReynolds to come home. Shelby threw home but McReynolds leveled Mike Scioscia before the ball arrived and the Mets had a 3-2 lead. Myers pitched a 1-2-3 ninth to give the Mets a 1-0 series lead.

Cone started Game 2 with a chance to put the Mets in the driver's seat. He was also writing a guest column in the New York Daily News for the series. He called Hershiser "lucky" and said Howell's curveball was like that of a "high school pitcher." Cone apologized and stopped writing but the Dodgers still jumped on for him for five runs in two innings. The Mets almost had some more ninth inning magic with Carter coming up with the bases loaded and two outs down 6-3 but he flied out to right against Alejandro Pena.

Game 3 was rained out, allowing Hershiser to come back against Darling. The Dodgers scored twice in the second and once in the third. The Mets got on the board with a Strawberry RBI double in the third. In the sixth, Hernandez led off with a single and Strawberry followed with one of his own but Hernandez stumbled on the muddy infield and was tagged out. With two on and two out, Carter singled to make it 3-2. Backman followed with an infield single to tie the game. Los Angeles loaded the bases against McDowell in the eighth and took the lead when Myers walked Mike Sharperson.

Howell entered the game and went to 3-2 on McReynolds before time was called. Johnson asked the umpires to check on the pitcher and it turned out Howell had pine tar in his glove to help with his grip in the cold weather. The umpires even brought the glove to NL President A. Bartlett Giamatti, sitting near the Mets dugout. Pena entered and walked McReynolds. With McReynolds on second and two outs, Backman doubled to tie the game. Dykstra drew a walk and Jesse Orosco came in. Wilson greeted him with a single to give the Mets a 5-4 lead. Jefferies was hit by a pitch to load the bases and Hernandez walked to make it 6-4. With Ricky Horton pitching, Strawberry's single made it 8-4. Cone came in from the bullpen to set down the Dodgers in the ninth to give the Mets the series lead.

Gooden was on the mound for Game 4 and quickly gave up two runs as Shelby singled home a pair. John Tudor pitched three scoreless innings before the Mets broke through. Hernandez singled and Strawberry homered to right, tying the game. Two pitches later, McReynolds homered to give the Mets a 3-2 lead. Carter's RBI triple in the sixth made it 4-2. Gooden was rolling and took a 4-2 lead into the ninth.

Shelby led off the inning with a walk after falling behind 0-2. Scioscia, who hit only three homers during the season was up. Johnson left Gooden in the game with Myers watching from the bullpen. Scioscia hit Gooden's first pitch into the bullpen to tie the game. With two outs in the 12th, Kirk Gibson, who was 1-16 in the series, homered off McDowell to make it 5-4.

There was still the bottom of the inning. Sasser and Mazzilli singled off Tim Leary. Jefferies flied out to left. Orosco came in and walked Hernandez, loading the bases for Strawberry. Strawberry popped up to second for the second out. Then Lasorda called on Hershiser to get the final out. McReynolds hit one to center but Shelby made a running catch to end it.

In Game 5 Sid Fernandez gave up six runs and didn't make it out of the fifth. Gibson's three-run home made it 6-0. In the bottom of the inning, Dykstra hit a three-run home run off Tim Belcher. In the eighth, Dykstra doubled and Jefferies singled to make it 6-4. After Horton fanned Strawberry and gave up a single to Hernandez, Holton came in with runners on first and second and one out. McReynolds hit a slow roller between third and short. Jefferies tried to jump over the ball but it took a higher bounce than expected and hit his cleat. Instead of bases loaded it was two on and two out for Carter, who flied out to end the inning. The Dodgers added a run in the ninth and Holton pitched a 1-2-3 inning.

It was up to Cone to save the season and he answered the bell, giving up one run on five hits in a 5-1 win. The big blow was McReynolds' two-run homer in the fifth. So the series came down to Game 7. Johnson said he felt good going against Hershiser, who would be making his third start in addition to the one relief appearance. But who would start for the Mets? Johnson went with Darling over Gooden.

A Gibson sacrifice fly gave the Dodgers a 1-0 lead in the first. The wheels came off in the second. Four hits and two errors gave the Dodgers a 6-0 lead. Darling was gone five batters into the second. Gooden pitched three shutout innings. Hershiser made the Mets pitching decision a moot point as he pitched a five-hit shutout.

1989

	W	L	GB	Pos
	87	75	6.0	2nd
RS/G	RA/G		Manager	
4.22	3.67		Davey Johnson	

Horrendous Trades and the End of an Era

The Moves

Wally Backman was traded to the Twins in December 1988. He hit .303 in 1988 but was in a crowded infield including Tim Teufel, Keith Miller and Gregg Jefferies, so Backman asked for a trade. The team had talked to the Dodgers about Backman but wanted another player in addition to lefty relief pitcher Rick Horton. The Mets also signed reliever Don Aase, who had made the 1986 All-Star team with the Orioles but had battled injuries since. He would make the team out of spring training after beginning without a major league contract.

The Situation

Coming off a heartbreaking NLCS loss to the Dodgers, the Mets still had lofty expectations for 1989. The roster was nearly identical, although Wally Backman was traded to Minnesota in December for three minor league pitchers. New York was interested in acquiring two-time MVP Dale Murphy, but Atlanta's asking price was deemed too high. The Braves wanted Howard Johnson, Lenny Dykstra, Keith Miller and David West. The Mets were only willing to give up Johnson and Dykstra.

Problems arose in spring training as Keith Hernandez and Darryl Strawberry had to be restrained after the latter threw a punch before posing for the team photo with Strawberry reportedly saying, "I've been tired of you for years."

Still, the Mets had won the division by 15 games the year before, so if they fell back a bit they were still expected to be superior. As Darryl Strawberry

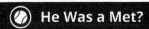

⚾ He Was a Met?

Don Aase spent 11 seasons in the AL before the Mets signed him as a free agent for 1989. Aase appeared in 49 games, but managed only a 1-5 record with a not-impressive ERA of 3.94. After one season with the Dodgers, Aase retired.

The Mets are famous for going through a lot of third basemen, but they've also had a knack of dealing for second basemen who go from the penthouse to the outhouse as soon as they joined the team. Juan Samuel (who was pegged for CF), Carlos Baerga, and Roberto Alomar were an unfortunate trio.

Player	Team	BA	HR	RBI	RS
Carlos Baerga	1995 Cle	.314	15	90	87
	1996 Cle/Mets	.254	12	66	59
Juan Samuel	1987 Phi	.272	27	100	113
	1989 Phi/Mets	.235	11	48	69
Roberto Alomar	1999 Cle	.336	20	100	113
	2000 Mets	.266	11	53	73

said before the season, "We have a really good chance of really running away with the whole thing if we get off to a good start. In our division, our toughest competition is ourselves."

Sports Illustrated was in agreement as Steve Wulf wrote, "The Mets are the only team that can beat the Mets. Their bench and second-line pitching would probably finish fourth in the National League East."

The Season

The Mets beat the Cardinals on Opening Day and New York seemed to be off and running. Whitey Herzog may have been trying to add pressure when he said, "To tell the truth, if any of the 25 other clubs had the Mets' pitching, they'd win."

The Mets would not run away with the division, starting the year 3-7. After losing to the Phillies on June 18, the Mets were 34-31, two games out of first. Then came one of the most infamous trades in team history, as Lenny Dykstra and Roger McDowell were sent to the Phillies for Juan Samuel. Dykstra had struggled against lefties and was in a platoon with Wilson in center while McReynolds and Strawberry were the corner outfielders. Samuel was slotted to play in center although it was his first year after moving from the infield. Samuel had hit 28 homers and drove in 100 runs in 1987, but was hitting .249 with eight home runs in 51 games so far in 1989.

New York would lose something more than stats, as Dykstra had now been exiled along with fellow wild boy Wally Backman.

Three years later, David Cone commented that the Mets heart and soul was being lost and that

 Final Resting Ground

Phil Lombardi played in 18 games as a Met before retiring in 1990. His main claim to fame in his brief career was being one of the few players to play for both the Yankees and Mets and no other teams.

FUTILE: JUAN SAMUEL

Juan Samuel came to the Mets in June of 1989 in blockbuster deal with the Phillies for Lenny Dykstra and Roger McDowell. Unfortunately for the Mets, Samuel's career was in the midst of falling off a cliff, as he batted only .228 with only 3 HR and 28 RBI in 333 ABs. Two years earlier Samuel had collected 80 EBH, 113 RS, 28 HR, and 100 RBI, but he never approached any of those totals again.

"The day it began was the day they traded Lenny Dykstra and Roger McDowell for Juan Samuel."

In late July, the Mets won six straight games to improve to 53-43 but then lost seven straight as they fell seven games out of first. Toronto signed Lee Mazzilli at the end of July, claiming him off waivers. Mazzilli was hitting .183 in 48 games for the Mets. He would play 28 games with the Blue Jays before retiring. The Mets landed 1988 Cy Young winner Frank Viola, sending Rick Aguilera, David West and minor leaguer Keven Tapani to the Twins.

Fan favorite Mookie Wilson joined Mazzilli in Canada, when the Mets traded him for southpaw Jeff Musselman. Wilson's contract was up at the end of the season and he was unlikely to return as a role player. Musselman had a 10.64 ERA in five appearances for Toronto at the time of the trade, although he had pitched well the previous two seasons. Wilson had only been batting .205 in 80 games with the Mets.

The moves seemed to spur the Mets who went 15-4, including a win over the Reds in which Tim Teufel charged the mound after being drilled by Rob Dibble. On August 19, the Mets were a season-high 14 games over .500 with a 68-54 record, only 2.5 games out of first. On August 20, the Mets led the Dodgers 3-1 with two outs in the ninth. After two singles, Willie

FABULOUS: SID FERNANDEZ

Fernandez had one of his best seasons for the Mets, with a fine ERA of 2.83, a career high 219.1 IP, and nearly a strikeout per inning. El Sid also won 14 and led the NL in winning percentage at .737.

Randolph hit his first homer of the season, a three-run shot to right-center off Don Aase. Randolph had been hitless in 10 at-bats in the series and had made the final out in the first two games of the series. The Dodgers would win 5-4.

New York would lose nine of the next 13 as the season slipped away. The Cubs surprisingly won the NL East, in part because they beat the Mets in seven of nine games at Wrigley Field. On September 27, Carter and Hernandez pinch-hit in the bottom of the ninth in their final home games at Shea Stadium. The game ended with Gregg Jefferies grounding out against McDowell, but the fun was just beginning as Jefferies charged McDowell and a brawl ensued. The Mets ended the season winning four straight in Pittsburgh to finish 87-75, six games behind the Cubs.

TOP BATTERS

Pos	Name	G	AB	H	BA	HR	RBI	RS	SB	OPS
2B	Gregg Jeffries	141	508	131	.258	12	56	72	21	.706
3B	Howard Johnson	153	571	164	.287	36	101	104	41	.928
LF	KevinMcReynolds	148	545	148	.272	22	85	74	15	.775
RF	Darryl Strawberry	134	476	107	.225	29	77	69	11	.779

TOP PITCHERS

Pos	Name	G	GS	W	L	SV	ERA	IP	SO	BB
SP	David Cone	34	33	14	8	0	3.52	219.2	190	74
SP	Sid Fernandez	35	32	14	5	0	2.83	219.1	198	75
SP	Ron Darling	33	33	14	14	0	3.52	217.1	153	70
SP	Bob Ojeda	31	31	13	11	0	3.47	192.0	95	78
CL	Randy Myers	65	0	7	4	24	2.35	84.1	88	40

Top 5 Highlights

1 The Mets completed a triple play on June 6 as Cubs third baseman Vance Law lined out to Dave Magadan at first, Magadan stepped on the bag and threw to Kevin Elster at second to triple up Lloyd McClendon and Damon Berryhill

2 On June 16, the Mets scored eight runs in the top of the first against Bruce Ruffin but the Phillies scored five times off David Cone in the bottom of the frame. Philadelphia led 10-9 after four innings and 11-10 after seven but the Mets battled back to win 15-11. Mackey Sasser's two-run double in the top of the eighth put the Mets ahead.

3 Dwight Gooden notched the 100th win of his career in a 5-3 victory over the Expos on June 19 at Shea. Gooden gave up three runs on five hits over seven innings. Doctor K became the third youngest pitcher in the modern era to win 100 games.

4 Frank Viola outduels Orel Hershiser in a matchup of 1988 Cy Young winners on August 28. Viola pitches a three-hit shutout and Hershiser gives up one run in eight innings, a Howard Johnson RBI single in the third.

5 The last home game of the season. The final appearance for Keith Hernandez and Gary Carter at home. Hernandez flies out to left as a pinch-hitter in the eighth and Carter doubles as a pinch-hitter in the ninth. Gregg Jefferies grounds out to end the game, then turns around and charges Roger McDowell to finish off the home schedule with a brawl.

Quiz #5: 1990s

1. (1991) What team was Ron Darling on for 16 days between his 8+-year stint with the Mets and 4+-year stint with Oakland? **[10 points]**

2. (1990s) Which Mets player homered in 4 consecutive Opening Days? **[10 points]**

3. (1991) This player from the 1986 Mets was a solid contributor for the Pittsburgh Pirates (.292 BA in 315 at bats), who beat out the Mets for the NL East crown by 4 games. **[10 points]**

4. (1990s) Tom Seaver famously fanned 19 batters in one game, including the last 10 (1970 vs Padres). Name the other Mets pitcher to reach that amazing single-game mark. **[6 points]**

5. Name the three pitchers on the Mets 1992 staff who won the Cy Young Award during their career? **[3 points for 1, 6 for 2, 10 points for all three]**

6. (1993) What player did the Mets receive in their trade of Vince Coleman to the Kansas City Royals in January 1994? **[10 points]**

7. Two Mets managers from the 1990s—Jeff Torborg and Dallas Green—did not prove themselves to be very good managers, and neither was a very good player during their careers, either. What positions did they play? **[5 points each]**

8. (1990s) Edgardo Alfonzo played for the Mets for eight seasons. With what team did he sign as a free agent after the 2002 season? **[10 points]**

9. (1990s) This lefthander played for the Mets in 1997 and part of 1998 before being traded to the Dodgers. After a year with the Dodgers, he signed with Colorado for 3 years, winning 12 games the first 2 but pitching to an ERA of 7.14 in 19 starts in what would turn out to be the last year of his career. Name him. **[8 bonus points]**

10. The son of a very successful major leaguer, this center fielder hit a career-high 21 home runs for the Mets in 1998 and played in 159 of the team's 162 games. **[10 points]**

11. Another son of a successful major leaguer and former first-round pick broke into the majors with the Mets in 1998, but was traded in May in one of the franchise's most consequential deals in their history. **[8 points]**

12. (1990s) Speaking of trades with the Marlins, who was the main piece given up by the Mets in the trade in which they acquired Al Leiter? **[12 points]**

13. (1990s) Name the first Mets player to collect 200 or more hits in a season. **[10 points]**

14. (1996) Dwight Gooden's final season with the Mets was 1994. With which team did he finish his career? **[8 points]**

15. Name the Mets pitcher who was traded to the Dodgers in June 1998 and then traded back to the Mets in July 1998. **[10 points]**

QUIZ #5: TOTAL POINTS – 134, BONUS POINTS – 8

1990

	W	L	GB	Pos
	91	71	4.0	2nd

RS/G	RA/G	Manager
4.78	3.78	Davey Johnson Bud Harrelson

Buddy's Mets Push Pirates in East

The Moves

The Mets had a new look for a new decade. Gary Carter was with the Giants. Keith Hernandez was with the Indians.

The team made a surprising trade, as Randy Myers was sent to the Reds for John Franco. The thought originally was that the Mets went into meetings thinking they wanted a right-hander to compliment Myers. Instead the New York native Franco, who played at St. John's with Frank Viola, was back in Queens.

Juan Samuel was sent to the Dodgers for right-handed reliever Alejandro Pena and first baseman Mike Marshall. The Dodgers were looking to solve leadoff and centerfield questions after they failed to sign Robin Yount. For the Mets, Marshall gave them options. Marshall hit 137 home runs in eight seasons with the Dodgers but fought through consistent back problems. The question would be if Marshall would be in left, moving Kevin McReynolds to center and Keith Miller to the bench, or if Marshall would platoon with Dave Magadan at first.

The Situation

Davey Johnson wasn't fired after a disappointing 1989 season but two of his coaches, Bill Robinson and Sam Perlozzo, were. Clearly the winningest manager in team history was on a short leash.

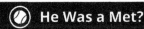

⚾ He Was a Met?

Pat Tabler's 17 games with the Mets in September were the only of his more than 1200 in the National League. Tabler, who batted over .290 5 times, did well for the Mets, batting .279 with 10 RBI in 43 at bats. Tabler finished his career as a backup for the Blue Jays, collecting a World Series ring in 1992.

Local Boy Makes (Very) Good

After signing with the Mets as a free agent after the 1989 season, Brooklyn native John Franco pitched in New York for the next 15 seasons (though he did miss the entire 2002 season due to injury). Franco was very good for a very long time, and probably doesn't get the recognition he deserves for the excellent career he had. He totalled 90 wins and 424 saves (fifth most all time), leading the league the latter 3 times. He appeared in 1119 games in his career (third most all time) and finished with an ERA of 2.89 (ERA+138).

Darryl Strawberry was entering the final year of his contract but focused turned to off-the-field matters as he was arrested for an alleged assault with a deadly weapon during an argument with his wife in January. He entered the Smithers Center for alcohol rehabilitation. Prosecutors declined to file charges because of insufficient evidence.

Expectations were still high for the team. Whitey Herzog said, "This is the sixth year in a row the Mets will be favored to win the division. Even I like 'em. I would certainly like to have some of their pitching. And they made a pretty good trade with the Dodgers." SI picked the Mets to finish behind St. Louis but ahead of the Expos in what was predicted to be a three-team race.

Dwight Gooden would get the Opening Day start, his first start since July 1 when he left after two innings because of a torn muscle in his shoulder. The rotation was so deep that Bobby Ojeda was sent to the bullpen.

Barry Lyons was the new Opening Day batterymate. "It was certainly an honor and something I looked forward to," Lyons said in an interview for this book. "Backing up Gary, unless he was injured, there was no chance of starting Opening Day."

The previous season, injuries to Hernandez and Carter meant more playing time for Lyons and Dave Magadan. Davey Johnson spoke to the pair on a plane ride to Montreal. "He didn't really confer with me personally or probably Mags either," Lyons said. "He sat with us on the way up and was complimentary of our patience and waiting and working towards our opportunity but said that our time was coming. He liked what we were doing and was more or less giving us a pat on the back." Unfortunately, Lyons was injured during the series on a foul tip and missed a month.

Final Resting Ground

After years as a Mets' nemesis for the rival St. Louis Cardinals and stops with 2 other teams, the Mets acquired Tom Herr for the 1990 season for Rocky Elli and Nikco Riesgo. Herr played the last 32 games of his career for San Fran after his release from the Mets, in August, 1991.

The Season

The 1990 season began later than usual. There was a lockout, which began in February and lasted a little over a month, throwing off the spring training schedule. No games were lost although Opening Day was pushed back to April 9. There was a resolution on March 19 but the result was abbreviated spring training.

The Mets got off to a 3-6 start with Gooden getting pounded in his first two starts. "I just know and believe in my heart that the shortened spring training and all the uncertainty and doubt as to when we were going to begin spring training and begin the season certainly caught us not as prepared as we could've been, and I think that played a part," Lyons said.

FABULOUS: FANK VIOLA

Frank Viola won his 20th game on the final day of the season, finishing 20-12 with a 2.67 ERA and three shutouts. Viola pitched one more season for the Mets, winning 13 games, before signing with the Red Sox as a free agent.

Frank Viola was keeping the season from falling apart fast, winning his first seven decisions. He won six of the team's first 10 games, seven of the first 13. David Cone suffered through an embarrassing moment on April 30 in Atlanta as two runs scored while he argued with first base umpire Charlie Williams.

Viola's complete game shutout on May 12 against the Dodgers gave the southpaw a 7-0 record with an 0.87 ERA. But the Mets lost eight of the next 12 to drop to 20-22 and Davey Johnson was fired.

"Our club was underachieving," Frank Cashen said. "The time had come for a new direction." Bud Harrelson was the new manager. "Nobody on the team has ever said anything bad about Buddy," said Dave Magadan. "He's got a good relationship with the players. As a coach, he's probably been able to see some things that Davey couldn't as manager."

Sports Illustrated said the team was "The Amazin' Mess." The team was 21-26 but then caught fire, winning 27 of 32. The team scored 43 runs in three wins against the Cubs. A franchise-record-tying 11 straight wins brought the team into a shocking tie for first on June 29. SI declared, "Meet the Mets," with the word "Mess" crossed out.

Ojeda went 3-0 in June, having joined the rotation with the scuffling Ron Darling being sent to the bullpen. Strawberry, who had been hitting .228 with four home runs on May 20, hit 10 home runs in June and raised his batting average to over .300. Magadan was on fire, including an 11-game hitting streak with six multi-hit games.

Gooden won seven decisions in a row in June and July. Mike Marshall was traded to the Red Sox in late July as Magadan's hot bat ensured

FUTILE: JEFF MUSSELMAN

Acquired for Mookie Wilson, southpaw reliever Jeff Musselman had a 5.63 ERA in 28 appearances in 1990. In a season and a half with the Mets he walked 25 batters and struck out 25.

TOP BATTERS

Pos	Name	G	AB	H	BA	HR	RBI	RS	SB	OPS
2B	Gregg Jeffries	153	604	171	.283	15	68	96	11	.771
3B	Howard Johnson	154	590	144	.244	23	90	89	34	.753
LF	Kevin McReynolds	147	521	140	.269	24	82	75	9	.808
RF	Darryl Strawberry	152	542	150	.277	37	108	92	15	.879

TOP PITCHERS

Pos	Name	G	GS	W	L	SV	ERA	IP	SO	BB
SP	Frank Viola	35	35	20	12	0	2.67	249.2	182	60
SP	Dwight Gooden	34	34	19	7	0	3.83	232.2	223	70
SP	David Cone	31	30	14	10	0	3.23	211.2	233	65
SP	Sid Fernandez	30	30	9	14	0	3.46	179.1	181	67
CL	John Franco	55	0	5	3	33	2.53	67.2	56	21

his spot at first base. New York and Pittsburgh took turns in first place. The Mets started August winning three, losing four, and winning three more.

Kelvin Torve was called up from the minors and on August 7 became the first Met since Willie Mays to wear number 24. Joan Payson had wanted Mays to be the last player to wear it, and Torve soon switched to 39.

In late August, the Mets went 2-5 in San Diego and Los Angeles. Darling had shuttled between the rotation and the bullpen and on August 25, he gave up a home run in the bottom of the 14th for a demoralizing 3-2 loss.

But then the Mets won seven straight and moved back into first, capped off by seven shutout innings from Gooden against the Cardinals. The team went to Pittsburgh on September 5 trailing the Pirates by a half-game. Pittsburgh won three straight, with the Mets scoring two runs in the series. In the final game, Harrelson started Julio Valera, who had won his MLB debut five days earlier, over Darling. Valera gave up five runs (four earned) on eight hits, failing to make it out of the third inning.

The Mets weren't done yet though and swept a two-game set from Pittsburgh at Shea the following week to get back to a half-game out. A five game losing streak, including a Shea sweep by the Expos, damaged the season. One last push put the Mets three games back with five to play but a pair of losses to the Cubs finished it off. Viola lost three straight crucial starts.

Pittsburgh clinched the division on September 30, with the score going final during the ninth inning of New York's 6-5 loss to the Cubs at Shea.

The season ended in Pittsburgh with the only drama left remaining was if Gooden and Viola could both win 20 games. Gooden was shelled in his start. Viola won number 20 on the final day of the season.

Top 5 Highlights

1 With the Mets and Astros tied in the top of 11th during their May 6 game, Doug Harvey calls John Franco for a balk, scoring Eric Anthony with the go-ahead run. In the bottom of the inning, Tim Teufel ties the game with a double and Kevin McReynolds wins it with a three-run homer to left off Dave Smith.

2 New York's offense explodes in a 19-8 win at Wrigley on June 12. McReynolds goes 3-4, with two homers and four RBI. Magadan goes 4-4 with a homer and six RBI. Gregg Jefferies and Tom O'Malley collect three hits apiece.

3 The Mets take a 10-3 lead into the bottom of the ninth at Veterans Stadium on July 25 but Wally Whitehurst and Julio Machado can't get anyone out and Franco has to come in. With the lead 10-9 and the tying run on third base with two outs, Tom Herr lined out to short, leading to Bob Murphy's famous call, "The Mets win the ballgame. They win the damn thing by a score of 10 to 9."

4 In front of 51,079 fans, the Mets win a critical September 13 game against the Pirates, with Gooden defeating Drabek. Strawberry hits a three-run homer and became the first Met with three 100-RBI seasons. Franco notches his 32nd save, a new team record.

5 Frank Viola wins his 20th game of the season in a 6-3 victory over the Pirates. The southpaw gives up three runs on seven hits over seven innings. New York scores a run in each of the last three innings and Dan Schatzeder and Alejandro Pena pitch an inning of scoreless relief. The game was also the last for Pirates starter Jerry Reuss, who made his debut in 1969.

1991

OPENING DAY LINEUP

Vince Coleman, CF
Gregg Jefferies, 3B
Dave Magadan, 1B
Hubie Brooks, RF
Howard Johnson, SS
Kevin McReynolds, LF
Tom Herr, 2B
Charlie O'Brien, C
Dwight Gooden, P

	W	L	GB	Pos
	77	84	20.5	5th
RS/G	RA/G		Manager	
3.98	4.01		Bud Harrelson Mike Cubbage	

Mets Feud and Struggle Through Summer

The Moves

Darryl Strawberry left for the Dodgers, signing a five-year deal for $20 million, the second biggest contract in baseball. The Mets needed to go out and get somebody to replace the most productive position player in team history. Figuring they couldn't replace the power of Strawberry, the team went in a different direction, signing speedster Vince Coleman. It was a four-year deal for almost $12 million, the first big free agent signing in team history. Coleman had stolen 549 bases in six seasons, including 77 in 1990, as he helped St. Louis edge out the Mets for division titles in 1985 and 1987. At one point, Coleman stole on 57 consecutive attempts against the Mets. Bud Harrelson said, "I telephoned him this morning and told him 'On behalf of our catchers, welcome to New York.'"

The Mets traded Bobby Ojeda to the Dodgers in return for Hubie Brooks. Brooks had hit 20 homers in 1991 and the Dodgers could afford to send away the outfielder after acquiring Strawberry and Brett Butler.

The Situation

One issue with the Mets was the defense, or possible lack thereof. Brooks would be new to right field, Jefferies moving to third and HoJo was at short.

He Was a Met?

People associate Rick Cerone with the Yankees, for whom he played 3 separate times, but also spent a season with the Mets, splitting time behind the plate with Mackey Sasser.

"There is concern, and it'd be kind of ridiculous to pretend otherwise," David Cone said. "The questions about the defense are legitimate. It's what we've all talked about among ourselves for more than a month." went on to say, "We've been through the backstabbing, the finger pointing about the defense. It tore us apart last year. Is it likely to be perfect this year? No. Could it be detrimental? Yes. We have to be prepared to play through it."

Another area of concern was the bullpen, specifically the middle relievers. "I don't want to hand the ball to anybody but Franco," one unnamed starter said. "I don't want a setup guy to have to get me to him."

And the offense struggled in spring training. "It's kind of strange the way the team didn't score any runs in the spring," Puhl said. "It kind of made you think that when and if this offense works it'll be if and when everyone hits."

After grueling negotiations, Dwight Gooden signed a three-year, $15.45 million contract extension one week before the start of the regular season. It gave him the second-highest salary in the majors, behind Roger Clemens, and ahead of Jose Canseco, Tony Gwynn and Strawberry.

Bud Harrelson was entering his first full season as manager. The Mets media guide had Harrelson with a faded image of Gil Hodges over his shoulder. And Harrelson shared his office with bench coach Doc Edwards.

"It's important for him to have a grip on the clubhouse," Ron Darling said. "But that has to be nurtured."

The Season

The Mets started the season by taking two of three from the Phillies and three of four from the Expos. But Gooden complained of stiffness after being left in for 149 pitches in a win over Montreal. Tom

Speed and Power: Howard Johnson

For the first 2 years after the Mets' trade of Walt Terrell to the Tigers for Howard Johnson in December 1984, it looked like the Tigers had gotten a steal. Terrell won 30 games and totalled nearly 450 IP, while Johnson managed only 21 HR/85 RBI/.243 combined. Terrell was even better in 1987, going 17-10 with 10 CG, but Hojo finally hit his stride, belting 36 home runs, driving in 99, and walking 83 times. It was the first of 5 consecutive productive years for Johnson, of which 1991 was the best. Johnson led the NL with 38 HR and 117 RBI, scored 108, and came in fifth in the MVP voting. He was beset by back problems after that and managed only 31 HR and never batted above .238 in the final four years of his career.

Final Resting Ground

After 15 years with St. Louis and San Diego, Gary Templeton found himself in the Mets' infield, acquired in a trade for Tim Teufel. Templeton backed up Kevin Elster at SS, but he also appeared in 25 games at 1B, fading into the sunset with a batting average of .228.

FABULOUS: HOWARD JOHNSON

Howard Johnson culminated a very productive 5-year stretch with a career year in which he lead the league in both HR (38) and RBI (117), while drawing 78 walks and stealing 30 bases. It was downhill from there for Johnson, however, as injuries limited him to a total of only 31 homers in the remaining 4 seasons of his career, during which he never batted higher than .238.

Herr struggled at the plate and was benched as a healthy Kevin Elster replaced a defensively-challenged Howard Johnson at short, Johnson moved to third and Gregg Jefferies moved to second.

Harrelson quit his radio show on WFAN, believing host Howie Rose and the tone of the show were too negative. Dallas Green was hired as a scout and loomed as a potential replacement. A pair of errors from Jefferies led to a loss against the Dodgers in mid-May.

Jefferies, sick and tired of being anonymously criticized, went on WFAN to read nine-paragraph letter that he wrote defending himself. The team traded Tim Teufel to the Padres for Garry Templeton. In early June, Harrelson and David Cone had to be separated by Hubie Brooks after a confrontation in the dugout in a game against the Reds. Cone had refused to pitch out although the reason may have been because it was called by unpopular coach Doc Edwards. The next day, the Mets lost 11-10 with Gooden giving up 11 hits for the third straight start and falling to 5-5 with a 4.25 ERA.

Still, the inconsistent Mets remained over .500 and won on June 25 when Kevin McReynolds hit a grand-slam in the bottom of the ninth to beat the Expos. New York won seven in a row heading into the All-Star break and the first three after returning from the break to improve to 49-34.

TOP BATTERS

Pos	Name	G	AB	H	BA	HR	RBI	RS	SB	OPS
1B	Dave Magadan	124	418	108	.258	4	51	58	1	.721
2B	Gregg Jeffries	136	486	132	.272	9	62	59	26	.711
3B	Howard Johnson	156	564	146	.259	38	117	108	30	.877
LF	Kevin McReynolds	143	522	135	.259	16	74	65	6	.738

TOP PITCHERS

Pos	Name	G	GS	W	L	SV	ERA	IP	SO	BB
SP	David Cone	34	34	14	14	0	3.29	232.2	241	73
SP	Frank Viola	35	35	13	15	0	3.97	231.1	132	54
SP	Dwight Gooden	27	27	13	7	0	3.60	190.0	150	56
SP	Wally Whitehurst	36	20	7	12	1	4.19	133.1	87	25
CL	John Franco	52	0	5	9	30	2.93	55.1	45	18

With Sid Fernandez ready to return from the disabled list, a combination of reliable Wally Whitehurst starts and Ron Darling struggles saw Darling traded to the Expos for Tim Burke.

Tim Teufel went from the spotlight to an afterthought in his 5+ seasons with the Mets. After several years of declining plate appearances, he was dealt to San Diego for Gary Templeton after having collected only 4 hits in 34 AB (.118).

Gooden beat Ojeda as the Mets improved to 53-38 before the wheels fell off. The team lost four in a row, won two of three, and then lost seven straight. Vince Coleman cursed out third base coach Mike Cubbage after he was told that he was hitting out of order in batting practice. Mark Carreon was disciplined for leaving a game early after he was pinch-hit for.

An 11-game losing streak in mid-August saw the team fall from 57-50 to 57-61. Whitehurst lost six straight decisions. Viola lost 10 of 11 decisions. Gooden left his August 22 start with shoulder tightness and was done for the season. Sid Fernandez didn't make it to September either, as his knee problem limited him to eight starts.

Harrelson was fired before the final home game of the season and Cubbage took over for the final week. The season ended on a high note with Cone tying a National League record by striking out 19 Phillies in a 7-0 win. In Frank Cashen's last year as general manager, New York finished 77-84, 20.5 games behind the Pirates.

Top 5 Highlights

1 In the second game of the season, Rick Cerone ties it with a home off Roger McDowell in the bottom of the ninth and Hubie Brooks wins it with a solo shot off Joe Boever in the bottom of the 10th to give the Mets a 2-1 triumph.

2 Down 4-2 in the bottom of the ninth of their May 4 game against the Giants, Mackey Sasser and Mark Carreon hit back-to-back pinch-hit homers off Jeff Brantley to tie it. Howard Johnson walks it off with a two-run homer in the 12th off Mike LaCoss.

3 One strike from defeat, Kevin McReynolds hits a grand slam off Montreal's Scott Ruskin to give the Mets an 8-5 win on June 25.

4 John Franco notches his 200th career save, striking out Philadelphia's Ron Jones with two on and two out to preserve a 2-1 win on July 6.

5 David Cone ties a National League record with 19 strikeouts on the final day of the season in a 7-0 win over the Phillies. He finishes with a league-high 241 strikeouts. Cone, who fanned 15 batters through six, sees his bid for 20 spoiled when Dale Murphy grounds out to short to end the game.

1992

	W	L	GB	Pos
	72	90	24.0	5th
RS/G	RA/G		Manager	
3.70	4.03		Jeff Torborg	

The Worst Team Money Can Buy

The Moves

Jeff Torborg, the 1990 AL Manager of the Year for leading the White Sox to a 94-68 record and a second place finish behind the powerhouse A's, was hired shortly after the 1991 season ended. It was lauded as a good hire of a baseball man – and Sandy Koufax's former catcher – who had dealt with plenty of drama as a Yankees coach in the 1980s.

Then the front office, with new general manager Al Harazin making moves after Frank Cashen's retirement, went to work improving the on-field product. Eddie Murray signed a two-year, $7.5 million deal. One of the premier sluggers of the '80s, Murray was 35 but was still coming off a 1991 campaign with the Dodgers during which he hit 19 homers with 96 RBI.

Bobby Bonilla, who helped the Pirates win two straight division titles, was signed to a five-year, $29 million deal. His $5.8 million yearly salary made him the highest paid player in team sports.

Signings of Murray and Bonilla made Kevin McReynolds expendable, as Murray would play first, Bonilla right, and Howard Johnson would move to center. Several days after the Bonilla signing, McReynolds, Gregg Jefferies and Keith Miller were sent to the Royals for two-time Cy Young winner Bret Saberhagen and infielder Bill Pecota.

Seven years to the day after the Mets traded him to the Expos, Hubie Brooks was traded to the California Angels for outfielder Dave Gallagher. The Mets

 He Was a Met?

D.J. Dozier scored the winning touchdown for Penn State in the 1987 Fiesta Bowl and spent five seasons in the NFL before switching to baseball. He worked his way through the minors and appeared in 25 games with the Mets, hitting .191.

The Unfortunate Anthony Young

Anthony Young was a combined 3-30 in 1992 and 1993, including a 27-game losing streak, during which he was 0-14 as a starter and 0-13 out of the pen. He did fill in well as closer at one point, pitching 23.2 consecutive shutout innings. At one point Young made 27 consecutive starts without a win, despite 13 quality starts. The Mets went 4-23 in those games. He later pitched for the Cubs and Astros and finished his career with a 15-48 record.

also signed Willie Randolph, the veteran second baseman, who grew up as a Mets fan.

The Situation

Baseball wasn't the main focus in spring training. Dwight Gooden, Daryl Boston and Vince Coleman were accused of rape by a woman who said the attack had taken place in March 1991. Several weeks later, it was announced that charges wouldn't be filed because there wasn't enough evidence. In late March, David Cone was hit with a lawsuit by three women, charging that he lured two women into the Shea Stadium bullpen in 1989 and masturbated in front of them.

Mets players called for a media boycott in the final days of spring training. The New York Times didn't write about the team for two days. The team eventually went back to talking after industry-wide pressure.

Howard Johnson was being moved to centerfield. "He hasn't shown the instincts yet," Torborg said in spring training.

There were plenty of questions about the Mets. Gooden was recovering from shoulder trouble. Sid Fernandez lost 40 pounds after surgery to repair torn cartilage in his left knee. But still, the Mets and their record $45 million payroll, were considered favorites to win the division.

The Season

Bonilla announced his presence immediately with two homers on Opening Day, including a 10th inning blast in a 4-2 win over the Cardinals. Jeff Innis picked up the win after not recording a win or save in 69 appearances in 1991. Met pitching was hammered in the next two games and then Coleman injured his hamstring beating out a bunt single. The outfielder was placed on the DL.

The Mets lost their first four home games, including a sweep at the hands of the Expos. But then the team got hot, winning 12 of 15.

 Final Resting Ground

Willie Randolph's playing career for the Mets was forgettable, as he batted .252 with only 15 RBI in 286 Abs. Thirteen years later, Randolph returned to the team as manager, a job he held for three-and-a-half seasons.

Torborg was still navigating his way through the National League game. "Our pitcher always seems to be coming up," he said after a loss in Montreal.

The fielding was an issue and Elster was lost for the season because of an injured shoulder. There was shoddy defense all around the field for the Mets. "I don't think we can ever afford to wait in a game," Expos manager Tom Runnells said. "But what I will say is that as long as we stay close, our chances improve of beating these guys because of their defensive lapses."

New York swept the Dodgers at Shea in May. Rodney McCray delivered a walk-off single. The next day, Magadan hit a three-run homer in the bottom of the ninth off Roger McDowell to beat LA 5-2.

But a trip the following week to Los Angeles wasn't as joyous. The Mets lost three of four and Saberhagen had to leave the one win with tendinitis in his right index finger. He was gone for more than two months and wouldn't win another game in 1992. At least there was Cone, who pitched consecutive shutouts late in the month to lower his ERA to 2.06. The Mets were shutout six times in May. Johnson was batting .201 with four homers at the end of the month as his mind was on learning to play his new position. On May 19, Bonilla hit his first homer since Opening Day. By the end of the month he was wearing earplugs to drown out the unhappy Shea Stadium fans.

A pair of wins to begin June improved the Mets' record to 27-24, a half-game behind the Cardinals and Pirates for first place. But then the team lost nine of 11. After a 15-1 win, the offense was shutout in back-to-back games, which included being one-hit by Montreal. Only an Anthony Young single stopped a no-hitter. The Mets committed six errors in an 8-2 loss in Montreal.

The team did put together a four-game winning streak late in the month. During an 8-2 win over the Cubs on June 22, Bonilla was hit by Chicago pitcher Shawn Boskie, leading to a bench clearing brawl. Several days later, the Mets gave up seven runs in the first inning in a 9-2 loss to the Cubs and didn't have a base hit until the sixth. Bonilla was charged with an error in the first inning and was seeing using the dugout phone to call the press box. "If I choose to use the phone, I'm going to use the phone," Bonilla said. "It's not the manager's dugout. It's the team's dugout."

FUTILE: LEE GUETTERMAN

After several strong seasons out of the pen for Seattle and the Yankees, Lee Guetterman bombed out in his one season for the Amazins, posting and ERA of 5.82 in 43 innings, allowing 57 hits and striking out only 15.

John Franco had been the best Met throughout the tough start. Through 21 appearances he was 6-0 with 11 saves and a 0.77 ERA. But on June 28 he blew a save in the 10th and lost in the 11th against St. Louis. It was his final appearance until August because of a strained elbow. And Coleman was lost for a month with another injury. The Mets entered the All-Star break 42-46 and seven games out of first.

In his first start after the break, Cone threw a six-hit shutout in a 1-0 win over the Giants. Torborg allowed Cone to throw 166 pitches. He would struggle in his next two starts but good run

TOP BATTERS

Pos	Name	G	AB	H	BA	HR	RBI	RS	SB	OPS
1B	Eddie Murray	156	551	144	.261	16	93	64	4	.759
LF	Daryl Boston	130	289	72	.249	11	35	37	12	.764
CF	Howard Johnson	100	350	78	.223	7	43	48	22	.666
RF	Bobby Bonilla	128	438	109	.249	19	70	62	4	.779
3B	Chico Walker	107	227	70	.308	4	36	24	14	.792

TOP PITCHERS

Pos	Name	G	GS	W	L	SV	ERA	IP	SO	BB
SP	Sid Fernandez	32	32	14	11	0	2.73	214.2	193	67
SP	Dwight Gooden	31	31	10	13	0	3.67	206.0	145	70
SP	David Cone	27	27	13	7	0	2.88	196.2	214	82
SP	Pete Schourek	22	21	6	8	0	3.64	136.0	60	44
RP	Jeff Innis	76	0	6	9	1	2.86	88.0	39	36

support picked him up. On July 24, Sid Fernandez pitched a three-hit shutout against the Padres. It was New York's sixth win in seven games and was the first time the Mets were at .500 since June 10. It would also be the last time they were at .500.

The Mets were blanked in three straight games. Johnson, who had been moved to left with young outfielder Pat Howell now playing in center, fractured his wrist sliding into second. He was placed on the DL in early August and was gone for the season. Bonilla went on the DL with an injured rib after he dove for a ball. Saberhagen, in his third start back, was removed in the fourth inning and placed back on the DL. He wouldn't return until September 11. Magadan was hitting .283 but broke his wrist breaking up a double play in Chicago on August 8. He was lost for the rest of the season.

After taking two of three from the Cubs to begin August, the Mets were 51-53, in third place and 5.5 games out of first. Then the team lost 12 of 13. Frustration mounted. There were three extra-inning losses to the Pirates, including a 16-inning loss at Shea.

On August 23, Cone gave up four runs (three earned) in seven innings in a loss to the Padres. It was his final start before being traded to the Blue Jays for infielder Jeff Kent and outfielder Ryan Thompson.

Bonilla's 3-run home run beat Rob Dibble 4-3 in a game in which Vince Coleman was ejected. Two nights later, Coleman was ejected again. The moody outfielder was called for strike three on a check swing. Coleman argued with home plate umpire Gary Darling. Torborg came out to separate player from umpire and was shoved by Coleman. Bonilla came out to settle down his teammate but was also shoved as Coleman walked through the dugout and into the clubhouse, later followed by Torborg.

FABULOUS: CHICO WALKER

The Mets picked up Walker off waivers from the Cubs and he did a solid job in the utility role. Walker spent time at 2B, 3B, and all 3 OF positions, and also pinch hit frequently. He finished with a .308 BA and 14 SB and 36 RBI in 227 AB. He filled a similar role for the Mets the next year, his last in the majors.

"I'm not going to be shown up," Torborg said. "There's a basic thought of respect that has to be honored. I'm in charge. That's the way it's going to be." Coleman believed Torborg should've been yelling at Darling instead of him. "His arguing at me doesn't defend me," Coleman said.

On September 5, the Mets led 5-4 in the top of the ninth and looking for more with Murray up, the bases loaded and one out. Murray asked second base umpire Terry Tata to move over but was perturbed when the umpire didn't move as far as he wanted. Murray reportedly cursed Tata and bumped home-plate umpire Ed Rapuano. He was ejected as were Torborg and Chico Walker. Pinch-hitter Mackey Sasser hit into a double play and Young gave up two runs in the bottom of the ninth for a painful 6-5 loss.

There were still more indignities. A seven-game losing streak in late September included a 4-3 14-inning loss at St. Louis. The game was scoreless through 13 but Kent's three-run homer in the top of the 14th made it 3-0. But the Cardinals scored four off Mark Dewey and Wally Whitehurst in the bottom of the inning.

Towards the end of the season, Gooden was asked what his lasting image of the season was. "I can't do it. I swear the season was so ugly it's a bad blur. I can't begin to say what will stay with me longest and most painfully."

Top 5 Highlights

1 Bobby Bonilla's 10th inning homer off Lee Smith gives the Mets a 4-2 win on Opening Day. It's Bonilla's second homer of the game. He homered off Jose DeLeon to begin the fourth. Down 2-1 in the ninth with runners on the corners and one out, Mackey Sasser beat out a throw that would've been a game-ending double play.

2 Eddie Murray hits his 400th career home run off Atlanta's Marvin Freeman in the top of the eighth on New York's 7-0 win on May 3. Murray's homer, his second as a Met, just clears the wall in left.

3 Dave Magadan's three-run homer in the bottom of the ninth off Roger McDowell gives the Mets a 5-2 in on May 9. Mitch Webster tied the game in the top of the eighth with a homer off Bret Saberhagen. The Mets scored twice in the first against Bobby Ojeda.

4 Dwight Gooden helps his own cause with a two-run homer off San Francisco's Bryan Henderson in a 4-1 win over the Giants on August 24. Gooden also pitches seven innings of one-run ball and picks up the win.

5 Dick Schofield, Jeff Kent and Eddie Murray combine for an acrobatic double play in September against the Expos. Darrin Fletcher hit a grounder up the middle. Schofield covered ground, snagged it, tossed the ball behind his back to Kent for one out, and then Kent made a spinning throw to Murray at first to complete the 6-4-3 double play.

1993

OPENING DAY LINEUP

Vince Coleman, LF
Tony Fernandez, SS
Eddie Murray, 1B
Bobby Bonilla, RF
Howard Johnson, 3B
Joe Orsulak, CF
Jeff Kent, 2B
Todd Hundley, C
Dwight Gooden, P

	W	L	GB	Pos
	59	103	38.0	7th

RS/G	RA/G	Manager	
4.15	4.59	Jeff Torborg Dallas Green	

Torborg Out, Dallas In, Mets Lose 103

The Moves

The Padres were having a fire sale and former Mets executive Joe McIlvane sent Tony Fernandez to New York for Wally Whitehurst, D.J. Dozier and Raul Casanova. Fernandez was a four-time All-Star and four-time Gold Glove winner. Sharing the left side of the infield with Fernandez would be Howard Johnson, who was back at third base after the failed outfield experiment of 1992.

Dave Magadan and Chris Donnels joined the expansion Florida Marlins. Daryl Boston was on the expansion Colorado Rockies. Mackey Sasser and Kevin Elster both left in free agency. The Mets signed outfielder Joe Orsulak. Pat Howell was traded to the Twins for Darren Reed.

Roger Mason was traded to San Diego for Greg Maddux's brother, Mike. The team also signed veteran lefty Frank Tanana, who had won 233 games in the American League.

The Situation

"We'll have a good team if we stay healthy," Jeff Torborg said. "No team in history had the number of injuries we had last year."

A major question was what the team would get out of Dwight Gooden, who suddenly looked ordinary but was still only 28. *Sports Illustrated* picked the Mets to finish fourth in the NL East.

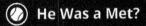

He Was a Met?

The Mets traded for Tony Fernandez after the 1992 season, but he struggled (.225/1/14) in 48 games, and was shipped back to Toronto for his second of three stints with the Blue Jays.

Vincent Van Ugh

Vince Coleman led the NL in stolen bases his first six seasons in the majors, averaging more than 90 per year. Then he came to the Mets, signing as a free agent after the 1990 season. The moody outfielder stole 99 in three seasons and cemented his place in team lore by dropping a powerful firecracker out the window of opponent Eric Davis's jeep into a crowd of fans, injuring three children. Felony charges were brought, community service time was served, and Coleman was traded in the off-season.

The Season

During the first week of the season, Bobby Bonilla threatened "to show the Bronx" to sportswriter Bob Klapisch after Klapisch and John Harper's book "The Worst Team Money Could Buy" hit bookshelves detailing the drama and disappointment of the 1992 Mets. Eddie Murray asked Klapisch to leave the clubhouse.

The Mets took two straight from the expansion Rockies to start the season. Gooden pitched an Opening Day shutout. The Mets took two straight from the Reds late in the month. It would be more than two months before the Mets won consecutive games again. John Franco closed out New York's win on April 16 but was lost for nearly a month with a tender left elbow.

Gooden pitched seven shutout innings against the Giants to improve to 2-2. Tanana went eight innings in a 6-1 win over the Padres to improve the Mets to 8-7. It would be the final time the team was over .500. Eddie Murray was off to a blazing start, hitting .368. Bonilla was hitting .268 with four homers and 13 RBI. Todd Hundley had 10 RBI. But the rest of the offense was struggling. Fernandez and Vince Coleman were batting under .230. Johnson was hitting .151.

Coleman was testing out some new golf clubs in the clubhouse when he hit Gooden on the right shoulder blade. The team tried covering up the story but eventually the truth came out. When a TV crew began setting up at Coleman's locker the next day, they were stopped by Franco, Bonilla and Murray.

🕐 Final Resting Ground

After 20 seasons in the majors, Frank Tanana made his way to the National League and went 7-15 with a 4.48 ERA before being traded to the Yankees. He picked up his first hit (he finished with nine) and took a no-hitter two outs into the seventh inning against the Giants on July 17 until Barry Bonds homered to break it up.

A seven-game losing streak had the Mets in last place, where they would spend the rest of the season, even looking up at the expansion Marlins. The Mets would split four games at Shea with the Marlins in an ugly series, which included Bonilla screaming at third base coach Mike Cubbage after dogging it on the bases.

Franco told writers the team lacked fire and questioned the preparation of some players. Torborg was unhappy that Franco spoke out in the papers about it. If the veterans were causing havoc, the younger guys were scuffling. Ryan Thompson was sent to the minors with a .125 average after being rushed into the lineup.

"The other day I looked at the scoreboard to see how the Phillies were doing," Saberhagen said. "But then I said, 'Why bother with the first place team? We've got six teams to worry about.' It's frustrating. One of the problems we have here is that we don't have that one dynamic player who gets everything going, like a Lenny Dykstra, who can do something every day to help you win."

After the Marlins left town, the Mets lost seven of eight, including four one-run games. On May 19, there was a rare win as Bonilla homered in the bottom of the 10th to beat the Pirates after the Mets scored three in the ninth to tie the game. The game was the last for Torborg as Mets manager. The beleaguered skipper was fired along with coaches Barry Foote and Dave LaRoche.

The new manager was Dallas Green, who had been scouting for the team. He had pitched in several games for the 1966 Mets. He led the Phillies to the title in 1980 and helped build the Cubs in the front office for the 1984 NL East title. "I'm not looking for him to win 15 or 20 straight and jump us back into contention with the Phillies," Harazin said. "But what I want to come from the rest of the season is the sense that the franchise is back going in the right direction."

The team lost 21 of 25 to begin June before taking two straight from the Marlins, the first time the Mets won consecutive games in more than two months. On June 11, Tony Fernandez was traded to the Blue Jays for Darrin Jackson. Fernandez hit .225 with six stolen bases in 48 games. Paul Gibson, and his 5.19 ERA, was released. He allowed a go-ahead three run homer to Philadelphia's Pete Incaviglia the night before.

Jeromy Burnitz was called up to the majors and made his debut on June 21. On June 29, he went 3-5 with two doubles, a homer and two RBI in a win over the Marlins.

In late June, Gooden had seven of New York's 21 wins. Green was asked how he dealt with all the

---

FUTILE: PETE SCHOUREK

Pete Schourek went 5-12 with a 5.96 ERA. He was 1-8 with a 6.46 ERA at Shea. Two years later, as a Red, he would finish second in the Cy Young voting.

FABULOUS: EDDIE MURRAY

In his final season in Queens, Eddie Murray hit .285 with 27 home runs and 100 RBI, the last 100-RBI season of his career. He drove in 93 in his other season in New York. Murray ended strong, hitting .365 with 7 HR and 21 RBI in Sept/Oct.

TOP BATTERS

Pos	Name	G	AB	H	BA	HR	RBI	RS	SB	OPS
1B	Eddie Murray	154	610	174	.285	27	100	77	2	.792
2B	Jeff Kent	140	496	134	.270	21	80	65	4	.765
LF	Vince Coleman	92	373	104	.279	2	25	64	38	.691
RF	Bobby Bonilla	139	502	133	.265	34	87	81	3	.874
OF	Joe Orsulak	134	409	116	.284	8	35	59	5	.730

TOP PITCHERS

Pos	Name	G	GS	W	L	SV	ERA	IP	SO	BB
SP	Dwight Gooden	29	29	12	15	0	3.45	208.2	149	61
SP	Frank Tanana	29	29	7	15	0	4.48	183.0	104	48
SP	Bret Saberhagen	19	19	7	7	0	3.29	139.1	93	17
SP	Sid Fernandez	18	18	5	6	0	2.93	119.2	81	36
RP	Dave Telgheder	24	7	6	2	0	4.76	75.2	35	21

losing. "Somehow you've got to bust it out of your system and get it over with, and some guys do it easier than others," he said. "I just beat the hell out of Sylvia and kick the dog and whatever else I've got to do get it out, and then I think about it the rest of the night and come back to the park and try to smile a little bit and get after it again."

Harazin left the organization in late June, rather than accept a demotion. McIlvane would return in August, after battling with Padres ownership.

The Mets entered the All-Star break 29-60. Bonilla, who was being shifted to third base, was the lone All-Star, having hit 20 home runs in the first half of the season. The team won eight of 11 in late July. Johnson hurt his hand sliding into second base. He would never play for the Mets again.

After a loss to the Dodgers Coleman threw a lit firecracker into a crowd of fans waiting for autographs. Three were injured, including a two-year-old girl. Saberhagen, who admitted to throwing a firecracker under a table of reporters who had been interviewing Anthony Young earlier in the month, sprayed three reporters with bleach in the clubhouse. Saberhagen's season would end in early August because of a knee injury.

Coleman played in a few more games but his time in New York was done. He was placed on "leave" on August 12. Fred Wilpon was so angry with the team that he made his first speech in the clubhouse since buying the team in 1980. During a late August press conference, Wilpon said Coleman would never wear a Mets uniform again.

Gooden was 11-10 in early August but lost four of five and then missed the final month of the season with a shoulder injury. On September 7, the Mets were no-hit in a 7-1 loss by Houston's Darryl Kile. The game marked the MLB debut of Butch Huskey, who went down on strikes in all three of his at-bats.

The team lost 100 games for the first time since 1967. The Mets did win their final six games of the season, including a 1-0, 17-inning victory over the Cardinals that saw Bobby Jones, who made his debut in August, throw 143 pitches over 10 shutout innings.

Top 5 Highlights

1. Dwight Gooden throws a four-hit shutout on Opening Day in a 3-0 win over the Rockies. Bobby Bonilla homers off David Nied in the fifth.

2. Frank Tanana, who made his MLB debut in 1973, delivers his first base hit in the majors on April 28 against the Giants. In the fifth inning of a scoreless game, Dusty Baker had Trevor Wilson intentionally walk Todd Hundley to load the bases for Tanana. Tanana singled home two runs with a hit to the left side.

3. Gooden homers off John Smoltz in the second inning of New York's 6-1 win over the Braves on May 22 at Shea Stadium. Gooden also gave up one run in eight innings.

4. Eddie Murray's double down the right field line off Florida's Bryan Harvey gives the Mets a 5-4 win on July 28 and snaps Anthony Young's 27-game losing streak. It looked like Young was going to lose number 28 in a row when Chuck Carr gave the Marlins a 4-3 lead in the top of the inning with a bunt single. In the bottom of the ninth, Ryan Thompson tied the game, with an RBI single to score Jeff McKnight. Two batters later, Murray's hit scored Thompson.

5. Sid Fernandez wins his final game as a Met, going seven innings in a 7-1 win over the Marlins on October 2. The lefty gives up one run on two hits. He won 98 games as a Met in 10 seasons, still good for fifth in team history.

1994

	W	L	GB	Pos
	55	58	18.5	3rd
RS/G	RA/G		Manager	
4.48	4.65		Dallas Green	

Gooden Era Ends in Strike-Shortened Season

The Moves

Vince Coleman was gone and Kevin McReynolds was back. It was a positive for the Mets as Fred Wilpon stated Coleman wouldn't play for the Mets again and there was thought that they might have to release him and another team could sign him for the minimum.

Howard Johnson signed with the Rockies. Sid Fernandez signed with the Orioles. Eddie Murray signed with the Indians.

Dave Gallagher was traded to the Braves for pitcher Pete Smith. The team signed outfielder John Cangelosi, the former White Sox, Pirates and Rangers player who had spent 1993 in the minors. Southpaw Mike Remlinger, who played for the Giants in 1991 before spending the next two seasons in Seattle's minor league system, was signed.

Charlie O'Brien signed with Atlanta and the Mets selected catcher Kelly Stinnett from the Indians in the Rule V Draft.

In late March, the Mets traded Kevin Baez to the Orioles for first baseman David Segui. Segui hit 10 homers in 1993 but was expendable after Baltimore signed Rafael Palmeiro. Anthony Young was sent to the Cubs for Jose Vizcaino, who would become the shortstop and leadoff hitter. The Mets looked to send Young to the Angels for J.T. Snow but when a deal fell through, it looked like

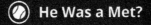 **He Was a Met?**

The Mets signed John Cangilosi as a free agent after he had missed the entire 1993 season. It was the fourth of seven teams for the lefty. He was released in July after driving in only 4 runs and collecting 4 EBH in 111 at bats.

Young would be back with the Mets as a fourth starter. His trade ensured Bobby Jones and Eric Hillman filling out the back of the rotation. Vizcaino hit .287 with the Cubs and played several positions. "We think this kid can really help us," Dallas Green said. "He's an everyday player, a leadoff, switch-hitting type that can play defense and he's a proven major league quality hitter."

The trade was a surprise for Fernando Vina, who had been told he would leadoff and play short. "I'm in shock," he said.

The Situation

For the first time in 10 years, the Mets entered a season with low expectations around baseball. "It is weird," Dwight Gooden said. "The last couple of years, at least we looked good on paper when the season started, even if it didn't turn out that way. This year, we don't even have that."

Bobby Bonilla's stay in New York was an unpleasant one both for him and the Mets. Bonilla came to Queens in a 5-year contract that made him the top-paid player in the game. A long slump in May in his first season dropped Bonilla's average to .222 and led to intense and widespread criticism from both the media and fans, which the sensitive Bonilla had trouble handling. He went on to be a productive hitter for the Mets, but alway remained a target of angry fans.

The Season

The Mets opened the season with a sweep of the Cubs at Wrigley Field. New York won 12-8 on Opening Day despite Gooden failing to make it out of the sixth and Cubs centerfielder Tuffy Rhodes hitting three homers.

The bullpen, baseball's worst in 1993, was still a work in progress. Mike Maddux and Jonathan Hurst blew an 8-3 eighth inning lead against the Cubs on April 14 but Jeff Kent saved the day with a two-run homer off Dan Plesac.

On April 21 in Los Angeles, Gooden was taken out in the sixth inning of

 Final Resting Ground

Kevin McReynolds returned after two seasons in Kansas City, traded for none other than Vince Coleman, and batted .256 with four home runs in 51 games in the final season of his career.

FABULOUS: RICO BROGNA

Rico Brogna showed great promise as a part-timer for the '94 Mets, putting up a slash line of .351/.380/.626 in 131 AB. He was fairly productive the next season and a half, but did his best work after being traded to Philadelphia, where he put up 2 100-RBI seasons.

a 13-3 loss to the Dodgers. It was his final start until June 9 as the right-hander would go on the DL with a toe injury. He reinjured it after initially injuring it on Opening Day.

A Vina single against the Padres on April 27 gave the Mets a 15-inning win and brought the team back to .500. There were still growing pains. On the last day of the month, the Mets blew a 10-5 eighth inning lead with Josias Manzanillo giving up home runs to Chris Gwynn, Mike Piazza and Tim Wallach. And on May 3, John Franco blew a ninth inning lead in a 6-5 loss to the Giants after Joe Orsulak gave the Mets the lead with a seventh inning grand slam.

But the Mets won six of seven to improve to 18-14. The heroics were shared. Bobby Bonilla hit two home runs in a win over the Giants. Bret Saberhagen and Jones pitched complete game victories over the Cardinals. Bonilla hit a go-ahead homer in the eighth against St. Louis. Segui hit a go-ahead homer in the eighth in a win over the Expos. Orsulak hit a go-ahead homer in the 10th in Montreal after Cangelosi tied the game with a single in the ninth.

Hillman's ERA was north of seven and he managed to anger Barry Bonds after hitting the slugger on the elbow with a pitch, forcing Bonds to miss two games. "If he hits me again, I'm chasing him around the clubhouse and out of the clubhouse, I'll take my bat out to the mound if he starts running away," Bonds said. "They can suspend me the whole year. I don't care. I'll knock him out."

There was no fight with the Giants but the Mets did brawl with the Braves on May 14. In the bottom of the fifth, Ryan Thompson hit a grand slam giving the Mets a 7-0 lead. Thompson's blast ended a two-for-36 stretch at the plate and he took his time around the bases. John Smoltz's next pitch drilled Cangelosi, who charged the mound.

New York lost six of seven. Jeromy Burnitz found himself in Green's doghouse after a slow start and was sent to the minors on May 11 with a .192 average. "He ran the bases poorly. He started to field the ball lackadaisically and throw the ball lackadaisically, and he took us out of some games because of it," Green said, adding that the outfielder "pouted."

FUTILE: JOSE VIZCAINO

The Mets made journeyman Jose Vizcaino their regular shortstop during the strike-shortened 1994 season. Vizcaino managed only 33 RBI and 47 RS in over 400 at bats and was an abysmal 1-for-12 in SB attempts.

The Mets ended May 25-25 but then came a June swoon, a 9-18 month. There were a pair of five-game losing streaks. And there was Gooden. He returned on June 9, giving up six

TOP BATTERS

Pos	Name	G	AB	H	BA	HR	RBI	RS	SB	OPS
C	Todd Hundley	91	291	69	.237	16	42	45	2	.746
2B	Jeff Kent	107	415	121	.292	14	68	53	1	.816
3B	Bobby Bonilla	108	403	117	.290	20	67	60	1	.878
CF	Ryan Thompson	98	334	75	.225	18	59	39	1	.735
RF	Joe Orsulak	96	292	76	.260	8	42	39	4	.651

TOP PITCHERS

Pos	Name	G	GS	W	L	SV	ERA	IP	SO	BB
SP	Brett Saberhagen	24	24	14	4	0	2.74	177.1	143	13
SP	Bobby Jones	24	24	12	7	0	3.15	160.0	80	56
CL	John Franco	47	0	1	4	30	2.70	50.0	42	19
RP	Doug Linton	32	3	6	2	0	4.47	50.1	29	20
RP	Josias Manzanillo	37	0	3	2	2	2.66	47.1	48	13

runs in four innings in a loss to the Expos. The 9-0 loss marked the first time the Mets were blanked and the first career shutout of Pedro Martinez. Gooden pitched better in Philadelphia but lost again. On June 19, he beat 46-year-old Charlie Hough and the Marlins, pitching eight innings and giving up one run on three hits. It would be his 157th and final win as a Met.

On June 24, he gave up nine runs (eight earned) in 5.1 innings, needing 119 pitches as he labored in a 9-4 loss to the Pirates. He was pitching distracted because he knew a suspension was imminent. The 29-year-old Gooden had failed another drug test. Several days later, the announcement came that he was suspended for two months.

On the field, the Mets kept losing. The Mets rallied from a 7-1 seventh inning deficit to take an 8-7 lead over the Cardinals, only to see Franco lose it in the ninth with help from a Bonilla error.

July would be much better as the team went 16-10. Southpaw starter Jason Jacome, called up for Gooden, won four straight starts, including a shutout at Dodger Stadium for his first win. Jim Lindeman's 10th inning homer off Rod Beck gave the Mets a 2-1 win over the Giants on July 4. Saberhagen went 4-0 in July. His two no-decisions included a 10 shutout innings against San Diego and nine innings in Pittsburgh when he gave up the tying hit one out away from a win. Saberhagen, who had seemed likely to be traded at the start of the season, was the one Met All-Star in Pittsburgh. Franco converted 10 of 11 save opportunities during the month.

The youth movement was also to thank for the improvement. Thompson had 18 home runs at the end of July. Todd Hundley had 16.

The Mets played the Braves tough, taking two of three at Shea to begin August. Meanwhile, the threat of a strike was looming. The owners wanted a salary cap implemented. The players' union rejected it. On July 28, a strike date of August 12 was set.

On August 11, the Mets lost in 15 innings to the Phillies at Veterans Stadium when Ricky Jordan singled with the bases loaded off Mauro Gozzo. On the eve of the strike, Bonilla got into a confrontation with reporter Art McFarland, who was asking about the impending work stoppage and noted that Bonilla would lose more money than any other player. Bonilla told the reporter to "shove that mic as far up your ass as you can stick it."

Then it was strike time. "Right now, it just seems like a day off," Franco said. "My daughter keeps asking me, and I said it could be one day, two days, three days, and it could be more. Who knows?"

Green said, "I don't anticipate too many of them going out and getting a job anytime soon. But a few of them might have to fire their gardeners and chauffeurs."

On September 14, the rest of the season, including the World Series was called off. It was a sad ending to baseball's 125th season. The Expos had baseball's best record at the time of the stoppage. Tony Gwynn was hitting .394 and looked to become the first player to hit .400 since Ted Williams in 1941. Matt Williams had 43 homers and looked to challenge Roger Maris' record of 61.

The Mets playoff hopes weren't damaged by the strike. In fact, it was a positive year, as the team nearly played .500 ball after a 103-loss season. Unfortunately, Gooden would be suspended for the entire 1995 season in November after failing another drug test.

Top 5 Highlights

1 The Mets outslug the Cubs for a 12-8 Opening Day win. Jose Vizcaino, Todd Hundley and Jeff Kent all homer. Vizcaino, Hundley, Kent, Kevin McReynolds, Bobby Bonilla and Ryan Thompson all have multi-hit games.

2 Bobby Jones throws 143 pitches in a 1-0 win over the Cardinals on May 7. McReynolds doubles in a run in the sixth for the only scoring. With two on and two outs in the bottom of the ninth, Jones gets Brian Jordan on a groundout to short.

3 The Mets score four runs in the top of eighth against Greg Maddux in a 5-2 win over the Braves on June 22. Maddux retired 16 straight batters and entered the eighth with a 2-1 lead. Three hits tied the game and Maddux threw away a Fernando Vina bunt, allowing two runs to score.

4 Jason Jacome pitches a six-hit shutout in a 3-0 win over the Dodgers on July 7 for his first MLB win. Jacome gets Eric Karros on a 6-4-3 double play to end the night. Hundley homered off Tom Candiotti in the top of the fourth.

5 The Mets hold off the Cardinals on July 26 in a 10-9, 11-inning win lasting four hours and six minutes. Brogna's two-run homer off Gary Buckels makes it 10-8. St. Louis rallies and cuts the lead to 10-9 and puts runners on the corners but John Franco strikes out Tom Pagnozzi to end it.

1995

OPENING DAY LINEUP

Brett Butler, CF
Jose Vizcaino, SS
Rico Brogna, 1B
Bobby Bonilla, 3B
Jeff Kent, 2B
David Segui, LF
Carl Everett, RF
Todd Hundley, C
Bobby Jones, P

	W	L	GB	Pos
	69	75	21.0	2nd
RS/G	RA/G		Manager	
4.56	4.29		Dallas Green	

A Strong Finish Is Not Nearly Enough

The Moves

In mid-April the Mets re-signed John Franco to a two-year, $5 million deal. Right-handed starter Pete Harnisch, a 1991 All-Star as a member of the Astros, was signed to a three-year, $9 million deal after being acquired in a trade with Houston for Juan Castillo. And they signed another 1991 All-Star, bringing in centerfielder Brett Butler for a one-year, $2 million contract.

Butler, who batted .314 with 27 stolen bases in 1994, solved New York's leadoff and center field questions. Several teams were interested in the popular player, but phone calls from Dallas Green, Fred Wilpon, Bret Saberhagen and Franco convinced Butler to come to the Big Apple. The deal seemingly made the Mets a wild card contender.

There were other offseason deals. The Mets traded Jeromy Burnitz, often a Dallas Green whipping boy, to the Indians for pitching prospects Dave Mlicki, Paul Byrd and Jerry Dipoto. Carl Everett, who had only played 27 games over two seasons in Florida, was acquired in late November as Quilvio Veras was sent to the Marlins. Fernando Vina was traded to the Brewers for right-handed reliever Doug Henry.

The Situation

The Mets entered 1995 coming off a season in which they nearly finished .500, unlike the year before when they entered coming off a 103-loss campaign.

He Was a Met?

The Mets signed 37-year-old Brett Butler before the 1995 season. Butler gave them what was expected - no power, a good batting average, and some walks - before they traded him back to the Dodgers for two players who never made the major leagues.

Managerial Miseries

The years between Davey Johnson and Bobby Valentine were tough for the Mets both on the field and at the manager position. Johnson was followed by Bud Harrelson in May of 1990, who was 70-49 for the remainder of the season. But one year later, company man Harrelson was replaced by the ineffectual Jeff Torborg (who was AL Manager of the Year in 1990 for the Chicago White Sox). Torborg hailed from Westfield, NJ but his straight-laced style seemed out of place in New York. Torborg was followed by another out-of-step "baseball man," Dallas Green, whose teams never attained .500 in parts of 4 seasons. Bobby V took over near the end of 1996 and the Mets were strong contenders for the next 4 years.

Major League Baseball was back after the strike was settled in late March. Each team would play 144 games and Opening Day was pushed back to April 26. And things seemed to be looking up as the wild card meant the Mets wouldn't have to edge the Braves in the NL East to make the playoffs.

The Mets plucked righty reliever Blas Minor off waivers from the Pirates. "When they picked me up during the offseason they said they were just collecting as many good arms as they could, they were going to throw us all in spring training and see who came out on top at the end," Minor said in an interview for the book. "That was when they had Pulsipher, Isringhausen, and Wilson down in the minor leagues and they said we have probably a year window we'd like to fill, and I'm like, 'Hey, regardless, I'm here to throw.' Anytime someone wants to give me a chance to pitch in the big leagues, I was ready to go."

Minor wanted to impress his new team after three seasons in Pittsburgh. "I had something to prove because the Pirates had let me go," Minor said. "You have to take advantage of those things and prepare yourself for the opportunity to be successful. Everybody in the bullpen was chomping at the bit to throw."

After the strike was ended and replacement players wouldn't be used, it was off to shortened spring baseball. "Once it was settled, everybody's kind of rushed over into spring training," Minor said.

The Season

A look at the starting lineup shows how many moves the Mets had made, as only Bobby Bonilla, Jeff Kent and Todd Hundley were around from the 1993 Opening Day lineup.

The Mets played the first two games at Coors Field in Colorado, losing both in walk-off fashion.

New York did return home to win two straight, including a 5-4, 11-inning win with Joe Orsulak singling to win it. The Mets would struggle mightily in May, going 11-17. Jason Jacome was 0-4 with an ERA over 10. He was demoted and later traded. The team also dumped Remlinger and Lomon, both of whom had ERAs north of six.

Fabulous to Futile in Flushing

The Mets lost two 3-2 games in 13 innings. They lost three straight games at Shea to the Dodgers for the first time since 1975. Light-hitting LA catcher Tom Prince tripled and then hit a homer the next night. Green said, "We ain't talking about Babe Ruth," when asked about Prince. The catcher delivered an RBI double the next night. The Mets lost six straight late in the month.

Bonilla was the force on offense, hitting .345 with seven homers through the end of May. Kent hit

> ## FABULOUS: JASON ISRINGHAUSEN
>
> *Jason Isringhausen took New York by storm in the second half of 1995, winning 9 of 14 starts and compiling an ERA of 2.81. But his true calling was as a reliever, which the Mets never realized. He went on to collect an average of 34 saves over an 8-year stretch for Oakland and St. Louis.*

five home runs in May. Segui was batting .324 and Orsulak was hitting .316.

The Mets stumbled through June as well, going 10-17. Early in the month, Josias Manzanillo was designated for assignment with a 7.88 ERA in 12 games. Green heavily criticized the team, suggesting he might get fired for the team's poor play. "You can say it's because of this or that, but I've made excuses for these guys for 40 to 50 days, saying it's still spring training on the 40th or 50th day," Green said. "But I'm running out of excuses for them."

Bonilla wasn't happy with the move of the Manzanillo. "If that was a sign, they should have done it a long time ago," he said. "What – putting Manzy on waivers is going to give us more offense? What area did they fix?"

Segui was traded to the Expos for Triple-A pitcher Reid Cornelius. With Brogna at first, the Mets made a deal for another pitcher. "This trade obviously doesn't help the major league club immediately but it gives us an opportunity to acquire another young quality arm," said Gerry Hunsicker, the assistant vice president for baseball operations.

The offense was struggling. Butler saw his batting average drop more than .100 points after a blazing start. Jose Vizcaino was hitting .232. Kent was batting .142 with runners in scoring position. Rookie Edgardo Alfonzo was batting at .210. He played both second and third before being placed at third for good, with Bonilla moving to left.

The Mets fell to the Astros in a 16-inning game at Shea on June 16. The next day marked the debut of Bill Pulsipher, the team's second round draft pick in 1991. He pitched well in the minors and was a Double-A Eastern League All-Star in 1994. Right-hander Mike Birkbeck went to play in Japan and Pulsipher was called up from Triple-A Norfolk, where he was 6-4 with a 3.14 ERA. GM Joe McIlvaine called it "a great day for the organization." With Jason Isringhausen and Paul Wilson highly touted and in the majors, the GM said it was "the tip of the iceberg."

"I'm definitely happy and I can't wait to get up there," Pulsipher said. "I don't expect to win 20 games or anything like that. But I do expect to hold my own."

TOP BATTERS

Pos	Name	G	AB	H	BA	HR	RBI	RS	SB	OPS
C	Todd Hundley	90	275	77	.280	15	51	39	1	.865
1B	Rico Brogna	134	495	143	.289	22	76	72	0	.827
2B	Jeff Kent	125	472	131	.278	20	65	65	3	.791
CF	Brett Butler	90	367	114	.311	1	25	54	21	.773
UT	Bobby Bonilla	80	317	103	.325	18	53	49	0	.984

TOP PITCHERS

Pos	Name	G	GS	W	L	SV	ERA	IP	SO	BB
SP	Bobby Jones	30	30	10	10	0	4.19	195.2	127	53
SP	Dave Mlicki	29	25	9	7	0	4.26	160.2	123	54
SP	Bret Saberhagen	16	16	5	5	0	3.35	110.0	71	20
SP	Jason Isringhausen	14	14	9	2	0	2.81	93.0	55	31
CL	John Franco	48	0	5	3	29	2.44	51.2	41	17

Pulsipher's first pitch went to the backstop and gave up five runs in the first. Green left him in for 131 pitches, even letting him leadoff in the bottom of the fifth down 6-2 after already throwing 98 pitches. The fans got on Butler, who misplayed two balls. After striking out in the third, he tipped his helmet to the booing fans. In the eighth he was thrown out trying to advance to third on a botched pickoff play. Butler called it one of the worst games he had in his career. In the eighth with runners on the corners and the Mets down by five, Bonilla flied out to right. Third base coach Mike Cubbage held the runner. Bonilla, unhappy about missing out an RBI, glared at Cubbage and then trashed a pair of water coolers in the dugout.

The Mets lost nine of 11 and dropped into last place behind the Marlins. The Mets went nearly a month without winning consecutive games. Pulsipher picked up his first win without 7.1 shutout innings against Florida on June 27. McIlvane spoke of making moves if he didn't see improvement in 10 days. "Why did they do that? It's stupid," Bonilla said. "You don't say you're going to wait 10 days to make changes. If you're going to make changes, make them. Now we've got guys sitting around here waiting for the bomb to drop. Nobody knows what's going to happen."

McIlvane pushed it back and said he would give his team until the All-Star break to turn it around. The team was fighting the perception that they were out of it and looking ahead to 1996, with Bonilla, looking for the team to be more aggressive, and the front office exchanging barbs.

Harnisch fell to 1-7 in a loss to the Cubs. The defense made four errors behind him. "I'm embarrassed all the time," Green said. "Nobody wants to watch this."

The Mets went into the break with a 25-44 record, only percentage points ahead of the Marlins away from the cellar in the NL. Bonilla, batting .315 with 13 home runs, was the lone All-Star.

But they got hot in the second half, winning six of seven. Isringhausen, who was 9-1 with a 1.55 ERA in Triple-A, was called up and made his debut on July 17, giving up two runs in seven innings against the Cubs. Brogna won a game against the Rockies with a single. But the team lost six straight to fall to 32-52.

FUTILE: REID CORNELIUS

To Cornelius's credit, he had a decision in all 10 of his starts. Unfortunately, only 3 were W's, due to an ERA of 5.15. Reid made a comeback with Florida a few years later with similar results - a 5-10 record, before calling it quits for good.

Bonilla, batting .325 with 18 home runs and 53 RBI, was traded to the Orioles late in July. The deal was in the works for a month but the Mets were able to hold out for Alex Ochoa, a minor league outfield prospect, along with Damon Buford. Bonilla was tied for the NL lead in total bases at the time of the deal.

Right before the deadline, the team sent Bret Saberhagen to the Rockies, who were making a playoff push in their third season. The Mets picked up pitching prospect Juan Acevedo. Colorado took on the majority of Saberhagen's contract. The team shed about $9 million in salary with the two deals. It was expected that Saberhagen, who was 5-5 with a 3.35 ERA and completed three of 16 starts, would be dealt but the Red Sox had been the expected team.

The only million-dollar Mets remaining were Franco, Harnisch and Vizcaino. The new-look Mets began August with five straight losses. The Mets won 16 of the next 22, including sweeps of the Phillies and Dodgers. Butler played his last game for the Mets on August 9. His mother died that day after a long battle with cancer. He returned to New York on the 18th and learned he was traded to the Dodgers, who were in town. Butler hit .311 and stole 21 bases in 90 games with the Mets.

The players still on the roster were rolling. Bill Spiers won a game with a squeeze bunt. Isringhausen pitched eight shutout innings in a win against the Phillies. Vizcaino won a game against the Giants with a single off Rod Beck. Chris Jones hit a walk-off homer to beat Pittsburgh, his second game-ending blast of the year. Carl Everett hit a grand slam in a victory over the Padres.

The Mets kept it going in September. There was a five-game winning streak in the middle of the month. The team split a four-game series in Atlanta, including Isringhausen beating John Smoltz. With six games remaining in the season, the Mets were 63-75, dead last in the division. The remaining games were at Shea against the Reds and Braves, two teams that had already clinched their divisions.

The Mets won six straight to end 1995. On the final day of the season, Tim Bogar drew a bases loaded walk against Brad Woodall in the 11th and the Mets had a 1-0 win. Combined with Philadelphia's loss to Florida, the Mets tied for second place.

The Mets were 44-31 after the All-Star break, the second-best record in the league. They also tied a franchise record with 11 straight home wins.

"I'm proud of our kids and the way they battled in the second half," Green said. "We got our act together and played as a team. There were some doubting Thomases as to whether the team could get it done or whether I could get it done. I enjoy getting those kind of challenges and beating them."

Franco said, "It's the first winter in a long while where we can walk around with our heads up high. I'm going to enjoy that."

Top 5 Highlights

1 The Mets win the home opener over the Cardinals 10-8 on April 28 in a game interrupted several times by rowdy fans in the first game at Shea since the strike ended. New York erases deficits of 6-2 and 7-6. Carl Everett, Bobby Bonilla and Rico Brogna all homer.

2 Todd Hundley hits in a pinch-hit grand slam in the top of the 11th off Montreal's Bryan Eversgard to give the Mets a lead in a 5-1 win over the Expos on May 4. Felipe Alou had Brogna intentionally walked to bring up John Franco's spot. Dallas Green countered by sending Hundley up. Mike Remlinger pitched a scoreless bottom of the 11th.

3 Chris Jones hits a pinch-hit three-run walk-off home run off Trevor Hoffman to give the Mets a 7-5 win over the Padres on May 31. The Mets scored three in the eighth to take a 4-3 lead but Eddie Williams led off the top of the ninth with a homer off John Franco. San Diego scored again in the 10th against Franco to take a 5-4 lead. Jeff Kent and Joe Orsulak singled in the bottom of the inning in front of Jones.

4 Jason Isringhausen defeats Rookie of the Year Hideo Nomo and the Dodgers in a 6-3 win on August 20. Nomo, who enters the game 10-3, gives up home runs to Jose Vizcaino, Carl Everett and Butch Huskey.

5 Bobby Jones pitches a three-hit shutout in a 5-0 win over the Expos on September 8. Jones takes a no-hitter into the seventh before Sean Berry breaks it up with a leadoff single.

1996

	W	L	GB	Pos
	71	91	25.0	4th

RS/G	RA/G	Manager	
4.60	4.81	Dallas Green Bobby Valentine	

Big Bats Buried by Weak Pitching

The Moves

Before the 1995 season, the Mets had signed Brett Butler as a leadoff hitter and centerfielder. For 1996, it was Lance Johnson filling in those roles. The Mets signed the outfielder who had led the American League in triples four times with the White Sox. Johnson would be the Mets ninth Opening Day centerfielder in the last nine seasons, a consistency that would make the drummers in Spinal Tap proud.

In January, the Mets traded three minor leaguers to the Cardinals for left fielder Bernard Gilkey, who had hit .298 with 17 home runs in 1995. The organization was looking at Gilkey to bring some leadership to Queens, despite being 29 years old.

Huskey's strong spring training, combined with Everett's brutal spring training, gave Huskey the starting job in right field. Huskey had played at first base in the spring after Rico Brogna sprained a knee ligament in early March, but Brogna was healthy for the start of the regular season.

The Mets traded Ryan Thompson and pitcher Reid Cornelius to the Indians for Mark Clark, who had been competing for the fifth starter spot in Cleveland. Clark was acquired because of injuries to Bill Pulsipher (strained left elbow), Pete Harnsich (recovering from surgery) and Juan Acevedo (strained right hamstring). The trade meant the Mets would begin the season with an all-righty rotation of Bobby Jones, Jason Isringhausen, Paul Wilson and Dave Mlicki and Clark.

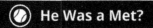

He Was a Met?

Catcher Brent Mayne spent 15 seasons in the majors or 7 different teams, and most notably was the winning pitcher for Colorado in a game in 2000. Mayne appeared in 70 games as a Met, but started only 16.

The Triumphant Trio

No threesome in the history of the Mets was stronger than Lance Johnson, Bernard Gilkey, and Todd Hundley. Johnson set team records with 227 hits and 21 triples, scored 117 runs, batted .333, and stole 50 bases. Gilkey also had a career year with .317 BA/30 HR/117 RBI/108 RS. His next best totals for HR and RBI were 18 and 78 the following year. Hundley, meanwhile, set a team record with 41 HR, which also established the record for home runs by a catcher in a single season, and drove in 112. The next most productive batter was Butch Husky with 15 HR and 60 RBI. This lack of depth, a poor pitching staff, and a record of 23-35 in 1-run games, put the Mets at 20 games below .500 for the season.

The Situation

There was a real anticipation for this Mets team for the first time in several years and this time it was because of young talent, labeled Generation K, not overpriced veterans past their prime coming to Queens.

"You've got to be excited about this year," Dallas Green said. "I am, I think our coaching staff is and I think the players are. I hope the fans are, too, because for the first time since I've been here, we come to spring training with a ball club that has a chance to be exciting and productive."

Part of the excitement came from the strong ending the Mets had to the 1995 season.

"We played well for 60 games last year," Green said. "The question is: Can we play well for 162? I think we can."

Sports Illustrated predicted the Mets would finish in second place behind Atlanta in the division.

The Season

The Mets began the season taking two out of three from St. Louis. It would be the high point of the season as New York's 2-1 record was the last time they would be over .500 in 1996.

 Final Resting Ground

Alvaro Espinosa came to the Mets in July 1996 as part of the Jeff Kent trade after 10 years in the AL. He was a remarkably unproductive hitter, but Espinosa batted a career high of .306 for the Mets, who nevertheless released him after the season. After 33 games with Seattle the following season, he was gone for good.

The Mets struggled for most of the season despite some solid individual performances. The team went 11-13 in April and 11-17 in May. New York was in last place and the phenoms on the mound weren't phenomenal. Wilson was 1-5 with a 7.13 ERA. Isringhausen was 2-7 with a much more respectable 3.84 ERA.

Whenever it looked like the season would go off the rails, the team rallied. After a 1-5 start, Mark Clark won nine of 10 decisions. Gilkey and

Hundley were providing power, and Lance Johnson was sparking the offense at the top of the lineup.

In late July, the Mets acquired three-time All-Star Carlos Baerga from the Indians, with Jeff Kent and Fernando Vina heading to Cleveland. Baerga was one of the premier infielders in baseball and helped the Indians win the 1995 American League pennant but was only hitting .267 with 10 home runs and 55 RBI at the time of the trade. Kent was batting .290 with 9 home runs and 39 RBI but carried a $2 million salary. The move also gave a bigger role to Edgardo Alfonzo.

> ## FABULOUS: BERNARD GILKEY, LANCE JOHNSON
>
> *Bernard Gilkey and Lance Johnson were a fearsome OF combo for the Mets in 1996. Gilkey had a career year with .317/30/117, while Johnson hit. 333, scored 117, and set the Mets' single-season record for hits (227) and triples (21).*

The Mets were 52-56 entering August but the wheels would fall off, with the team losing 20 of 27. The Mets committed seven errors in a 13-9 loss to the Pirates on August 1. Robert Person gave up eight runs on nine hits in consecutive starts. The team went to Los Angeles and was swept by the Dodgers.

The Mets were 13-24 over a six-week stretch that was the second worst in the National League. With the Mets sitting at 59-72, the Dallas Green era was over. In addition to the lackluster record, the organization was not happy with comments he made to reporters about his struggling starters.

"These guys don't belong in the big leagues," Green said of Isringhausen and Wilson. "That might sound harsh and negative, but what have they done to get here?"

In came Bobby Valentine, who had been acquired for Dave Kingman in the Midnight Massacre of 1977 but would go on to become a fan favorite as manager. Valentine was a third-base coach with the Mets before leaving to manage the Rangers. He was managing the Triple-A team in Norfolk when Green was fired. Pitching coach Greg Pavlick was also fired and replaced by Bob Apodaca. "Our hope with this change is that the younger players can begin to blossom more," McIlvane said.

> ## FUTILE: PAUL WILSON
>
> *Part of Generation K, Paul Wilson was 5-12 with a 5.38 in his only season as a Met. In August he went 0-5 with an 8.42 ERA. Injuries would keep him out until 2000. Wilson ended up having 4 seasons of over 150 IP, but posted a winning record only once in his career, 11-6 for the 2004 Reds.*

The Mets finished 12-19 under Valentine, 71-91 overall.

TOP BATTERS

Pos	Name	G	AB	H	BA	HR	RBI	RS	SB	OPS
C	Todd Hundley	153	540	140	.259	41	112	85	1	.906
1B	Butch Huskey	118	414	115	.278	15	60	43	1	.754
LF	Bernard Gilkey	153	571	181	.317	30	117	108	17	.955
CF	Lance Johnson	160	682	227	.333	9	69	117	50	.841

TOP PITCHERS

Pos	Name	G	GS	W	L	SV	ERA	IP	SO	BB
SP	Mark Clark	32	32	14	11	0	3.43	212.1	142	48
SP	Bobby Jones	31	31	12	8	0	4.42	195.2	116	46
SP	Pete Harnisch	31	31	8	12	0	4.21	194.2	114	61
CL	John Franco	51	0	4	3	28	1.83	54.0	48	21
RP	Dave Mlicki	51	2	6	7	1	3.30	90.0	83	33

Top 5 Highlights

1 Rey Ordonez introduces himself on Opening Day as he throws out Royce Clayton at home plate from his knees. The Mets would erase a 6-0 deficit to beat the Cardinals.

2 John Franco notches his 300th career save with a shutout inning against the Expos to preserve a 3-2 win on April 29. (The Mets hold John Franco Day on May 11 to celebrate his 300th save. Franco is ejected in the fifth inning along with seven others after a brawl with the Cubs.)

3 Bobby Valentine wins his first game as Mets manager on August 31 against the Giants. Roberto Petagine and Alvaro Espinoza hit back-to-back home runs in the sixth inning of the 7-2 victory.

4 Derek Wallace only pitched in 19 games with the Mets but made his mark in the books when he became the first pitcher in team history to strikeout four batters in one inning. Wallace picked up the save on September 13 against Atlanta by striking out Terry Pendleton, who reached on a passed ball, Chipper Jones, Ryan Klesko and Mike Mordecai.

5 Todd Hundley hits his 41st home run of the season, a game-tying, three-run homer off Atlanta's Greg McMichael, to set the single-season record for a catcher, passing Roy Campanella.

1997

OPENING DAY LINEUP

Lance Johnson, CF
John Olerud, 1B
Bernard Gilkey, LF
Todd Hundley, C
Butch Huskey , 3B
Carlos Baerga, 2B
Carl Everett, RF
Rey Ordonez, SS
Pete Harnisch, P

	W	L	GB	Pos
	88	74	13.0	3rd
RS/G	RA/G		Manager	
4.80	4.38		Bobby Valentine	

Bobby V and Mets Win Surprising 88

The Moves

John Olerud, the Blue Jays first baseman who hit .363 and finished third in the MVP voting in 1993, was acquired, with Robert Person going to Toronto. Olerud went through struggles up north, batting .274 in 1996, including a .219 mark against lefties. The Blue Jays even paid $5 million of his $6.5 million salary and manager Cito Gaston predicted he wouldn't handle the pressure in New York well. Olerud seemed to enjoy the new surroundings and had a great spring.

The team was trying to deal with Generation K falling apart. Bill Pulsipher's elbow was hurt and he would miss the season. Paul Wilson had a torn shoulder capsule, keeping him out for the season. Jason Isringhausen needed surgery on his shoulder and elbow, sidelining him until late August.

New York's pitching staff looked different. Paul Byrd was traded to the Braves for reliever Greg McMichael. Jerry Dipoto was dealt to the Rockies for Armando Reynoso, who had gone 30-31 with a 4.65 ERA in four seasons with the Rockies. Rico Brogna was sent to the Phillies for relievers Toby Borland and Ricardo Jordan. Brogna once looked like a major piece in the team's rebuilding process but only played 55 games in 1996 because of a shoulder tear.

The team signed Todd Pratt, a former part-time catcher with the Phillies and Cubs, was out of the majors in 1996, working part-time delivering pizzas for Domino's and working as an instructor at Bucky Dent's baseball school. He lost out on the backup catching job in spring training but played well in Triple-A and would be called up.

He Was a Met?

Cory Lidle finished his rookie season as a Met 7-2 with a 3.53 ERA. He was claimed in the expansion draft. He played nine seasons before being killed in a plane crash in New York City in 2006.

Manny Alexander, Cal Ripken Jr.'s backup in Baltimore, was acquired to help the infield. The Mets assigned him No. 8 – Ripken's number – but he arranged with Carlos Baerga to switch to No. 6. The No. 8 "is a bad number," Alexander said. "Bad luck. I don't want that number to follow me."

Tim Bogar as traded to Houston for infielder Luis Lopez. Looking for a lefty reliever, the Mets picked up Yorkis Perez days before the start of the season. And the team added right-hander Barry Manuel from Montreal.

Bobby V at the Helm

Things were never boring where Bobby Valentine was concerned. His controversial comments ticked off players, the front office, and the media, and he famously returned to the bench in fake nose and glasses after being ejected. Critics accused him of overmanaging, but he was widely praised for outmanaging Dusty Baker and Tony La Russa in the 2000 playoffs. Valentine began managing at the big-league level in 1985 for the Texas Rangers at the young age of 35. He lasted there nearly 8 seasons, then managed the Mets for 6+ years. After 10 years off the field, Valentine came back in 2012 with the Red Sox, which did not go well as Boston finished last with 93 losses.

The Situation

Sports Illustrated picked the Mets to finish fourth in the division. There were plenty of questions with the team. Rey Ordonez's throws weren't sharp in spring training. Baerga struggled at the plate.

The Mets were interested in making a deal with San Diego for Japanese pitcher Hideki Irabu but would have to watch as the Padres dealt him to the Yankees.

There were seven pitchers going for five spots in the rotation. Pete Harnisch and Mark Clark struggled mightily but made the rotation. Bobby Jones and Dave Mlicki made it as well. Joe Crawford and Juan Acevedo went to the minors. The fifth starter would be Rick Reed, who pitched for four teams and spent 1996 in Triple-A Norfolk. Valentine and pitching coach Bob Apodaca liked him, though the manager asked some team leaders how they felt about Reed, who played during the strike. "I heard everything from 'I've forgotten about it' to 'Well, I still may need a little time,'" Valentine said. "But I never heard, 'I'll be the first to burn his uniform.'"

The Season

Harnisch started on Opening Day in San Diego. He had been nearly sleepless for a week after quitting chewing tobacco but pitched five shutout innings and took a 4-0 lead into the sixth. Chris Gomez, Rickey Henderson and Quilvio Veras hit back-to-back-to-back home runs to knock Harnisch out of the game. Perez entered and three batters later, the game was tied. Borland came in and walked three of the four batters he faced, including Gomez with the bases loaded as the Padres took a 5-4 lead. Manuel was called on and he plunked

FABULOUS: RICK REED

After 8 seasons in which he won a total of only 10 games, Rick Reed began a streak of 6 years with double figure wins, going 13-9 and finishing 6th in the league in ERA at 2.89.

Henderson, then walked Veras. Tony Gwynn's two-run single and Steve Finley's two-run double made it 11-4. The Mets would lose 12-5.

Harnisch was scratched from his next scheduled start because he was "mentally unprepared" to pitch. Suffering from depression and insomnia, he went on the DL and wouldn't be back until August.

The Mets started the season 3-6 on the West Coast, with three extra-inning losses. Perez was sent to the minors after two games.

The home opener was rained out and then the team lost a doubleheader to the Giants. Todd Hundley was batting .200 and Baerga was hitting .182. The Mets lost again the next day to fall to 3-9. New York won the final four games of the month to improve to 12-14. Jones had four of the 12 wins. Clark won his final three starts of the month. Olerud was batting .356. Edgardo Alfonzo brought his average up to .268.

On May 6, the Mets lost a 12-11 slugfest in Colorado. Borland gave up four runs in 1.1 innings of relief and his ERA increased to 6.08. It was his last game as a Met, as he would be sent to Boston with Rick Trlicek coming to New York. Trlicek would have an ERA of eight in nine appearances with the Mets.

Isringhausen got himself in some hot water when, after a conference call with reporters, called the team's public relations director Jay Horwitz "Jew boy." "We all talk to Jay like that," Isringhausen said. "Jay's almost like my brother. He is to everybody. That's stupid to think anybody would think anything bad about Jay." Isringhausen apologized and Horwitz said he wasn't offended.

Hundley was named NL Player of the Week after batting .444 with three home runs and 11 RBI. He hit two homers in a win at Colorado and had 10 through May 6. The Mets were rolling. Jones and John Franco combined to blank the Cardinals and the next day Carl Everett's ninth inning homer beat St. Louis and put the Mets over .500 for the first time all year.

FUTILE: PETE HARNISCH

Long Island native Pete Harnish won in the double digits five times in his career, but his 2+ year tenure with the Mets was a bust, as he went 10-20 in 44 starts. In 1997, before the Mets shipped him off to the Brewers in a trade deadline deal, Harnisch made 5 starts and relieved in one other game, going 0-1 with an ERA of 8.06.

The Mets finished May 18-9. Jones went 5-0 during the month, culminating with shutout of the Expos. Cory Lidle gave the Mets a reliable arm in the bullpen, going 3-0 with an ERA of one in his first seven outings. Reynoso improved to 4-0. Baerga busted out, batting .368 with 15 RBI during the month.

TOP BATTERS										
Pos	Name	G	AB	H	BA	HR	RBI	RS	SB	OPS
C	Todd Hundley	132	417	114	.273	30	86	78	2	.943
1B	John Olerud	154	524	154	.294	22	102	90	0	.889
3B	Edgardo Alfonzo	151	518	163	.315	10	72	84	11	.823
LF	Bernard Gilkey	145	518	129	.249	18	78	85	7	.755
RF	Butch Huskey	142	471	135	.287	24	81	61	8	.822

TOP PITCHERS										
Pos	Name	G	GS	W	L	SV	ERA	IP	SO	BB
SP	Rick Reed	33	31	13	9	0	2.89	208.1	113	31
SP	Dave Mlicki	32	32	8	12	0	4.00	193.2	157	76
SP	Bobby Jones	30	30	15	9	0	3.63	193.1	125	63
CL	John Franco	59	0	5	3	36	2.55	60.0	53	20
RP	Greg McMichael	73	0	7	10	7	2.98	87.2	81	27

Jones outdueled Pedro Martinez on June 3 and then beat the Reds in Cincinnati, winning eight straight starts to tie the club record, set by Tom Seaver in 1969 and tied by David Cone in 1988. Reynoso pitched a five-hit shutout in Florida to improve to 5-0. The Mets hit four homers in a 10-6 win over the Cubs at Wrigley Field.

Interleague play began for the first time, with the Red Sox taking two of three at Shea Stadium. Clark took a no-hitter into the eighth inning and even homered off Tim Wakefield in a 5-2 win over Boston. Then the Mets traveled to Yankee Stadium for three games. In the first, Mlicki pitched a shutout, striking out eight, with six Yankees going down looking.

The Yankees won the next two. Back at Shea, the Mets won six straight, including three walk-offs. Jason Hardtke's single beat the Pirates 7-6. Everett hit a walk-off homer in the 10th to beat the Pirates 12-9. Baerga was the hero against the Braves on June 24. He tied the game with a homer in the eighth and won it with a single in the ninth to beat Atlanta 6-5 and the Mets closed to within four games.

Atlanta avoided a sweep with Chipper Jones hitting two home runs off Bobby Jones in a 14-7 beatdown. The Mets pitching went into a funk. The team went to Detroit and gave up 31 runs in three games. Back in Queens, Reynoso gave up eight runs in 1.2 innings in a 10-4 loss to the Marlins.

A week after the All-Star break, McIlvaine was fired as GM, with 34-year-old assistant GM Steve Phillips taking his place two weeks before the trade deadline. "I had no idea this was coming," McIlvaine said. Owner Fred Wilpon said it was areas like finance, traveling with the team and meeting with the media that needed improvement. "The business of baseball has changed dramatically and the function of a general manager has changed dramatically," Wilpon said. "You can't be here and all over America."

Valentine said he knew people would blame him for the move. "In this situation, all I know is my hands are going to be dirtied, or bloodied, or whatever term they want to use," Valentine said. "But in time, they'll be cleansed."

Eight wins in 10 games improved the team's record to 59-43 and the Mets were in a race for the wild card, though an injury ended Reynoso's season. In early August, the team looked to improve its bullpen, acquiring Mel Rojas and Turk Wendell, along with outfielder Brian McRae. Lance Johnson, Clark and Alexander went to the Cubs. Rojas would set-up Franco. The right-hander was once reliable but had become a whipping boy at Wrigley Field for his struggles. Johnson was a reliable hitter at a time when Olerud and Gilkey were struggling. "We lose, in my opinion, the best leadoff hitter in the game," Hundley said. "We'll see how this works out in the long run."

There was also controversy surrounding Everett. A child-care worker at Shea noticed bruises on Everett's five-year-old daughter who was being taken care of the ballpark, along with her four-year-old brother. Police were called and the Administration for Children's Services took the kids away from the Everett's custody. Ultimately, a family court judge ruled the children would be placed in foster care until a hearing in October.

The team slumped through the month. Teams started accusing the Mets of videotaping managers, third base coaches and pitchers. The Phillies went as far as to speak to the league office about it.

Hundley was struggling, batting .195 in August. Valentine was asked about Hundley's injured elbow and sore toe and the manager suggested that the catcher get more sleep. Valentine said Hundley was always in his room for curfew and noted that he was dealing with his mother's illness and wife's pregnancy. But asked if there was a reference to Hundley's drinking or smoking, Valentine replied, "You said that, not me. I didn't say that." Days later, Valentine was given a contract extension that would take him through 2000.

Harnisch returned in August. After a few unimpressive starts, he was moved to the bullpen and his ERA ballooned to 8.06. He was traded to the Brewers after demanding more playing time. Harnisch called Valentine a "very low-grade person" and accused him of speaking with a "forked tongue." He did say he didn't mind being released by "people he didn't have respect for," meaning Valentine and pitching coach Bob Apodaca. Harnisch and Valentine got into an altercation at the lounge of a hotel where the team was staying.

The Mets were 6.5 games behind the Marlins after a 6-2 loss to the Giants but the team won six of seven, scoring 15 runs in a win against the Giants and 13 more in a win against the Orioles. The team swept the Blue Jays at Shea to begin September. The Mets lost four of five to fall to 77-66. They were seven games back of the wild card with 19 games remaining. New York showed one more spark, winning five of six, including two extra-inning wins and a 1-0 victory. The team even won a game they trailed 6-0 in the bottom of the ninth.

The fun ran out with a five-game losing streak, with the offense being held to two runs or less in four of the five games. The Mets would finish 88-74, four games behind the wild-card Marlins. The Braves and Marlins finished with the two best records in the NL. The Mets tied for the seventh-best record in all of baseball.

Top 5 Highlights

1 Carl Everett's pinch-hit two-run home run off Dennis Eckersley gives the Mets a 5-4 lead in the ninth on May 11. Butch Huskey follows with a homer and John Franco pitches a scoreless inning to close out New York's 6-4 win.

2 Dave Mlicki pitches a shutout in a 6-0 win over the Yankees on June 16, in the first regular season meeting between the two teams. The Mets jumped on Andy Pettitte for three runs in the first and John Olerud finishes with three RBI. Mlicki strikes out Derek Jeter looking to end the game.

3 Alex Ochoa's 10th inning home run off Mike Bielecki gives the Mets a 7-6 lead and Franco saves it for a come-from-behind win on July 13. Bobby Jones gave up six runs in the first. Huskey hit a two-run homer in the second, and a three-run shot in the fourth off Denny Neagle. The Mets tied the game in the fifth and the game remained tied until Ochoa's shot.

4 Carlos Baerga draws a bases loaded walk in the 11th to beat the Padres 9-8 on August 22. The Mets trailed 5-1 but scored four in the seventh to tie it. San Diego took an 8-5 lead in the ninth against Yorkis Perez and Mel Rojas. With two outs in the bottom of the ninth, Olerud's RBI double made it 8-6 and Todd Hundley tied the game with a two-run home run off Trevor Hoffman.

5 Bernard Gilkey's three-run home run off Mike Thurman gives the Mets a 9-6 win in 11 innings on September 13 against the Expos. The Mets trailed 6-0 in the ninth and had been held to one hit over the first eight innings. Down to the final out, Roberto Petagine singled in two runs, ending Hermanson's day. Luis Lopez singled off Shayne Bennett. Matt Franco singled off Ugueth Urbina to load the bases. Everett hit a 3-2 pitch over the wall in right-center to tie the game.

1998

	W	L	GB	Pos
	88	74	17.0	2nd
RS/G	RA/G		Manager	
4.39	3.98		Bobby Valentine	

Piazza and Leiter Lead a Second-Place Finish

The Moves

The Mets didn't acquire Gary Sheffield but they did take some talent from the World Series champion Marlins during their fire sale. Al Leiter, a 1996 All-Star, came to Queens in exchange for three minor leaguers, including A.J. Burnett. And the team traded two minor leaguers for lefty reliever Dennis Cook.

The outfield underwent an overhaul. Alex Ochoa was dealt to the Twins for Rich Becker. Ten days later, Carl Everett was sent to the Astros for John Hudek, a reliever who put up a 5.98 ERA in 40 games in 1997. Steve Phillips said Everett's situation – city officials taking his children into custody – had no bearing on the move.

The Situation

Bob Murphy was reminded of the Miracle Mets when he saw the 1998 squad. "What people forget about the '69 Mets is that all through April, you looked in the clubhouse, you saw a bunch of nobodies," he said. "There was no magic associated with the '69 team until after they won. This year you have a roster filled with solid, dependable guys, without a single marquee name among them. I think the club is poised to do something special."

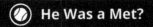

🎾 He Was a Met?

The only Opening Day catcher for the Mets from 1992 to 2005 not named Hundley or Piazza, Tim Spehr played 21 games before fracturing his wrist. He had two hits on Opening Day. Spehr's eight-year career included three stints with the Royals.

Al Leiter pitched for the Mets for 8 seasons, reaching double-digit wins in all of them. His best year was his first, 1998, when he won 17 games in 28 starts, finishing third in the league in ERA at 2.47. Leiter also pitched the Mets into the postseason with a brilliant 2-hit shutout in Game 163 against the Reds in 1990. In seven tough-luck postseason starts for Leiter for the Mets in 1999-2000, the lefty went 0-2, but posted a strong ERA of 3.57.

The bullpen was better as the Mets hoped they could rely on more than just John Franco and Greg McMichael. Phillips looked at the AL champion Indians for inspiration. "They have good starting pitching but they're not aces," he said. "And with a number of good starters and a very deep bullpen, they were proof that you can get to a World Series."

Tim Spehr was signed from Atlanta. The catcher with nine career homers launched five in March to win the starting job in place of an injured Todd Hundley. Masato Yoshii, who was signed in January from Japan, won a job in the rotation after pitching to a 2.05 ERA in 22 innings.

The Season

The exciting Mets pulled out one late win after another early in the season. Alberto Castillo's single with two outs in the bottom of the 14th gave the Mets a 1-0 Opening Day win. New York also pulled out consecutive walk-off wins against the Pirates, including a 13-inning victory on a Rich Becker single.

 Final Resting Ground

For some reason, the Mets picked up 39-year-old Tony Philips on July 31st, after more than 2000 games played in the AL. He played regularly for the last 2 months of the season. Philips moved on to Oakland for his age 40 season, after which retiring.

The Mets jumped out to a 13-7 start. Leiter won three straight starts, including back-to-back starts pitching seven shutout innings. But a six-game losing streak brought the Mets down to .500. Dave Mlicki struggled in April, going 0-3 with a 7.27 ERA. Edgardo Alfonzo and Bernard Gilkey were two of 10 players the team had to put on the Disabled List. Carlos Baerga was healthy but batting .198. New

York was 14-14 and scored three or fewer runs eight times in nine games. And Spehr was lost with a broken bone in his left wrist while tagging out Arizona's Kelly Stinnett.

An uneven start to the month saw the Mets return home from a west coast trip with a 20-19 record. The Mets found a fix for the offense: they acquired superstar catcher Mike Piazza from the Marlins for several minor leaguers including Preston Wilson. Piazza, a perennial

FABULOUS: JOHN OLERUD

In his second season with the Mets after being acquired from Toronto for Robert Person (!), John Olerud set single-season records for BA (.354) and OBA (.447). Olerud had another great year in 1999 before departing for Seattle as a free agent.

All-Star with the Dodgers, had been dealt to the Marlins a week earlier. Phillips had told Hundley he wouldn't be acquiring Piazza because they already a power-hitting catcher but then pulled the trigger.

Hundley said, "it makes us a better team, but where do we both play if we're in the lineup together? They made the trade. They have to decide."

The Mets won seven straight after acquiring Piazza to end the month on a nine-game winning streak. Rick Reed went 5-0 in May, giving up six earned runs in 36.1 innings. Yoshii went 3-0 during the month, including a complete game victory against the Reds. Bobby Jones also went 3-0 in May.

Piazza hit his first homer as a Met on June 1 in Pittsburgh but the Mets started the month getting swept by the Pirates. On June 4, the Mets and Dodgers made a deal for disappointing starters as Mlicki and his 5.68 ERA was sent to LA for Hideo Nomo. The 1995 NL Rookie of the Year was 2-7 with a 5.05 ERA. Also in the deal were McMichael, going from New York to LA and Brad Clontz coming to Queens. The Mets struggled in mid-June, losing six of eight in one stretch to the Marlins and Expos, including three walk-offs.

While several relievers scuffled such as Hudek and Brian Bohanon, nobody fell off like Mel Rojas. The right-hander had a 1.93 ERA in early June before losing it. Three earned runs in 0.2 innings in Florida on June 14; two earned runs on five hits and a walk in a 5-4 loss to the Expos on the 17th; two more earned runs in an inning on the 20th against the Marlins.

FUTILE: MEL ROJAS

Mel Rojas had a 6.05 ERA in 50 games. He had an ERA of 8.59 in August, giving up 14 earned runs in 14.2 innings. Rojas is best remembered for giving up a three-run homer to Paul O'Neill in the first regular season Mets-Yankees game at Shea.

On June 26, the Yankees came to Shea for the first time in the regular season. The Mets were holding on to a 4-3 lead in the seventh when Bobby Valentine brought in Rojas to pitch to Paul O'Neill instead of lefty Brian Bohanon. O'Neill greeted him with a three-run homer to left and the Yankees went on to win 8-4.

TOP BATTERS

Pos	Name	G	AB	H	BA	HR	RBI	RS	SB	OPS
C	Mike Piazza	109	394	137	.348	23	76	67	1	1.024
1B	John Olerud	160	557	197	.354	22	93	91	2	.998
3B	Edgardo Alfonzo	144	557	155	.278	17	78	94	8	.782
CF	Brian McRae	159	552	146	.264	21	79	79	20	.822

TOP PITCHERS

Pos	Name	G	GS	W	L	SV	ERA	IP	SO	BB
SP	Rick Reed	31	31	16	11	0	3.48	212.1	153	29
SP	Al Leiter	28	28	17	6	0	2.47	193.0	174	71
SP	Masato Yoshii	29	29	6	8	0	3.93	171.2	117	53
CL	John Franco	61	0	0	8	38	3.62	64.2	59	29
RP	Dennis Cook	73	0	8	4	1	2.38	68.0	79	27

Leiter, who had won six straight decisions before Rojas blew the lead to the Yankees, was lost for several weeks with an injury.

The Blue Jays battered the Mets 15-10 on July 1 as Nomo failed to make it out of the third inning. Rojas came in with the Mets leasing 8-7 in the eighth: single, single, three-run homer, hit by pitch, walk. Hudek came in, struggled andwas traded two days later to the Reds for Lenny Harris.

In the final game before the All-Star break, the Mets lost 3-2 when Atlanta's Michael Tucker scored on a sac fly to left despite appearing to never touch home plate. Franco would later be suspended three games for bumping home plate umpire Angel Hernandez during the ensuing argument.

Back from the break, Franco gave up a go-ahead single in an 11-inning loss to the Expos. The next night, Franco had the Expos down to their final out in a 6-5 game but Mark Grudzielanek singled to tie it and Mark Andrews followed with a two-run triple to stun the Mets. How to improve the bullpen? The Mets reacquired McMichael with Bohanon going to LA. "It's a strange situation," McMichael said. "I should ask for a raise for mental stability."

Hundley returned to play left field on July 11. John Olerud stole the night though with a pair of homers in a win over the Expos as the first baseman raised his average to .330. Brian McRae also homered, the first of six he would hit in July. After a 3-1 loss to the Pirates on July 20, the Mets were 48-46 but the team responded by winning six straight, including doubleheader sweeps in Milwaukee and Chicago.

At the trade deadline, the team sent Pulsipher, who had a 6.91 ERA in 15 games, to the Brewers for minor league infielder Mike Kinkade. The team also sent Bernard Gilkey to Arizona for Jorge Fabergas and Willie Blair. The Mets also acquired utility player Tony Phillips from Toronto. Gilkey was hitting a disappointing .227 with four homers in 82 games. Blair was 4-15 with a 5.34

ERA. The acquisition of Fabergas meant Todd Pratt was optioned to Triple-A despite batting .313 in 24 games as Piazza's backup.

Armando Reynoso returned from surgery in late July and Valentine went to a six-man rotation. Reynoso came back sharp, winning his first five starts with a 1.54 ERA. Reed went 5-1 in August, including a complete game win against the Dodgers. Piazza hit eight homers in the month. The Mets began the month 16-7 to improve to 72-57 and took the lead in the NL wild card race.

In early September, the Mets even took three of four from the Braves. Phillips hitting a two-run homer as a Met in the bottom of the eighth to give New York a 5-4 lead in the second game of the series and two nights later Alfonzo hit a two-run homer off John Rocker in the bottom of the eighth to give the Mets an 8-7 lead.

The Mets gave up seven homers in Philadelphia on September 8 in a 16-4 loss (Rojas gave up three in his final appearance as a Met) but New York took the next two. After losing two of three in Montreal, the Mets took three of four from the first place Astros in Houston. Down to their final strike in the series finale, Piazza launched a three-run homer off Billy Wagner. Cook blew the save but Hundley put the Mets ahead with a pinch-hit homer in the 11th. How sweet it was for Hundley who saw his outfield experiment end in late August because of the misadventures on fly balls as well as runners taking extra bases on his arm. His batting average was at .164 when he was removed from the outfield and relegated to pinch-hitting status.

But in their first game back home from the Texas triumph, Franco blew a 6-4 ninth inning lead to the Marlins for a stunning 7-6 loss. The Mets did recover to win the next two games and were 88-69 with five left to play, leading the Cubs in the wild card race by one game.

Reynoso couldn't hold a three-run lead against the Expos and the Mets lost 5-3 in the first of a two-game series, with the Mets being held scoreless for the final eight innings. The bats didn't wake up the next night as Carl Pavano and five Montreal relievers combined to blank the Mets on three hits in a 3-0 game. Still, the Mets were tied for the wild card with three games left and a trip to Atlanta left.

In the series opener, the Mets trailed 5-3 when Olerud came up with two on and two out. He singled off Rudy Seanez to make it 5-4, but Jay Payton, in his 14th career game, was easily thrown out trying to advance to third with Piazza on deck. Atlanta added an insurance run in the bottom of the eighth but the Mets fought back, scoring once in the ninth and getting the tying run to third before Pratt struck out against Rocker to end the 6-5 loss.

Still tied for the wild card with two games left, Leiter pitched five shutout innings before surrendering three runs in the sixth in what became a 4-0 loss. Needing a win on the final day of the season and losses from the Cubs and Giants to stay alive, Valentine had to choose between starting Reynoso, who was 7-2, and Nomo, who was 6-12, had not pitched in 18 days but had better numbers against Atlanta. Valentine approached Nomo about starting. Nomo declined. Reynoso gave up gave up five runs in 1.2 innings and the Mets lost

7-2. Nomo pitched four innings of shutout relief. Both the Cubs and Giants lost but it didn't matter.

The season was over after a stunning five-game stretch in which they scored 10 runs in 44 innings.

Top 5 Highlights

1 Alberto Castillo singles off Ricky Bottalico in the bottom of the 14th to give the Mets a 1-0 win in a four-hour, 35-minute Opening Day. Bobby Jones and Curt Schilling matched zeroes before the game was handed off to the bullpens.

2 Mike Piazza delivers a fifth inning RBI double off Milwaukee's Jeff Juden on May 23 in his first game as a Met. Al Leiter pitches a complete game shutout and even collects two hits.

3 Rick Reed retires the first 20 Devil Rays and pitches a three-hit shutout in New York's 3-0 win on June 8. Wade Boggs doubles with two outs in the seventh for the first Tampa Bay hit.

4 Luis Lopez's sac fly gives the Mets a 2-1 win over the Yankees on June 28. Facing Ramiro Mendoza with Carlos Baerga on third and Brian McRae on first, Lopez flies out to Paul O'Neill in right. O'Neill throws the ball to first, not in time to get McRae. After some initial confusion, it's ruled that Baerga crossed the plate in time and the Mets win.

5 Mike Piazza hits a three-run homer to right-center off Billy Wagner to give the Mets, down to their final strike, a 3-2 lead in Houston on September 16. Brad Ausmus homers off Cook in the bottom of the ninth but Todd Hundley hits a pinch-hit homer off Sean Bergman in the top of the 11th and Turk Wendell strikes out the side to preserve the win.

1999

	W	L	GB	Pos
	97	66	6.5	2nd

RS/G	RA/G	Manager	
5.23	4.36	Bobby Valentine	

Mets Just Miss World Series

The Moves

Mike Piazza signed the richest contract in baseball history, a $91 million deal for seven seasons. (Less than two months later, the Dodgers signed pitcher Kevin Brown for $105 million.) "This tells the fans that we appreciate the fact that they came back to watch us play after we acquired Mike," Nelson Doubleday said. "They wanted a marquee player, we needed a marquee player and we got them a marquee player."

Steve Phillips took a brief absence as a former employee threatened to sue him for alleged sexual harassment. Frank Cashen returned to serve as temporary GM. It was during Cashen's time that a trade was completed sending Mel Rojas to the Dodgers for Bobby Bonilla, a deal including two of the least popular Mets of all time. The Dodgers had hired Davey Johnson as manager, and there was little chance of the team keeping Bonilla, who had feuded with Johnson in Baltimore. The Mets were hoping for a Bobby Bo that was a bit mellower than he was in the earlier part of the decade. "My hope is he blends in more this time," Steve Phillips said. "There aren't the same expectations. And now we have other quote makers on the team."

Roger Cedeno and Armando Benitez were acquired in a three-team deal that saw Todd Hundley got to the Dodgers. Cedeno would give the team a speedy outfielder and Benitez would be the set-up man for Franco. The Mets outbid the Orioles for third baseman Robin Ventura, giving him four years, $32 million. The All-Star and five-time Gold Glove winner was at the hot corner

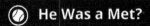

He Was a Met?

Brooklyn native Shawon Dunston came to the Mets in a trade deadline deal, played outfield exclusively, and batted .344 in 93 at bats. That winter he was gone, as quickly as he had arrived.

Forty-year-old Rickey Henderson played a significant role on the 1999 Mets, putting up a slash line of .315/.423/.466. He also scored 89 runs and stole 37 bases in 121 games. The Mets released him in May 2000 after a slow start.

with Edgardo Alfonzo moving to second base.

Rickey Henderson, who turned 41 on Christmas, was signed. He batted a career-low .236 with Oakland in 1998 but led the league in walks and stolen bases. His 66 steals were four more than the Mets had as a team.

Right-handed pitcher Pat Mahomes was signed. He had gone 18-28 with a 5.82 ERA with the Twins, and had an ERA of 6.85 in two seasons with the Red Sox. In the final days of spring training, Orel Hershiser was signed. The 1988 NL Cy Young winner had been released by Cleveland and the Mets needed a starter as Hideo Nomo struggled in March. Nomo would be let go.

The Situation

The Braves still looked to be the team to beat in the NL East, but the revamped Mets were a popular pick for the wild card spot and there was a possibility of the first Mets-Yankees World Series.

The Season

Mets' first 13 games were against the Marlins and Expos, and New York went 8-5. Bobby Jones hit a homer in the home opener and won his first three starts. John Franco notched his 400th career save. The team played around .500 with Mike Piazza on the DL with a right knee injury. A six-game winning streak from late April to the beginning of May improved the team to 17-9. John Olerud was on fire, batting .364. Henderson went on the DL in early May and Cedeno moved into the leadoff spot. He hit .344 and stole 23 bases during the month.

 Final Resting Ground

The Mets traded Greg McMichael to the Dodgers in June 1999, and 5 weeks later the Dodgers traded him back to the Mets. Three weeks later, the Mets traded McMichael to Oakland where he finished the 1999 season, and after a mini-farewell tour in 2000 with his original team, the Braves, McMichael went to where he could be traded no more.

He credited Bobby Valentine with giving him a green light on the bases after coming from the Dodgers, who had tried to reign him in.

After the 17-9 start, the team lost nine of 13. Jones was pounded in three straight starts late in the month, went on the DL and didn't return until mid-September. After missing 1998, Jason Isringhausen returned to the rotation but was moved to the bullpen for the first time since college after posting a 7.30 ERA in five starts. On May 29, Allen Watson made his first start in a month and failed to make it out of the fourth inning. He would be traded to Seattle after two more relief appearances. The Mets improved to 27-20 with Hershiser, off to a bad start to the season, beating the Pirates.

> **FABULOUS: EDGARDO ALFONZO**
>
> *Alfonzo blossomed into a star in 1999, putting up a slash line of .304/.384/.502, driving in 107 runs while scoring 123. Alfonzo played 2B exclusively in 1999, and he was outstanding, committing only 5 errors all season.*

Returning to Shea, the Mets could nothing right. They were swept by the Diamondbacks, giving up 18 runs in the final two games. Then the Reds came to Queens and swept the Mets. John Franco blew his first save on June 2, after converting his first 14 opportunities. Fred Wilpon and Phillips said Valentine would remain manager for the rest of the season.

The team went to Yankee Stadium and lost the first two games of the series, falling under .500. Valentine wasn't fired, but pitching coach Bob Apodaca, bullpen coach Randy Niemann and hitting coach Tom Robson, were. The Mets had a 4.84 ERA, 12th in the NL, with the starters struggling, going 18-24 with a 5.69 ERA. And despite leading the NL in on-base percentage, the Mets were eighth in runs scored. Apodaca had been with Valentine on the coaching staff in Triple-A and Robson had been on Valentine's staff with the Rangers. Valentine's relationship with Phillips was becoming increasingly strained. Dave Wallace was the new pitching coach, Al Jackson the bullpen coach and Mickey Brantley the hitting coach. Valentine then put his own job on the line. "I'm not worried about my job. I believe, though, that if in the next 55 games we're not better, I shouldn't be the manager. If we're dealing with 55 games and if it just cost a few guys their jobs, I can't see lasting much past that. That's fine with me."

On June 6, the Mets began to turn their season around. Al Leiter, entering the night 2-5 with a 6.39 ERA, gave up one run in seven innings and Piazza homered off Roger Clemens in a 7-2 win. Even the struggling Bonilla, who was batting under .170, had a two-run

> **FUTILE: BOBBY BONILLA**
>
> *Bobby Bonilla came back to the Mets in the winter of 1998 in a trade with the Dodgers for pitcher Mel Rojas (1998 ERA 6.05). Bonilla got into 60 games for the Amazins, going 19-for 119, good for a BA of .160, and collected 4 HR.*

double. Three days later, Valentine was ejected arguing a catcher's interference call but reappeared in the dugout with a fake moustache and sunglasses. The Mets won in 14, but the TV camera picked up Valentine and he was fined and suspended for two games. New York was hot, winning 15 of 18. On June 15, the team hit six home runs in an 11-3 win in Cincinnati. The team won three of four in St. Louis and swept the Marlins at Shea. The Mets even pounded the Braves 10-2 in a win at Turner Field. Benny Agbayani hit 10 home runs in his first 73 at-bats. Piazza hit seven home runs in 14 games. Leiter went 5-0 with a 2.62 ERA in June. Rick Reed won three straight starts.

Despite the hot stretch, Atlanta was still ahead. The Braves won two of three in Atlanta and two of three at Shea a week later, including a 16-0 win on fireworks night, though Matt Franco did strike out Andruw Jones. Adding injury to insult, an injured finger put John Franco on the DL for two months. Benitez would step in and save eight games in nine opportunities in July.

The Mets avoided a sweep with a 7-6 win on July 4, with Alfonzo hitting a go-ahead three-run homer off John Smoltz in the seventh. The team wouldn't lose a series until early August. The Mets took a series from the Yankees for the first time, with Piazza going deep in both wins. Hershiser beat the Expos for his 200th career victory. Octavio Dotel made his debut in late June and after losing his debut would win seven straight decisions.

Kenny Rogers was acquired from Oakland in late July. The Mets couldn't pull off a deal for him in the offseason but finally landed the veteran southpaw, who pitched for Valentine in Texas. His first win was in Milwaukee on August 4, and he even delivered an RBI single. Rogers would win his first five decisions. Veteran infielder Shawon Dunston was acquired from St. Louis. Isringhausen and Greg McMichael were sent to Oakland for right-hander Billy Taylor. Brian McRae and Rigo Beltran were sent to the Rockies for outfielder Darryl Hamilton and southpaw Chuck McElroy. McRae was batting .221 and Hamilton was batting .303 at the time of the deal. The Mets had been trying to move McRae – and Bonilla – for weeks. McRae had been critical of Valentine's lineup changes and also said the Expos played better against the Mets than other teams because they hated Valentine.

The team moved into the lead for the wild card in late July. The team took two of three at Wrigley Field, coming back from a 7-2 deficit to win 10-9 with Mahomes pitching 4.2 innings of relief, and then delivering the go-ahead single in the 13th two days later. The long reliever was 5-0 and was also batting .400. His reliable pitching was helpful in keeping games from turning into blowouts and also lowered pressure on other relievers. Dennis Cook and Turk Wendell also provided solid relief as a lefty-righty tandem. When Hershiser beat the Brewers on August 3, the Mets moved into first place. Reed had to go on the DL, leaving the second inning of a game against the Dodgers. He would miss a month.

New York won four of six out West, with Ventura hitting his third grand slam of the season in a win against the Giants. Rogers pitched a complete game and then took a shutout into the ninth against Houston. Cedeno set the team stolen base mark, swiping his 59th bag on August 30. Hamilton hit a grand slam

TOP BATTERS

Pos	Name	G	AB	H	BA	HR	RBI	RS	SB	OPS
C	Mike Piazza	141	534	162	.303	40	124	100	2	.936
1B	John Olerud	162	581	173	.298	19	96	107	3	.890
2B	Edgardo Alfonzo	158	628	191	.304	27	108	123	9	.886
3B	Robin Ventura	161	588	177	.301	32	120	88	1	.908
LF	Rickey Henderson	121	438	138	.315	12	42	89	37	.889

TOP PITCHERS

Pos	Name	G	GS	W	L	SV	ERA	IP	SO	BB
SP	Al Leiter	32	32	13	12	0	4.23	213.0	162	93
SP	Orel Hershiser	32	32	13	12	0	4.58	179.0	89	77
SP	Masato Yoshii	31	29	12	8	0	4.40	174.0	105	58
CL	Armando Benitez	77	0	4	3	22	1.85	78.0	128	41
RP	Dennis Cook	71	0	10	5	3	3.86	63.0	68	27

against the Rockies. John Franco returned on September 5, though Benitez would remain as closer.

The infield of Ventura, Ordonez, Alfonzo and Olerud made the cover of *Sports Illustrated* with the headline "The Best Infield Ever?" The four combined for 27 errors. Ordonez, who had to miss several games after being punched on the team bus by Luis Lopez, even hit a grand slam in an 11-1 win over the Phillies. An 8-6 win against the Phillies improved the record to 92-58, one game behind Atlanta and were heading to Atlanta for a three-game series, though New York was still 3.5 games ahead of the Reds for the wild card. The rotation was moved to get Leiter a start. Dotel was eliminated from the six-man rotation, going to the bullpen. Facing Smoltz, Tom Glavine and Greg Maddux, the Mets scored six runs and were swept.

A trip to Philadelphia against the sub-.500 Phillies was next but again the Mets were held to six runs in three games and were swept. Valentine, like he did in June, put himself on the hot seat. "If we don't get into the playoffs, I shouldn't come back," he said. The Braves came to Shea Stadium and annihilated Hershiser, knocking him out in the first inning of a 9-3 win. The Mets got a much-needed win the next night, with Olerud hitting a grand slam off Maddux in a 9-2 victory. In the finale, Atlanta edged out the Mets in 11 innings, seemingly delivering a knockout punch to the Mets' season.

The Mets were two games behind the Reds with three games left, and the Reds were in Milwaukee to play the fifth-place Brewers. The Pirates came to Shea and Rogers pitched a gem, striking out 10. Ventura and Piazza homered and Rogers took a 2-0 lead into the eighth. But the Pirates cut the lead to 2-1 and then tied it with Franco on the mound. With the bases loaded, Franco struck out Adrian Brown looking at a 3-2 pitch. In the bottom of the 11th, Ventura's single with two outs and the bases loaded off Scott Sauerbeck gave the Mets a 3-2 win. Combined with Milwaukee's comeback over the Reds, the Mets were one game back.

On October 2, the Brewers beat the Reds 10-6, meaning a win would put the Mets in a tie for the wild card. Piazza hit his 40th home run and Reed pitched a three-hit shutout, striking out 12 and improving to 11-5.

Hershiser started Game 162 and fell behind 1-0 in the first. The Mets tied the game on Hamilton's RBI double in the fourth. The Pirates put two on with two outs in the ninth but Benitez fanned Aramis Ramirez. In the bottom of the ninth, Melvin Mora and Alfonzo singled, putting runners on the corners. Olerud was intentionally walked, loading the bases for Piazza. Brad Clontz came in from the bullpen and threw his first pitch to the backstop, allowing Mora to score the winning run. The Mets were still alive. The Reds beat the Brewers to tie the Mets after waiting out a nearly six-hour rain delay.

The Mets traveled to Cinergy Field for the 163rd game of the season. The winner would go on to the NLDS. The loser would go home. Facing Steve Parris, Henderson led off with a single and Alfonzo homered. Two batters in, it was 2-0. Ventura later walked with the bases loaded, Henderson homered off Denny Neagle and Alfonzo added an RBI double. It was more than enough for Leiter, who pitched a two-hit shutout and fanned seven in the 5-0 win. After being written off after losing eight of nine, the Mets were in the postseason for the first time since 1988.

Top 5 Highlights

1 Mike Piazza's two-run homer off Trevor Hoffman gives the Mets a 4-3 win over the Padres on April 28. San Diego had won 181 straight games when leading after eight innings.

2 Matt Franco's two-run single with two outs and two strikes off Mariano Rivera beats the Yankees 9-8 on July 10. The Yankees hit six home runs in the back-and-forth affair. Piazza's three-run homer off Ramiro Mendoza put the Mets up 7-6 in the seventh. The home run went 482 feet and landed on the picnic area behind the bleachers. Jorge Posada's two-run homer in the eighth off Dennis Cook put the Yankees up 8-7.

3 Edgardo Alfonzo's walk-off single off Ricky Bottalico gives the Mets an 8-7 win over the Cardinals on August 22. Joe McEwing led off with a home run and Mark McGwire hit his 49th and 50th homers of the season, including a shot off the Shea scoreboard. The Met trailed 6-1 in the eighth when Olerud hit a grand slam and Piazza followed with a game-tying home run off Rick Croushore. The Cardinals took the lead in the top of the ninth but the Mets rallied in the bottom of the inning. After two walks, Rickey Henderson tied the game with a double to right.

4 Alfonzo goes 6-6 with three home runs in a 17-1 win over the Astros on August 30. Alfonzo homered in the first off Shane Reynolds, doubled in the second, hit a fourth inning home run off Brian Williams, hit a sixth inning home run off Sean Bergman, singled to left in the eighth and doubled off Trever Miller in the ninth.

5 Al Leiter pitches a two-hit shutout on October 4 in Cincinnati, sending the Mets to the playoffs for the first time in 11 years. Alfonzo and Henderson go deep in the 5-0 win.

1999 NLDS

The Mets would face NL Cy Young winner Randy Johnson in Game 1 of the NLDS. The Arizona Diamondbacks went 100-62 in the second season of the franchise. Alfonzo again put the Mets on the board with a first inning homer. Olerud hit a two-run home run off Johnson in the third. After Arizona scratched out a run against Yoshii in the third, Ordonez's squeeze bunt extended the lead to 4-1. Erubiel Durazo's fourth inning homer cut the lead to 4-2. In the sixth, Luis Gonzalez tied the game with a two-run blast. The game remained tied until the ninth. Ventura led off with a single. With one out, Ordonez singled and Mora walked. Right-hander Bobby Chouinard came in and got Henderson to ground into a 5-2 force. With two outs, Alfonzo hit a grand slam to left. Benitez pitched a 1-2-3 bottom of the ninth and the Mets had a 1-0 series lead.

Arizona tied the series the next night with a 7-1 victory, jumping on Rogers for four runs in 4.1 innings but at least the Mets had a split heading back to Shea. Piazza wouldn't be available as he aggravated a thumb injury and Todd Pratt was in the lineup batting seventh, with Agbayani moved to the cleanup spot. The Mets took a 3-0 lead against Omar Daal but Turner Ward's two-run homer in the fifth off Reed cut it to 3-2. New York broke the game open with a six-run sixth.

It was a pair of southpaws, Leiter and Brian Anderson, on the mound in Game 4. Alfonzo gave the Mets a 1-0 lead with a fourth inning homer and Greg Colbrunn tied it with a homer in the fifth. Agbayani's RBI double made it 2-1 in the sixth. Leiter retired the first two batters in the eighth but walked Ward and allowed a single to Tony Womack, ending his day. Jay Bell greeted Benitez with a two-run double and Arizona had a 3-2 lead. Roger Cedeno then tied it at 3 with a sacrifice fly. The game was still 3-3 in the 10th when Pratt came to the plate. He hit Mantei's 1-0 pitch deep to center. Steve Finley went back and jumped for the ball but couldn't grab it.

1999 NLCS

In Game 1 of the 1999 NLCS, Maddux gave up one run in seven innings and the Braves beat Yoshii 4-2. The Mets took a 2-0 lead against Kevin Millwood in the second game, with Mora hitting a home run. In the sixth, Brian Jordan tied the game with a home off Rogers. Andruw Jones followed with a single. Valentine left Rogers in and watched as Eddie Perez homered to make it 4-2. The Mets scored once in the eighth but Smoltz closed it out in the ninth.

Back at Shea, Leiter and Glavine dueled. The Braves scored an unearned run in the first inning and that was it. Glavine pitched seven shutout innings. John Rocker entered the game in the ninth. Rocker, who said "I hate the Mets" in September, was becoming public enemy No. 1 in Queens. "The hell with New York fans," he said. "They're a bunch of stupid asses anyway." Rocker pitched a scoreless ninth against the quiet Mets offense.

Reed and Smoltz were in a scoreless duel until Olerud homered in the sixth. In the eighth Jordan and Ryan Klesko hit back-to-back homers to give the Braves a 2-1 lead. In the bottom of the inning Olerud hit a grounder up the with runners on second and third driving in two runs. Benitez pitched a 1-2-3 ninth to keep the Mets alive.

Henderson led off Game 5 with an infield single off Maddux and Olerud hit a two-run home run. Yoshii pitched three shutout innings but the Braves tied the game with three straight hits in the fourth. Hershiser pitched 3.1 innings of shutout relief. In the top of the sixth, Maddux came up with the bases loaded and one out. The Met turned an inning-ending double play as failed to get a bunt down and Klesko was caught stealing home. In the eighth, Andruw Jones flied out against Mahomes with the bases loaded. It was still 2-2 in the 13th when Chipper Jones doubled to right off Dotel but the Mets turned a relay, Mora to Alfonzo to Piazza, to nail Keith Lockhart at the plate. In the 15th, Lockhart's RBI triple gave the Braves a 3-2 lead. Dunston led off with a single against Kevin McGlinchy and Matt Franco followed with a walk. Alfonzo and Olerud was intentionally walked to load the bases. Pratt worked a walk to tie the game. Ventura came up and hit a 2-1 pitch over the wall in right-center to end the five-hour, 46 minute game. Ventura was mobbed by teammates before reaching second base, so it went in the books as a single and a 4-3 win.

Back at Turner Field, the Braves knocked Leiter out in the first and took a 5-0 lead. The Mets scored three in the sixth but Jose Hernandez's two-run single off Cook made it 7-3. Facing Smoltz in the seventh, Franco and Henderson doubled to cut the lead to 7-4. Two batters later, Olerud singled to make it 7-5. Then Piazza homered to right-center, tying the game. In the eighth, Mora's RBI single off Remlinger gave the Mets an 8-7 lead. But Atlanta tied the game against John Franco. Perez singled, pinch-runner Otis Nixon stole second, moved to third on a Piazza error and scored on Brian Hunter's single. The Mets took a 10th inning lead on Pratt's sacrifice fly off Rocker. But Guillen's RBI single off Benitez tied the game. Rogers took the mound in the 11th and Gerald Williams led off with a double. Bret Boone bunted him over and the next two batters were intentionally walked. Andruw Jones worked the count to 3-2 and Rogers threw ball four, ending the series and the season.

Quiz #6: 2000s

1. Who was the Mets starting RF in the pennant-winning 2000 season? He suffered a high ankle sprain after only one AB in Game 1 of the NLDS and did not appear again in the postseason. **[10 points]**

2. Mike Hampton and Al Leiter won 15 and 16 games, respectively, for the 2000 Mets, and their other 3 starters each won 11. Who were the other 3? **[10 points for 2, 4 bonus points for all 3]**

3. (2000) The Mets won the critical Game 3 of the NLDS against the SF Giants 3-2 in 13 innings. How did the winning run score? **[8 points]**

4. (2000) Who was the winning pitcher in the Mets' only victory in the 2000 World Series, Game 3 a 4-2 victory. **[8 points]**

5. (2000) Who paced the Mets with 8 hits and a .400 BA in 2000 World Series (though he drove in and scored only 1 run)? **[12 points]**

6. Trades between the Mets and Yankees are rare. Who are the 2 big-name players the teams swapped in the winter of 2001? **[5 points for each]**

7. What was Todd Zeile's notable accomplishment in the last game of his career on October 3, 2004? **[8 points]**

8. (2000s) Name the Mets player—known for his strong defense—who in the first of his 2 seasons with the team led the Amazins' with 30 HR. **[10 points]**

9. (2000s) Name the Mets manager with the second highest overall winning percentage behind Davey Johnson's sparkling .588. **[8 points]**

10. What team beat out the Mets by one game for the 2007 NL East title? **[8 points]**

11. (2000s) Name the infielder who despite six solid years in the minors and two years as a backup for the Mets, was claimed off waivers in the winter of 2003 and went on play 11 for seasons, mostly in the AL, achieving a 100-RS season, an All-Star selection, and lifetime BA of .277 in nearly 5000 career at bats. **[12 points]**

12. (2006) Who is the Hall of Fame pitcher the Mets KO'd after 4 innings on their way to sweeping the Dodgers in the clinching game of the 2006 NLDS? **[10 points]**

13. 2006 What was the decisive blow against the Mets' in their Game 7 loss to the St. Louis Cardinals of the 2006 NLCS? What pitcher allowed it? **[4 points for batter, 4 points for pitcher]**

14. (2007) Name the two pitchers who tied for the team lead in wins, posting identical 15-10 records. **[6 points each]**

15. (2000s) Who holds the Mets record for most RBI in a game? **[8 points]**

16. For which team did Justin Turner make his major league debut (in 2009)? **[8 bonus points]**

Quiz #6: TOTAL POINTS – 142; BONUS POINTS – 12

2000

	W	L	GB	Pos
	94	68	1.0	2nd
RS/G	RA/G		Manager	
4.98	4.56		Bobby Valentine	

New Acquisitions Help Mets Win NL

The Moves

The Mets received an early Christmas present when they acquired Houston ace Mike Hampton on December 23. Hampton, a 22-game winner in 1999, came to Queens along with Derek Bell in a trade that sent Roger Cedeno, Octavio Dotel and minor league pitcher Kyle Kessel to the Astros. "We've waited for this opportunity for a long time to secure a starter of Mike Hampton's ilk," Steve Phillips said.

John Olerud signed with Seattle and the Mets responded by signing Todd Zeile, after they failed to pull off a trade for Toronto first baseman Carlos Delgado. Zeile hit .293 with 24 home runs and 98 RBI in 1999 at third base for Texas. Ken Griffey Jr. vetoed a trade from the Mariners to the Mets, not surprising because of his desire to play in Cincinnati. Bobby Bonilla was released, despite still being owed $5.9 million. Bonilla and his agent made a deal with the Mets: the team would pay him $1.19 annually every July 1 from 2011 through 2035.

Masato Yoshii was sent to the Rockies for lefty pitcher Bobby M. Jones. Luis Lopez was traded to the Brewers with Bill Pulsipher returning to Shea Stadium. The team also signed shortstop Kurt Abbott.

Jesse Orosco came back to the Mets in a deal that sent Chuck McElroy to Baltimore. The problem was this gave the Mets four left-handed relievers. It came down to Orosco and the college roomate of Steve Phillips, Rich Rodriguez. Orosco was sent to St. Louis for utility infielder Joe McEwing.

Charlie Hayes hit .386 in spring training but was released.

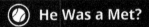

He Was a Met?

When you think of the NL champ 2000 Mets, Derek Bell's name does not jump to mind, but Bell was the full-time right fielder, playing in 144 games, finishing with 18 HR, 69 RBI and 87 RS.

The Situation

The Mets had four pitchers competing for the final spot in the rotation, with Glendon Rusch beating out southpaw Bobby M. Jones, knuckleballer Dennis Springer and Pulsipher. Jesse Orosco came back to the Mets in a deal that sent Chuck McElroy to Baltimore. The problem was this gave the Mets four left-handed relievers. It came down to Orosco and the college roomate of Steve Phillips, Rich Rodriguez. Orosco was sent to St. Louis for utility infielder Joe McEwing. Benny Agbayani asked to be traded as an option to Triple-A looked likely, but the Mets kept him with the major league club as Agbayani was on the Opening day roster.

Turk Wendell

Turk Wendell set a team record by pitching in 80 games in 1999 and 77 more in 2000. But the reliable righty reliever was popular with fans for his quirks, including jumping over foul lines on his way to and from the mound, slamming the rosin bag before facing batters, and his shark-tooth necklace. Wendell won a total of 3 games in the postseason for the Mets in 1999 and 2000, but lost Game 1 of the 2000 World Series Wendell was also quite outspoken, and at the height of the steroids era, broken off from the players' code of silence and called out Barry Bonds and Sammy Sosa by name.

"Clearly we look like an improved team, but you never know how things will mesh until you go out and play. I've been on teams with great talent that just don't work out. Everyone has to come through," Ventura said.

The Season

After a 5-7 start, the Mets won nine straight and 11 of 14 to end April. The team scored at least 10 runs five times in the 14-game stretch. Bell was batting .385 with four home runs, including a go-ahead shot in the eighth inning in the first game at Shea, quickly winning over the fans. Piazza was batting .368 with five home runs. Alfonzo was hitting .348 with four home runs. Agbayani was hitting .321 and Zeile was batting .302. Melvin Mora hit his first home run, a walk-off shot to beat the Brewers. The Mets were winning despite Hampton losing his first three starts and going 2-4 with a 6.48 ERA early in the season.

May began with the Mets losing four straight in San Francisco, a series which saw Jeff Kent beat the Mets with a three-run home run and the benches clear after Dennis Cook hit Marvin Bernard. The Mets quickly fell to .500 and were already seven games out of first. The team was 7-0 when Leiter started and 12-19 when he didn't. Rickey Henderson, batting .219 with two RBI, was let

⊘ Final Resting Ground

Dennis Springer started two games for the Mets - his 6th team in 6 seasons - allowing 20 hits and 11 runs in 11.1 innings. His career ended after 5 more appearances with the Dodgers, finishing with a 24-48 W-L mark.

FABULOUS: MIKE PIAZZA

Mike Piazza hit .324 with 38 home runs and 113 RBI, playing through pain. He drove in 32 runs in June. The catcher looked on his way to winning the MVP award before batting .222 in September and ending up third behind Jeff Kent and Barry Bonds.

go. The outfielder, who had been upset since the start of spring training with the team not raising his salary, had to settle for a single against the Marlins after starting a home run trot. He was criticized by Bobby Valentine and later shouted at a reporter. The Mets played better late in May, winning nine of 12, including sweeps over the Diamondbacks and Cardinals. McEwing, who was called up after Henderson's departure, had three hits, including a homer, against Randy Johnson in a win against Arizona. Hampton won four straight starts, going at least eight innings in three of them. Ordonez was lost for the season after breaking his left forearm while making a tag against the Dodgers. The Mets would use Abbott and Mora at short.

In late June, the Mets won seven straight. The team scored at least 10 runs three times and Hampton pitched a shutout against the Pirates. The Mets played 75 games before meeting Atlanta in an NLCS rematch. Security at Shea was tightened because of John Rocker, who had made racist and homophobic statements regarding the city to *Sports Illustrated* and also criticized Mets fans. Before the first game of the series, Rocker apologized to Mets fans for his comments during a press conference. The lefty pitched a 1-2-3 eighth in the first game of the series. The Mets won the next two and had a chance to pull into a first-place tie but the Braves jumped on Glendon Rusch in a 10-2 game in the finale. Rusch had won five of his last six decisions before the start.

On July 8, the Mets and Yankees took part in a two-stadium doubleheader because of a rain out the month before. In the first game, Dwight Gooden returned to Queens and beat the Mets. In the second inning of the nightcap at Yankee Stadium, Clemens beaned Piazza, who was 7-12 with three home runs against him. Piazza was on the ground for two minutes before getting up,

FUTILE: RICH RODRIGUEZ

Rodriguez was behind Dennis Cook and John Franco on the Mets' LHP depth chart...way behind. In 32 appearances Rodriguez pitched 37 innings, compiling an ERA of 7.78 while allowing 59 hits and 7 HR, walking another 15 and fanning just 18.

suffering his second concussion in six weeks. "It's one of the worst things I've ever seen in baseball," Todd Pratt said. "If he meant it or not, it didn't look good. I lost a lot of respect for Roger Clemens." Piazza, who was batting .348 with 24 home runs and 72 RBI, would have to miss the All-Star Game. "I guess he was just a little off his game," Valentine sarcastically said about Clemens. "The guy is going to the Hall of Fame, he doesn't have that bad control."

TOP BATTERS

Pos	Name	G	AB	H	BA	HR	RBI	RS	SB	OPS
C	Mike Piazza	136	482	156	.324	38	113	90	4	1.012
1B	Todd Zeile	153	544	146	.268	22	79	67	3	.823
2B	Edgardo Alfonzo	150	544	176	.324	25	94	109	3	.967
3B	Robin Ventura	141	469	109	.232	24	84	61	3	.777
RF	Derek Bell	144	546	145	.266	18	69	87	8	.773

TOP PITCHERS

Pos	Name	G	GS	W	L	SV	ERA	IP	SO	BB
SP	Mike Hampton	33	33	15	10	0	3.14	217.2	151	99
SP	Al Leiter	31	31	16	8	0	3.20	208.0	200	76
SP	Glendon Rusch	31	30	11	11	0	4.01	190.2	157	44
SP	Rick Reed	30	30	11	5	0	4.11	184.0	121	34
CL	Armando Benitez	76	0	4	4	41	2.61	76.0	106	38

In the first game after the break, Piazza's RBI single gave the Mets a 3-2 lead in Boston but Mora booted what could've been a game-ending double play and the Red Sox took advantage, coming back to win 4-3. Mora committed five errors in his previous 15 games at short and had the team looking into different options, even considering moving Alfonzo from second. The Mets looked to have a deal for Reds star Barry Larkin but the future Hall of Famer nixed the trade when the Mets wouldn't give him an extension. Instead the Mets traded Mora to the Orioles for Mike Bordick, who was batting .297 with 16 home runs and had committed nine errors during the season, as opposed to Mora's seven in 44 games. Phillips also acquired outfielder Bubba Trammell and reliever Rick White from Tampa Bay with Paul Wilson and outfielder Jason Tyner going to the Devil Rays. Bordick and Trammell both homered in their first Met at-bats and the Mets won six straight with sweeps over the Expos and Cardinals.

On a roll, the Mets went 20-9 in August, moving into a tie for first. And this was with a struggling Ventura batting .229 in the month and Bell hitting .176. That was thanks to Alfonzo, who hit .360 with five home runs and 19 RBI, and Piazza, who hit .342 with four homers and 16 RBI. Agbayani hit .311 with four homers and Payton hit .310 with three home runs. The team knocked out Randy Johnson in the fourth inning of a win against Arizona. Hampton and Jones went 3-0 during the month. Jones had improved since being sent down to Triple-A for a pair of starts in June. Before the All-Star break he was 3-4 with a 6.98 ERA. In the second half he went 8-2 with a 3.98 ERA. Reed won four games in August. Leiter pitched eight shutout innings in a win against the Giants. Benitez saved 11 games during the month.

The Mets lost on three straight walk-offs in St. Louis to begin September. The Mets lost seven of eight to start the month, reminding fans of September struggles of the previous two seasons. But the team had enough distance between themselves and the rest of the NL in the wild card chase. The team scored 10 runs three times in five games. Jay Payton hit a walk-off homer to beat the Brewers. Alfonzo hit .319 with seven home runs in the final month. The Mets won eight of nine to end the season, including a win over the Braves on September 27 to clinch a playoff berth. Timo Perez was a September call up. The outfielder was batting .222 on September 22 but collected eight hits over the next week and found himself on the postseason roster. Piazza batted .222 in September, costing him MVP votes. He would finish third behind a pair of Giants, Jeff Kent and Barry Bonds.

Top 5 Highlights

1 Benny Agbayani's 11th inning grand slam puts the Mets ahead in a 5-1 win against the Cubs on March 30 in Japan. A single and two walks loaded the bases for Agbayani, who went deep off Danny Young. Rick Reed gave up one run in eight innings.

2 Mike Piazza hits a grand slam off Roger Clemens to give the Mets a 4-0 lead in the third against the Yankees in an eventual 12-2 win. Al Leiter gave up two runs in seven innings.

3 Piazza's go-ahead three-run homer off Terry Mulholland caps off a 10-run eighth inning in an 11-8 win against the Braves on June 30. The Mets trailed 8-1 and were down 8-2 with two outs in the inning before rallying. Three consecutive bases loaded walks cut the lead to 8-6 and Edgardo Alfonzo's single tied the game.

4 Bubba Trammell hits a three-run homer off St. Louis' Garrett Stephenson in his first at-bat as a Met in a 4-2 win on July 30. The day before, Mike Bordick homered off Andy Benes in his first Mets at-bat.

5 Armando Benitez strikes out Kevin Lockhart to finish a 6-2 win over the Braves on September 27, as the Mets clinch the NL Wild Card. Alfonzo hit a two-run homer in the fifth off Kevin Millwood.

2000 NLDS

The Mets traveled to San Francisco for the NLDS. Valentine went with Hampton, 9-0 in his career against the Giants, as the Game 1 starter. The Giants jumped on Hampton for a run in the first but Payton's sacrifice fly tied it in the third. In the bottom of the inning, Hampton thought he struck out Bonds on a pitch on the outside corner but it was called a ball. Bonds then ripped one down the line in right. The ball caromed off the ball wall and back toward the infield. Bell had to make a quick turn and he rolled his ankle. Bonds had an RBI triple and Bell was done for the postseason. Hampton walked Kent on four pitches and Ellis Burks followed with a homer to make it 5-1. That was all the scoring and the Mets were down 1-0 in the NLDS.

Perez was now in right and leading off Game 2. The injury to Bell, who was hitting .360 in late May but finished with a .266 average, turned out to be a blessing in disguise. In the second, Perez delivered a two-run single off Shawn Estes to put the Mets in front. Burks doubled off Leiter in the bottom of the inning but it was all the Giants would get for the first eight innings. Still 2-1 in the ninth, Perez singled for his third hit of the night and Alfonzo followed with a two-run home run off Felix Rodriguez. Leiter gave up a leadoff double to Bonds in the bottom of the inning and was removed after throwing 123 pitches. Kent singled off Benitez. Two batters later, J.T. Snow hit a three-run homer down the line to tie the game. Giants manager Dusty Baker still had Rodriguez on the mound in the 10th instead of Robb Nen, when Hamilton doubled with two outs. Payton followed with an RBI single to center, giving the Mets a 5-4 lead. Armando Rios singled off Benitez to begin the bottom of the inning and Valentine called on John Franco. A sacrifice moved Rios to second. Bill Mueller hit a grounder to short but Rios tried to make it to third. Bordick easily threw him out. It came down to Bonds against Franco. Franco got Bonds looking at a 3-2 changeup to end the game and tie the series. A defiant Kent said, "I believe we're the better ballclub," adding, "We'll stick it to them."

The Mets received good news during the first inning of Game 3: The Cardinals had completed a sweep of the Braves in the other NLCS.

In Game 3, the Giants broke a scoreless tie in the fourth with Bobby Estalella and Marvin Bernard delivering RBI singles off Reed. Russ Ortiz took a no-hitter into the sixth inning before the Mets got something going. Bordick walked, Hamilton singled and Perez followed with an RBI single. In the eighth, a rested Nen came in with Harris on first and two outs. Harris stole second and then Alfonzo doubled to left, tying the game. The top of the ninth featured a Franco-Bonds rematch and again Franco fanned the slugger. With two on and two outs in the top of the 13th, White got Bonds to pop-up to second. With one out in the bottom of the inning, Agbayani homered to left-center off Aaron Fultz, bringing an end to the five-hour, 22 minute game.

Ventura hit a two-run homer in the first off Mark Gardner to give the Mets an early Game 4 lead. Jones was given the start and cruised against the Giants. He retired the first 12 batters before Kent doubled to start the fifth. With two on and two outs, Jones pitched around Doug Mirabelli to bring up the pitcher's spot. Baker let Gardner hit for himself and the pitcher popped up to second. Gardner only lasted four more batters, with an Alfonzo double scoring two runs. The Giants made quick outs over the final four innings, with Jones retiring the final 13 batters. Bonds, who went 4-17 with one RBI in the series, flied out to end the 4-0 win.

2000 NLCS

The Mets went to St. Louis for the NLCS. In Game 1, the Mets scored twice off Darryl Kile in the first inning. Alfonzo added an RBI single in the fifth. Hampton pitched seven shutout innings. In the ninth, homers by Zeile and Payton made it 6-0. The Cardinals scored two unearned runs off Benitez in the bottom of the ninth but the Mets had a 1-0 series lead.

New York took a 2-0 first inning lead against a wild Rick Ankiel, who walked three batters and threw two wild pitches. In the third, Piazza homered off Britt Reames to make it 3-1. RBI doubles from Edgar Renteria and Will Clark off Leiter tied the game in the fifth. In the eighth, Alfonzo's RBI single scored Perez and Zeile added an RBI single to extend the lead to 5-3. But the Cardinals came back again with J.D. Drew tying the game with a double off Wendell. Ventura reached to begin the ninth on a Clark error at first. After an Agbayani bunt, Payton singled in Ventura to make it 6-5. Benitez pitched a scoreless ninth and the Mets were up 2-0.

Back at Shea, the Cardinals jumped on Reed for five runs (four earned) in 3.1 innings and added three against White in an 8-2 shellacking of the Mets. Andy Benes gave up two runs in eight innings.

In Game 4, Jim Edmonds' two-run homer off Jones gave the Cardinals a first inning lead. La Russa started Kile on three days' rest. The first four Mets doubled and New York scored four runs in the inning on five doubles. In the second, Zeile's bases loaded double scored two runs and Agbayani's RBI single made it 7-2. Clark homered in the fourth but Piazza answered with a shot of his own in the bottom of the inning off James to make it 8-3. The Cardinals knocked Jones from the game in the fifth and cutting the lead to 8-6. The Mets scored two unearned runs in the sixth thanks to two errors from third baseman Fernando Tatis to go up 10-6. Rusch pitched three shutout innings in relief. With a four-run lead in the ninth, Benitez put the first two Cardinals on. With two on and two outs, Edmonds worked the count full before flying out.

Game 5 was never in doubt. The Mets scored three times in the first against Pat Hentgen and Zeile's three-run double in the fourth made it 6-0. Hampton pitched a three-hit shutout, striking out eight and not allowing a runner to reach second. Rick Wilkins flied out to Perez to end the game. It was Perez who had seven hits and scored eight runs in the series.

2000 World Series

Valentine tabbed Leiter to start Game 1 at Yankee Stadium. Leiter and Andy Pettitte matched zeroes for five innings. In the top of the sixth, with Perez on first and two outs, Zeile hit an 0-2 pitch deep to left. It just missed going over the wall. David Justice threw the ball back in to Derek Jeter who threw it home to nail Perez, who had broken into a trot near second base. Then Justice did it at the plate, doubling in two runs in the bottom of the inning. In the top of the seventh, Agbayani and Payton singled, and Pratt walked to load the bases. Trammell delivered a two-run single to left to tie the game. Two batters later, Alfonzo's single off Jeff Nelson gave the Mets a 3-2 lead. Benitez was on the mound in the bottom of the ninth when Paul O'Neill worked a 10-pitch walk. Luis Polonia and Luis Vizcaino followed with singles to load the bases and Chuck Knoblauch's sacrifice fly tied it. The Mets went nine up, nine down in extra innings. In the bottom of the 12th, the Yankees won it when Vizcaino singled with the bases loaded and two outs off Wendell.

Game 2 marked the first Clemens-Piazza meeting since the July 8 beaning. In the first inning, Piazza fouled off a pitch and his bat shattered. A piece of the bat went to Clemens, who threw it in Piazza's direction. The benches cleared but there were no ejections. Clemens stayed in and pitched eight shutout innings, giving up two hits, both to Zeile. Hampton wasn't as sharp, giving up RBI singles in the first to Tino Martinez and Jorge Posada. Scott Brosius homered in the third. The Yankees led 6-0 heading into the ninth. Alfonzo singled and Piazza homered. Jay Payton's three-run homer off Mariano Rivera cut the lead to 6-5 but Abbott struck out looking to end the game. The Mets were down two games to none though the main topic was Clemens and Piazza.

Hampton said he wanted to fight the Yankees and would have been more likely to retaliate in a regular season game. "You can't make something happen if guys aren't going to defend themselves."

Reed and Orlando Hernandez traded strikeouts early in Game 3. Ventura's homer put the Mets on the board in the second and Justice tied it with an RBI double in the third. An O'Neill triple in the fourth made it 2-1 Yankees. Zeile tied the game in the sixth with an RBI double and the Mets loaded the bases with nobody out but couldn't take the lead. Hernandez was still in when Zeile singled with one out in the eighth. Agbayani followed with a double to left-center that went all the way to the wall, allowing Zeile to score the go-ahead run. Trammell's sacrifice fly made it 4-2. Benitez came on to close it out. With the tying run at the plate, Benitez got Justice to pop up to Alfonzo.

The first pitch of Game 4 became a home run off the bat of Jeter. The Yankees added a run in the second and another in the third, when Jeter tripled and scored on a groundout. In the bottom of the third, Piazza hit a two-run homer off Denny Neagle. With two outs in the fifth, Piazza was up again. Torre brought in David Cone. The veteran righty got Piazza to pop up to second. Though the Mets bullpen kept it a 3-2 game, the offense couldn't mount a comeback. Nelson and Mike Stanton combined to blank the Mets for two innings and then Rivera was called on to get six outs. The closer pitched two scoreless innings to give the Yankees a 3-1 lead. The Mets only mustered two hits in 4.1 innings against the bullpen.

It was Leiter and Pettitte again in Game 5. Bernie Williams, who had been hitless in the series, homered to give the Yankees a 1-0 lead in the second. The Mets scored twice in the bottom of the inning but Jeter tied the game in the sixth with a home run. With two on and two outs in the ninth, Luis Sojo hit Leiter's 142nd pitch up the middle, just getting past the middle infielders. Posada rounded third and kicked Payton's throw home into the dugout, also allowing Brosius to score. With two outs and Agbayani on second, Piazza hit a fly ball to center. Off the bat it looked like it could tie the game, but it settled into Williams' glove.

2001

	W	L	GB	Pos
	82	80	6.0	3rd
RS/G	RA/G		Manager	
3.96	4.40		Bobby Valentine	

Mets Uplift City but Finish Third

The Moves

The team didn't sign Alex Rodriguez with Steve Phillips not want a "24-plus-one-man roster" and now wanting to destroy the "fabric of the team." Mike Hampton left the Mets for an eight-year, $121 million deal with the Rockies, although the 2000 NLCS MVP pointed to the lifestyle as well as the school system in the Denver area as reasons why he went to pitch at Coors Field as opposed to the huge contract.

The Mets filled a hole in the rotation by signing Kevin Appier to a four-year, $42 million deal. Appier had been an All-Star in 1995 with the Royals and had once led the AL in ERA. In 2000, Appier had gone 15-11 with Oakland.

The team also acquired Steve Trachsel. Trachsel was 68-84 but was tough to beat when on top of his game, as evidenced in game 163 of the 1998 season, when he took a no-hitter into the seventh inning against the Giants as the Cubs won the wild card, and in 2000 when he won back-to-back 1-0 games at Fenway Park and Yankee Stadium with the Devil Rays. Bobby Jones would sign with San Diego. John Franco returned after flirting with the idea of signing with the Phillies to become a closer instead of setting up Armando Benitez.

Derek Bell signed with the Pirates and the Mets filled the outfield void with Tsuyoshi Shinjo, a seven-time Gold Glove winner in Japan who hit .278 with 28 homers and 85 RBI for the Hanshin Tigers in 2000. Bubba Trammell was

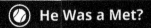 **He Was a Met?**

The Mets signed Kevin Appier in the winter of 2000 and he was a solid contributor, going 11-10 with a fine ERA of 3.57 in 206.2 IP. After the season, the Mets traded Appier to the Angels for Mo Vaughn.

traded to the Padres for righty reliever Donne Wall.

Desi Relaford, claimed on waivers from the Padres, would be the backup shortstop as Kurt Abbott signed with the Braves and Mike Bordick went back to the Orioles.

A few days before the season, tragedy struck when top prospect Brian Cole was killed in a car crash in Florida. The team would wear a patch honoring him and 1969 Met Tommie Agee, who had passed away in January, in the home opener.

The Mets played host to the Braves 10 days after 9/11, the first sporting event in the city after the tragedy. The crowd was subdued most of the night and Atlanta led 2-1 in the bottom of the eighth. With one on and one out, Mike Piazza launched a Steve Karsay pitch to center, putting the Mets ahead, who then hung on for a 3-2 win. The blast proved cathartic for the still-mourning New York crowd and lives on as a symbol of The Big Apple's resilience. Piazza is shown here at a press conference following his election to the Hall of Fame.

The Situation

The Braves were still the defending division champs, and 11 of 12 ESPN writers polled picked Atlanta to win the East, with Matt Szefc going with the Mets. Five of the 12 picked the Rockies to win the West, in part because of the Hampton signing. Szefc and Tom Tippett picked Al Leiter to win the Cy Young, and Bob Klapisch picked Mike Piazza to win the MVP.

Could it finally be the year Atlanta's reign at the top would end? "They're starting to show cracks now," said Turk Wendell, never one to shy away from giving his honest opinion. "They don't have the depth in power they had. They don't have Galarraga. You look around that field, who do you really have to worry about as far as power hitters? Chipper and Andruw Jones. That's not the thunder that they had in there. They had Galarraga, Chipper, Gerald Williams. And Javy Lopez is banged up right now, too. They have guys getting older. Smoltz is hurting. I'm sure there's questions about Millwood; he didn't have a very good spring."

FABULOUS: ARMANDO BENITEZ

The burly right-hander put up his second consecutive 40+ save season, collecting 43, along with 6 wins, and fanning 93 in 76 IP.

The Season

The Mets took four of six from the Braves in the first week-and-a-half of the season but couldn't beat anyone else. They were swept by the Expos in Montreal, with the pitching staff giving up 10 runs in back-to-back games. The Reds came to Shea and swept the Mets, with the meager offense scoring three runs in three games. Edgardo Alfonzo was hitting .109 through 12 games and was dropped to fifth in the order with Todd Zeile moving up to second. "We've tried different orders and tried to get some fresh faces in there," Zeile said. "But at this point, we've run up against a bunch of walls."

Jay Payton missed the three games in Montreal with a throat infection. Benny Agbayani was out for two weeks with a fractured left wrist. Timo Perez went on the Disabled List with a strained left groin. Al Leiter was 0-3 with a 5.87 ERA in April and went on the DL with a strained left elbow. A four game losing streak late in April dropped the Mets to 8-14, with the pitching staff giving up 21 runs in the final two losses. Brett Hinchcliffe was called up after the Leiter injury and failed to make it out of the third inning in Milwaukee, giving up eight runs on nine hits. Even the defense was struggling, making multiple errors in two straight games in Milwaukee.

The final loss of the month was a 12-1 drubbing in St. Louis with the Mets committing four errors and Glendon Rusch giving up seven runs on 11 hits in 2.1 innings. The bullpen wasn't helping Valentine much. Southpaw Tom Martin had a 10.95 ERA before being sent down. Wall had a 6.39 ERA in April.

New York looked to sweep Houston at Shea but but the bullpen gave up five homers in three innings in an extra-inning loss.

Ten losses in 15 games to begin May put the Mets at 15-25. Jay Payton was hitting .315 but lost for a month-and-a-half, tearing his hamstring while running to first. Trachsel was healthy but couldn't get anybody out. On May 17, he gave up seven runs in 2.1 innings, surrendering four home runs in the third. Relaford had to pitch the ninth inning of a 15-3 loss. Valentine called the right-hander's approach "unacceptable." Trachsel, who was 1-6 with an 8.24 ERA, was sent down to the minors. "I absolutely stunk it up tonight and I'm very embarrassed about it," he said after the ugly start. Zeile said the game "reached a new low for this season. It's embarrassing."

Rey Ordonez was unhappy with his playing time dwindling but such was life as Relaford's batting average was more than .100 points higher. Veteran outfielder Darren Bragg was leading off, though he would only last 18 games. Darryl Hamilton was batting .129 with Valentine throwing him a back-handed compliment one day, noting "He swung it today in BP the way I wish he swung at least once during the season." During a six-game losing streak, the Mets were swept in

FUTILE: GLENDON RUSCH

Glendon Rusch won only 8 of his 33 starts (losing 12), compiling an ERA of 4.63. He was even worse at the plate, collecting only 3 hits in 54 ABs with 1 BB and zero runs scored.

Colorado with Hampton throwing a seven-hit shutout on May 9. Highly-touted prospect Alex Escobar made his debut on June 8 but was sent back down after a week. The Mets lost all six games he played in.

Leiter returned from the DL and won two straight starts. The Mets won six of eight but ended the loss with four straight losses. On May 28, Mike Piazza tied the game with a ninth-inning homer off Philadelphia's Jose Mesa but in the top of 10th, Pat Burrell hit a two-run homer off Benitez. Burrell was becoming a Met-killer in the mold of Chipper Jones. The next day, he hit a three-run eighth inning homer off Turk Wendell to put the game out of reach.

Rusch was struggling mightily, 3-5 with a 6.43 ERA in mid-June. Even a trip to Tampa Bay to play the lowly Devil Rays resulted in two losses in three games. The Mets found a bit of a spark on June 17, scoring six runs in the bottom of the eighth, capped off by Piazza's 19th homer of the year, to beat the Yankees. But a four-game win streak was followed by a six-game skid. The Braves swept the Mets at Shea, including a 9-3, 11-inning win on June 23. Trachsel returned, lost three more games, but then pitched a gem in a win against the Braves. But that was followed by giving up seven runs in 2.2 innings in a 13-4 loss to the Cubs. One bright spot was Rick Reed, who began the season 7-2 with a 2.62 ERA and made the All-Star team.

An 8-3 loss at Yankee Stadium on July 6 dropped the Mets to last place. Hamilton was released following an argument with Valentine over his playing time. The team did win five straight in the middle of the month. On July 22, the Mets lost a tough one in Philadelphia. Bobby Abreu's eighth inning homer made it 3-2 and was the first time a lefty hit a homer off John Franco since Pittsburgh's Dave Clark did it in 1993. The Mets traded Todd Pratt to the Phillies for backup catcher Gary Bennett. Vance Wilson was emerging as Piazza's backup and Pratt was batting .163 with two homers and four RBI. Bennett would be traded to Colorado a month later.

TOP BATTERS

Pos	Name	G	AB	H	BA	HR	RBI	RS	SB	OPS
C	Mike Piazza	141	503	151	.300	36	94	81	0	.957
1B	Todd Zeile	151	531	141	.266	10	62	66	1	.732
2B	Edgardo Alfonzo	124	457	111	.243	17	49	64	5	.725
3B	Robin Ventura	142	456	108	.237	21	61	70	2	.778

TOP PITCHERS

Pos	Name	G	GS	W	L	SV	ERA	IP	SO	BB
SP	Kevin Appier	33	33	11	10	0	3.57	206.2	172	64
SP	Al Leiter	29	29	11	11	0	3.31	187.1	142	46
SP	Steve Trachsel	28	28	11	13	0	4.46	173.2	144	47
SP	Rick Reed	20	20	8	6	0	3.48	134.2	99	17
CL	Armando Benitez	73	0	6	4	43	3.77	76.1	93	40

After beating the Phillies 6-1 at Shea on July 27, the Mets traded Dennis Cook and Turk Wendell to the Phillies for starter Bruce Chen. Wendell was 4-3 with one save and a 3.51 ERA in 49 games. Cook was 1-1 with a 4.25 ERA in 43 games. "You can't take the heart of our bullpen out of there without thinking they're throwing in the towel," Wendell said.

In the first game after the trade, Ventura hit a walk-off homer off Wendell. The next day, Piazza hit a walk-off homer of Rheal Cormier. Needing offense, Phillips traded Reed to the Twins for Matt Lawton.

A sweep of the Brewers in early August was followed by a seven-game losing streak, dropping the team to 54-68, matching as many losses as they had in 2000, with 40 games remaining.

But then the Mets got hot. The team won 11 of 14, including a pair of walk-off wins in the 11th inning. Leiter even tripled in a game against the Marlins. Shinjo was 10-20 with two homers in a five-game stretch. Ordonez hit .389 over 11 games. Alfonzo and Zeile were hitting as well. Agbayani was lost for the year with a broken bone in his hand but the team kept winning. A loss to the Marlins ended a 13-game homestand but then the Mets won six straight. A win on September 8, brought the Mets to within one game of .500. Down in the ninth, Lawton delivered a two-run double off Antonio Alfonseca and the Mets won 9-7 in Florida. New York couldn't get back to .500 on September 9, losing 4-2 and heading to Pittsburgh eight games back with 18 to play.

The Mets were off Monday. On Tuesday morning, the nation was stunned by terror attacks that took nearly 3,000 lives. Shea Stadium became a location for volunteers and supplies as baseball became secondary.

The games resumed on September 17. New York swept Pittsburgh to pull within five games of first. The team was 74-73. It was the first time since 1973 that the Mets had gone from at least 10 games under .500 to having a winning record.

Baseball returned to the city on Friday night, September 21. There had been discussions about moving the series to Turner Field and moving the series the following week from Atlanta to Shea as the stadium was being used as a staging area for the rescue effort but the decision was made to keep the games at Shea. Atlanta led 2-1 in the bottom of the eighth when Piazza crushed a homer to center off Steve Karsay, giving the Mets a 3-2 lead and helping the city heal.

On a roll, the Mets beat the Braves again the next day. Greg Maddux left two batters into the game with a hyperextended right elbow and New York won 7-3 to move within 3.5 games of first. Benitez even delivered an RBI groundout. Trachsel won his 10th game of the season, giving up one run on five hits over seven innings. But the next day, Benitez blew a 4-1 ninth inning lead with two outs. Brian Jordan hit a two-run homer and three batters later, B.J. Surhoff's single made it 4-4. In the top of the 11th, Jordan homered off Jerrod Riggan and the Braves were 5-4 winners.

The scrappy Mets went to Montreal and swept the Expos. The team went to Atlanta for a three-game series, three games back with nine to play. The

Phillies were one game behind Atlanta for the division lead. The Braves took the opener behind Tom Glavine 5-3.

On September 29, Leiter pitched eight stellar innings and the Mets took a 5-1 lead in the bottom of the ninth. But Leiter had thrown 121 pitches and was pinch-hit for in the top of the ninth. Benitez entered. He recorded two outs but two singles, a walk, a two-run double and an intentional walk later it was 5-4 with two on and two out. Franco came in and walked Wes Helms. Then Jordan came up. Franco used a pair of changeups to get ahead of Jordan 0-2. Then he went with the fastball. "When I saw [Piazza] put down a fastball in, I said, 'No way,' said Leiter who was watching on TV in the clubhouse. Jordan hit a grand slam to left. The Mets had given up seven in the ninth and the season was unofficially over, now down five games with seven left to play. "It's a crime to lose a game like that," Piazza said.

The Mets won 9-6 to avoid a sweep, with Benitez striking out the side in the ninth, but the Mets lost four of six at home to end the season.

Top 5 Highlights

1 Robin Ventura's 10th inning homer off Kerry Ligtenberg gives the Mets a 6-4 win in Atlanta on Opening Day. Ventura's eighth inning homer off John Rocker had given the Mets a 4-2 lead. Mike Piazza hit a two-run homer in the first off Tom Glavine.

2 Piazza's two-run homer off Carlos Almanzar in the eighth gives the Mets an 8-7 lead over the Yankees on June 17. The Mets trailed 7-2 heading into the bottom of the eighth but rallied against Randy Choate and Almanzar. Roger Clemens was originally slated to start the Sunday night game but pushed him back and started Ted Lilly instead.

3 Glendon Rusch and Armando Benitez combine to pitch a one-hitter in a 2-0 win over the Red Sox on July 14. Trot Nixon's first inning bunt single is the only Boston hit. Rusch pitches eight shutout innings, striking out 10. Mark Johnson drives in both Mets runs, including a second inning home run.

4 In the first game in New York after 9/11, Piazza hits a go-ahead two-run homer off Steve Karsay in the eighth and the Mets win 3-2 on an emotional night in Queens. Atlanta had taken the lead in the top of the eighth on a Brian Jordan double off Benitez. Edgardo Alfonzo drew a walk in front of Piazza, with Karsay believing he had Alfonzo struck out looking.

5 Lenny Harris becomes the all-time pinch-hit leader with a sixth inning single off Montreal's Carl Pavano in a 4-0 win on October 6. His 151st pinch-hit passed Manny Mota.

2002

OPENING DAY LINEUP

Roger Cedeno, LF
Roberto Alomar, 2B
Mo Vaughn, 1B
Mike Piazza, C
Edgardo Alfonzo, 3B
Jeromy Burnitz, RF
Jay Payton, CF
Rey Ordonez, SS
Al Leiter, P

	W	L	GB	Pos
	75	86	26.5	5th
RS/G	RA/G	Manager		
4.29	4.37	Bobby Valentine		

Star-Studded Lineup Finishes Last

The Moves

Steve Phillips went to work after missing the playoffs. The team traded for 12-time All-Star Roberto Alomar, sending several pieces, including Alex Escobar and Matt Lawton to the Indians. Alomar, a 10-time Gold Glove winner, would play second and Edgardo Alfonzo would move back to third.

The Mets had traded Robin Ventura to the Yankees for David Justice, then turned around a week later and flipped Justice to Oakland for southpaw reliever Mark Guthrie. The Mets tried signing slugger Juan Gonzalez but the two-time MVP signed with Texas.

Roger Cedeno returned to the Mets, signing a four-year, $18 million deal. He hit .293 and stole 55 bases in 2001. The team also signed reliever David Weathers, who posted a 2.41 ERA with the Brewers and Cubs in 2001.

Tsuyoshi Shinjo and Desi Relaford were dealt to San Francisco for lefty starter Shawn Estes, a 1997 All-Star averaging 29 starts over the previous five seasons.

The Mets also added former AL MVP Mo Vaughn, sending Kevin Appier to the Angels. Vaughn was a three-time All-Star with 299 career home runs but had missed the entire 2001 season after surgery to repair his biceps tendon and muscle on his left arm. Vaughn looked forward to playing in the Big Apple.

A few weeks later, the Mets landed Jeromy Burnitz in a three-way trade with the Brewers and Rockies. Benny Agbayani and Todd Zeile went to Colorado, while

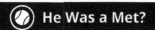

🎾 He Was a Met?

John Valentin spent his last season in the majors in Queens, batting .240 with three home runs. He appeared in his 1,000th career game on April 14 against the Expos and had a four-RBI game on May 3 in Houston.

Lenny Harris and Glendon Rusch went to Milwaukee. Burnitz had averaged 32 homers and 102 RBI over the last five seasons, very different numbers than he put up with the Mets in the early 90s. Burnitz hit 34 home runs in 2001. The entire Mets outfield hit 40.

New York also received righty starter Jeff D'Amico in the deal. The Mets signed right-handed starter Pedro Astacio and seven-time Japanese All-Star Satoru Komiyama, known as the "Japanese Greg Maddux." Red Sox veteran infielder John Valentin also joined the team after playing in 30 games the previous two seasons.

The Fred Wilpon Era

Fred Wilpon bought a 1% share of the Mets in 1980 when the Payson family sold the team to Doubleday & Company. During another transfer of ownership, Wilpon negotiated his stake up to 50%. Then, in 2002, he became the sole owner Chairman of the Board of the Mets, ending more than 20 seasons of Nelson Doubleday's say in the team. It has been a rocky nearly 20 years at the helm for Wilpon, with at best mixed results on the field. On the business front things have also been challenging, as Wilpon and the Mets' finances were heavily tied up with the criminal enterprise of Bernie Madoff, and they suffered a serious blow when the Madoff empire collapsed.

The Situation

The Mets had not had a dramatic roster turnover since the 1992 season, although the team hoped this would go better than that nightmare. "This isn't the same [situation]," Steve Phillips said. "The character I see here is outstanding. Mo and Alomar are quality people and teammates. All of our new players are."

Jim Caple and Bob Klapisch picked the Mets to finish first. Michael Morrissey of the *New York Post* predicted that the Mets would win the World Series.

The Season

In the early days of the season, the Mets would improve the bullpen, trading Bruce Chen to the Expos for Scott Strickland. Surgery would keep John Franco out for the entire season.

The Mets lost two of three to start the season against the Pirates but went to Turner Field and took two of three from the Braves. New York scored nine runs in the ninth in an 11-2 win on April 6. The Mets took of three from the Cubs, two of

 Final Resting Ground

Mo Vaughn came to the Mets one year removed from a 6-year stretch in which he averaged 38 HR and 118 RBI. But he was out of action the entire year between, and he totaled only 26/72 for the Mets. He played in 27 games the following year before hanging them up for good.

three from the Expos and two of three from the Braves again. On April 15, the Mets erased a five-run lead in the seventh and beat Atlanta on Alfonzo's game-winning single in the bottom of the 11th.

New York won the final five games of the month to end April 16-10 and in a tie for first. And the team did it even with Vaughn missing two weeks after being hit on the hand by a pitch. The team swept Milwaukee with both Estes and Astacio taking no-hitters into the seventh. Armando Benitez converted all seven save opportunities. Al Leiter beat the Diamondbacks on April 30, making him the first pitcher to defeat all 30 teams. Leiter went 3-1 with a 0.92 ERA during the month, including a two-hit shutout against the Expos.

FUTILE: JOE MCEWING

Joe McEwing put up a slash line of .199/.242/.296, drawing only 9 walks while fanning 50 times in 214 plate appearances. McEwing did play five positions, but did not do well at the challenging ones, posting a fielding average .921 at SS and .900 at 3B.

A six-game losing streak in early May included a sweep at San Francisco. The inconsistent Mets lost back-to-back games in 13 innings but then rolled off five straight wins. Astacio pitched a two-hit shutout over the Dodgers. The next night, D'Amico did the same. It was the first time the Mets posted consecutive shutouts since David Cone and Bret Saberhagen 10 years earlier. In a 13-4 win in San Diego, Piazza hit a grand slam and the team turned a 5-4-3 triple play. Benitez returned to pitch an inning after the clubhouse door at Shea closed on his right index finger days earlier.

Several days later, the focus would shift to Piazza's personal life. Bobby Valentine said the league was "probably ready for an openly gay player." The *New York Post* noted, "There is a persistent rumor around town that one Mets star who spends a lot of time with pretty models in clubs is actually gay and has started to think about declaring his sexual orientation." Piazza denied the rumors about his personal life. "I'm not gay. I'm heterosexual," he said, adding "I can't control what people think. I date women."

On the field, the Mets ended the month with a 29-25 record, only a half-game out of first. The team lost five straight to begin the month. The team took two of three in Cleveland but then lost two of three to the White Sox. The Mets lost 2-1 in the finale.

Chris Chambliss was hired as hitting coach with Dave Engle dismissed. "Having played in New York and succeeded, having coached in New York and succeeded, having been a left-handed slugging first baseman, he's going to have a real impact in dealing with our hitters," Phillips said. Perhaps the left-handed slugging first baseman reference was putting the onus on Vaughn, who was batting .230 with four home runs. "I don't teach everybody the same thing about hitting," Chambliss said. "I don't believe in having a system. I think it's important to know all styles of hitting. I use what I think I need to help a major-league hitter."

TOP BATTERS

Pos	Name	G	AB	H	BA	HR	RBI	RS	SB	OPS
C	Mike Piazza	135	478	134	.280	33	98	69	0	.903
1B	Mo Vaughn	139	487	126	.259	26	72	67	0	.805
3B	Edgardo Alfonzo	135	490	151	.308	16	56	78	6	.851
RF	Jeromy Burnitz	154	479	103	.215	19	54	65	10	.677

TOP PITCHERS

Pos	Name	G	GS	W	L	SV	ERA	IP	SO	BB
SP	Al Leiter	33	33	13	13	0	3.48	204.1	172	69
SP	Pedro Astacio	31	31	12	11	0	4.79	191.2	152	63
SP	Steve Trachsel	30	30	11	11	0	3.37	173.2	105	69
CL	Armando Benitez	62	0	1	0	33	2.27	67.1	79	25
RP	David Weathers	71	0	6	3	0	2.91	77.1	61	36

It wasn't just Vaughn struggling. Burnitz was batting .197. In the first game with Chambliss as coach, the Mets blew a ninth inning lead to the Yankees and lost in 10 with Ventura hitting a go-ahead two-run homer in the top of the 10th.

FABULOUS: MIKE PIAZZA

Piazza had the last of 4 consecutive exceptional years at the plate for the Mets, during which he surpassed 30 HR and 90 RBI each season. In 2002, he won his 10th Silver Slugger Award and legged out 2 of the 8 triples of his career.

The next day featured Roger Clemens pitching against the Mets for the first time since Game 2 of the 2000 World Series when he threw a broken bat at Piazza and then pitched eight shutout innings. Estes threw behind Clemens in the top of the third. In the bottom of the fifth, Estes hit a two-run homer to left. Then Piazza hit a solo shot off Clemens in the sixth. When it was over the Mets had an 8-0 win. In the rubber game, David Wells took a shutout into the eighth but Vaughn hit a go-ahead three-run homer and Benitez closed the door in the ninth.

Late in the month, the Mets lost two of three to the Braves at Shea. Before a game, Cedeno and Alomar got into a spat in the clubhouse and dugout after Cedeno made fun of Alomar's rookie card hung over his locker. "Just a little personal thing," Valentine said. "A little Latin yelling. I thought we were up for the game. There was a lot of fluids going. I loved it."

What Valentine didn't love was Alomar's .260 average and Cedeno's .245 average at the end of the month, which finished with the team losing two of three at Yankee Stadium. The Mets went 11-15 in June and with the Braves going 21-5, the Mets were suddenly 10.5 games out of first. The Mets were five out of the wild card, which was where attention would shift. It wasn't just the offense struggling. D'Amico went 0-3 in June and saw his ERA increase by more than a run-and-a-half.

The Mets lost four of seven to open July and went to the All-Star break with a 43-44 record. In the first days of the second half, Fred Wilpon sued co-owner Nelson Doubleday to sell his half of the team at a price already set by a mutually agreed-upon appraiser. The breach-of-contract suit came two weeks after Doubleday vowed to sue to prevent the sale, saying he was low-balled by MLB appraiser Robert Starkey, who set the Mets value at $391 million. One month later, Wilpon bought Doubleday's 50 percent of the team.

Moving into second place, the team won 11 of 16 to finish the month. Alfonzo was hitting .320 through the end of the month. Vaughn delivered a walk-off single against the Reds. Piazza hit seven homers during the month. New York was 4.5 out of the wild card with two months remaining.

Phillips acquired Rockies starter John Thomson and Padres reliever Steve Reed at the deadline. Jay Payton was sent to Colorado. Reed had a 1.98 ERA in 40 appearances. Thomson as 1-6 with a 5.74 ERA in his last 11 starts but wouldn't have to pitch at Coors Field.

August began with five straight home losses. Arizona came to town and took four straight including a doubleheader sweep on August 3. In the first game, the Mets led 5-4 in the ninth when Craig Counsell, who had one homer on the year, went deep off Benitez. Erubiel Durazo hit a three-run homer in the 10th off Strickland. In the nightcap, Thomson gave up seven runs in six innings though only three were earned. The Mets took three of four to improve to 58-57, then lost 12 straight. The Padres came to Shea with a 17-40 road record and swept the Mets. The team celebrated its 40th anniversary on august 17 and then Astacio gave up eight runs on 12 hits in three innings. The offense scored three runs in four games.

Valentine had an emotional clubhouse speech, saying there weren't enough disciples on the team but said he didn't criticize any players. Kind of. "I've never criticized my players in public, and I'll never do it again," he said.

The manager also said some players – meaning Leiter and Alfonzo – were more concerned about negotiating contracts after the season.

The team was one out away from dropping a 13th straight game when Timo Perez hit a two-run homer off Colorado's Jose Jimenez to give the Mets a 3-2 lead. The team would score two more runs and hold on for a 5-2 win.

The month ended with a 1-0 loss at home to the Phillies. The Mets had gone 0-13 at Shea in August. Then they lost the first two games in September. Finally, the Mets beat the Marlins 11-5. Then they beat the Marlins 11-3 the next day. The team won six straight, scoring 11 runs three times.

During the week, MSG broadcaster Keith Hernandez said "The club has no heart. The Mets quit a long time ago." Piazza criticized "voices from the grave." Piazza added, "Personally, I'm not going to come back five years [after retirement] and rip guys. That shows me envy and jealously. If I'm doing that, just shoot me."

Later in the month the team had three walk-off wins in five games but more notable was a Newsday report that at least seven players smoked marijuana during the season, including Tony Tarasco, Mark Corey and Grant Roberts. A picture of Roberts smoking appeared in the paper but Phillips said it was taken in 1998. "I guarantee you no one was in uniform and smoking marijuana, unless they were running around with a whole lot of Visine in their eyes," Valentine said. "I grew up in the '60s. I think I could tell by looking in a guys' eyes if he was smoking dope."

Fans brought signs to Shea that read "At Least They're Hitting Something" and "2002 Mets: Up In Smoke."

In the final days of the season, Rey Ordonez said he wanted out. "I don't want to play here no more. The fans here are too stupid. You have to play perfect every game. You can't make an error. You can't go 0-for-4. Are we like [bleeping] machines?"

The team lost six straight before beating the Braves on the final day of the season. Two years after winning the pennant, the Mets were a last place team.

Valentine, the second-longest tenured manager in team history behind Davey Johnson, was fired.

Phillips and Valentine clashed but the general manager downplayed that. "There are points that you will disagree," Phillips said. "Our relationship wasn't any different today than it was when we went to the World Series. It was functional." Phillips remained as general manager.

Top 5 Highlights

1 Pedro Astacio pitches six no-hit innings before Geoff Jenkins breaks up the bid with a single with one out in the seventh in New York's 2-1 win on April 27. The night before, Shawn Estes took a no-hitter into the seventh before Eric Young singled to lead off the inning.

2 Al Leiter gives up one run on three hits in seven innings in a 10-1 win against the Diamondbacks on April 30, becoming the first pitcher to beat all 30 teams. The Mets scored all 10 runs in the first three innings. Mike Piazza homered twice off Rick Helling.

3 Steve Trachsel induces Wiki Gonzalez into a 5-4-3 triple play in the fifth inning of New York's 13-4 win on May 17. With the Mets up 5-1 in the fifth, Deivi Cruz singled and Sean Burroughs drew a walk. Gonzalez then hit into a triple play, turned by Edgardo Alfonzo, Roberto Alomar and Mo Vaughn.

4 Shawn Estes hits a two-run homer off Roger Clemens, two innings after throwing behind the defending Cy Young winner in the Mets' 8-0 win on June 15. Mike Piazza homered the next inning. Rey Ordonez broke it open with a three-run triple in the eighth.

5 Mo Vaughn's eighth inning home run off Atlanta's Kevin Gryboski hits the giant Budweiser sign on the Shea scoreboard and goes an estimated 505 feet from home plate. It's Vaughn's second home run of the game.

2003

OPENING DAY LINEUP

Roger Cedeno, CF
Roberto Alomar, 2B
Cliff Floyd, LF
Mike Piazza, C
Mo Vaughn, 1B
Ty Wigginton, 3B
Jeromy Burnitz, RF
Rey Sanchez, SS
Tom Glavine, P

	W	L	GB	Pos
	66	95	34.5	5th
RS/G	RA/G		Manager	
3.99	4.68		Art Howe	

Howe Bad Can You Get?

The Moves

Art Howe "lit up" the room when he spoke to Fred Wilpon and was named the new Mets manager a few weeks after Howe's A's lost to the Twins in the ALDS. Howe had led Oakland to the playoff three straight seasons and finished second in the Manager of the Year voting four times in a row. Howe had a calm, likeable demeanor and was seemingly the right guy to take over. The Mets wouldn't give up players to get Lou Piniella from Seattle and couldn't wait for Dusty Baker's playoff run with the Giants to end before talking to him. "I may not have been the first choice, but I'm the right choice," Howe said at his introductory press conference.

In early December, the Mets signed two-time Cy Young winner and five-time 20-game winner Tom Glavine to a three-year deal, taking him away from the arch-rival Braves. The Mets weren't the only division rival trying to sign him, as the Phillies were also interested, but Glavine felt the veteran presence of the Mets was better for him.

The team also signed outfielder Cliff Floyd, a 2001 All-Star. Former Yankees relievers Mike Stanton and Graeme Lloyd both signed as well. Rey Sanchez signed on to play shortstop as Jose Reyes was still in the minors. Tsuyoshi Shinjo returned, after playing with the Giants National League championship team in 2002.

⚾ He Was a Met?

After years as a reliable lefty out of the bullpen for the Brewers, Yankees, and other teams, Grahame Lloyd found himself in the Mets bullpen as a free agent signee. He put up pedestrian numbers before being dealt to the Royals where a 10.95 ERA signaled the end of his career.

Jay Bell, the 38-year-old infielder who scored the winning run for Arizona in the 2001 World Series, signed a minor league contract and was brought in to compete for a spot in spring training. Tony Clark, a 2001 All-Star with the Tigers, also signed with the Mets.

David Cone was talked out of retirement by John Franco and Al Leiter, and attempted to latch on with the team. The 40-year-old Cone had gone 9-7 with the Red Sox in 2001 before sitting out the 2002 season. Cone would battle Jason Middlebrook, Mike Bacsik and Aaron Heilman for the last spot in the rotation.

The Legendary Bob Murphy

The 2003 season was the final one in the booth for Bob Murphy, after 41 years with the team. Murphy's distinctive nasal twang, love of the Mets, and dedication to the details and flow of the game and his team made him a highly popular and acclaimed announcer, particularly after shifting to a radio-only role. Murphy's signature was the "Happy Recap" he provided after every Mets win. Murphy was inducted into the Hall of Fame in 1994, and after his retirement the Mets broadcast booth was named after him, an honor that continued when the Mets moved to Citi Field.

The Situation

The Mets had a team bonding moment in March when they brawled with the Dodgers after Guillermo Mota drilled Mike Piazza in the back with a fastball. The two had also been in a scuffle the year before in spring training. Piazza charged the mound as Mota threw his glove and ran away.

I think we're a playoff-caliber team," Steve Phillips said. "That's our goal – get to the postseason, and from there the World Series and win it."

Scott Strickland had high expectations: "If everybody plays the way they're capable of, there's no reason we shouldn't be a World Series-type team. Look at the names of these people and what they've done. The only reason why we wouldn't be is if we beat ourselves like we did last year."

The Season

Reality set in fast as the Cubs crushed Glavine on Opening Day en route to a 15-2 win. One of the bright spots of the season came in the fourth game of the year, as Cone returned to pitch five shutout innings against the Expos, only allowing two hits to opposing pitcher Tomo Ohka. It was his only win in 2003 and he would retire after five appearances.

 Final Resting Ground

Jay Bell was an All-Star with the Pirates and Diamondbacks, hitting 38 home runs in 1999 for Arizona. He also scored the winning run in Game 7 of the 2001 World Series. As a Met, Bell hit .181 in his final season in the majors. He appeared in his 2,000th career game on April 13 against the Expos.

FABULOUS: STEVE TRACHSEL

Steve Trachsel was a solid starter for the Mets over the years, reaching double digits in wins 5 times. In 2003, he won a career high 16 games and pitched a pair of one-hit shutouts.

The Mets were 11-16 after April and though they went 14-14 in May, it was a terrible summer as the team went 10-16 June and 9-18 in July. Injuries to Piazza and Vaughn took away expected power from the middle of the lineup as the Mets would finish the season with the third-fewest runs scored.

Steve Phillips was fired in mid-June. The firing of Phillips wasn't the only noteworthy about the Mets trip to Texas as Jose Reyes made his MLB debut on the day before his 20th birthday, going 2-4 with two runs scored.

The team was involved in three straight one-hitters the next week. Steve Trachsel pitched a complete-game one-hitter against the Angels on July 15, allowing only a sixth-inning single to David Eckstein. The next day, Marlins rookie sensation Dontrelle Willis beat the Mets 1-0, allowing only a fourth-inning single to Ty Wiggington. The following night, Jae Seo, David Weathers and Benitez pitched a combined one-hitter in a 5-0 win against the Marlins. Juan Encarnacion singled in the fifth but was caught stealing second. It was the first time Mets pitching faced the minimum 27 batters in a game.

With the team out of contention, new general manager Jim Duquette traded Alomar to the White Sox on July 1 for three minor leaguers. The future Hall of Famer never got it going in the Big Apple and was hitting .262 in 73 games at the time of the trade.

Jeromy Burnitz finally performed like the hitter the Mets expected but with the team out of contention, he was traded to the Dodgers in mid-July. Burnitz hit .274 with 18 home runs. Despite playing in only 65 games he would finish as the Mets home run leader along with Floyd. Armando Benitez was traded to the Yankees days later. Benitez, who had blown four games in April, blew his final save opportunity as a Met on July 13 against the Phillies.

FUTILE: TSUYOSHI SHINJO

After trading him to the Giants after his 2001 rookie season, the Mets resigned Shinjo after the Giants released him the next winter. Bad move. Shinjo put up a slash line of .193/.238.246, and drove in 7 and scored 10 in 114 at bats, the last of his major league career.

Lloyd and Sanchez were traded at the end of the month. Sanchez had seen his playing time dwindle after Reyes was promoted and but became part of Mets lore with a story of him receiving a haircut in the clubhouse during a blowout loss early in the season.

Playing out the string, the Mets put together their first winning month, going 15-12 in August before a 7-19 September to end the season. The Mets lost 16 of 17 from September

TOP BATTERS

Pos	Name	G	AB	H	BA	HR	RBI	RS	SB	OPS
1B	Jason Phillips	119	403	120	.298	11	58	45	0	.815
3B	Ty Wigginton	156	573	146	.255	11	71	73	12	.714
LF	Cliff Floyd	108	365	106	.290	18	68	57	3	.894
RF	Roger Cedeno	148	484	129	.267	7	37	70	14	.698

TOP PITCHERS

Pos	Name	G	GS	W	L	SV	ERA	IP	SO	BB
SP	Steve Trachsel	33	33	16	10	0	3.78	204.2	111	65
SP	Jae Weong Seo	32	31	9	12	0	3.82	188.1	110	46
SP	Al Leiter	30	30	15	9	0	3.99	180.2	139	94
CL	Armando Benitez	45	0	3	3	21	3.10	49.1	50	24
RP	David Weathers	77	0	1	6	7	3.08	87.2	75	40

4 through the 21st. The only late season was drama was seeing if the Tigers would break the 1962 Mets record of 120 losses. Detroit was 38-118 after 156 games but won five of their final six to finish 43-119.

Top 5 Highlights

1 Wearing number 16 as a nod to Dwight Gooden, David Cone wins his first start as a Mets since 1992, pitching five shutout innings against the Expos on a cold night at Shea. It would be his 194th and final win in the majors.

2 On May 10, Mike Piazza's two-run homer off Jaret Wright in the bottom of the 10th gives the Mets a 4-2 win over the Padres and sends the fans home happy on Mo Vaughn bobblehead day.

3 In his first at-bat in the majors, Jose Reyes singles to right off Rangers starter John Thomson. It's the first of 1,534 hits Reyes would collect as a Met.

4 Jason Phillips delivers a walk-off single to beat the Phillies 4-3 on July 13 on the day the Mets honored the 1973 NL champions. Philadelphia had tied the game on a Mike Lieberthal single with two outs in the ninth but Phillips saved the day with his hit off Terry Adams.

5 Steve Trachsel pitches his second complete game one-hit shutout of the season in an 8-0 win against the Rockies on August 18. The only batter to reach was Colorado pitcher Chin-Hui Tsao, who doubled over the head of Timo Perez in center with two outs in the sixth.

2004

	W	L	GB	Pos
	71	91	25.0	4th
RS/G	RA/G		Manager	
4.22	4.51		Art Howe	

Ugly Second Half Sinks Mets

The Moves

The Mets signed Kazuo Matsui, a four-time Gold Glove winner in Japan, setting up what looked like an exciting middle infield for the future with Matsui and Jose Reyes.

Reyes would play at second. Coach Matt Galante, who helped convert Craig Biggio from a catcher to a Gold Glove second baseman with the Astros, would attempt to help Reyes. Mike Piazza was in the process of moving from behind the plate to first base, another new look in the infield.

Braden Looper signed on to be the closer after saving 28 games and winning Game 4 of the World Series for the Marlins. Looper became expendable when the Marlins signed Armando Benitez. The Mets signed former Yankees outfielders Shane Spencer and Karim Garcia. Todd Zeile made a return to Queens. Veteran pitchers like Scott Erickson, Ricky Bottalico and James Baldwin signed as well.

The plan in the outfield was for Garcia and Spencer to platoon in right, Cliff Floyd in left and ike Cameron in center. Because of the outfield squeeze, Timo Perez was traded to the White Sox for pitcher Matt Ginter, who the Mets envisioned as a setup man down the road. Roger Cedeno was traded to the Cardinals for Wilson Delgado and Chris Widger.

🌀 He Was a Met?

A former AL wins leader, Scott Erickson was placed on the DL in early April and made his Mets debut on July 19. He was traded to Texas after a pair of unimpressive starts.

Glavine's Stay a Mixed Bag

Atlanta Braves' icon Tom Glavine was treated shoddily by the Braves after 2002 (18-11, 2.96) and signed a 4-year contract with the Mets after the season. The veteran had trouble adjusting to his new team and struggled to a 9-win, 4.52 season in 2003. The next two years he was pretty much the old Glavine, with ERAs well below the league average, but poor offensive support and a leaky bullpen cost him many wins and he went 24-27. His fortunes were better the next 2 years (28-15, including career win 300), but his last 3 starts with the Mets, during their September collapse of 2007, were disastrous (10.1 IP, 17 ER).

The Situation

There was an issue with the middle infield of dreams, as Matsui strained his right wrist and Reyes aggravated his right hamstring. The Mets made a trade with Cleveland for Ricky Gutierrez as insurance. "Playing in New York is always an honor with all the great players that have played through there, so going there, I was excited," Gutierrez said in an interview for the book. "I was excited to be able to go play for the Mets."

The trade was made on March 29 and Gutierrez was put in the starting lineup for the next day's game before he had even arrived. "Art just welcomed me in, my record spoke for itself and he was just excited to have me on board," Gutierrez said. "They got me just to do what I could to help the team win."

As an Astro, Gutierrez had the lone hit against Kerry Wood on the afternoon in 1998 when Wood struck out 20 Astros. Gutierrez had been in the majors since 1993 and was getting a close look at a lot of former opponents. "It was a good group of guys, it was a lot of guys that in my career I played against," Gutierrez said. "Mike Piazza, Glavine, guys I played against my whole career that I was able to be a teammate now. Cliff Floyd, Mike Cameron, Todd Zeile. So it was a team that I was going into with guys I knew. They welcomed me in and it was just a good group of guys and we were trying to do something special in New York."

Outside the clubhouse, expectations weren't high, especially after finishing spring training 13-20-1, leading the NL in errors and battling injuries. *Sports Illustrated* picked the Mets to finish last in the division, the Phillies winning the NL East and the Braves, who lost Greg Maddux to the Cubs in free agency, falling to third. Al Leiter was drilled in the face by a line drive, although he avoided serious injury and the disabled list. Matsui had been injured twice in spring training and hit .192 in the exhibition

 Final Resting Ground

Shane Spencer set New York on fire as a rookie who hit 10 HR in only 67 Abs after his callup, and then 2 more in that fall's ALDS. Five years and two seasons later he joined the Mets. Spencer hit .281 in 185 at bats for the Amazins, but went deep only 4 times, and after the season was out of baseball at age 32.

games while leading the team in strikeouts. And Reyes would start the season on the disabled list. On a positive note, Eric Valent came to the Mets as a Rule V pick from the Reds and nearly hit .300 while playing well defensively, earning a spot on the major league club.

The Season

Matsui homered on the first pitch he saw, a shot off Atlanta's Russ Ortiz, propelling the Mets to a 7-2 win over the Braves on Opening Day. The Mets lost the next two but took two of three from the Braves in the first home series of the season. But after a 5-4 start, the Mets lost eight of 10. The team scored one run in six of the losses and was shutout in another. In a three-game sweep at Wrigley Field, the Mets were 2-for-29 with runners on base. They were no-hit into the seventh inning in the final game of the series. "It's pretty bad," Piazza said. "What are you going to do? It's frustrating because we think we're getting decent pitching. We went from bad team offense to worse."

Spencer was swinging a hot bat but Art Howe wasn't getting much production from anyone else as he tinkered with the lineup day after day. Cliff Floyd missed a month with a strained right quadriceps. The Mets won four in a row in early May, including a sweep of the Giants. Piazza hit his 352nd home run as a catcher, breaking Carlton Fisk's record, with a shot off Jerome Williams on May 5. The next night he hit a walk-off homer. A week later, he would begin primarily playing at first base.

The Mets won nine of 12 in late May to improve to 23-22 and were only two games out of first. Tom Glavine was 6-2 with a 2.13 ERA after throwing a one-hit shutout against the Rockies on May 23. Steve Trachsel went 3-0 during the month.

New York swept the Phillies in Philadlephia, including a 5-3, 10 inning win with Zeile tying the game with a three-run homer in the eighth and putting the Mets ahead with a two-run blast. When the Mets left Kansas City on June 13, they were 28-33. A walk-off loss to the Royals saw Howe screaming at his players in a postgame meeting with someone throwing a garbage can against the clubhouse door.

TOP BATTERS

Pos	Name	G	AB	H	BA	HR	RBI	RS	SB	OPS
1B	Mike Piazza	129	455	121	.266	20	54	47	0	.806
SS	Kazuo Matsui	114	460	125	.272	7	44	65	14	.727
LF	Cliff Floyd	113	396	103	.260	18	63	55	11	.814
CF	Mike Cameron	140	493	114	.231	30	76	76	22	.798
RF	Richard Hidalgo	86	324	74	.228	21	52	46	3	.759

TOP PITCHERS

Pos	Name	G	GS	W	L	SV	ERA	IP	SO	BB
SP	Tom Glavine	33	33	11	14	0	3.60	212.1	109	70
SP	Steve Trachsel	33	33	12	13	0	4.00	202.2	117	83
SP	Al Leiter	30	30	10	8	0	3.21	173.2	117	97
CL	Braden Looper	71	0	2	5	29	2.70	83.1	60	16
RP	Mike Stanton	83	0	2	6	0	3.16	77.0	58	33

The team fired hitting coach Denny Walling and replaced him with bench coach Don Baylor. The Mets were batting .246, second-worst in the majors ahead of only Montreal, and were somehow 6-for-59 with the bases loaded, a .102 average. Howe, though unsurprised, was not happy of the firing of his former Astros teammate. "I know the offense has had problems. Everybody knows how much trouble we've had scoring runs," he said. "You realize something like this can happen and it has. Denny did everything possible to get the guys going. It just did not happen. Sometimes things don't sink in."

New York's pitching staff was keeping the Mets in the division race. The team's 3.61 ERA led the National League. And back at Shea, the Mets won six of seven including back-to-back walk-off hits from Cameron against Detroit. There were different bats in the lineup. The team traded for Astros outfielder Richard Hidalgo, sending David Weather and Jeremy Griffiths to Houston. Hidalgo hit .309 with 28 homers and 88 RBI in 2003 but was only hitting .256 with four homers and 30 RBI at the time of the trade and had lost his job to Jason Lane. The trade was made after the Mets had contacted the Royals about Carlos Beltran but balked when Kansas City asked for David Wright, who was still in Triple-A.

Also in the lineup was Jose Reyes, who played his first game of the season on June 19. His strained right hamstring had sent him to the DL on March 15. In his first game back, he tripled in the bottom of the 10th of a tied game and the Mets would win several batters later.

The Mets were 38-39 when the Yankees came to Shea for a series on fourth of July weekend. The Mets clobbered Mike Mussina and the Yankees staff 11-2 in the opener, with Matsui hitting two homers and Hidalgo homering. The Mets won a wild Saturday afternoon game 10-9 with Tanyon Sturtze unable to field Spencer's tapper back to the mound as Matsui scored to win it. The sweep was completed the next day as Ty Wigginton homered off Tom Gordon in the eighth to give the Mets a 6-5 lead and Looper got Alex Rodriguez on a grounder to end the game. Suddenly the Mets were 41-39, the first time they were two games over .500 since August 2002, and only two games out of first.

Though the team lost the next night in Philadelphia, Hidalgo became the first Met to homer in five consecutive games. On July 15, Wigginton delivered a game-winning single as the Mets improved to 45-43 and were one game out of first. The Phillies, Braves, Mets and Marlins were separated by one game.

But then the Mets lost four of five. On July 20, Trachsel gave up six runs in the first and Piazza had to leave in the second after a collision at first that would keep him out a week. The Mets came back to take a 7-6 lead in the third inning but lost 9-7 with a struggling John Franco picking up the loss. By mid-July, Franco was being used as a situational lefty in the middle innings.

Wright made his highly-anticipated debut on July 21 against the Expos and collected his first career hit the following afternoon. But the Mets lost four straight to drop to 47-51. Scott Erickson made his second start on July 26 and gave up seven runs (six earned) in two innings and the Mets would go on to lose 19-10 with Zeile pitching the bottom of the eighth.

With the season slipping away, Jim Duquette went to the phones and made some deals before the deadline. The team acquired starting pitchers Kris Benson and Victor Zambrano.

First the team traded Triple-A catcher Justin Huber to the Royals for minor leaguer Jose Bautista. Then the Mets sent Bautista, Wigginton and Double-A pitcher Matt Peterson to Pittsburgh for Benson and minor league shortstop Jeff Keppinger. Wigginton had been batting .285 with 12 homers but with Wright and Reyes the future on the left side of the infield, he was a goner. Benson was 8-8 with a 4.22 ERA with the Pirates.

Then Duquette got Zambrano, who was 9-7 with a 4.43 ERA, from the Devil Rays but it cost them top pitching prospect Scott Kazmir. Duquette believed that Kazmir, who was blowing away batters in the minors, was still a ways away. "We're still in the hunt and we're still in the mix. Let's go for it," Duquette said. "With these guys added to the rotation, we're going to have a chance to win every night."

But the new look Mets were swept in Atlanta and suddenly the team that was going for it was 49-55, nine games out of first and 8.5 out of the wild card. Benson lost his first start, giving up seven runs in five innings. The Mets swept the Brewers in Milwaukee but then went to St. Louis and were swept by the Cardinals. The Mets returned home but Glavine had to miss a start after being involved in a taxi accident. Reyes also missed a week as he turned his ankle on the dirt cutout around second base. Reyes was left in the game and aggravated the injury, which kept him out several days. "Sometimes, you've just got to spit on it and let's go," Howe said.

The injuries were piling up. Matsui was out with back spasms and Piazza was on the DL with a swollen knee. Zambrano would win his first two starts but then go on the DL with an elbow injury and was done for the season.

The Mets won an 11-9, 12-inning marathon on August 21 in San Francisco to improve to 59-62. But the season went off the rails as the team lost 16 of the next 17. Floyd said, "There isn't any light at the end of the tunnel right now."

At 63-82, it was announced Howe would be fired. The announcement was supposed to be made at the end of the season but when the news broke early, Duquette and Howe acknowledged the inevitable. Howe finished the rest of the season. Many believed Howe, who would often speak of how the team "battled" in defeat, was too laid back. When Howe told the team of the news, Hidalgo and Zambrano walked in after the meeting had started. When a writer asked Floyd what was said at the start of the meeting, Floyd admitted he missed that part.

The Mets were able to play spoiler as they took two straight from the Cubs at Shea, dealing a blow to Chicago's wild card hopes. On the final day of the season, the Mets beat the Expos 8-1. It was the final game the Expos played before moving to Washington and becoming the Nationals. Zeile homered in his final at-bat in the majors.

Top 5 Highlights

1 Mike Piazza sets the all-time home run record for catchers with a solo shot off San Francisco's Jerome Williams in the first inning of New York's 8-2 win over the Giants on May 5.

2 Tom Glavine beats Randy Johnson and the Diamondbacks in a 1-0 duel on May 12 in Arizona. Kaz Matsui leads off the game with a homer. Glavine gives up three hits in 7.2 innings and Braden Looper records the final four outs. Johnson gives up three hits in 7 innings.

3 The Mets finish off their first sweep of the Yankees since interleague play began with a 6-5 win at Shea on July 4. After the Mets squander a 4-1 lead, Richard Hidalgo homers in the seventh to make it 5-4. And after the Yankees tie it in the eighth, Ty Wigginton homers in the bottom of the eighth.

4 David Wright collects his first hit in the majors with a fifth inning double off Montreal's Zach Day on July 22. In the ninth, Wright singles off Chad Cordero for hit number two.

5 Craig Brazell hits his first career homer, a solo shot off Kent Mercker in the bottom of the 11th to give the Mets a 4-3 win over the Cubs on September 25. Down to their final strike, Victor Diaz tied the game with a three-run homer off LaTroy Hawkins in the ninth.

2005

	W	L	GB	Pos
	83	79	7.0	4th
RS/G	RA/G		Manager	
4.46	4.00		Willie Randolph	

Strong Team Underachieves and Finishes Third

The Moves

Omar Minaya was the new general manager after spending three seasons in the same capacity with the Expos. He liked what he heard when speaking the Fred Wilpon. "I said, 'Fred, full autonomy?' He said, 'Full autonomy.' As a baseball man, that is a baseball man's dream."

The final choices for manager were former Astros and Angels manager Terry Collins, Rangers hitting coach Rudy Jaramillo and Yankees coach Willie Randolph. Minaya hired Randolph, who grew up as a Mets fan in Brooklyn and played for the team in 1992. Randolph, who had been a Yankees coach since 1994, had interviewed for a number of jobs over the years but had always been passed over.

Minaya's first trade was with the Yankees. In a deal of southpaw relievers, Mike Stanton waived his no-trade clause to go back to the Bronx and Felix Heredia joined the Mets. Al Leiter also went back to a former team, signing with the Florida Marlins. "I did not want to leave the Mets and I did not want to leave New York," Leiter said. "The reason I am leaving is that Omar Minaya did not want me." He said he accepted an offer from Minaya who then rescinded it. John Franco was also gone, signing with the Astros.

Minaya made a splash, signing three-time Cy Young winner Pedro Martinez, who had helped the Red Sox win the World Series for the first time since

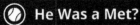 **He Was a Met?**

An All-Star with the Dodgers and Red Sox, Jose Offerman spent the final 53 games of his MLB career with the Mets. He hit a pinch-hit home run off Cory Lidle on June 29.

David Wright, seen here in 2016, was a highly-touted prospect who, if anything, exceeded expectations in his tremendous career. In his first full season in 2005, Wright .306/.388/.523 with 102 RBI, the first of 5 100+ RBI seasons. Despite back troubles that sharply curtailed his production after age 30—and likely derailed his shot at the Hall of Fame—Wright is the all-time leader in most offensive categories for the Mets.

1918. The six-time All-Star led the league in ERA five times, strikeouts three times and winning percentage three times. But there was some concern from fans about giving Martinez four years and $53 million after he ended the 2004 season with a career-high 3.90 ERA.

Martinez would form a battery with Mike Piazza, notable because Piazza said the pitcher had no class after being drilled by him in 1998 and Martinez said the catcher was a coward after Piazza fought Guillermo Mota in 2003. "It is resolved already, because he's my teammate," Martinez said. "And whatever happens before when we were not teammates or whatever – whatever words were said – have to be forgotten the first moment I became a teammate."

In January, the team signed outfielder Carlos Beltran, whose impressive postseason helped take the Astros to Game 7 of the NLCS. Beltran, who had almost returned to Houston, was given seven years and $119 million.

Other moves included signing Marlins catcher Ramon Castro to backup Piazza, Toronto utility man Chris Woodward, and veterans Marlon Anderson and Miguel Cairo. Roberto Hernandez, the 40-year-old two-time All-Star, was signed to provide help in the bullpen.

 Final Resting Ground

Gerald Willams' 14-year career had been in decline for a few years when he joined the Mets in 2004, when he batted. 233 in 57 games. In limited action in 2009, he replicated the .233 average, became a free agent, went unsigned and retired.

The Mets traded for Boston first baseman Doug Mientkiewicz after Carlos Delgado accepted a deal from the Marlins. Mientkiewicz had won a Gold Glove with the Twins in 2001. Jason Phillips was traded to the Dodgers for pitcher Kaz Ishii, who was acquired to replace an injured Steve Trachsel.

The Situation

Beltran's signing moved Mike Cameron to right, despite being a two-time Gold Glove winner. And Martinez was a hard-thrower on a team that hadn't had one. "Pedro gives us a defense mechanism, the feeling that he can stop any losing streak," Cameron said. "That's the difference in this team: We've got a lot more bullets." Piazza's first base experiment was over.

Reyes and Matsui flipped position with Reyes going to short and Matsui now at second. "If [Matsui] can play shortstop, he can play second," Mientkiewicz said. "Obviously, he's got great feet and great hands."

Sports Illustrated still picked the Mets to finish third. "Shortcomings abound. New general manager Omar Minaya hasn't made the Mets great. Merely intriguing."

The Season

Martinez fanned 12 batters in six innings, including eight Reds in a nine-batter stretch, in his first start as a Met, dominating after Adam Dunn's first inning three-run homer. The Mets took a 6-4 lead into the ninth and Looper came in. Austin Kearns singled, Dunn homered to tie it and Joe Randa homered to win it. Randa hit a grand slam the next game and the Reds finished off a sweep with a 6-1 win over Ishii. Then the Mets went to Atlanta and dropped the first two. Cameron found himself on the DL with tendinitis in his left wrist and would be gone until the first week of May.

Aaron Heilman lost a start filling in for injured Kris Benson. It was Benson's wife, Anna, who was drawing attention even more than the pitcher who agreed to a three-year, $22.5 million deal in the offseason. Shortly after, Benson went on Howard Stern's show and said she would sleep with every Met player and staffer if she found her husband cheating.

In the home opener, the Mets trailed 4-3 in the eighth when they busted out for five runs, including a two-run single from Floyd off John Franco. In the next game, Ishii matched Roger Clemens for seven shutout innings and Reyes delivered a game-winning single in the 11th. Heilman pitched a one-hit shutout against Florida. The Mets would follow their 0-5 start with six straight wins. The sixth straight win saw Martinez and Leiter duel. The Mets took a 3-2 lead into the ninth but Looper blew the lead. Castro played the hero when he singled in the bottom of the ninth off Mota.

The Mets offense exploded for seven homers in a 16-4 laugher over the Phillies on April 19. The

**FABULOUS:
PEDRO MARTINEZ**

In his first year with the Mets, signed as a free agent, Martinez had the last good season of his career, posting a 15-8 record, fanning nearly a batter an inning, posting a sparkling ERA of 2.82, and leading the league in WHIP.

team scored 10 runs in a win in Florida and 10 more in a win over the Nationals. New York lost its final four to end April. Zambrano lost on April 30, falling to 1-3 with a 5.81 ERA. On the bright side, Floyd was hitting .366 through the end of April. Wright was hitting .303, Diaz was at .292 and Beltran was hitting .284. Reyes was hitting .281 through May 2 but was yet to draw a walk.

FUTILE: HEATH BELL

Before blossoming into a star reliever as soon as the Mets traded him to San Diego, Heath Bell had 2 consecutive seasons with a +5.00 ERA, including 2005, when in 42 games he went 1-3 with a 5.59.

Randolph flipped Floyd and Piazza in the lineup. Floyd had a 15-game hitting streak and a team-high six homers while Piazza was batting .222.

The Mets won six of seven to begin the month. Heilman was moved to the bullpen because of the amount of starters available. The Mets lost five of seven, then swept the Reds to improve to 22-19. The Mets beat Randy Johnson on a Saturday at Shea but the bullpen blew a late lead the next day for Martinez and then went to Atlanta and were swept by the Braves. The Mets were shutout in consecutive games for the first time since September 2003. Beltran missed a few games with a quad injury. Piazza had a stretch of 11 hitless at-bats with seven strikeouts. Floyd was in a seven-for-64 slump.

New York started June with four wins in five games but then lost nine of 11. Ishii struggled mightily, losing three straight starts and saw his ERA increase to 5.40. Benson went 3-0 during the month. Glavine failed to make it out of the third inning in a loss to the Mariners and saw his ERA go over five. Matsui went on the DL with a bruised knee and would miss nearly two months.

The team was three outs from sweeping the Yankees in the Bronx but Looper blew a ninth inning lead in a 5-4 loss on June 26. The mediocre Mets went 13-13 in June, ending the month 39-39 and in last place.

There had been talk of Mike Cameron going to the Yankees and Gary Sheffield coming to the Mets but Sheffield's tirade about the report killed any chance of that. Beltran was only hitting .258 at the end of June. The team did sign veteran All-Star Jose Offerman, who had hit .182 with the Phillies early in the season.

The team entered the All-Star break 44-44. Martinez gave up one run on five hits in seven innings in the last game before the break, so he didn't pitch in the midsummer classic. Piazza and Beltran were both voted in as starters. Piazza had only hit .260 with nine homers in the first half but in the first game after the break, his three-run homer in the bottom of the eighth off Blaine Boyer gave the Mets a 6-3 win over the Braves. The Mets won seven of 10 on their homestand, including a four-game sweep over the Padres. Woodward's pinch-hit two-run homer in the bottom of the 11th gave the Mets a 3-1 win on July 19. Martinez won three straight starts to improve to 12-3. Ishii even pitched six shutout innings in a win over San Diego. Benson tossed eight shutout innings in a win over the Dodgers.

TOP BATTERS

Pos	Name	G	AB	H	BA	HR	RBI	RS	SB	OPS
C	Mike Piazza	113	398	100	.251	19	62	41	0	.778
SS	Jose Reyes	161	696	190	.273	7	58	99	60	.687
3B	David Wright	160	575	176	.306	27	102	99	17	.912
LF	Cliff Floyd	150	550	150	.273	34	98	85	12	.863
CF	Carlos Beltran	151	582	155	.266	16	78	83	17	.744

TOP PITCHERS

Pos	Name	G	GS	W	L	SV	ERA	IP	SO	BB
SP	Pedro Martinez	31	31	15	8	0	2.82	217.0	208	47
SP	Tom Glavine	33	33	13	13	0	3.53	211.1	105	61
SP	Kris Benson	28	28	10	8	0	4.13	174.1	95	49
RP	Aaron Heilman	53	7	5	3	5	3.17	108.0	106	37
RP	Roberto Hernandez	67	0	8	6	4	2.58	69.2	61	28

The team couldn't land Boston slugger Manny Ramirez at the deadline and the team went 2-5 on a roadstand to end the month. Ishii was sent down to Triple-A in early August. The southpaw was 3-9 with a 5.04 ERA. Seo was called back up and won four straight starts, giving up three runs in 30.1 innings. During a 2-1 loss in San Diego on August 11, Cameron and Beltran collided while diving for a ball. Beltran wouldn't play until the 17th. Cameron got the worst of it, suffering a concussion and multiple fractures of his nose and cheekbones. He would be out for the rest of the year.

On the day Beltran returned to the lineup, the team learned that Piazza had a hairline fracture in his wrist and would be out for several weeks. On August 18, the Mets were shutout on three hits in a loss to the Pirates, dropping the team to 61-59. But the Mets won seven of the next eight, bookending the stretch with 1-0 wins. The stretch also included a 9-8 win in a game the Mets blew an 8-0 lead and 32 runs in two games in a beatdown of the Diamondbacks. Trachsel returned and pitched eight shutout innings in San Francisco.

The new star was Mike Jacobs who homered in his first at-bat and four of his first 13. Jacobs was called up from Double-A when Piazza went on the DL.

After Trachsel's gem against the Giants the Mets were 68-60 and 1.5 out of the wild card. The season would suddenly fall apart with the Mets losing 15 of 18. Martinez gave up four homers in a loss to the Phillies. The Mets lost two of three in Florida and then were swept at that old house of horrors, Turner Field.

Looper blew his seventh save of the season in a loss on September 15. Randolph still kept Heilman, who had an 0.56 ERA in 20 games since July 16, as his set-up man. Martinez pitched a shutout in a win over the Braves but would lose his next and final start of the year. He would later write that Fred Wilpon ordered him to pitch through an injury in order to increase attendance.

The Mets would get hot too little, too late, winning 11 of 14. There were back-to-back walk-off wins against the Marlins and a Glavine shutout against the Rockies. The final day of the season was an emotional one as it was the final game in a Mets uniform for Piazza, who would not be resigned. He grounded out in three at-bats against Colorado's Aaron Cook and was replaced in the top of the eighth by Mike Difelice.

New York finished with its first winning record since 2001. The team finished six games out of the wild card, though they did win one more game than the NL West champion Padres.

Top 5 Highlights

1 Carlos Beltran's two-run homer in the eighth off John Smoltz gives the Mets a 2-1 lead and New York goes on to win 6-1 over the Braves on April 10. It's the team's first win after five losses to begin the season. Pedro Martinez earns his first win as a Met, giving up one run on two hits and retiring the final 16 Braves in a 101-pitch complete game.

2 Dae-Sung Koo takes a legendary trip around the bases, doubling off Randy Johnson and scoring from second on a Jose Reyes bunt in a 7-1 win over the Yankees on May 21. Koo also pitched 1.1 innings, striking out three batters.

3 Down to the final strike, Cliff Floyd hits a three-run homer off Brendan Donnelly to give the Mets a 5-3 win in 11 innings. The Mets trailed 2-1 in the ninth when Marlon Anderson hit an inside-the-park home run. Steve Finley failed to make a diving catch and kicked the ball away with Anderson narrowly beating a play at the plate.

4 Mike Piazza draws a bases loaded walk as the Mets beat the Brewers 9-8 in 11 innings on August. The Mets trailed 8-7 in the ninth when Mike Cameron homered off Derrick Turnbow. The Mets trailed 6-2 in the second inning after Victor Zambrano was hit hard.

5 Martinez pitches a six-hit shutout against the Braves in a 4-0 win on September 16. Atlanta loads the bases in the ninth, but Jeff Francoeur flies out to left to end the game. Martinez strikes out 10 and throws 122 pitches. Mike Jacobs homered in the second off Smoltz.

2006

	W	L	GB	Pos
	97	65	12.0	1st
RS/G	**RA/G**		**Manager**	
5.15	4.51		Willie Randolph	

Division Champs and Playoffs Heartbreak

The Moves

The Mets solidified the middle of the lineup, acquiring superstar slugger Carlos Delgado from the Marlins. Delgado hit 30 home runs for nine straight seasons. Mike Jacobs and two prospects went to the cost-cutting Marlins. "Cleanup hitters, left-handed power hitters, do not come along too often," Omar Minaya said. "And when they do, I think you just have to react. He's a force."

The team opened the checkbook for four-time All-Star closer Billy Wagner, giving him $43 million for four years. And the team traded for Paul Lo Duca, answering the catching question by acquiring the three-time All-Star.

Omar Minaya made other moves. Mike Cameron was traded to the Padres for Xavier Nady. Jose Valentin was signed, as was 47-year-old Julio Franco, who made his MLB debut in 1982. The team improved the bullpen by signing Chad Bradford and veteran southpaw Darren Oliver. Outfielder Endy Chavez was signed.

Jae Seo was traded to the Dodgers for reliever Duaner Sanchez. Kris Benson was dealt to the Orioles, with pitching prospect John Maine coming to Queens. His wife, Anna, had worn a revealing Mrs. Claus dress to Kris' Santa Claus at the team holiday party. She also criticized Delgado for not standing for the national anthem when he played with the Blue Jays. "If they traded Kris

⚾ He Was a Met?

Chan Ho Park is in the history books for several reasons. He gave up two grand slams in one inning to Fernando Tatis. He gave up a home run to Cal Ripken Jr. in the 2001 All-Star Game. And he gave up Barry Bonds' record-breaking 71st (and 72nd) home run of 2001. As a Met, Park surrendered two homers in his April 30 start. He gave up seven runs in four innings in a 9-6 loss to the Marlins, his only game with the Mets.

because of what I've done, then that's a dirty, nasty, rotten trick," she said. Minaya said the move was strictly baseball-related.

The Situation

Sports Illustrated picked Atlanta to win the division again. The Mets had added talent on the field and leadership in the clubhouse. "We thought we needed some leadership when we looked at the team last year," Minaya said. There were the new acquisitions, while Jose Reyes and David Wright were expected to take a step forward.

Heartbreak in the NLCS

The Mets, who had won 97 games during the season and swept the Dodgers in the NLDS lost to a hard-fought 7-game series to St. Louis, who finished the seasson 83-79. Jeff Suppan, who held the Mets to 3 hits in 8 innings in a Game 3 win, handcuffed New York again in Game 7, allowing only 2 hits and one run in 7 innings. After the Cardinals scored 2 runs in the top of the 9th, the Mets loaded the bases in the bottom half, only to see Carlos Beltran, who had had a phenomenal season, take a called third strike to seal one of the most heart-breaking losses in the team's history.

"Right now we're phenomenal on paper," Wright said. "There's a difference between having the tools and having the pieces and fitting that together." Lo Duca said the Mets, barring injuries, were the team to beat.

Aaron Heilman wanted to be a starter and seemed to be the winner of the Benson trade. Brian Bannister pitched 19 innings in the spring with a 0.95 ERA and took the fifth starter spot, sending Heilman back to the bullpen as a set-up man for Wagner.

The Season

The Mets came out of the gate on fire, starting 8-1 on the strength of a seven-game winning streak. Nady was hitting .353 with two homers. Wright was batting .429. Delgado was hitting .378 and Reyes .326. Beltran went 5-10 with two homers in a sweep over the Nationals. From the third game on, the Mets would be at the top of the division. Delgado hit nine home runs in April.

Martinez won five games in April, including two against Washington and two against Atlanta. After Martinez, Tom Glavine and Steve Trachsel, the team struggled to find dependable starters. Bannister and Zambrano got hurt, and Geremi Gonzalez was ineffective and was traded to the Brewers. Minaya traded for Orlando Hernandez, who had won three titles with the Yankees and White Sox, but was 2-4 with a 6.11 ERA in nine starts for the Diamondbacks.

Final Resting Ground

Jose Lima reached the fifth inning only once in four starts, and gave up at least four earned runs in each one. He gave up a grand slam to Dontrelle Willis in the final game of his career.

FABULOUS: CARLOS BELTRAN

Beltran got comfortable in his second year with the Mets and had perhaps the best year of his great career. Beltran put up career highs in HR (41), RBI (116), and RS (127) - in only 140 games. He also walked 95 times and finished fourth in the MVP voting.

"We're adding a starter, a guy who can compete," Minaya said. "He's a big-game pitcher. The later the season gets, the more impact he has."

The Mets were coming through in the clutch, winning eight games on walk-offs from May 1 through June 3. Wright had two walk-off hits, 10 days apart. "He's been clutch for us all year," Willie Randolph said. "He's been our leader."

Kaz Matsui and his .200 batting average were traded to the Rockies for Eli Marrero. It marked the end of a brief era of Mets history. Matsui homered in his first at-bat of the season in each of his three seasons with the Mets.

An eight-game winning streak in June put the division away early. The offense exploded, scoring at least nine runs in five of the wins. The Mets became the third team since 1900 to score in the first inning in eight straight games on the road.

Lastings Milledge was called up in late May with Nady on the DL. The highly-touted outfielder was 21 years old and showed some immaturity. His first home run was a game-tying shot off Armando Benitez with two outs in the bottom of the 10th against the Giants. When he went out to right field for the 11th, Milledge high-fived fans down the line. Randolph said it wouldn't happen again. He was thrown out at home trying to score from first on a double as he was jogging in a game in Philadelphia. Then he showed up late to the ballpark for a game. "I never had to deal with any teaching because I pretty much played the game well enough that people left me alone," he said. "Here, with everything being so crucial, there are things I need to know and work on."

The back of the rotation was still in flux, though Glavine eased the burden with a 5-0 May. Martinez was lost for a month due to injury. Maine, who made one start in May before going back to the minors, was recalled. Mike Pelfrey made his debut on July 8 and was the winning pitcher as the Mets pounded out a 17-3 win over the Marlins but he would only make four starts before being sent back to the minors.

FUTILE: VICTOR ZAMBRANO

Zambrano started 5 games for the Mets in 2006, winning 1 and losing 2 and pitching only 21 innings. He tore a ligament in his elbow while pitching and was done for the season. Zambrano came back with Toronto, but appeared in only 13 more games before being out of the majors for good.

The Mets were 53-36 at the break and well represented at the All-Star Game. Lo Duca, Wright, Beltran, Glavine, Martinez and Reyes were

TOP BATTERS										
Pos	Name	G	AB	H	BA	HR	RBI	RS	SB	OPS
C	Paul Lo Duca	124	512	163	.318	5	49	80	3	.783
1B	Carlos Delgado	144	524	139	.265	38	114	89	0	.909
SS	Jose Reyes	153	647	194	.300	19	81	122	64	.841
3B	David Wright	154	582	181	.311	26	116	96	20	.912
CF	Carlos Beltran	140	510	140	.275	41	116	127	18	.982

TOP PITCHERS										
Pos	Name	G	GS	W	L	SV	ERA	IP	SO	BB
SP	Tom Glavine	32	32	15	7	0	3.82	198.0	131	62
SP	Steve Trachsel	30	30	15	8	0	4.97	164.2	79	78
SP	Pedro Martinez	23	23	9	8	0	4.48	132.2	137	39
CL	Billy Wagner	70	0	3	2	40	2.24	72.1	94	21
RP	Pedro Feliciano	64	0	7	2	0	2.09	60.1	54	20

selected. Wright participated in the home run derby, advancing to the final round before losing to Ryan Howard. Wright hit .327 with 10 home runs and 29 RBI in June but would only hit eight home runs over the final three months. He hit .245 in August before rebounding with a .371 mark over the final month. On July 16, Cliff Floyd and Beltran both hit grand slams in the sixth inning of a 13-7 win against the Cubs. The Mets ended August with a 3-game sweep of the Braves at Turner Field.

Sanchez had emerged as one of the best set-up men in the game, going 5-1 with a 2.60 ERA. The night before the trade deadline, he suffered a season-ending shoulder injury during a late-night cab accident. Working quickly, Minaya sent Nady – who was batting .264 with 14 home runs and 40 RBI in 75 games – to the Pirates with Roberto Hernandez returning to the Mets bullpen, and struggling southpaw Oliver Perez also coming to Queens. Milledge returned from the minors and would split time in right with Chavez, substituting speed for power in Nady's absence.

Heilman became the eighth-inning man and 13 of his next 14 outings were scoreless. Wagner blew a save in Florida on August 1, but then closed out his final 18 opportunities. Guillermo Mota was acquired from the Indians and went 3-0 with an ERA of 1.00 in 18 games. The team added Shawn Green from the Diamondbacks. The outfielder was batting .283 with 11 home runs and 51 RBI.

The Mets closed in on the division, though the one problem was hitting left-handed pitching after the Nady trade. The team went 7-15 against southpaw starters. Another issue was Martinez. He returned on September 15 after missing a month, was hit hard by the Pirates and was seen crying in the dugout. He was hit hard in his next two starts. Martinez would miss the playoffs with an injured leg and then it turned out an injured pitching shoulder would keep him out for most of 2007.

For the first time since 1988, the Mets won the NL East, clinching on September 18 against the Marlins. Valentin hit two homers. He would hit 18, after hitting none in April. In the final days of the season, Beltran hit his 41st home run in a win at Atlanta, tying Todd Hundley for the team record.

The Mets won 97 games and won the division by 12 games. They led the NL East by double-digits since late June.

Top 5 Highlights

1 David Wright's double in the bottom of the 14th gives the Mets an 8-7 win over the Braves on May 5. The Mets trailed 7-6 in the 11th when Cliff Floyd tied the game with a home run off Chris Reitsma. Atlanta led 6-2 but the Mets scored four in the seventh to tie it.

2 Wright's hit off Mariano Rivera goes over the head of Johnny Damon in center, scoring Paul Lo Duca to beat the Yankees 7-6 on May 19. Lo Duca doubled and Carlos Delgado was intentionally walked to bring up Wright. Carlos Beltran and Xavier Nady homered off Randy Johnson as the Mets erased a 4-0 first inning Yankee lead.

3 Beltran's 16th inning home run wins it 9-8 ends a five-hour, 22-minute marathon over the Phillies on May 23. Ryan Madson pitched seven shutout innings before surrendering the home run. The Mets trailed 6-2 in the fifth and were down 8-5 in the eighth. Jose Reyes' two-run homer off Ryan Franklin tied the game.

4 Beltran's two-run home run off Jason Isringhausen completes a six-run comeback to beat the Cardinals 8-7 on August 22. Delgado homered to give the Mets a 1-0 lead. Albert Pujols hit a three-run home run in the fourth. Pujols hit a fifth inning grand slam to make it 7-1 but Delgado answered with a grand slam in the bottom of the inning, the 400th home run of his career.

5 Josh Willingham flies out to Cliff Floyd in left as the Mets clinch the NL East title for the first time since 1988 with a 4-0 win over the Marlins on September 18. Jose Valentin homers twice off Brian Moehler and Steve Trachsel pitches 6.1 shutout innings.

2006 NLDS

With a 2.01 ERA in five September starts, Hernandez was named the starter for Game 1 of the NLDS against the Dodgers. Running in the outfield the day before the playoffs began, the right-hander suffered a right calf tear and would have to miss the postseason.

Instead it was Maine who started the first game. In the top of the second inning, Jeff Kent and J.D. Drew singled. Russell Martin drilled a pitch off the wall in right but Kent got a bad read from second. On a relay, the Mets threw Kent out at the plate and Drew was tagged right behind him for a double play. Marlon In a back-and-forth game, in the bottom of the seventh the Mets took a 5-4 lead with Delgado's RBI single off Brad Penny. Wright followed with an RBI double. In the ninth, Ramon Martinez's RBI double cut the lead to 6-5 and Garciaparra came up with the tying run on second but Wagner struck him out to end the game.

Glavine took the mound in Game 2 and the playoff veteran tossed six shutout innings. The Mets manufactured offense against Dodger pitching. Reyes had an RBI groundout. Lo Duca's sacrifice fly made it 2-0. A run scored when Franco hit into a force out. Then Reyes added an RBI single. The Mets bullpen retired nine of 11 batters in the 4-1 win and went back to California with a 2-0 series lead.

The Mets jumped on Greg Maddux for three runs on five hits in the first inning, with RBI singles from Wright, Floyd and Green. Green's RBI double in the third extended the lead to 4-0. Trachsel worked in and out of trouble but was pulled in the fourth when James Loney's single drove in two runs. LA took the lead in the fifth as Kent homered off Darren Oliver to tie it and Loney drew a bases loaded walk to make it 5-4. New York took back the lead in the sixth with three runs off Jonathan Broxton, with RBI singles from Reyes, Lo Duca and Beltran. The Mets added two more in the eighth to make it 9-5 and achieve a Mets sweep.

2006 NLCS

Awaiting the Mets in the NLCS were the 83-win Cardinals, in their third straight NLCS and fifth in seven seasons. Glavine and Jeff Weaver dueled for six innings until Beltran homered to give the Mets a 2-0 lead. Glavine pitched seven shutout innings and Mota and Wagner pitched an inning apiece in the 2-0 win.

Delgado's three-run homer off Chris Carpenter gave the Mets a 3-0 first inning lead in Game 2. Yadier Molina drove in two runs with a second inning double. After a Reyes RBI single made it 4-2, Jim Edmonds tied the game with a homer in the third. In the fifth, Delgado homered off Carpenter again. Lo Duca's RBI double in the sixth made it 6-4. Mota retired the first two batters in the seventh before walking Albert Pujols on the 11th pitch of the at-bat. Edmonds drew a four-pitch walk to bring up Scott Spiezio, who was starting at third in place of a slumping Scott Rolen. Spiezio hit an 0-2 pitch deep to right. Green prevented a home run but both runners scored to tie the game. So Taguchi, who hit two home runs in 2006, had entered as a defensive replacement for Chris Duncan, who hit 22 homers during the season. Leading off the ninth, Taguchi homered off Wagner. St. Louis added two more runs and won 9-6.

The Cardinals jumped on Trachsel in Game 3. Spiezio had a two-run triple in the first. Opposing pitcher Jeff Suppan homered leading off the second. Trachsel left in the second inning with a right thigh contusion after being hit by a Preston Wilson liner. Trachsel stayed in, walked Pujols and left. The Cardinals led 5-0 after two and that was the final score. Oliver rescued the bullpen with six shutout innings and was mentioned as a possible Game 7 starter.

Perez was given the Game 4 start. Molina's RBI single gave the Cardinals a 1-0 lead in the second. Beltran and Wright homered off Anthony Reyes in the third but Juan Encarnacion's triple in the bottom of the inning tied the game. Then the offense took over. Delgado hit a three-run homer off Brad Thompson in the fifth. David Eckstein homered off Perez to make it 5-3 but the Mets blew it open with six runs in the sixth. Valentin's three-run double was the big blow. Beltran homered off Braden Looper in the seventh to make it 12-5. Beltran scored four runs and Delgado drove in five.

Glavine and Weaver met again in Game 5. Valentin's two-run double gave the Mets a fourth inning lead. In the bottom of the inning, Pujols homered and Ronnie Belliard tied the game with a single. In the fifth, Wilson's RBI double drove in Eckstein to give St. Louis the lead. Duncan's homer off Feliciano in the sixth made it 4-2. The Mets were blanked for the final five innings.

Facing Carpernter, Reyes hit a leadoff homer. In the fourth, Green's single made it 2-0. Maine pitched 5.1 innings of two-hit shutout ball. Lo Duca's single off Looper in the seventh extended the lead to 4-0. Bradford, Mota and Heilman kept the Cardinals off the board and Wagner entered in the ninth. He quickly ran into trouble, giving up a single to Encarnacion and a double to Rolen. He settled down, getting Belliard on a groundout and Molina on a fly ball. Taguchi doubled to left, scoring two and bringing the tying run to the plate. Eckstein grounded out to second and the Mets survived to tie the series.

Perez, who went 3-13 with a 6.55 ERA during the season, was the Game 7 starter. The only other time he started on three days' rest was in September 2005, following an outing in which he was ejected in the second inning. Suppan, who won Game 7 of the 2004 NLCS, would start on full rest for St. Louis. Wright's single in the first scored Beltran to give the Mets an early 1-0 lead. The Cardinals tied the game in the second on a squeeze bunt from Belliard. The game was still 1-1 in the top of the sixth when Perez walked Edmonds with one out. Randolph came out to talk to his pitcher and left him in. Rolen hit the next pitch over the wall in left but Chavez robbed a home run and began a relay to double off Edmonds.

With two outs in the top of the eighth, Heilman intentionally walked Pujols with nobody on base. Heilman struck out Encarnacion to end the inning. Beltran led off the eighth with a walk, ending Suppan's day. Flores struck out Delgado and Wright. Green grounded out to send the game to the ninth. Heilman was back on the mound for the ninth instead of Wagner. With one out, Rolen singled. Then Molina, who hit .216 with six home runs, crushed one into the Cardinals bullpen in left, giving St. Louis a 3-1 lead. Facing Wainwright, Valentin and Chavez led off the bottom of the ninth with singles. Randolph called on Floyd, making his third at-bat of the series, looking for power instead of using Anderson Hernandez to bunt the runners over. Randolph's faith was not rewarded as Floyd struck out. Reyes lined out to center and Lo Duca walked, loading the bases for Beltran. Beltran struck out looking on an 0-2 curveball and the season was suddenly over.

2007

OPENING DAY LINEUP

Jose Reyes, SS
Paul Lo Duca, C
Carlos Beltran, CF
Carlos Delgado, 1B
David Wright, 3B
Moises Alou, LF
Shawn Green, RF
Jose Valentin, 2B
Tom Glavine, P

	W	L	GB	Pos
	88	74	1.0	2nd

RS/G	RA/G	Manager	
4.96	4.63	Willie Randolph	

Mets Choke Away Division in 17 Games

The Moves

The biggest acquisition of the offseason was six-time All-Star Moises Alou. He batted .300 six times, including a .301 mark in 2006 with the Giants, though injuries limited him to 98 games. "I watched the Mets' playoff games while I was in the Dominican and I was very excited and hoped they would show interest in me," he said. An excited Jose Valentin switched to No. 22, so Alou could have 18.

New York also signed a number of veteran role players including Damion Easley, David Newhan, Fernando Tatis and Ricky Ledee. The Mets signed right-handers Aaron Sele and Jorge Sosa. Southpaw reliever Scott Schoeneweis was given a three-year, $10.8 million deal to become the set-up man after Chad Bradford signed with the Orioles.

Guillermo Mota was suspended for 50 games for using performance-enhancing drugs but the team still signed him two a year-deal the next month.

The Situation

There were rotation questions behind Tom Glavine and Orlando Hernandez, as Pedro Martinez wouldn't pitch until after the All-Star break. John Maine, Mike Pelfrey and Oliver Perez rounded out the rotation. Six of 10 ESPN experts

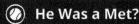

⊘ He Was a Met?

Yes, though barely. The Mets signed Chan Ho Park as a free agent after he went 7-7 4.81 for the Padres the season before. Park's season, and career with the Mets, lasted one game, a start in which he allowed 7 runs in 4 IP and took the loss.

picked the Mets to repeat as division champions.

Phillies shortstop Jimmy Rollins had a statement of his own: "I think we are the team to beat in the NL East – finally. But that's only on paper."

The Season

It certainly didn't make up for the NLCS but the Mets opened the season with a sweep of the Cardinals in St. Louis. The Mets finished off the sweep with a 10-0 win. Beltran hit two home runs and Maine pitched seven

A Collapse Down the Stretch

Playoff tickets were being printed as the Mets coasted towards the postseason, leading the Phillies by 7 games with 17 remaining. Then New York fell apart, finishing 5-12 while the Phillies went 13-4 to capture the NL East. The collapse started with a 3-game sweep at the hands of the Phillies, and included 2 5-game losing streaks. After tying for first on Game 161, they were humiliated on the last day of the season when Tom Glavine faced 8 batters in the first inning, allowing 5 hits, 2 walks, and 7 runs to the lowly Florida Marlins, and the Mets limped to an 8-1 loss.

innings of one-hit ball. The Mets went to Atlanta and pounded the Braves 11-1 to improve to 4-0 for the first time since 1985.

In the first series at Shea, the Mets took two of three from the Phillies. On April 17, the Mets went to Philadelphia and won 8-1 with Alou, who was hitting .341 through 12 games, homering twice. The Phillies were off to a 3-9 start.

The Mets jumped out to a 15-8 start, with Maine improving to 4-0 with a 1.35 ERA after throwing seven innings of three-hit shutout ball in Washington. The offense was blazing. Reyes and Beltran were hitting .356. Shawn Green was batting .355 and Alou .349. The bats were clicking even with David Wright and Carlos Delgado off to slow starts.

New York went 5-2 on the West Coast in early May, including a 5-3 win over the Giants with Wright winning the game with a two-run double off Armando Benitez in the ninth. Not everything was perfect. Alou strained his quadriceps and was lost for two-and-a-half months. Speedy outfielder Carlos Gomez was promoted to take his place. After a loss to Milwaukee, Pelfrey was 0-5 with a 6.53 ERA and was demoted. The good news was that Jorge Sosa, who had been bypassed in a crowded pitching field that also included Chan Ho Park, Aaron Sele and Jason Vargas, entered the rotation in early May. On May 16, Sosa beat the Cubs and the Mets moved into first place, where they would remain until the final days of the season. In fact, Sosa became the first Met pitcher to win six of his first seven starts with the team, culminating with eight shutout innings of the Tigers in Detroit.

In a Subway Series showdown, the Mets took two of three from the Yankees at Shea with Perez outpitching Andy Pettitte in the opener. Endy Chavez hit a two-run homer to give the Mets the lead and also threw out Johnny Damon at second. The speedy fourth outfielder was batting .352. The next afternoon, the Mets took an 8-2 lead after four innings and held on for a 10-7 victory. Glavine improved to 5-1 but wouldn't win a game for more than a month.

Delgado started to find his swing. After batting .224 with three home runs through May 25, he had a pair of two-home run games late in the month, including a walk-off blast off Benitez.

The Mets also had a Lastings Milledge problem. In spring training he said he learned how to handle responsibility. In May, his voice could be heard a rap record recorded by his childhood friend with some questionable content. The team released a statement saying it disapproved of the "content, language and message of this recording."

The Mets struggled in the first half of June, losing 13 of 16. The Phillies came to Shea and swept the Mets. Chase Utley's 11th inning homer was the difference in the first game. The next night, Hernandez pitched six shutout innings but Pat Burrell hit a three-run home run in the seventh off Aaron Heilman. In the final game, Delgado, Wright and Paul Lo Duca hit back-to-back-to-back home runs in the sixth and the Mets took a 3-2 lead into the ninth. But Burrell tied it with a homer off Billy Wagner and the Phillies scored three in the 11th.

Chavez was on the DL, joining Alou and Shawn Green as the outfield became banged up. Ben Johnson started eight games in the outfield, batting .185. Valentin broke a bone in his leg when he fouled off a pitch. A rare highlight during the slump was Perez outdueling Roger Clemens at Yankee Stadium. The worst game was a 9-0 loss to the Twins with the Mets making four errors. A slumping Beltran saw his average drop 36 points in two weeks.

The team got hot and won seven of eight to end June. The Mets swept Oakland, with two blowouts and a 1-0 win with Wright delivering a walk-off double. Lo Duca was suspended for two games and fined $2,000 for a tirade after a called strike call from Marvin Hudson. He had to be restrained by Willie Randolph as his eyes bulged. Walking to the dugout, he threw his helmet, bat and elbow guard toward first base. Once in the dugout, he tossed his shin guards into foul territory and his chest protector. The Mets took two of three from St. Louis. Then they took three straight in Philadelphia before the Phillies took the final game, defeating Pelfrey, who had returned from the minors. Both Perez and Sosa were on the DL. Pelfrey lost again to Houston, falling to 0-7 with a 6.10 ERA and wouldn't start again until September. At least there was Maine, who won four straight starts to improve to 10-4.

> **FABULOUS: DAVID WRIGHT**
>
> *David Wright hit .325 with 30 homers and 107 RBI, stole 34 bases, reached base nearly 42% of his plate appearances, earned a Gold Glove and a Silver Slugger and finshed fourth in the MVP voting. An argument could be made for his winning the award.*

Reyes, Wright, Beltran and Wagner represented the Mets at the All-Star game in San Francisco. Marlon Anderson returned to the Mets, after the Dodgers let the veteran go. In his first game back with the Mets, he had two hits and two RBI in a 13-9 win at Dodger Stadium. Beltran homered in three straight games but went on the DL. Delgado hit five homers in July, giving him 17.

At the deadline, the Mets acquired three-time All-Star second baseman Luis Castillo from the Twins. Ruben Gotay had played at second since Valentin's injury. Castillo not only filled a hole at second but allowed the Mets to have three switch-hitters at the top of the lineup, between Reyes and Beltran.

A struggling Sosa was sent to the bullpen and Brian Lawrence was promoted. He won his first start against Milwaukee but didn't win any of his next five starts. The Mets won seven of eight in the middle of August, with Castillo delivering a walk-off single off Trevor Hoffman to beat the Padres. During the month, Reyes set the team record with his 67th stolen base.

In late August, the Mets, with a six-game lead in the division, traveled to Philadelphia for a four-game series. Lawrence was crushed in the opener with Burrell and Utley going deep. In the second game, Delgado hit a two-run homer off Adam Eaton and Glavine pitched seven innings before being taken out. Rollins led off the eighth with a homer off Pedro Feliciano and Aaron Rowand singled off Heilman to tie it. Ryan Howard's 10th inning home run off Guillermo Mota ended it. The next night, the Mets trailed 3-2 in the ninth with runners on the corners and one out for Green. He hit a grounder to short. Rollins flipped to Tadahito Iguchi at second for one out but Anderson's take out slide broke up the throw to first, allowing the Mets to tie the game. Or not.

FUTILE: MIKE PELFREY

Mike Pelfrey struggled in his first full season with the Mets, going 3-8 with a 5.57 ERA. After 3 seasons with double-digit wins, Pelfrey resumed his losing ways, going 25-62 in parts of seven seasons, mostly in the American League.

C.B. Bucknor ruled interference, ending the game. The Mets couldn't believe the call. "Don't even ask me about that play," Lo Duca said. "I'm not getting myself in trouble." Anderson did slide wide with his forearms raised but his foot did hit second. "As far as I know, as long as I've been playing in the major leagues that's a pretty routine slide," Anderson said.

In the finale, the Phillies jumped out to a 5-0 lead against Hernandez. The slumping offense came to life, tying the game at five. Sele gave up three runs as the Mets fell behind 8-5. But in the top of the eighth, New York scored five runs. Chavez's two-run single tied it. An error from catcher Carlos Ruiz allowed Reyes to score the go-ahead run. Randolph called on Wagner for a six-out save, after the lefty hadn't pitched in several days. Burrell hit a home run, his second of the game, but the Mets still led 10-9 heading into the ninth. Jayson Werth singled, stole second and then stole third. Iguchi singled to tie it, then stole second. Rollins was intentionally walked and Utley singled to stun the Mets 11-10. "It's one of those games it's either going to be a huge win or a tough loss and unfortunately, it was a tough loss," Green said, adding that the series "obviously changes everything."

Happy to get out of Philadelphia, the Mets traveled to Atlanta to take on a Braves team only three games out of first. The Mets swept the Braves in an impressive series. Maine beat Tim Hudson in the opener with Delgado hitting his 20th home run. Pelfrey pitched a gem, taking a no-hitter into the seventh in a 5-1 win Atlanta. Delgado homered again and Beltran hit his 26th homer. In the finale, Glavine beat John Smoltz, with Wright hitting a two-run homer.

Martinez made his first start of the year, picking up a win and striking out the 3,000th batter of his career in a 10-4 as Delgado, Wright and Alou homered. The team announced the launch of online random drawings on the team website for the opportunity to purchase potential playoff tickets. The offense kept rolling, scoring 11 runs against the Reds with Beltran hitting his 27th home run and Lo Duca going deep twice. But Delgado had a strained flexor and would be gone for two-and-a-half weeks. Still, two days later, the Mets scored 11 runs against the Astros, with Beltran again hitting a home run. After the four-game sweep to the Phillies, the Mets won 10 of 12. On September 12, Mota gave up a two-run single against Atlanta in the eighth – the beleaguered reliever's ERA was near six – but Green's single in the bottom of the inning put the Mets ahead and Wagner closed out the win. The Mets were 83-62 and leading the division by seven games with 17 remaining.

The Phillies came to Shea down 6.5 games. The Mets had a chance to put the division out of reach. Wright homered off Jamie Moyer and Alou added an RBI single but Utley tied the game with a two-run homer off Glavine in the sixth. The game remained tied until the top of the 10th. Heilman was on the mound and Mike DiFelice was behind the plate after Lo Duca was ejected after making the last out of the ninth. Werth led off with a single. Ruiz tried a bunt but popped it up. DiFelice couldn't make the catch. Ruiz then laid down a bunt. Heilman went for the lead runner and threw it into center. The Phillies would score on a sacrifice fly and won 3-2. "There's still 16 games left," Lo Duca said. "So this division is not over with. So we need to go out and take it."

"Nobody in here is just riding our way to October," Wright said. "We know it's still a fight and that's when a team is most dangerous, when it's backed into a corner and they come out swinging. That's what they've done so far."

The Mets took a 3-2 lead into the eighth the next night but gave up three runs and lost. The crushing blow was a two-run triple from Rollins after Beltran misread the ball and took a step in, allowing the ball to go over his head. It was a sloppy game on the bases. Castillo was doubled off on a fly ball in the first, apparently forgetting how many outs there were. Both Gotay and Reyes were caught stealing in the sixth. Reyes was caught stealing third with Wright at the plate to end the inning. Philadelphia finished the sweep with a 10-6 as the Mets committed six errors. A Greg Dobbs grand slam was the big blow. "They kicked our butts," Randolph said. But the Mets still led the division by 3.5 games and wouldn't have to play the Phillies again. "We're in first place and they're in second place," Beltran said. "We just need to continue to win ballgames."

Attempting to hold onto the lead, the Mets went to Washington, who was battling with the Marlins for last place. Hernandez was scratched from starting with right foot pain and Lawrence was recalled from Triple-A. The Mets took a 4-0 lead but the Nationals tied it in the fourth. Then Washington scored eight runs against the bullpen and the defense made four more offenses. "Obviously it's been about as bad as it can get the last four days and we've got to find a

TOP BATTERS

Pos	Name	G	AB	H	BA	HR	RBI	RS	SB	OPS
1B	Carlos Delgado	139	538	139	.258	24	87	71	4	.781
SS	Jose Reyes	160	681	191	.280	12	57	119	78	.775
3B	David Wright	160	604	196	.325	30	107	113	34	.963
LF	Moises Alou	87	328	112	.341	13	49	51	3	.916
CF	Carlos Beltran	144	554	153	.276	33	112	93	23	.878

TOP PITCHERS

Pos	Name	G	GS	W	L	SV	ERA	IP	SO	BB
SP	Tom Glavine	34	34	13	8	0	4.45	200.1	89	64
SP	John Maine	32	32	15	10	0	3.91	191.0	180	75
SP	Oliver Perez	29	29	15	10	0	3.56	177.0	174	79
CL	Billy Wagner	66	0	2	2	34	2.63	68.1	80	22
RP	Aaron Heilman	81	0	7	7	1	3.03	86.0	63	20

way to turn it around tomorrow," Green said. Lo Duca was even more to the point: "It needs to turn around quickly or we're going home."

The Mets staked Maine to leads of 4-0, 5-1 and 7-3 the next night after the team had its first players meeting of the season but things fell apart with Ronnie Belliard hitting a three-run homer to give the Nationals an 8-7 lead in the fifth. The Mets trailed 9-7 with two outs in the ninth but three singles made it 9-8 with runners on the corners. Chad Cordero struck out Gotay to end the game. The division was lead was down to 1.5 with 12 to play. "If I told you I'm not worried, I'd be lying," Alou said. But Randolph, who was questioned for leaving in Maine so long, remained calm. "When we're sipping a little champagne in a little while this will all seem like a long time ago," the skipper said.

New York won four of the next five, including taking three of four in Florida, to improve to 87-68 with a 2.5 game lead. The Nationals came to Shea and again played spoiler. On September 24, Washington scored 13 runs over the final six innings in a 13-4 win. "We just came out flat tonight," Lo Duca said. "There's just no excuse. You can't expect to win a division the way we played and the way we've been playing." Pelfrey gave up seven runs (six earned) with Mota and Dave Williams each giving up three runs. "It's embarrassing, with the season on the line and seven games left, to go out there and get embarrassed on our home field," Wright said.

Glavine gave up six runs in five innings the next night, putting the Mets in a 4-0 first inning hole and giving up three home runs. The Mets trailed 10-3 heading into the bottom of the ninth before almost pulling out a miracle. Reyes' three-run homer and then two singles and a walk loaded the bases for Alou, who doubled to right, clearing the bases and cutting the lead to 10-9. Delgado struck out with pinch-runner Chavez stealing third. With the tying run 90 feet away, Lo Duca flied out to right.

Looking to avoid a sweep, Beltran hit two home runs and the Mets took an early 5-0 lead with Philip Humber, making his first start of the season, on the mound. Still up 6-2 in the fifth, Humber, Joe Smith and Feliciano gave up five runs as the lead slipped away. Wagner gave up two more in the ninth and the offense went quiet late in a 9-6 loss.

The Cardinals came to town for a Thursday night game, a make-up from a rainout three months earlier. Martinez gave up three runs in the first three innings and the Mets were shutout on three hits in a 3-0 loss against Joel Pineiro, who went eight innings. The Phillies beat the Braves to move into a tie for first. The Mets were also one game behind the Padres for the wild card. "Guess we've got a new season. Start from scratch," Randolph said. "We're tied now, so now we've got three games to get it done." It was the first time the Mets weren't alone in first since taking over the lead on May 16.

With the Marlins in town, Perez gave up six runs in 3.2 innings and the Mets lost 7-4. The erratic lefty hit three batters in the third. The Phillies beat the Nationals and suddenly Mets were in second place. "We know what it's like to be chased," Wright said. "Now it's the Phillies' turn."

Maine pitched a masterpiece the next day, taking a no-hitter two outs into the eighth before Paul Hoover's infield single broke up the historic bid. The Mets scored eight runs in the first three innings and won 13-0. A fight broke out in the fifth after Harvey Garcia threw behind Castillo. The teams came on the field but there was no action. Marlins manager Fredi Gonzalez came to the mound to make a pitching change and catcher Miguel Olivo went down to third and threw a punch at Reyes, later saying Reyes was talking trash. Third base coach Sandy Alomar Sr. got between the two. And perhaps Milledge woke up the Marlins with his excited home run celebration. The Phillies lost to the Nationals and the division was tied again. The Mets were also one game behind the Padres for a wild card spot, with the Rockies having an identical record to the Phillies and Mets.

Wagner criticized Randolph and pitching coach Rick Peterson as part of the problem with the bullpen, in a magazine story hitting newsstands during the week, but the interesting quotes came out before the final game. "We've been throwing four innings a night – for months!" Wagner said. "Our pitching coach has no experience talking to a bullpen. He can help you mechanically, but he can't tell you emotions. He has no idea what it feels like. And neither does Willie. They're not a lot of help, put it that way."

Plenty of playoff permutations existed when Glavine took the mound on the final day of the season. With one on and one out, Jeremy Hermida singled to right. Miguel Cabrera singled to make it 1-0. Cody Ross doubled to right, scoring two runs. Glavine's throw to third to get Ross got away, scoring him to make it 4-0. A single, walk and another single loaded the bases. Then Glavine plunked Dontrelle Willis to bring in another run, ending Glavine's day. Two batters later, Dan Uggla doubled off Sosa and it was 7-0 in the first inning.

New York did score a run and loaded the bases for Ramon Castro in the bottom of the first. The catcher drove Willis' 2-0 pitch to deep left but it was caught in front of the wall. The Mets would lose 8-1. The Phillies beat the Nationals 6-1. The Mets finished the season 5-12 and the Phillies went 13-4. "This is just a tough life lesson in baseball," Randolph said. "Any time you have an opportunity to finish the deal and don't capitalize on it, it will come back to haunt you. And it sure did with us. The bottom line is that we spit away an opportunity to win the division. It's going to be a tough winter living with that."

"It's obviously painful," Wright said. "It hurts. But at the same time, we did it to ourselves. It's not like it blindsides us. We gradually let this thing slip away. In all honesty, we didn't deserve to make the playoffs."

Top 5 Highlights

1 Endy Chavez lays down a drag bunt for an infield single, scoring Shawn Green with two outs in the 12th to beat the Rockies 2-1 on April 24. The Mets trailed 1-0 in the 10th when Damion Easley hit a homer to left-center off Brian Fuentes.

2 Carlos Delgado's two-run single off Scott Eyre gives the Mets a 6-5 win over the Cubs on May 17. The Mets trailed 5-1 heading into the ninth but two singles and a walk loaded the bases for Chavez, who drew a walk to make it 5-2. Ruben Gotay singled to left, cutting bases, then a walk and a single cut the lead to 5-3. Eyre came in to replace Ryan Dempster. David Wright delivered a pinch-hit single to make it 5-4 and Delgado singled to win it.

3 Delgado's 12th inning home run off Armando Benitez beats the Giants 5-4 on May 29. Delgado homered earlier in the game off Tim Linceum. The Mets trailed 4-3 in the 12th when Jose Reyes walked to begin the inning and was balked to second. With two outs and Reyes dancing off third, Benitez balked again, scoring Reyes with the tying run. Then Delgado hit a 2-2 pitch over the wall in right-center.

4 Carlos Beltran's RBI single gives the Mets a 17th inning lead and New York beats the Astros 5-3 on July 7. In the bottom of the 14th, with a runner on first and two outs, Luke Scott drove a Joe Smith pitch deep to center but Beltran made a running, falling catch on the hill located in deep center at Minute Maid Park to save the game.

5 Tom Glavine wins his 300th game, giving up two runs on six hits in 6.1 innings in an 8-3 win over the Cubs on August 5. The lefty also had an RBI single.

2008

	W	L	GB	Pos
	89	73	3.0	2nd

RS/G	RA/G	Manager
4.93	4.41	Willie Randolph Jerry Manuel

OPENING DAY LINEUP

Jose Reyes, SS
Luis Castillo, 2B
David Wright, 3B
Carlos Beltran, CF
Carlos Delgado, 1B
Angel Pagan, LF
Ryan Church, RF
Brian Schneider, C
Johan Santana, P

Shea Goodbye: Mets Falter Late Again

The Moves

In early February, the Mets made a splash, landing two-time Cy Young winner Johan Santana from the Twins for Carlos Gomez and Philip Humber. The Mets signed the lefty to a six-year, $137.5 million deal. It was a huge move for a team reeling from the final 17 games of 2007. "It's like we were on the Titanic and he is our lifeboat," said pitching coach Rick Peterson. "Someone is coming who can rejuvenate us, who can help us heal."

It looked like the Mets were the team to beat again in the division. "We felt good about ourselves going into spring training as it was," Willie Randolph said. "But when you add a person like Santana, a guy of his caliber, you have a little bit of swagger going."

There were other moves. Lastings Milledge was traded to the Nationals for outfielder Ryan Church and catcher Brian Schneider. "I thought we needed to change it up a little," Omar Minaya said. "Names like Schneider and Church are not known names, but they give us balance."

Guillermo Mota was traded to the Brewers and Paul Lo Duca signed with the Nationals. For behind the plate, the Mets signed Raul Casanova, who would back up the recently resigned Ramon Castro. Nelson Figueroa, who hadn't pitched in the majors since 2004, was signed after pitching overseas.

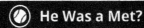 He Was a Met?

The Mets picked up Trot Nixon from Arizona (for whom he never played) after an 11-year career in the American League. Nixon got into 11 games for the Mets, collecting 6 hits, including a homer.

The Situation

The team was banged up in spring training, including Moises Alou dealing with a hernia, Carlos Delgado's forearm injury and Luis Castillo's knee. Jose Reyes showed up with a different, more serious attitude. Pedro Martinez's fastball was strong.

Sports Illustrated, MLB.com, Beckett and ESPN the Magazine picked the Mets to win the division. Athlon and Lindy's predicted the Phillies would make it two straight division titles and The Sporting News went with the Braves.

Jose Reyes, pictured in 2016, had his fourth consecutive tremendous year offensively in 2008, with 204 hits, 19 triples, and 113 runs scored. Reyes reached double-figures in triples 6 times for the Mets, leading the league in 4 of them.

The Season

The Mets took two of three to begin the season, but Martinez hurt his hamstring and wouldn't return until June. The team was inconsistent during the month. Five straight wins were followed by five losses in six games. Carlos Beltran and Carlos Delgado were off to slow starts. Beltran hit .211 in April. Delgado hit .198.

On April 29, the Mets beat the Pirates in 11 innings, with the bullpen working 5.1 innings. Perez failed to make it out of the second inning the next day, walking five of 13 batters he faced in a 13-1 loss. "Perez has honestly got to step up and know that we've just used every guy in our bullpen the night before," Billy Wagner said. "He can't come out there and decide that, gee, he hasn't got it today and so be it." Randolph later said he thought the comments should've been kept in-house.

The inconsistent play continued throughout May. Wagner criticized teammates for ducking "being accountable" with the media after some players weren't available to media after a 1-0 loss to the Nationals. "You should be talking to the guys over there," he said to reporters, gesturing toward the lockers of Beltran, Delgado and Luis Castillo. "Oh, they're not there. Big shock."

 Final Resting Ground

Moises Alou joined the Mets in 2007 for his age 40 season and put up some very good numbers for any age, including a BA of .341 and OPS+ of 137. Injuries took away almost the entire next season for Alou, though he did collect 17 hits in 49 at bats, good for .347, before he called it quits.

FABULOUS: CARLOS DELGADO

Carlos Delgado hit 38 homers and drove in 115 runs, the second time he reached those levels in 3 years with the Mets. Early the next season, he injured his hip, and after two surgeries and comeback attempts, Delgado was forced to retire. Despite 473 HR in his career 9 100+ RBI seasons, he received only 3.8% of HOF votes his first year of eligibility and fell off the ballot.

The walls were closing in on Randolph, who wondered if criticism he was enduring from SNY had something to do with his race. "In my 17 years of major league baseball and 10-plus years of being up here in the booth, I've just never heard of a manager make those kinds of comments before, and I'm really quite surprised that Willie made those comments," Keith Hernandez said. Ron Darling added, "It's stopping you from doing what you're supposed to be doing: getting ready for the game. Part of the problem we have now is that the manager has chosen to make comments about things that you would think that for him should be water under the bridge. Who cares what anyone says? You care about wins."

Minaya gave Randolph a vote of confidence, though the manager told the media he wasn't promised he would finish the season in a meeting with ownership. Gary Carter, managing an independent team in California, even stumped for the job. The team lost seven of eight in late May.

In early June, the team lost six of seven. The team lost four straight to the Padres, including three straight 2-1 games. Tony Clark's three-run homer off Wagner in the final game was the big blow. On June 12, Santana pitched seven shutout innings against Arizona and left with a 4-0 lead but Joe Smith gave up two runs in the eighth and Wagner gave up two more in the ninth. Heilman gave up the losing run in the 10th, raising his ERA to 5.88. The Mets were 31-34. SI.com columnist Jon Heyman reported that Randolph was on thin ice and was unlikely to last past an upcoming road trip. Joel Sherman of the *New York Post* reported Randolph had the weekend series against the Rangers to save his job. The Mets took two of three from Texas and then went to California to play the Angels.

The Mets beat the Angels 9-6, with Beltran hitting two home runs to improve to 34-35. Then fans woke up the next morning to the news that the team had a new manager. Randolph was fired, along with pitching coach Rick Peterson and first-base coach Tom Nieto. Bench coach Jerry Manuel, who was the 2000 AL Manager of the Year with the White Sox, was the new skipper. The team took a lot of criticism for flying the staff out and then firing Randolph in the middle of the night.

There were other issues with the team. There were bullpen woes, Moises Alou was gone for the year with a torn hamstring. Church was batting over .300 but suffered multiple concussions.

Reyes led off Manuel's first game as manager with a single but his hamstring tightened and looked uncomfortable. Manuel came out and tried to remove

TOP BATTERS

Pos	Name	G	AB	H	BA	HR	RBI	RS	SB	OPS
1B	Carlos Delgado	159	598	162	.271	38	115	96	1	.871
SS	Jose Reyes	159	688	204	.297	16	68	113	56	.833
3B	David Wright	160	626	189	.302	33	124	115	15	.924
CF	Carlos Beltran	161	606	172	.284	27	112	116	25	.876
RF	Ryan Church	90	319	88	.276	12	49	54	2	.785

TOP PITCHERS

Pos	Name	G	GS	W	L	SV	ERA	IP	SO	BB
SP	Johan Santana	34	34	16	7	0	2.53	234.1	206	63
SP	Mike Pelfrey	32	32	13	11	0	3.72	200.2	110	64
SP	Oliver Perez	34	34	10	7	0	4.22	194.0	180	105
CL	Billy Wagner	45	0	0	1	27	2.30	47.0	52	10
RP	Joe Smith	82	0	6	3	0	3.55	63.1	52	31

him. Reyes walked away, eventually walking back to the dugout but tossed his helmet. The Mets went 8-9 in Manuel's first 17 games.

Then the Mets won 10 straight, including four shutouts, and moved into a tie for first. The Mets took three of four in Philadelphia and then three of four from the Phillies at Shea later in the month, though the team blew a win for Santana, giving up six runs in the ninth of an 8-6 loss. Delgado hit .357 with nine homers and 24 RBI during the month. Wright hit .317 with five home runs and 19 RBI. Pelfrey won his first four decisions of the month, giving him seven wins in a row after a 2-6 start.

Wagner was lost for the season in early August with a torn tendon and ligament in his left elbow. Daniel Murphy was called up and provided a hot bat in left field. Heilman was the story of August. On August 1, Heilman gave up an eighth inning grand slam in a 7-3 loss to the Astros. The next night, he allowed both runners he faced to get on and was charged with the loss when Pedro Feliciano allowed the run to score. Wagner had blown a two-run lead in the ninth. On August 7, Martinez left with a 5-1 lead. It was a 5-4 game in the ninth when Heilman allowed a game-tying single. Schoenweis allowed a two-run single and the Mets lost 7-5. In mid-August, the team picked up Luis Ayala, who had a 5.77 ERA with the Nationals. Heilman blew a seventh inning lead on August 24 and the Mets lost when Feliciano gave up two in the 10th. On August 30, he walked in the winning run in a loss to the Marlins. Maine was lost for the season with a bone spur in late August, though he would volunteer to close games in September.

Still, the Mets entered September in first place. Reyes was batting over .300. Wright was just under the mark. Delgado drove in 24 more runs in August.

The Mets won six of eight to begin September, scoring 23 runs in two wins against the Nationals. There were still bullpen issues. On September 14, Ayala blew a ninth inning lead to the Braves. But the team was 48-28 since firing Randolph. New York was 82-63 and 3.5 games ahead of the Phillies with 17 to go. "We don't worry about what happened last year, because this year is the year for us."

FUTILE: ENDY CHAVEZ

Endy Chavez probably won a game or two with his glove, appearing in 133 games. But no doubt he lost that many or more with his bat, however, hitting only 1 HR and driving in 12 in 270 at bats.

The Mets lost two of three at home to the Braves. Then the team went to Washington to play the last-place Nationals, who were heading toward a 102-loss season. John Lannan outpitched Martinez in the first game. Odalis Perez and two relievers blanked the Mets in a 1-0 game the next night. The Mets won three straight, and led the Phillies by a half-game with nine to go. On September 21, Schoenweis, Smith and Heilman combined to blow an eighth-inning lead in Atlanta.

There were six home games remaining in the season. The Mets trailed the Phillies by 1.5 games, but were ahead of the Brewers by 1.5 in the wild card. The Mets and Cubs split two games. On September 24, the Mets blew an early 5-1 lead but looked to win it in the ninth. In a 6-6 game, Daniel Murphy led off with a triple. Wright got ahead 3-0 but struck out. Delgado and Beltran were walked intentionally. Church grounded into a force at the plate. Castro struck out to end the inning. Ayala gave up three runs and the Mets were 9-6 losers. Manuel called it "at this juncture probably our toughest defeat." The team did rally to win in the ninth the next night.

The Marlins came to Queens for the final series in the history of Shea Stadium. The Mets were one game behind the Phillies and tied with the Brewers for the wild card. Chris Volstad and four Marlins relievers kept the Mets in check and Pelfrey lost the opener 6-1. Santana pitched a three-hit shutout the next day, throwing 117 pitches, four days after throwing 125 in a win against the Cubs.

Philadelphia clinched the division but the Mets and Brewers were tied for the wild card. Perez and Scott Olsen matched zeroes for five innings before the Marlins scored twice in the sixth. Olsen came into the game with an 0-3 record and a 6.95 ERA against the Mets during the year. Beltran tied the game with a two-run shot in the bottom of the inning. Wes Helms led off the eighth with a home run off Schoenweis. Dan Uggla followed with a homer off Ayala. The Mets put two on with two outs in the eighth but Delgado flied out to end the inning. Milwaukee won with C.C. Sabathia pitching a complete game, his seventh in 17 starts since being acquired by the Brewers. In the bottom of the ninth, Damion Easley kept the season alive with a two-out walk but Matt Lindstrom got Church to fly out to center.

"It feels like a wasted season," Wright said. "It burns. It's a bad feeling, and this is just the beginning."

Jeff Wilpon tried to soften the blow, saying "I feel totally different this year than last year. Last year I felt we underachieved. This year I felt we overachieved."

Top 5 Highlights

1 Damion Easley's 10th inning homer off Justin Speier gives the Mets a 5-4 lead in the 10th and Billy Wagner pitches a 1-2-3 bottom of the inning as New York defeats the Angels on June 18 to give Jerry Manuel his first win as Mets manager. With two outs in the ninth, David Wright's single scores Jose Reyes to tie the game.

2 Carlos Delgado sets a team-record with nine RBI in a 15-6 win over the Yankees in the first game of a two-stadium doubleheader on June 27. In the fifth, Delgado's double off Edwar Ramirez scores two runs. In the sixth, he hits a grand slam off Ross Ohlendorf. In the eighth, he hits a three-run homer off LaTroy Hawkins.

3 Wright's homer to left in the bottom of the ninth off San Diego's Heath Bell gives the Mets a 5-3 win over the Padres on August 7. It's the only walk-off home run Wright would hit in his career.

4 Down to the final out, Carlos Beltran hits a grand slam off Florida's Kevin Gregg to give the Mets a 5-2 lead on August 29. Luis Ayala gives up two runs but gets Wes Helms to groundout to short with the tying and winning runs on base to hold on to the 5-4 win. There had been two outs with nobody on in the ninth but Luis Castillo and Wright singled, and Delgado was hit by a pitch to bring up Beltran.

5 Johan Santana pitches a three-hit shutout on September 27 in a 2-0 win over the Marlins. On three-days rest, the ace pitches the Mets back into a tie for the wild card. It's the final Mets win at Shea Stadium.

2009

	W	L	GB	Pos
	70	92	23.0	4th
RS/G	RA/G		Manager	
4.14	4.67		Jerry Manuel	

New Stadium Sees Mets Sink to Fourth

The Moves

After watching the bullpen blow up in 2008, the Mets went out and signed Francisco Rodriguez, who set the all-time record with 62 saves with the Angels. Then the team picked up 2007 All Star J.J. Putz in a 12-player deal. Players involved included Aaron Heilman, Endy Chavez, Joe Smith and Jason Vargas going to Seattle for Putz, reliever Sean Green and outfielder-first baseman Jeremy Reed.

"All I kept on hearing in the streets of New York when you go get bagels in the morning was, 'Omar, please address the bullpen,'" Minaya said. "Well, to all you Mets fans, we've addressed the bullpen."

In 2008, there were eight closers with 15 saves who struck out more than 10 batters per nine innings and the Mets suddenly had two of them. "To get one closer like Frankie would have been a good winter," Minaya said. "I think to get two guys like this is a great winter."

Other free agent signings included catcher Omir Santos, pitcher Tim Redding, infielder Alex Cora and veteran starter Livan Hernandez. Just before the start of the season the team signed Gary Sheffield. "He's going to help this team," Minaya said. "That I can guarantee you."

The Situation

Phillies starter Cole Hamels called the Mets choke artists. Carlos Beltran responded by saying "hopefully we'll kill him."

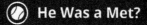

He Was a Met?

Livan Hernandez pitched for 9 teams in his career including, yes, the Mets, who signed him as a free agent for the 2009 season. Hernandez managed a 7-8 record despite an ERA of 5.47 and the Mets released him in August.

The Mets lost seven games when they led entering the ninth inning in 2008 and were eliminated on the final day of the season. Now they had Rodriguez and Putz, the latter saying during the spring that it was the best camp he had ever been in.

"I actually think in '08 we overachieved, given a lot of injuries," Minaya said. "We gave it away in '07. We basically had it. In '08 we never had it. The issue is, we have to win. We have to close it out before 162."

The New York Post predicted the Mets would win 94 games and the division before losing to the Cubs in the NLCS. *Sports Illustrated* had even higher expectations, saying the Mets would defeat the Angels in the World Series.

Citi Field, which opened in 2009, is "retro" in the fans' proximity to the field, with all the gastronomic amenities (and astronomic pricing) of contemporary ballparks. The change was a long time coming, as Shea had become quite dilapidated over the years as ownership chose not to maintain it while the new venue was planned for and built.

Nine Mets competed in the World Baseball Classic. One was Oliver Perez, who had signed a three-year, $36 million contract in the offseason. "He's out of shape," pitching coach Dan Warthen said after Perez was battered around by the Tigers in a spring training game. He would give up six runs in the first inning against the Red Sox in an exhibition game at the new home park, Citi Field.

The stadium was the new home of the Mets. It was reminiscent of Ebbets Field and a rotunda for Jackie Robinson greeted fans. The seats were green like the Polo Grounds. There was a rightfield overhang like the one at Tiger Stadium. Fans would note the lack of Mets memorabilia around the stadium.

The Season

The Mets won on Opening Day in Cincinnati. Daniel Murphy homered, Johan Santana picked up the victory and the bullpen retired 10 of 11 Reds batters. The team won two of three in Cincinnati with Perez giving up eight runs in 4.1 innings in the loss. "All my pitches were working," Perez said. Catcher Ramon Castro was asked by reporters if he knew what Perez meant. "No."

Final Resting Ground

Carlos Delgado seemed like a sure bet to reach 500 career home runs, finishing his age 36 season with 38 and a total of 469. But hip injuries sidelined him in May of 2009, and he was never again able to play in the majors, finishing with 473 career dingers and more than 1500 RBI.

New York went to Florida and lost two of three to the Marlins. In the final game, Santana lost 2-1 because of two unearned runs after Murphy committed an error in left in the second inning. "It was just one mistake that he made cost us the whole ballgame," Santana said.

After splitting six road games, it was time to open Citi Field. Tom Seaver threw out the ceremonial first pitch to Mike Piazza. An excited crowd of 41,007 was quickly silenced when Padres centerfielder Jody Gerut hit Mike Pelfrey's third pitch over the right field wall for a homer. The Mets erased a 5-1 deficit in the fifth with David Wright tying the game with a three-run home run. But in the sixth a Ryan Church error in right put Luis Rodriguez on and Pedro Feliciano balked him in. The Mets lost 6-5 and would drop the series to San Diego.

On April 17, Sheffield hit his 500th career home run to tie the game in the seventh and Luis Castillo's single beat the Brewers two innings later. The next day, Santana pitched seven shutout innings with Putz and Rodriguez following with scoreless frames in a 1-0 win. The Mets lost the finale, then went to St. Louis and were swept.

In the first game of the series, Perez blew a 4-0 lead, Beltran was thrown out at home in a tie game in the eighth because he didn't slide, and then Murphy misplayed a ball in left which put the go-ahead runner on third. "Things are moving fast [in the outfield], but I'm working hard," Murphy said. "I feel like I'm slowing the game down, but I could definitely relax more."

FUTILE: OLIVER PEREZ

Oliver Perez appeared in well over 500 games in the 2010s as a lefty specialist. But believe it or not, he led the NL in games started in 2008 with 34. The workload took its toll, however, as in 2009 Perez went 3-4 in 14 GS, sporting an ERA of 6.82.

Five days later, Perez was tagged by the last-place Nationals as his ERA soared to 9.31. Beltran reached base for the 23rd straight game but was thrown out attempting to steal second as he pulled up, thinking Wright had made contact. On a fly to left, Murphy turned the wrong way and fell while spinning to recover on what was ruled a double.

On May 2, there was a familiar feeling as the Phillies beat the Mets on a walk-off with Shane Victorino drawing a bases loaded walk against Green. More pressing was Perez, who failed to make it out of the third and saw his ERA increase to 9.97.

Jerry Manuel finally took the lefty out of the rotation. Perez wasn't the only struggling starter. Pelfrey had an ERA of six, though good run support made him 3-0. Hernandez had a 6.75 ERA through April. The team gave up trying to send Perez down to the minors and instead moved him to the bullpen. "He won't be the first guy I call, there's no question about that," Manuel said. But then the team placed him on the DL with a knee injury and the southpaw wouldn't return until July 8.

The Mets rolled off seven straight wins, with two wins over the Braves, two more over the Phillies and a three-game sweep of the Pirates. But the final win was the final game for Carlos Delgado. He was batting .298 with four home runs and 23 RBI in 26 games. On May 16, Delgado underwent arthroscopic surgery on his hip and would be gone for the rest of the year. Outfielder Angel Pagan returned from the DL, allowing Manuel to use Reed, Murphy and Fernando Tatis at first.

The idea of Murphy didn't inspire confidence in Manuel. "I'm scared to death," the skipper said. "If he can't catch it out there, how's he going to catch it in here?"

FABULOUS:
JEFF FRANCOEUR

Francoeur came to the Mets in July and hit very well, with a .311 batting average, along with 11 HR and 41 RBI in less than half a season. In the field, he collected 5 assists and made only 1 error. "Frenchy's" total lack of plate discipline, however, limited his value, and he was shipped to Texas the following summer.

The Dodgers swept a series in Los Angeles. In the first game, it looked like Pagan's triple to right-center scored Church to give the Mets an 11th inning lead. But LA appealed and it turned out Church didn't touch third base. "It's hard to miss third base," Manuel said. "I don't know if I ever remember seeing anyone miss third base in a situation like that. I don't have any explanation for it." In the bottom of the inning, Pagan and Beltran misplayed a fly ball, putting runners on second and third with nobody out. With the bases loaded and one out Brian Stokes got Orlando Hudson to hit a grounder to first. Jeremy Reed's throw home was off the mark and Mark Loretta scored to end the game.

Reyes went on the DL with tendinitis in his right calf, then tore the hamstring during an extended spring training game. The shortstop was batting .279 with 11 stolen bases in 36 games. Early reports hoped he would be back in July but he wouldn't play for the Mets again until 2010. Top prospect Fernando Martinez was called up. In his second game, he hit a pop-up which fell in front of the plate but he never moved and was thrown out.

New York won six of seven to move into first place. Santos was a hero twice, hitting a game-winning home run at Fenway Park and then beating the Marlins several nights later with a walk-off single in the 11th.

Despite the injuries – Beltran missed a few days and Church was out two weeks – the Mets were 28-21 and a half-game out of first at the end of May. Wright was batting .333. Luis Castillo was batting .294.

Pittsburgh took three straight from the Mets to begin June. In the first game, Putz pitched to five batters, giving up four singles and intentionally walking the fifth batter. In the third game, he gave up two runs on three hits in one inning as his ERA increased to 5.22. He had pitched his final game for the Mets. The reliever had surgery on his elbow to remove a bone spur. Two months later, an MRI found new fraying and a slightly torn ulnar collateral ligament in his right elbow.

TOP BATTERS

Pos	Name	G	AB	H	BA	HR	RBI	RS	SB	OPS
1B	Daniel Murphy	155	508	135	.266	12	63	60	4	.741
2B	Luis Castillo	142	486	147	.302	1	40	77	20	.732
3B	David Wright	144	535	164	.307	10	72	88	27	.837
LF	Gary Sheffield	100	268	74	.276	10	43	44	2	.823
CF	Carlos Beltran	81	308	100	.325	10	48	50	11	.915

TOP PITCHERS

Pos	Name	G	GS	W	L	SV	ERA	IP	SO	BB
SP	Mike Pelfrey	31	31	10	12	0	5.03	184.1	107	66
SP	Johan Santana	25	25	13	9	0	3.13	166.2	146	46
SP	Tim	30	17	3	6	0	5.10	120.0	76	50
CL	Francisco Rodriguez	70	0	3	6	35	3.71	68.0	73	38
RP	Pedro Feliciano	88	0	6	4	0	3.03	59.1	59	18

The Mets were three games behind the Phillies when the defending champions came to town on June 9. New York took the first game behind Santana, who improved to 8-3. The next night the Phillies erased a three-run seventh inning deficit with help from a Wright error and Chase Utley homered off Bobby Parnell in the 11th. In the final game, Raul Ibanez hit a go-ahead three-run homer off Ken Takahashi in the top of the 10th.

John Maine was placed on the DL with shoulder fatigue and wouldn't be back until mid-September.

The Subway Series began on June 12. A back-and-forth game saw the Mets leading 8-7 in the bottom of the ninth despite four Yankees home runs. With Derek Jeter on second with two outs, Mark Teixeira was intentionally walked, bringing up Alex Rodriguez. Francisco Rodriguez got the Yankee third baseman to pop-up a 3-1 pitch to second. But Castillo dropped the ball. Jeter scored. Castillo picked up the ball and threw it to second. Teixeira scored. The Mets lost 9-8. Santana was crushed in the final game of the series, giving up nine runs in three innings in a 15-0 loss.

Two weeks later, the Yankees came to Citi Field and swept the Mets. The Mets were outscored 18-3 in the series. The finale was the most embarrassing. Chien-Mien Wang entered the game 0-6 with an 11.20 ERA but kept the Mets in check. In the top of the ninth with the bases loaded and two outs, Rodriguez walked Mariano Rivera.

Beltran was batting .336 with eight home runs but had to miss a-month-and-a-half with a knee injury as the DL became more crowded. Still, the Mets were only one game out of first after a 9-8 win over the Pirates on July 2, despite a 39-39 record.

The Mets went to Philadelphia but were swept, scoring three runs in three games. The fielding was also an issue as the team missed a pop-up and dropped a fly ball in the sixth inning of the second game. "Right now, I think we're the worst defensive team in the league," Cora said. The Mets were blanked twice more in the next four games. In three weeks, the team went from one game back to 10 back. Church was traded to the Braves for rightfielder Jeff Francoeur in a swap of outfielders who had fallen out of favor. Fernando Nieve won his first three starts, lost his next three and then was gone for the season with a muscle tear in his right thigh. Sheffield would go on the DL in late July with a hamstring injury.

It was reported that Tony Bernazard, the team's vice president for player development, pulled off his shirt and challenged the Double-A team to a fight in a postgame tirade. Bernazard also verbally assaulted a Mets official after a seat he wanted behind home plate at Citi Field was occupied. And there had been a verbal confrontation with Rodriguez on the team bus after an 11-0 loss in Atlanta.

Bernazard was fired but the story became stranger when Minaya took aim at ESPN's Adam Rubin during the press conference, saying the writer had been lobbying for a player development position. "So what you're alleging is that – the only conclusion I can draw from that is that you're trying to allege that I tried to tear everyone down so that I could take their position," Rubin said. "Is that what you're saying?" He added, "It seems pretty despicable to say that." Jeff Wilpon issued an apology to Rubin, and Minaya would later offer one of his own.

The Mets lost 17 of 24 before winning five straight in late July. With his team 6.5 games out of the wild card at the deadline, Minaya stood pat at the deadline. "But being six games out, as the general manage I've been six games out before and it's kind of hard to go out and make a trade," he said. "It's not a situation of [needing] one player. It's a situation of a couple of players."

On August 3, Nelson Figueroa returned to the team from Triple-A. He gave up six runs on 10 hits in 1.2 innings. The next night, Rodriguez blew a 7-5 lead in the ninth after Santana pitched eight innings. St. Louis scored twice in the ninth and five more times in the 10th, including an Albert Pujols grand slam off Green. The Mets won 9-0 the following afternoon but Jon Niese was lost for the season. The lefty, in his third start back from the minors, did the splits covering first base and then crumbled in pain on the mound after tossing a warmup pitch.

San Diego took three of four from the Mets out West. On August 7, the Mets led 2-1 heading into the ninth. Rodriguez couldn't retire any of the five batters he faced, giving up a walk-off grand slam to Everth Cabrera. "If I suck, I suck," the beleaguered closer said.

Wright was batting .324 when he stepped to the plate against San Francisco's Matt Cain in the fourth inning of a scoreless game. Cain's 0-2 pitch beaned Wright, who was momentarily motionless at the plate. "It's been a crazy, a crazy year," Beltran said. "I have no explanations. All the injuries have been one month, two months, long injuries. It's terrible." Santana threw behind

Pablo Sandoval in the seventh and the Giants third baseman followed with a homer. The Giants won 5-4 in 10 as Bengie Molina homered off Rodriguez.

Bobby Parnell gave up eight runs in the second inning of a 15-2 loss to the Braves. The Phillies came to Citi Field and took three of four. On the night the 1969 Mets were honored, Tim Redding pitched five shutout innings. Manuel took him out for Pat Misch, who immediately issued a walk and gave up a two-run homer to Utley. The Mets lost 4-1. The next day, Perez gave up three-run homers in the first to Jayson Werth and Carlos Ruiz. After falling behind 3-0 to Pedro Martinez, Manuel came out to pull the pitcher. "I've never seen that situation with Oliver," Martinez said after the game. "That's something I don't like. I know he didn't do his job. But a 3-and-0 count? I don't know if that's disrespect. I don't know how Ollie feels. But definitely, it was really weird." The Mets cut the lead to 9-7 in the ninth with runners on first and second with nobody out and Francoeur at the plate. With the count 2-2, Manuel started the runners. Francoeur lined out to Eric Brunlett at second, who stepped on the bag and tagged the runner to end the game with an unassisted triple play. Perez would be diagnosed with patellar tendinitis in his right knee and underwent season-ending surgery.

Perez joined Santana, who was shut down for the year after undergoing season ending arthroscopic surgery to remove bone chips in his left elbow. Minaya was asked if the surgery was related to the elbow pain he felt in spring training but Minaya said he didn't remember the ace was hurt in March because "Spring Training was such a long time ago."

Hernandez was released to make room for Billy Wagner, who returned to pitch two scoreless innings and then was traded to the Red Sox.

Sheffield was getting fed up, as he asked the team for an extension, became verbally abusive when he was told it wouldn't happen, demanded to be traded or released to the Marlins, threatened to return home to Florida and pulled himself from the starting lineup. The Giants had claimed him on waivers but the Mets pulled him back, despite him not being in the plans for 2010.

Wright returned to the lineup with an oversized helmet that resembled the Great Kazoo. He admitted he was flinching a bit after returning from the DL after the beaning. The team lost 10 of 11 in the middle of September. On September 16, the Mets led the Braves 5-4 in the ninth with Rodriguez on the mound. Garrett Anderson doubled to start the inning despite Murphy guarding the line, later saying he thought the ball was foul. "Regardless if it's a foul ball, that ball should not go through," an unforgiving Rodriguez said. The game ended with Murphy booting a grounder off the bat of Church, allowing David Ross to score from second. "I don't understand why he just didn't block the ball and keep it in play," Manuel said. "After he muffed the ball he seemed to panic."

The Mets ended September by losing three straight to the last-place Nationals in Washington. In the finale, Rodriguez was on the mound with New York leading 4-2. With two outs, he walked in a run to make it 4-3. Justin Maxwell followed with a grand slam to left to beat the Mets.

TOP BATTERS

Pos	Name	G	AB	H	BA	HR	RBI	RS	SB	OPS
1B	Daniel Murphy	155	508	135	.266	12	63	60	4	.741
2B	Luis Castillo	142	486	147	.302	1	40	77	20	.732
3B	David Wright	144	535	164	.307	10	72	88	27	.837
LF	Gary Sheffield	100	268	74	.276	10	43	44	2	.823
CF	Carlos Beltran	81	308	100	.325	10	48	50	11	.915

TOP PITCHERS

Pos	Name	G	GS	W	L	SV	ERA	IP	SO	BB
SP	Mike Pelfrey	31	31	10	12	0	5.03	184.1	107	66
SP	Johan Santana	25	25	13	9	0	3.13	166.2	146	46
SP	Tim	30	17	3	6	0	5.10	120.0	76	50
CL	Francisco Rodriguez	70	0	3	6	35	3.71	68.0	73	38
RP	Pedro Feliciano	88	0	6	4	0	3.03	59.1	59	18

The season ended with the Mets taking three straight from the Astros at Citi Field, giving up two runs in three games to reach the 70-win mark. For one final indignity, Mets fans were subjected to a Yankees-Phillies World Series.

Top 5 Highlights

1 Oliver Perez gives up one run in six innings as the Mets beat the Padres 7-2 on April 15 for the team's first win at Citi Field. Carlos Delgado homered off Luis Perdomo in the eighth.

2 Gary Sheffield becomes the 25th player with 500 home runs, hitting the milestone blast on April 17 off Milwaukee's Mitch Stetter to tie the game in the seventh. It was his first hit as a Met. At 40 years, 150 days, Sheffield became the fourth-oldest player to hot 500, behind Willie McCovey, Eddie Murray and Ted Williams.

3 Omir Santos hits a two-run home run off Jonathan Papelbon to give the Mets a 3-2 lead over the Red Sox with two outs in the ninth at Fenway Park on May 23. At first it was ruled a double but the umpires checked the video and awarded Santos the home run, which made it just over the Green Monster. Putz pitched a scoreless ninth.

4 Pat Misch pitches an eight-hit shutout over the Marlins in a 4-0 win on September 27. The lefty retires the final 13 Florida batters.

5 On the final day of the season, Nelson Figueroa pitches a four-hit shutout in a 4-0 win over the Astros. The right-hander throws 113 pitches, striking out seven and walking none.

Quiz #7: 2010s

1. (2010s) Who holds the Mets' single-season record for appearances by a pitcher? **[8 points]**

2. Name the pitcher from the Japanese major leagues who joined the Mets in 2010 late in his career and appeared in 53 games, including 12 starts and 8 saves. **[12 points]**

3. Two Mets players have collected 6 hits in one game, one of whom did it in the 2010s. Name them. **[5 points each]**

4. (2010s) Who holds the Mets record for most pinch hit home runs in a season? **[8 points]**

5. Who are the 2 Mets first-round picks from the 2010s who became strong contributors to the team and are on the roster as of spring 2020? **[5 points each]**

6. Name the 3 Mets to record 40+ saves in a season, one of whom did it twice in the 2010s. **[4 points each]**

7. 2013 Name the catcher who had a phenomenal first month with the team (9 HR 25 RBI) only to fade quickly and be traded to Pittsburgh that August. After 97 at bats the following year, his career was over. **[10 points]**

8. Which Mets pitcher won 2 games against the Dodgers in the Mets' 3-2 series win against the LA Dodgers in the 2015 NLDS? **[10 points]**

9. The Mets swept the Cubs in the 2015 NLCS in dominating fashion, holding the Cubs to 8 runs in the 4 games. Name the 4 starters who each won a game. **[2 points for 1, 4 for 2, 8 points for 3, 5 bonus points for all 4]**

10. The Mets lost Game 1 of the 2015 World Series 5-4 in 14 innings after blowing a 1-run lead in the 9th inning. Which Royals player hit the home run off Jeurys Familia to tie the game? **[10 points]**

11. Which Mets player hit 3 home runs in the 5-game 2015 World Series? **[8 points]**

12. Who led the Mets in home runs in their championship 2015 season? **[10 points]**

13. What position did Jacob DeGrom play in college before he was converted to pitcher? **[6 points]**

14. Name the Mets pitcher who appeared in 80 games in 2016, finishing with a 4-2 record, 1.97 ERA, and fanning 91 in 77.2 IP. **[8 points]**

15. (2010s) Who holds the Mets single-season record for HBP for a batter? **[8 points]**

16. In addition to Pete Alonso's 53 long balls in 2019, who are the 4 other Mets broke the 20-home run mark? **[2 points each]**

QUIZ #7: TOTAL POINTS – 146; BONUS POINTS – 5

GRAND TOTAL POINTS – 1000, GRAND TOTAL BONUS POINTS – 80

2010

	W	L	GB	Pos
	79	83	18.0	4th
RS/G	RA/G	Manager		
4.05	4.02	Jerry Manuel		

Mediocre Thy Name Is Mets

The Moves

After hitting the fewest homers in 2009, the Mets needed power. So Omar Minaya went out and signed Jason Bay for four years and $66 million. Bay was a three-time All-Star who hit .267 with 36 homers and 119 RBI in Boston in 2009.

In January, Carlos Beltran surprised the team by having knee surgery after the team wanted to discuss medical options with its staff. Beltran said he didn't defy any team wishes. Either way, he wouldn't be available until mid-July.

Soon after, the team traded Brian Stokes to the Angels for Gary Matthews Jr., who would become the Opening Day centerfielder. The slumping outfielder wanted more playing time and the Angels paid $21.5 million of his $23.5 million salary.

The Mets signed free agent catcher Rod Barajas after Bengie Molina decided to re-sign with the Giants. Veteran Frank Catalanotto was signed. Mike Jacobs returned to Queens and became the Opening Day first baseman. Knuckleball pitcher R.A. Dickey was given a spring training invite and was eventually called up from Buffalo in May.

Daniel Murphy was injured his knee late in spring training and then suffered an MCL tear attempting to turn a double play in a minor league game in June. He would miss the entire season.

 He Was a Met?

Gary Matthews Jr. had a forgettable end to his career, batting .190 in 36 games, with 1 RBI. The Mets had traded him for another forgotten Met, Brian Stokes, who had appeared in 69 games for New York in 2009.

The Situation

Minaya and Jerry Manuel entered 2010 on the hot seat. Jeff Wilpon's October press conference had put them on notice. After years of heartbreak, the 2009 season had been a disaster but perhaps it could be chalked up as a fluke due to injuries if they could bounce back. The Mets entered te season with an opening day payroll of $133 million, the fifth-highest in the majors. Spring training gave the Mets some optimism after seeing good performances from Jenrry Mejia, Ike Davis, Fernando Martinez, Ruben Tejada and Jon Niese.

There was increased attention paid to fundamentals that had haunted the Mets in 2009. "My thought process was, 'how can I address these issues?'" Manuel said. "And so we spent hours on baserunning and defense, with the coaches doing a tremendous job of creating specific drills, applying action to the emphasis we wanted."

Left Field Losers

In the winter of 1982 the Mets traded for slugger George Foster and signed the 33-year-old to a 5-year, $10M contract. Foster was a disaster for the Mets in 1982, hitting only 13 home runs and driving in 70 after totaling 22HR/90RBI in 108 games the year before. Foster bounced back somewhat the next 3 seasons, averaging 24 HR and 84 RBI, but he remained Mets fans' number 1 target.

Fast forward to January 2010 when the Mets inked Jason Bay to a 4-year, $66M contract. After averaging nearly 30 home runs and 100 RBI in the previous 6 seasons, Bay totally bombed out for the Mets, hitting only 6 HR and 47 RBI in 2010 and missing two months with a concussion. From there, things only got worse before the Mets bought out Bay after three painful seasons in which he totaled 26 HR and 124 RBI (with a BA in 2012 of .165!)

The Season

The Mets quickly found themselves in last place, losing seven of 10. The team did outlast the Cardinals in a 20-inning marathon in St. Louis. The team rolled off eight straight wins to end the month and sat in first place at the end of April. Mike Pelfrey was the star of the month, going 4-0 with a 0.69 ERA and a save.

Barajas hit five homers in April while David Wright and Jeff Francoeur hit four apiece. Angel Pagan had taken over for a slumping Matthews in center. Matthews would be released in mid-June. Pagan was leading off and Reyes was moved to third in the order, something Manuel had been contemplating for some time. Davis made his debut on April 19 and hit .324 in the month.

 Final Resting Ground

Fernando Tatis landed with the Mets in 2008, his fifth team. Tatis hit over .280 in his first two seasons. But he fizzled out in 2010, batting just .185, though he was 7-for-22 as a pinch hitter.

FUTILE: LUIS CASTILLO

Luis Castillo is remembered for dropping a pop-up that cost the Mets a game at Yankee Stadium in 2009, but it was in 2010 when he hit .235 and really drew the ire of fans. He struggled throughout the season, his final in the majors.

May began the Phillies scoring 21 runs in two games started by Pelfrey and Johan Santana. The Mets lost 13 of 18 to begin the month. Jeff Wilpon even went to meet with Manuel and Minaya in Atlanta but there were no firings.

The pitching was in trouble. Niese's right hamstring put him on the DL. Oliver Perez was moved to the bullpen after an 0-3 start with a 5.94 ERA. John Maine had a 6.13 ERA and was removed from his May 20 start after one batter. Maine screamed at Manuel in the dugout and voiced his displeasure after the game. "I didn't get asked a chance [to stay in] and that's what I'm most upset about. There's no f---king reason I should be seeing a doctor tomorrow." Pitching coach Dan Warthen said Maine was a "habitual liar" when it came to his health. The right-hander had shoulder surgery and was gone for the season.

The Mets then won five straight against the Yankees and Phillies. Mets pitching didn't give up a run in three games against the Phillies but then lost three of four to end the month, including an 18-6 laugher at the hands of the Padres. Perez was hit hard again out of the bullpen. Perez had refused a demotion to the minors, much to the chagrin of anonymous teammates. The unhappy lefty was placed on the DL in early June with patella tendinitis in his left knee. He began a rehab stint in the minors at the end of the month and would be back with the Mets in late July. Luis Castillo, who was in competition with Perez for least popular player among fans, was sent to the DL in early June with feet problems.

TOP BATTERS

Pos	Name	G	AB	H	BA	HR	RBI	RS	SB	OPS
1B	Ike Davis	147	523	138	.264	19	71	73	3	.791
SS	Jose Reyes	133	563	159	.282	11	54	83	30	.749
3B	David Wright	157	587	166	.283	29	103	87	19	.856
CF	Angel Pagan	151	579	168	.290	11	69	80	37	.765

TOP PITCHERS

Pos	Name	G	GS	W	L	SV	ERA	IP	SO	BB
SP	Mike Pelfrey	34	33	15	9	1	3.66	204.0	113	68
SP	Johan Santana	29	29	11	9	0	2.98	199.0	144	55
SP	R. A. Dickey	27	26	11	9	0	2.84	174.1	104	42
CL	Francisco Rodriguez	53	0	4	2	25	2.20	57.1	67	21
RP	Hisanori Takahashi	53	12	10	6	8	3.61	122.0	114	43

A hot June saw the Mets go 18-8, including an eight-game win streak. Dickey made an immediate impact, winning his first six decisions. Reyes was hitting .344 in his first five weeks after being placed back in the leadoff spot. Hisanori Takahashi, who had been moved into the rotation, pitched six shutout innings in a win at Yankee Stadium. "We're showing emotion, we're playing well," Francoeur said. "Everybody's kind of firing each other up and we're feeding off that. It's fun to come to the park when you're playing that way."

**FABULOUS:
ANGEL PAGAN**

In his first year playing full time, Pagan rapped out 168 hits and batted .290 for the season. He added 31 doubles and 37 steals and played brilliantly in the field, with a defensive WAR of 2.2. Pagan backtracked the next season and was dealt to the Giants for two nobodies.

The Mets cooled off but still entered the All-Star break 48-40, four games out of first place and only one game out of the wild card. Reyes and Wright were selected to the team. Reyes missed the game due to injury. Wright had a .314 average after hitting .258 through May.

Coming back from the break, the team lost 13 of 18 to fall to .500. The Mets were blanked four times in the first 11 games after the break. Bay suffered a concussion in late July when he ran into the wall at Dodger Stadium and was gone for the rest of the season. He hit .259 with six homers and 47 RBI.

The lowly Diamondbacks swept the Mets in Arizona. Alex Cora snapped at Pelfrey and a number of reporters who were laughing in the clubhouse. "A little respect please. They stuck it up our [butts]."

Perez was back and gave up a walk-off homer to James Loney in a 13-inning loss in his second appearance since being recalled. The Mets hovered around .500 into August.

Francisco Rodriguez had 25 saves in 30 opportunities and a 2.24 ERA after a save against Colorado on August 10. But after the Mets lost the next night, he went into the family lounge, threw his girlfriend's father into a tunnel and "repeatedly hit him in the face and hit his head against a wall," according to the NYPD. The pitcher was arrested and released without bail. The team suspended him for two games. He pitched a scoreless ninth inning against the Phillies on August 14. But it turned out Rodriguez tore a thumb ligament during the fight and was sidelined for the rest of the season. "Obviously I'm disappointed, discouraged, frustrated," Manuel said. "When you get this kind of news it's ... we've just been through a lot. We seem to continue to have difficulties keeping things from – having these type of injuries or these type of setbacks. Every year it seems like we get a little something here or there."

Beltran had returned in mid-July but struggled. Early in September he was hitting .211 with two homers.

Santana's season ended early, needing shoulder surgery after his September 2 start. A four-game sweep over the Pirates improved the team's record to 74-73 but the team lost its next six. Even the final game of the season, often a quick game for teams, took 14 innings with the Nationals winning 2-1 and Perez giving up the losing run with a hit batter and three walks.

Minaya and Manuel were dismissed. Money spent on underperforming players did Minaya in. "I think some of the free-agent signings turning out the way they did, and the money we misspent, is probably the biggest piece of it," Jeff Wilpon said.

Top 5 Highlights

1 Mike Pelfrey closes out New York's 2-1 win over the Cardinals on April 17, after allowing two runners on in the 20th inning. The game was scoreless through 18 innings when St. Louis manager Tony La Russa had position player Joe Mather pitch the 19th. Jeff Francoeur's sacrifice fly scored Jose Reyes. But with two outs in the bottom of the 19th, Yadier Molina delivered an RBI single off Francisco Rodriguez. A Reyes sac fly in the 20th made it 2-1. With two on and two out, Ryan Ludwick grounded out to end the six-hour, 53 minute affair.

2 Henry Blanco's homer off Guillermo Mota in the bottom of the 11th gives the Mets a 5-4 win over the Giants on May 8. The day before, Rod Barajas hit a two-run homer in the bottom of the ninth off Sergio Romo to win it 6-4.

3 Mets pitchers shutout the Phillies in a late May sweep. R.A. Dickey and Raul Valdes combine for the blanking in the first game. Hisanori Takahashi and three relievers do it the next night. Mike Pelfrey and a pair of relievers finish it off.

4 Ike Davis' 11th inning homer off Edward Mujica beats the Padres 2-1 on June 8.

5 Johan Santana pitches a three-hit shutout and homers off Matt Maloney in a 3-0 win over the Reds on July 6. It's the first, and last, homer of Santana's career.

2011

	W	L	GB	Pos
	77	85	25.0	4th
RS/G	RA/G	Manager		
4.43	4.58	Terry Collins		

Lack of Horses Does in Collins

The Moves

The new general manager was Sandy Alderson, who had built the powerhouse A's teams of the 1980s and early 1990s, and spent the previous year-and-a-half as a consultant to the league. MLB commissioner Bud Selig recommended Alderson pursue the job.

The managerial search was narrowed down to Terry Collins, Clint Hurdle and Bob Melvin as fan favorite Wally Backman didn't make the cut. Hurdle, a former Met who managed the Rockies to the 2007 World Series, took the Pirates job. Melvin was 2007 NL Manager of the Year and took the Diamondbacks to the NLCS. But Alderson picked Collins, who hadn't managed in the majors since 1999 but had been the Mets' minor league field coordinator in 2010. He had been one of three finalists to replace Art Howe before the 2005 season.

Free agent signings included relievers D.J. Carrasco, Taylor Buchholz, Blaine Boyer and Tim Byrdak, starters Chris Capuano and Chris Young and catcher Ronny Paulino. The team signed 38-year-old Jason Isringhausen, who hadn't pitched since elbow-ligament replacement surgery in June 2009, to a minor league contract.

⊘ He Was a Met?

In his 17th season in the majors, Miguel Batista joined the Mets, going 2-0 with a 2.64 ERA in nine appearances (four starts). He pitched a two-hit shutout against the Reds on the final day of the season.

Terry Collins

Terry Collins, who spent 2010 as the Mets Minor league field coordinator, was hired as manager for the 2011 season. He hadn't managed in the majors since the Angels in 1999, and before that Houston in 1996. But Collins had mellowed by the time Sandy Alderson hired him and he knew the players in the organization. Some saw Collins as a placeholder, but instead the veteran manager would become the longest-tenured skipper in team history—7 full seasons. The Mets finished below .500 in 5 of Collins' 7 seasons, but they did win 90 games in 2015 and made it to the World Series.

The Situation

Outfielder Willie Harris, who hit .183 with Washington in 2010, was given a minor league invite and made his way into the Opening Day lineup. The Mets released Oliver Perez and Luis Castillo, two of the lightning rods for fans. The team had tried Perez as a situational lefty after falling out of competition in the rotation but struggled out of the bullpen. Brad Emaus would be the Opening Day second baseman as Justin Turner was optioned to the minors and Daniel Murphy would be a utility infielder.

Johan Santana was out with his shoulder injury, not to return until 2012. Jason Bay would miss the first few weeks of the season. Expectations were low and any hope of competing for a division title seemed to diminish as the powerhouse Phillies added Cliff Lee in free agency.

The Season

Mike Pelfrey got the Opening Day start but failed to make it out of the fifth inning with Marlins catcher John Buck delivering a grand slam. The Mets won the next two in Florida and then beat up Cole Hamels in Philadelphia to improve to 3-1.

New York split the first two games against Washington before dropping the rubber match in 11 innings. Boyer, who gave up four runs in the 11th, was designated for assignment and Isringhausen was promoted. Lucas Duda misplayed a fly ball in the eighth inning, running in only to see it go over his head. Duda, who was batting .118, was demoted. Duda would return for two games in May when Bay went on maternity leave and then would go back to the minors until June.

 Final Resting Ground

Free agent signee Willie Harris fulfulled his role as super utlity man in 2011, playing 5 positions plus DH! Willie appeared in 126 games and performed decently. A .114 batting average in 25 games for the Reds next year signaled the end for Harris.

The loss was the first of seven straight for the team as they fell to 4-11 after a doubleheader sweep at the hands of the Braves. The start matched their third worst in team history and was the first time they lost 11 of the first 15 in 30 years.

After losing two of the next three, the team got hot and won six straight. Collins was ejected in the first inning of a 9-1 win over Arizona, perhaps injecting life into the team. The Mets scored four in the ninth to beat Washington for the sixth straight win.

The Mets avoided a sweep in Philadelphia with a 2-1, 14 inning win on Sunday night baseball to begin May. Ronny Paulino, in his first start with the Mets, had five hits. And during the ninth inning, the news of Osama bin Laden's death had Mets and Phillies fans joining together to chant "U-S-A."

> ### FABULOUS: JOSE REYES
>
> *Reyes led the NL in batting average at .337 and in triples (for the fourth time in his career) with 16. He also scored 101 runs in only 126 games. That winter, he signed with the Florida Marlins and his career turned south with him, as he never again hit .300 or scored 100 runs in his career.*

Young gave up one run in seven innings and had a 1.88 ERA in four starts before being lost for the season as he needed shoulder surgery. The Mets won 10 of 14, including a 2-1 win at Yankee Stadium with RA Dickey and three relievers combining to shut down the Yankees. But David Wright, who was hitting .226, was on the DL with a stress fracture in his back. It was his first stint on the DL and he wouldn't return until late July. And Ike Davis, who had at least one RBI in nine of the team's first 10 games, had been lost after a collision with Wright going for a pop-up on May 10. He missed the rest of the season.

Attention drifted from the field to the owner's box as Fred Wilpon criticized several players in a New York Magazine story. On Reyes: "He thinks he's going to get Carl Crawford money. He's had everything wrong with him. He won't get it." On Wright: [He is] "a really good kid. A very good player. Not a superstar." On Beltran: "We had some schmuck in New York who paid him based on that one series. He's 65 to 70 percent of what he was."

After getting back to .500 the team lost eight of 11, culminating with an ugly 9-3 loss to the Pirates at Citi Field. "I'm running out of ideas here," Collins said. "I sit here every night trying to figure out what we can do to get us over the top. I don't have the answers. I'm searching. I'm wringing the rag dry coming in here and having to look at you guys and you look at me like I'm a stinking fool."

The Mets fell behind 7-0 the next day but rallied for a 9-8 win. After Collins' rant, the team won 16 of 25. Dillon Gee started the season 7-0. In late June, the Mets scored 52 runs in four road wins against the Rangers and Tigers.

Francisco Rodriguez, who saved 23 games and had a 3.16 ERA, was traded to the Brewers as payroll relief. The deal was surprising in that it was announced after the All-Star game ended but unsurprising in that the closer had a $17.5 million vesting option for the following season.

TOP BATTERS

Pos	Name	G	AB	H	BA	HR	RBI	RS	SB	OPS
1B	Daniel Murphy	109	391	125	.320	6	49	49	5	.809
2B	Justin Turner	117	435	113	.260	4	51	49	7	.690
SS	Jose Reyes	126	537	181	.337	7	44	101	39	.877
3B	David Wright	102	389	99	.254	14	61	60	13	.771
RF	Carlos Beltran	98	353	102	.289	15	66	61	3	.904

TOP PITCHERS

Pos	Name	G	GS	W	L	SV	ERA	IP	SO	BB
SP	R. A Dickey	33	32	8	13	0	3.28	208.2	134	54
SP	Chris Capuano	33	31	11	12	0	4.55	186.0	168	53
SP	Dillon Gee	30	27	13	6	0	4.43	160.2	114	71
SP	Jon Niese	27	26	11	11	0	4.40	157.1	138	44
CL	Francisco Rodriguez	42	0	2	2	23	3.16	42.2	46	16

FUTILE: CHIN-LUNG HU

The Taiwanese middle infielder came over from the Dodgers after batting .130 in LA in limited play. Things got even tougher for Chin-Lung with the Mets, as he managed only 1 hit in 20 at bats, fanning 11 times. By 2013 he found himself in the Chinese Professional Baseball League where he has thrived ever since.

The team entered the All-Star break with a 46-45 mark. Reyes and Beltran were All-Stars but Reyes missed the game with a strained left hamstring. Beltran was traded to the Giants on July 28 to San Francisco for pitching prospect Zack Wheeler. The team was 53-51 at the time of the trade but Alderson spoke of the deal helping the team in the future.

Reyes told the team he wouldn't discuss his contract until after the season. The Mets didn't trade him and then lost him for three weeks due to his troublesome left hamstring that he reinjured in a loss to the Braves on August 7. Murphy's season came to an end during the same game. Atlanta's Jose Constanza slid into second and his spike collided with Murphy's lower leg, causing a Grade 2 MCL tear.

After improving to 55-51 in late July, the team lost 17 of 22. One problem in the bullpen was Bobby Parnell, who was struggling in higher-leverage roles after the Rodriguez trade. He lost two games in late July and struggled in early August.

The Mets won 10 of 13 to climb to 70-71 with a .500 finish within reach. But then the team lost eight of nine including a four game sweep at home against the Nationals, capped off by a 10-1 finale. The 1-8 home stand was the team's worst in seven years. "Perception is reality in our game and the perception I have right now is that we've folded it up," Collins said. "And I won't stand for that. You want to see me be intense? You guys are going to see that."

The only drama left was to see if Reyes would win the batting title. On the final day of the season, Reyes led off with a bunt single and removed himself from the game. Milwaukee's Ryan Braun went hitless and Reyes won the batting title by five points.

Collins was happy to see his shortstop win the batting title but addressed the criticism of leaving in the first inning. "I heard some comments in the stands," he said. "I don't blame them. People pay a good price to come to these games. You've got to understand that I ask these players to do a lot. We worked hard to get their respect this year, and they deserve ours."

Top 5 Highlights

1 Jason Bay singles with two outs and the bases loaded off Yankees righty Hector Noesi to give the Mets a 3-2, 10-inning win on July 3. Facing a sweep, the Mets were down to their final out against Mariano Rivera in the ninth when Bay walked, Duda singled and Paulino delivered an RBI single to tie it.

2 Angel Pagan's 10th inning homer off Fernando Salas gives the Mets a 6-5 win over the Cardinals on July 20. New York trailed 4-0 early and tied it twice. SNY announcers Gary Cohen, Ron Darling and Keith Hernandez called the game from the Pepsi Porch and the homer nearly made it to the makeshift broadcast booth.

3 Jason Isringhausen saves his 300th game in the Mets' 5-4, 10-inning win in San Diego on August 20. The Padres had the potential tying and winning runs in scoring position with two outs but Isringhausen got Logan Forsythe on a grounder to short to end the game.

4 Chris Capuano pitches a two-hit shutout and strikes out 13 Braves in a 6-0 win on August 26. The lefty throws 79 of his 122 pitches for strikes and pitches to one batter above the minimum.

5 Though it's not without controversy, Jose Reyes becomes the first player in team history to win the batting title, finishing with a .337 mark. In his final at-bat, Reyes lays down a bunt single against Cincinnati's Edinson Volquez.

2012

OPENING DAY LINEUP

Andres Torres, CF
Daniel Murphy, 2B
David Wright, 3B
Ike Davis, 1B
Jason Bay, LF
Lucas Duda, RF
Josh Thole, C
Ruben Tejada, SS
Johan Santana, P

	W	L	GB	Pos
	74	88	24.0	4th
RS/G	RA/G		Manager	
4.01	4.38		Terry Collins	

Johan No-No but Mets a No-Go

The Moves

It was the end of an era when Jose Reyes signed a six-year, $106 million deal with the Marlins, who were looking to make a splash in their new stadium. General manager Sandy Alderson talked about Angel Pagan as a possible leadoff hitter but the night before Reyes signed with Miami, Pagan was traded to the Giants for outfielder Andres Torres and reliever Ramon Ramirez.

Alderson also went to work improving the bullpen, signing set-up man Jon Rauch and closer Frank Francisco from the Blue Jays. The team also signed Pittsburgh shortstop Ronny Cedeno.

The Situation

After three years of struggles at the plate, the walls at Citi Field were lowered from 12 feet to eight feet and moved in, four feet in left field and up to 12 feet in left-center. Expectations were low.

As Grant Brisbee wrote for SB Nation when previewing the Mets season: "It should be a tough National League East this year, with four teams that are looking to contend for a division title. And another team. This is the other team."

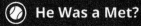

He Was a Met?

Andres Torres was injured on Opening Day and missed most of April. He finished the season batting .230 with three homers. Traded for Angel Pagan, Torres was the Mets' main center fielder (132 games), but with his poor production, the Mets let him go after the season.

Johan Hurls a No-No

Johan Santana tossed the first no-hitter in team history on June 1. There was help from Mike Baxter, who made a great catch in left, and third base umpire Adrian Johnson, whose missed call of a Carlos Beltran liner kept the no-no intact. Santana only won three games in the majors after that and Terry Collins took some heat for leaving him in for 134 pitches. But Santana had missed the entire 2011 season with a shoulder injury, and his comeback year really went down hill when Reed Johnson stepped on his ankle as he covered first base. He went 6-9 with a 4.85 ERA in his final season.

Jonah Keri wrote, "merely avoiding last place would be a coup, given the Mets' lack of talent and the possibility of four over-.500 (or better) teams duking it out for playoff spots.

The Season

When Daniel Murphy singled off Washington's Henry Rodriguez to score Mike Baxter in the bottom of the ninth on April 9, the Mets were 4-0. Johan Santana had returned and pitched five shutout innings in the opener, combining with four relievers to blank the Braves 1-0.

The Mets would finish April 13-10. R.A. Dickey went 3-1, with his only loss in the rain in Atlanta as he struggled to grip his knuckleball. New York swept the Marlins, with Reyes going 1-for-12 in the three games. Kirk Nieuwenhuis won the final game of the series with an RBI single in the bottom of the ninth. The rookie outfielder would hit .325 in April. Josh Thole was hitting .367 through April 27. David Wright was off to a blazing start, hitting .389 during the month. He also passed Darryl Strawberry's team record for RBI.

Mike Pelfrey was lost for the season with swelling in his left elbow. Chris Schwinden, who made four starts in 2011, was given a chance to start but gave up five runs in four innings in a pair of starts. Jason Bay was gone from late April to early June with a broken rib he suffered while making a diving catch.

FABULOUS: R. A. DICKEY

R.A. Dickey became perhaps the unlikeliest Cy Young winner ever, notching 20 wins at age 37, leading the league in starts, complete games and strikeouts. The journeyman knuckleballer pitched 44.2 consecutive scoreless innings at one point and pitched back-to-back one-hit shutouts.

After dropping to 13-13, the Mets won five straight. New York swept three straight in Philadelphia. Pinch-hitter Jordany Valdespin's first career hit was a three-run homer in the ninth off Jonathan Papelbon for a 5-2 win in the first game of the series. After the sweep, the Mets were a half-game out of first. First and fourth place were separated by 2.5 games.

Francisco lost two games in Miami in May, blowing a 5-4 lead on May 11 and then combining with Manny Acosta to squander an extra-inning lead two days later with Giancarlo Stanton ending the game with a grand slam off Acosta. Francisco had an ERA of 6.10 through May. He was ejected after being taken out of the May 13 game.

The star of the month was Dickey, who went 4-0 and lowered his ERA nearly a run and a half. The infield was becoming depleted as Ruben Tejada and Cedeno went down with injuries and Justin Turner went down with a sprained ankle. Omar Quintanilla was called up from Triple-A and got off to a hot start but soon slumped and was sent to Baltimore.

FUTILE: JASON BAY

In the second coming of George Foster, Jason Bay was signed before 2010 after a tremendous year with the Red Sox (36 HR, 119 RBI). Bay was at his worst in 2012, batting just .165 in 194 ABs. For their nearly $43,000,000, Bay produced a grand total of 26 HR and 122 RBI in three seasons.

Santana pitched a shutout on 96 pitches against the Padres on May 26. His next start was on June 1 with Thole, who had spent three weeks on the DL with a concussion, coming back to catch. Santana pitched the first no-hitter in team history as the Mets beat the Cardinals 8-0. It wasn't without controversy. Carlos Beltran, in his first game in Queens since being traded, hit a sixth-inning liner that kicked up on chalk on the line but was called foul by third base umpire Adrian Johnson. Two innings later, Santana hit Shane Robinson with a pitch but home plate umpire Gary Cedarstrom said it hit Robinson's bat. Santana struck Robinson out. Mike Baxter, who was hitting .323, would miss nearly two months after smashing into the wall to rob Yadier Molina of an extra-base hit. Collins would be questioned for leaving Santana in for 134 pitches, the final out striking out David Freese to make history. It was Santana's 11th start back from his shoulder injury. "My whole thing was my heart told me to take him out due to the fact that I'm playing with a huge part of the organization," Collins said. "If this guy goes down, it'd be pretty drastic."

The next day, Dickey pitched a shutout. Then, on Sunday night baseball with John Franco being inducted into the Mets Hall of Fame, Jon Niese fanned a career-high 10 batters in a 6-1 win. The Mets were in a three-way tie for first. But then the Mets lost six of seven. The team lost two of three in Washington and were swept by the Yankees, with Santana giving up six runs in five innings.

It was a streaky month for the team. Getting swept by the Yankees was followed by sweeping the Rays. Then the Mets were swept by the Reds, took four straight from the Orioles and Yankees, then lost four straight to the Yankees and Cubs before winning four straight. Bay was gone for another month after suffering a concussion against the Reds.

Dickey went 5-0 in May, improving to 12-1 and lowering his ERA to 2.15. He went 44.2 innings without allowing an earned run. He pitched consecutive one-hitters against Tampa Bay and Baltimore, striking out 25 in the two games. The journeyman knuckleball pitcher was a stunning story in a season that began with his autobiography detailing how he was the victim of sexual

TOP BATTERS										
Pos	Name	G	AB	H	BA	HR	RBI	RS	SB	OPS
1B	Ike Davis	156	519	118	.227	32	90	66	0	.771
2B	Daniel Murphy	156	571	166	.291	6	65	62	10	.735
3B	David Wright	156	581	178	.306	21	93	91	15	.883
RF	Lucas Duda	121	401	96	.239	15	57	43	1	.718

TOP PITCHERS										
Pos	Name	G	GS	W	L	SV	ERA	IP	SO	BB
SP	R. A. Dickey	34	33	20	6	0	2.73	233.2	230	54
SP	Jon Niese	30	30	13	9	0	3.40	190.1	155	49
SP	Dillon Gee	17	17	6	7	0	4.10	109.2	97	29
CL	Frank Francisco	48	0	1	3	23	5.53	42.1	47	21
RP	Bobby Parnell	74	0	5	4	7	2.49	68.2	61	20

abuse from his babysitter, his father's absence, mother's alcoholism and his own failings as a family man. Dickey led the league in all three triple crown categories and was 10 games over .500 only 68 games into the season. "I've never seen anything like this," Collins said. "Never. I've seen some dominant pitching but nothing like what he's going through right now."

The team exploded for 17 runs in shellacking of the Cubs in late June. Wright had five RBI, while Murphy, Ike Davis and Scott Hairston had four apiece. Murphy hit his first two homers of the season and Davis brought his average over .200 for the first time after a brutal start to the season.

Santana looked like he got his groove back, winning three of four starts after the Yankees beat him. The wins included six shutout innings against the Orioles and eight more zeroes against the Dodgers. But in the fifth inning of his start on July 6, Chicago's Reed Johnson stepped on his ankle as Santana went to cover first. Santana gave up five runs in the inning before being taken out. The Mets won the next day to improve to 46-39 but then dropped 12 of 13 with a Dickey win in Washington the only victory. Santana gave up six runs in consecutive starts and was placed on the DL with an ankle injury. He joined Gee, who had gone to the DL after a blood clot was removed from his shoulder. Gee, who was 6-7 with a 4.10 ERA, would miss the rest of the season.

The team also lost consecutive extra-inning games by at least five runs for the first time in team history: first an 8-3, 12-inning loss to the Dodgers with Ramirez getting shelled late and an 8-2, 10-inning loss to the Nationals with Tim Byrdak and Pedro Beaton getting hit. The Mets released Miguel Batista after he pitched three innings in a start against the Dodgers. Frustration was mounting. Beato uncorked a wild pitch in Washington and said, "I tried to get it down on the floor, so he can swing over it. And I yanked a little too far. Unfortunately, Thole wasn't able to get it and it got away from him." He apologized to his catcher the next day.

Tim Byrdak lost his temper after giving up a homer on a fastball to Adam LaRoche after Byrdak shook off Thole's requests for a fastball. Byrdak argued with Thole as LaRoche rounded the bases and was taken out. Upon learning the pitch call came from the bench, Byrdak got into a jawing match with pitching coach Dan Warthen. "There's frustration all around this clubhouse," Bydak said. "There's a lot of guys that are pissed. Everybody is pissed off … I didn't execute the pitch. Again, as a bullpen, we need to keep it close out there."

It was time to call up Matt Harvey. The confident right-hander was the seventh overall pick in the 2010 draft thought he should have made the team out of spring training though Alderson said, "aside from Matt himself – and I love that he thinks this way – there is no one in the organization who feels he is ready to be in the major leagues." He became an International League All-Star and with the team struggling and looking for a spark in the rotation, Harvey made his debut on July 26 in Arizona. Harvey fanned 11 batters in 5.1 innings and became the first player in modern baseball history to strikeout at least 10 batters and get two hits in his debut. It was a bright spot in a 7-17 month. Chris Young went 0-4 in July. Even a three-homer outburst from Davis on July 28 against Arizona couldn't put the Mets in the win column as the Mets lost 6-3.

Santana returned on August 11 and gave up eight runs in 1.1 innings, blaming the horrific performance on rust. On the 17th in Washington, he retired the first nine batters before falling apart. Mike Morse hit a fourth inning grand slam and Bryce Harper doubled two runs in an inning later. It was his final start as he was placed on the DL with lower back inflammation. He finished the season 6-9 with a 4.85 ERA.

The Mets lost four straight at home to the last-place Rockies, who came into Citi Field with a 46-73 record. The Mets scored five runs in the series.

Harvey at least won two games in August, including a win over the eventual-division champion Reds in Cincinnati, giving up one run on four hits in 7.2 innings. The team did win seven of eight before falling off a cliff, losing 11 of 12. A three-game sweep by the Braves marked the final trip to Queens by Chipper Jones, who drew a pinch-hit walk against Francisco in his last plate appearance.

There was still history to make, good and bad. A 16-1 loss at home to the Phillies made the Mets the first team since the 1980 Angels to lose 25 home games in a 29-game stretch. The team also went 16 straight home games without scoring more than three runs, joining the 2010 Mariners as the only team to do so since 1949. On September 26, Wright became the Mets all-time hit leader with an infield single off Pittsburgh's Jeff Locke.

Dickey won his 20th game in the home finale, a 7-5 win over the Pirates. Dickey gave up three runs in 7.2 innings and fanned 13. Dickey, who had never won more than 11 games in a season, became the first knuckleballer to win 20 games in a season since Houston's Joe Niekro in 1980.

Top 5 Highlights

1 Johan Santana strikes out David Freese for the first Mets no-hitter in game number 8,020. As Gary Cohen said, "It has happened!"

2 R.A. Dickey pitches his second straight one-hitter in a 5-0 win over the Orioles on June 18. Wilson Betemit's two-out fifth inning single is the only Baltimore hit. Dickey becomes the first pitcher to throw consecutive one-hitters since Toronto's Dave Stieb in 1988. Dickey is the first National Leaguer to accomplish the feat since Boston Braves pitcher Jim Tobin.

3 Ike Davis hits a walk-off home off Houston's Wilton Lopez to beat the Astros 2-1 on August 26. It was his second homer of the game. Jeremy Hefner took a shutout into the ninth before the Astros tied the game.

4 David Wright breaks Ed Kranepool's franchise hits record. Number 1,419 comes against the Pirates in a 6-0 win at Citi Field on September 26.

5 R.A. Dickey becomes the fifth Mets pitcher to win 20 games in a season, with a 7-5 win over the Pirates on September 27. Wright hits a three-run homer in the fifth to put the Mets up 6-3. Jon Rauch gives up a two-run homer in the ninth but Bobby Parnell retires the final two batters to close out the win.

2013

	W	L	GB	Pos
	74	88	22.0	3rd
RS/G	RA/G		Manager	
3.82	4.22		Terry Collins	

Mets Stay Stuck on 74 Wins

The Moves

The Mets locked down David Wright, signing the third baseman to an eight year, $138 million contract. He was later named the fourth captain in team history.

After weeks of shopping R.A. Dickey around, the Mets traded the Cy Young winner to the Blue Jays for top prospects Travis d'Arnaud and Noah Syndergaard. The deal, heavy on catchers, also saw Josh Thole and Mike Nickeas go to Toronto with John Buck coming to New York.

Jason Bay's contract was terminated in November. In three seasons as a Met, he hit .234 with 26 homers and 124 RBI. The Giants signed Andres Torres as a free agent and Scott Hairston signed with the Cubs. The Mets acquired Collin Cowgill from Oakland and signed veteran outfielder Marlon Byrd. Byrd was a 2010 All-Star who had been suspended in 2012 for PED use.

Before the Byrd signing the only outfielders on the roster were Cowgill, Mike Baxter and Kirk Nieuwenhuis, who had less than 300 games of combined MLB experience.

The Situation

Many pundits had the Mets finishing in fourth place, only ahead of the lowly Marlins. Johan Santana tore the anterior capsule in his pitching shoulder, the

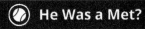

He Was a Met?

LaTroy Hawkins pitched for 11 different teams in the majors, including both the Mets and Yankees. Signed to a 1-year free agent contract, the 40-year-old was very effective - appearing in 72 games, saving 13, with an ERA of 2.93. That winter, he moved on to Colorado.

Daniel Murphy showed some signs in 2013 of the batting star he would become in Washington, with 188 hits, 78 RBI, and 92 RS.

same injury that made him miss 2011. He would be done for the season and, it turned out, his career was over. Zack Wheeler only pitched two innings in spring training because of a strained oblique and would begin the season in the minors.

The Season

Matt Harvey was the story in April. He won his first four starts with a 0.93 ERA and 32 strikeouts. He took a no-hitter into the seventh inning in Minnesota and then outpitched Stephen Strasburg in a highly-anticipated matchup at Citi Field. John Buck made an immediate impact at the plate. He hit six homers and had 19 RBI in the first 10 games. He would finish April with nine home runs and 25 RBI.

Jordanny Valdespin's walk-off grand slam against the Dodgers improved the Mets to 10-9 but it would be the last time they were over .500 for the year. The Mets lost six straight to end the month, including consecutive walk-off losses in Miami. The April 29 game was billed as a Harvey duel with Jose Fernandez though Fernandez lasted four innings and Harvey threw 121 pitches in 5.1 innings. The Marlins tied the game in the ninth against Bobby Parnell, the Mets scored in the 15th but Miami scored twice off Shaun Marcum in the bottom of the frame. The next night, Jeremy Hefner looked to save the bullpen, taking a 1-0 lead into the ninth but the first two batters reached and Miami scored twice with Brandon Lyon on the mound with the winning run scoring on a wild pitch. "I am extremely pissed off," Terry Collins said.

The offense struggled, putting up a .202 batting average over 12 games in late April and the beginning of May. Nieuwenhuis was sent down to the minors with Juan Lagares getting promoted. Cowgill, who hit an Opening Day grand slam, was sent to the minors after hitting .155 in his next 46 at-bats as Andrew Brown was called up.

 Final Resting Ground

The long and winding career of Rick Ankiel came to the end with the Mets at age 33. Picked up after his release by Houston, he played regularly for the Mets. But less than a month later, they had second thoughts and sent Ankiel and his .182 BA on their way.

At least there was Harvey. On May 7 against the White Sox, Harvey retired the first 17 batters before pinch-hitter Alex Rios broke up the perfect game with an infield single. He was the only batter to reach against Harvey and the Mets won in the 10th on Baxter's single off Nate

Jones. Two nights later, Baxter delivered another winner off Pittsburgh's Jason Grilli.

Valdespin hit a homer off Jose Contreras in the bottom of the ninth of an easy Pirates win but his showboating didn't sit well with either team. The next day, Collins sent him up as a pinch-hitter and Valdespin was drilled. "I would have been bothered had it been somewhere up in the neck area," Collins said. "If nothing else, he grew by it and that's the most beneficial thing that could happen."

What wasn't beneficial was a six-game losing streak that dropped the Mets to 14-23. Another five-game skid made them 17-29. Through May 25, Ike Davis was hitting .148 and striking out in what felt like every at-bat. Ruben Tejada was hitting under .230. So was Lucas Duda. Dillon Gee was 2-6 with a 6.34 ERA.

The Mets rolled off five straight wins, including a four-game sweep of the Yankees. But the good feelings quickly disappeared as the team went to Miami to play the 13-41 Marlins and were swept away. Marcum dropped to 0-6 with a 5.71 ERA in the first game. Collin McHugh lost his first start of the year the next day. Even Harvey couldn't stop the bleeding in the finale, giving up four runs in five innings. Still, he left with a 6-4 lead but Scott Rice walked three straight batters in the sixth and all three Marlins scored. Greg Dobbs' three-run blast off LaTroy Hawkins in the eighth capped off the 11-6 embarrassment.

FABULOUS: MARLON BYRD

Marlon Byrd gave the Mets some pop, hitting .285 with a team-leading 21 homers along with 71 RBI in 117 games before being traded to Pittsburgh, along with John Buck, for Dilson Herrera and Vic Black.

After leaving Miami, the Mets lost seven of nine, including two extra inning losses at home to the Marlins. On June 8, the Marlins won 2-1 in 20 innings. Marcum pitched his best game as a Met, working eight innings out of the bullpen, but still fell to 0-7, giving up a 20th inning RBI single to Adeiny Hechavarria. The Mets avoided a sweep by the Cubs as Nieuwenhuis hit a three-run homer to beat Chicago 4-3.

On June 17, Gee took a 1-0 shutout into the ninth inning in Atlanta but gave up a two-run homer to Freddie Freeman. Gee had also delivered an RBI single in the seventh. The season was already all but over but there was excitement the next day as Harvey and Wheeler, making his debut, started in a doubleheader. Harvey pitched six no-hit innings and the Mets held on for a 4-3 win in the opener. Wheeler pitched six shutout innings in the nightcap, a 6-1 Mets win. The two young pitchers beating the first-place Braves gave some hope for the future.

The team acquired Eric Young Jr. from the Rockies as the Mets looked for a spark at the top of the lineup. McHugh was sent to Colorado. Cowgill was designated for assignment and would go to the Angels. In his first home start,

TOP BATTERS

Pos	Name	G	AB	H	BA	HR	RBI	RS	SB	OPS
C	John Buck	101	368	79	.215	15	60	38	2	.652
2B	Daniel Murphy	161	658	188	.286	13	78	92	23	.733
3B	David Wright	112	430	132	.307	18	58	63	17	.904
RF	Marlon Byrd	117	425	121	.285	21	71	61	2	.848

TOP PITCHERS

Pos	Name	G	GS	W	L	SV	ERA	IP	SO	BB
SP	Dillon Gee	32	32	12	11	0	3.62	199.0	142	47
SP	Matt Harvey	26	26	9	5	0	2.27	178.1	191	31
SP	Jon Niese	24	24	8	8	0	3.71	143.0	105	48
CL	Bobby Parnell	49	0	5	5	22	2.16	50.0	44	12
RP	LaTroy Hawkins	72	0	3	2	13	2.93	70.2	55	10

Wheeler gave up five runs in 4.2 innings and catcher Anthony Recker pitched the ninth inning in a 13-2 loss to Washington.

In mid-July, Valdespin, and his .188 batting average, was sent to Triple-A. Valdespin reportedly called Collins a "cocksucker" during a confrontation following the demotion. He would later be suspended for 50 games for using performance-enhancing drugs. He had played his last game for the Mets.

The Mets were 41-50 heading into the All-Star break but it was an exciting time as Bruce Bochy named Harvey the starter for the midsummer classic at Citi Field. Harvey pitched two shutout innings in the American League's 3-0 win.

Brandon Lyon and his 4.98 ERA was released in July. So was Marcum, who was unlikely to pitch again anyway because of thoracic outlet syndrome. He was 1-10 with a 5.29 ERA.

Harvey pitched his first shutout, a 5-0 win over the Rockies on August 7. Wilmer Flores delivered a three-run double, his first hit in the majors. He was called up after Wright went on the DL with a strained right hamstring he suffered beating out an infield single. Wright wouldn't return until late September.

FUTILE: SHAWN MARCUM

Veteran righty Shaun Marcum followed five consecutive winning seasons with other teams by going 1-10 with a 5.29 ERA in 14 games (12 starts) in his one season with the Mets.

Even more concerning would be an injury to Harvey. The team was monitoring Harvey, with Collins announcing he wouldn't be allowed to pitch more than 215 to 220 innings. The ace started on August 24 against the Tigers and gave up 13 hits in 6.2 innings though he held Detroit to two runs. He admitted to being "pretty tired" and told team officials he was experiencing an abnormal level of forearm discomfort. An MRI revealed a partially torn ulnar collateral ligament in his right elbow. The Mets would later announce that he would have Tommy John surgery, keeping him out for all of 2014.

"I didn't feel a snap," said Harvey, who finished 9-5 with a 2.27 ERA, striking out 191 batters in 178.1 innings. "I didn't feel a pop. No tingling or anything like that. It was just some tightness in my forearm – that's why I was pretty shocked."

The pitcher injuries were piling up. Hefner was done, getting Tommy John surgery. Jenrry Mejia underwent season-ending surgery to remove a bone spur in his pitching elbow. And Niese had been out for nearly two months. Bobby Parnell, who saved 22 games, was lost for the last two months of the season with a herniated disk in his neck. The Mets signed former Boston star Daisuke Matsuzaka, who would lose his first three starts with a 10.95 ERA.

Byrd and Buck were traded to the Pirates with the deal being announced on Marlon Byrd t-shirt night at Citi Field. Byrd led the team in home runs (21) and RBI (71), while Buck was second with 15 and 60. Murphy was the only player in the lineup with more than 30 RBI. "We just went from struggling for three runs a game to struggling for one," an unnamed Met said. D'Arnaud was called up in late August. The team also called up Matt den Dekker, a defensive-first outfielder. The deal with the Pirates brought the Mets Dilson Herrera, their possible second baseman of the future, as well as reliever Vic Black.

There was little excitement at Citi Field in September, outside of two walk-off wins in three games, courtesy of d'Arnaud and Josh Satin. Mike Piazza was inducted into the Mets Hall of Fame on the final day of the season. If only he could still suit up.

Top 5 Highlights

1 Collin Cowgill hits an Opening Day grand slam in the seventh inning off San Diego's Brad Brach in the Mets' 11-2 win over the Padres.

2 Jordany Valdespin hits a walk-off grand slam to beat the Dodgers 7-3 on April 24. The 10th inning blast came off Josh Wall. David Wright delivered an RBI single with two outs in the ninth to tie the game.

3 Lucas Duda singles off Mariano Rivera to beat the Yankees 2-1 on May 28. Trailing 1-0 heading into the bottom of the ninth, Daniel Murphy doubles, Wright singles and goes to second on the throw home and Duda follows with a single. It's the first time Rivera, who threw out the ceremonial first pitch to John Franco, fails to record an out in a save opportunity.

4 Matt Harvey pitches two shutout innings in the All-Star Game at Citi Field. The game starts with a Mike Trout double and Robinson Cano hit by pitch but the ace retires the next six batters. Miguel Cabrera, Jose Bautista and Adam Jones are strikeout victims.

Harvey pitches a four-hit shutout in a 5-0 win over the Rockies on August 7. With two outs in the ninth, Charlie Blackmon hits a liner off Harvey and reaches first but Harvey is good enough to remain in the game and gets Troy Tulowitzki on a pop-up to end it.

2014

OPENING DAY LINEUP

Eric Young Jr., 2B
Juan Lagares, CF
David Wright, 3B
Curtis Granderson, RF
Andrew Brown, LF
Ike Davis, 1B
Travis d'Arnaud, C
Ruben Tejada, SS
Dillon Gee, P

	W	L	GB	Pos
	79	83	17.0	3rd

RS/G	RA/G	Manager
3.88	3.81	Terry Collins

Wright Nearing End as Mets Slumber Again

The Moves

The Mets made a splash by signing Curtis Granderson to a four-year, $60 million deal. The power hitting outfielder averaged 36 home runs in his first three seasons with the Yankees although he was limited to 61 games in 2013.

A few days after signing Granderson, the Mets signed another former Yankee, giving Bartolo Colon a two-year, $20 million contract. Colon, who had pitched for the Yankees in 2011, had won 18 games for Oakland in 2013. It was a case of the team signing a veteran in the absence of Matt Harvey, and not wanting to push prospects like Noah Syndergaard and Rafael Montero ahead of schedule.

The team added a few more arms. Southpaw John Lannan, who had picked up his first complete game victory and later his first complete game shutout against the Mets as a member of the Nationals, was signed. Kyle Farnsworth, who had already pitched for seven different teams, including the Tigers and Braves twice, was brought in. Lefty Dana Eveland, who had pitched for seven teams and spent 2013 playing in South Korea, was signed in February. Buddy Carlyle was signed the following day. Carlyle had made his major league debut

 He Was a Met?

You'd be forgiven if you forgot Kyle Farnsworth was on the Mets. He was signed as a free agent in February 2014 (the 8th team of his career) and then let go in May of that year, after picking up losses in three of his 19 appearances. Farnsworth got into 16 games for the Astros, who picked him up, after which the reliever called it a career.

Curtis Granderson came to the Mets in 2014 as a free agent. His best year was the championship season of 2015, in which Grandy scored 98 runs, walked 91 times, and belted 26 home runs, adding 3 more in that year's World Series.

in 1999, and was a 4-A player, who spent years in the minors, and had not pitched in the majors since 2011. Outfielder Chris Young was signed to a one-year, $7 million deal.

One surprise move was naming Jenrry Mejia the fifth starter over Daisuke Matsuzaka.

The Situation

After five straight losing seasons, including two straight seasons at 74-88, eyebrows were raised when it was reported that general manager Sandy Alderson spoke about a 90-win season. "Was I surprised by the skepticism? Am I concerned about the optics? No. It's time for us to get better. What you can measure, you can improve. You can't really measure competitiveness," Alderson said. It wasn't a guarantee. It wasn't a prediction. It was a challenge, OK? A challenge to all of us internally: How do we get there?"

While few expected the team to win 90 games, could they finish at .500? Adam Rubin predicted the team would go 76-86 and finish in

 Final Resting Ground

After a tremendous 16-year career in which he had 8 seasons with 100 or more RBI, RS, and BB, Bobby Abreu signed on with the Mets before the 2014 season, after not playing at all in 2013. Abreu's contributions were limited, including going only 5-for-39 as a pinch hitter. He did steal one base to give him a career total of 400.

FABULOUS: LUCAS DUDA

Lucas Duda hit 30 home runs and his 92 RBI were fifth in the league. And he did it as virtually the only threat in the lineup as nobody else drove in more than 66. Duda came back with 27 dingers the next year and 30 in 2017 (split between New York and Tampa Bay), but has struggled as a part-time player the last two seasons.

fourth place. Joe Lemire of *Sports Illustrated* wrote that the Mets would win 82 games.

The Season

The Mets were one out from an Opening Day win but Bobby Parnell blew the save and the Mets gave up four in the 10th in a 9-7 loss. It turned out Parnell had a partially torn elbow ligament and he would miss the rest of the season. Daniel Murphy missed the first two games of the season on paternity leave. WFAN's.

Murphy made two errors in his first game back as the Mets were swept at home in a season-opening series for the first time ever. The final game was an 8-2 drubbing, lasting three hours and 21 minutes with a struggling bullpen giving up five runs (four earned) in three innings.

Lucas Duda hit two homers against the Reds in the team's first win of the season. The first base job was his, though Ike Davis came off the bench to deliver a walk-off pinch-hit grand slam the next day. Davis would be traded to the Pirates on April 18. Davis was hitting .208 with a homer and five RBI in 24 at-bats. Duda was starting and the team had right-handed Josh Satin to back him up.

New York picked up the pace and went 15-11 in April. Anthony Recker's 13th inning homer gave the team a 7-6 win over the Angels. Granderson delivered two-walk off RBI. And Murphy hit .304 in April.

But the team would struggle in May. The team lost three of four in Colorado, including a six-run blown lead in an 11-10 loss. Terry Collins left Mejia in as he gave up eight runs in the fifth of the May 3 game. The Mets came back to take a 10-9 lead but Farnsworth allowed a two-run homer to Charlie Culberson in the bottom of the ninth. Still, the Mets left Colorado one game out of first in a bunched up NL East.

The Mets went to Miami and were swept by the Marlins. Two of the losses were on walk-offs and the Mets were blanked twice. The Mets took two games at Yankee Stadium, busting out for 21 runs in two wins but it would be the last time the team would be at .500. Dillon Gee was gone for two months with a lat injury. Jose Valverde had struggled in the closer's role and gave way to Farnsworth. But the latter was released in mid-May. The intense right-hander had a 3.18 ERA in 18 appearances but was 0-3 with a 5.40 ERA since April 26. "Hopefully I'll find a team to play against this team," an angry Farnsworth said.

TOP BATTERS

Pos	Name	G	AB	H	BA	HR	RBI	RS	SB	OPS
1B	Lucas Duda	153	514	130	.253	30	92	74	3	.830
2B	Daniel Murphy	143	596	172	.289	9	57	79	13	.734
3B	David Wright	134	535	144	.269	8	63	54	8	.698
CF	Juan Lagares	116	416	117	.281	4	47	46	13	.703
RF	Curtis Granderson	155	564	128	.227	20	66	73	8	.714

TOP PITCHERS

Pos	Name	G	GS	W	L	SV	ERA	IP	SO	BB
SP	Bartolo Colon	31	31	15	13	0	4.09	202.1	151	30
SP	Jon Niese	30	30	9	11	0	3.40	187.2	138	45
SP	Zack Wheeler	32	32	11	11	0	3.54	185.1	187	79
SP	Jacob deGrom	22	22	9	6	0	2.69	140.1	144	43
CL	Jenrry Mejia	63	7	6	6	28	3.65	93.2	98	41

Mejia and his 5.06 ERA became the new closer. Rafael Montero and Jacob deGrom made their debuts on consecutive days against the Yankees at Citi Field. Montero was the more anticipated of the two. Both received no run support and both lost. DeGrom gave up one run in seven innings, perhaps setting the tone for the offensive backing he would receive in many starts over the years. In deGrom's start, the Mets struck out 14 times, including seven looking. The beleaguered offense was struggling as Sandy Alderson stressed patience at the plate. Wright and Murphy were both hitting over .300 but most of the other players were scuffling.

FUTILE: CHRIS YOUNG

A free agent signing who topped 20 HR in a season 3 times with Oakland, Young hit .205 with eight homers in 88 games before being let go. He went to the Yankees and hit .282 with three homers in 23 games.

After 17 losses in 24 games, hitting coach Dave Hudgens was fired. On his way out the door, Hudgens took a shot at the team's announcers. "The naysayers, the guys who disapprove of us, the guys who I listen to on TV all the time, those guys that know everything about the game, I'm just amazed at it," Hudgens told Newsday. "What's wrong with getting a good pitch to hit? I just shake my head at the old-school guys that have it all figured out. Go up there and swing the bat. Well, what do you want to swing at? . . . That's one thing. I'm glad I don't have to listen to those guys anymore."

The team also released Valverde, who had given up four runs and allowed five of seven batters to reach in a loss to the Pirates. He had a 5.66 ERA in 21 games.

The Mets won six of seven, culminating with an 11-2 laugher over the Phillies but then lost six straight, getting swept by the Cubs and Giants. They scored four runs or fewer in each game. Frustratingly, the Mets led in five of the six losses. Wright hit .155 during losing streak. Travis d'Arnaud and his .180 batting average were sent to Triple-A. He had been 3-26 since returning from a concussion. Wheeler was 2-6 with a 4.19 ERA.

The Mets hung around. Five wins in six games put the team at 36-41, 5.5 games out of first. A 10-1 win over Oakland on June 24 saw the Mets hit four homers, including two from the struggling Young and one from d'Arnaud. And Colon won his sixth decision in a row, to improve to 8-5.

But seven losses in eight games followed. Wright missed seven games with shoulder discomfort. The team lost three of four in Pittsburgh and was swept in Atlanta. Alderson defended the roster, saying "We kind of like our team. If you look at the run differential, we should be a .500 team. We're not. At the same time, it doesn't mean we should throw everyone overboard." Then the Mets got hot, winning nine of 11. After a 1-5 start, deGrom won four straight starts, giving up two runs during the stretch.

August began with a four-game series against the Giants. San Francisco took three of four: a two-hour, six-minute breeze in which the Mets were limited to one run on two hits by Ryan Vogelsong; Madison Bumgarner pitching a two-hit shutout with 10 strikeouts on Sunday afternoon; and the final game of the series, with Pablo Sandoval doubling down the line off Mejia in the ninth to beat the Mets 4-3.

The Nationals took five of six from the Mets during the month, including a sweep at Citi Field. Bryce Harper hit a homer in the 13th inning off Carlos Torres to end a game in Washington. Young was released with a disappointing .205 average and eight homers. Den Dekker and Eric Campbell platooned in left.

Mejia took two tough losses. The first was August 10, in a game the Mets once led 6-1. Philadelphia cut the lead to 6-5 in the ninth. The Phillies tied the game at six and had Marlon Byrd on and two outs with Chase Utley at the plate. Byrd stole second on a 2-2 pitch and with the count full, Collins called for an intentional walk. Ryan Howard followed with a game-ending hit. A week later, Mejia gave up a tie-breaking ninth inning homer to Starlin Castro in a 2-1 loss to the Cubs.

The next day, Carlos Torres had to make a spot start despite pitching in relief the day before because Colon left the team following his mother's death. He pitched five shutout innings but the Mets still lost 4-1. It was the fifth straight game in which the Mets were held to four hits or fewer. It was Granderson who seemed to be slumping the worst as the outfielder hit .147 with one homer and two extra-base hits in August. One Mets person told the Daily News "the guy has been invisible. And remember, he was supposed to be our cleanup hitter." Wright only hit .232 in August as he battled a hurt shoulder. Bobby Abreu was released with one hit in his last 21 at-bats but then the team signed him again and brought him back in September.

Contributing to the lineup was d'Arnaud and the team even had internal discussions about a possible move to the outfield to keep his bat in the lineup and to avoid more concussions. Murphy went on the DL in late August with a strained right calf and the team called up Dilson Herrera.

September began with seven wins in nine games, but Wright was finished for the season. His injury was initially diagnosed as a bruised rotator cuff, but additional tests showed torn ligaments in his shoulder. New York did take a game from the Nationals, with Mejia striking out Ian Desmond with the potential tying and go-ahead runs on base. Mejia celebrated by standing in front of the mound and pretending to reel in Desmond. Collins met with Mejia, who often waved his arms and stomped his right foot after a save and told him to "tone it down."

 The drama late in the season was if Duda could get to 30 homers. Number 29 was a two-run walk-off shot in Game 161 and hit number 30 in his final at-bat of the season. And deGrom added to his Rookie of the Year case winning both September decisions and lowering his ERA.

Top 5 Highlights

1 Ike Davis launches a walk-off grand slam off Cincinnati's J.J. Hoover to beat the Reds 6-3 on April 5. The ninth inning rally included the first replay in Mets history, with Juan Lagares being called safe at second on an attempted force play.

2 Zack Wheeler pitches a three-hit shutout in a 1-0 win over the Marlins on June 19. David Wright's homer in the first off Andrew Heaney was all the offense Wheeler would need, throwing 111 pitches and striking out eight.

3 The Mets beat the Giants 4-2 as starters Jacob deGrom and Jake Peavy both take no-hit bids into the seventh inning. Pablo Sandoval's double in the top of the inning was the first Giants hit. A Daniel Murphy double to left was the first Mets hit. New York scored four times in the seventh off Peavy.

4 In the last at-bat of his career, Bobby Abreu singles in the fifth inning off Houston's Nick Tropeano and leaves to a standing ovation on the final day of the season. It was the 2,470th hit for the two-time All-Star.

5 In the last at-bat of his season, Lucas Duda hits his 30th homer of the year, a two-run blast off Mike Foltynewicz in the Mets' 8-3 win over the Astros.

2015

	W	L	GB	Pos
	90	72	7 GA	1st
RS/G	RA/G		Manager	
4.22	3.78		Terry Collins	

Deadline Help, Arms Lead Mets to Pennant

The Moves

Michael Cuddyer, a childhood friend of David Wright's and the 2013 NL batting champion, signed a two-year deal with the team. Cuddyer hit .332 with 10 home runs in 2014 but injuries limited him to 49 games. The team signed John Mayberry Jr., who showed some pop with the Phillies. The Mets also traded for lefty Jerry Blevins.

The Situation

Washington won the NL East in 2014 and then improved by signing superstar pitcher Max Scherzer. Still, based on the rotation including Matt Harvey and Jacob deGrom, the Mets were picked by some writers to win the division. Dillon Gee beat out Rafael Montero for the fifth starter spot. Anthony Recker beat out Johnny Monell to remain as backup catcher. Eric Campbell, who the Mets were hoping to use as a super-sub, struggled in spring training.

Major League Ambassador for Inclusion Billy Bean visited the spring training clubhouse. Daniel Murphy, a devout Christian, said, "I do disagree with the fact that Billy is a homosexual. That doesn't mean I can't still invest in him and get to know him," adding "you can still accept them but I do disagree with the lifestyle, 100 percent." The infielder later said he wouldn't talk to the media

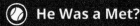

He Was a Met?

A fifth-round draft pick by the Mets in 2011, Jack Leathersich pitched decently for the Mets in 2015, putting up solid if fairly typical LOOGY numbers (17 G, 12.1 IP, 0-1, 2.31). Since being waived by the Mets that summer, Leathersich has appeared in 14 major league games for two other teams.

about his religious beliefs and would "stick to baseball."

The Season

The Mets beat Scherzer in Washington, with the help of shoddy Nationals defense, on Opening Day. It was shades of 1986 as the Mets started 2-3 and then won 11 in a row. A win in Atlanta was followed by sweeps at home against the Phillies, Marlins and Braves. Bartolo Colon won his first four starts. Harvey would go 4-0 in April. The bad news was that David Wright injured his hamstring sliding into second base and went on the DL. While on the DL, he was diagnosed with lumbar spinal stenosis and would be out until the final week of August. Travis d'Arnaud and Blevins suffered broken bones. Jenrry Mejia was suspended for 80 games for being suspended for performance-enhancing drug use. In July, he would be suspended for 162 games after failing another drug test. Jeurys Familia stepped into the closer's role and converted his first 13 save opportunities.

New York's offense fell into a slump. Nine times in May the Mets were shutout or held to one run. There were back-to-back 1-0 losses at home to the Nationals. Noah Syndergaard, a top prospect who was 3-0 with a 1.82 ERA with 34 strikeouts in 29.2 innings in Triple-A, was called up to the majors with Dillon Gee going to the DL with a mild groin strain.

A June swoon sent the spiraling Mets under .500. Daniel Murphy went on the DL with a left quad strain. On June 9, they were no-hit by San Francisco's Chris Heston in a 5-0 loss to the Giants.

A seven-game losing streak put the Mets at 36-37. The team scored nine runs in the seven games. The Mets, 26-11 at home, were 10-26 on the road. Southpaw Steven Matz made his MLB debut on June 28, beating the Reds. Not only did he pitch into the eighth but he also collected three hits and four RBI. However, he would go on the DL with a partial tear of the left lat muscle.

On July 12, Kirk Nieuwenhuis became the first Met to hit three

3 in a Game at Home - Finally!

In all, 12 Mets players have hit 3 home runs in a game. But somewhere along the way it was realized that no one had ever done it at home. The amazing streak continued into the 2010s and past 50 years until 2015, when on July 12 none other than Kirk Nieuwenhaus became the first, the 3 longballs making up 75% of his total for the season. Seventeen days after Kirk's career day, a more legit power hitter, Lucas Duda, duplicated the feat, and the two offensive explosions remain the only two times a Mets player has gone deep 3 times in a game at home.

 Final Resting Ground

John Mayberry Jr. batted .164 in 59 games with the Mets before being released in his final season in the majors. He became the poster boy for a struggling offense when Terry Collins batted him cleanup despite hitting .170 with three homers. He was four for his last 48 before being released.

home runs in a home game in a win against Arizona. John Smoltz, working for Fox Sports, said the Mets rotation was "way better" than the one Atlanta had in the 1990s featuring Smoltz, Greg Maddux and Tom Glavine. "They've got more talent that we could ever have," he said.

But the offense was still scuffling. July 23 saw Clayton Kershaw retire the first 18 Mets in a 3-0 win. Cleanup hitter John Mayberry Jr. entered the night batting .170. Campbell, batting fifth, was batting .179. Finally, Alderson called in reinforcements for the team with a .233 batting average. The team sent two minor league pitchers to the Braves for Juan Uribe, who was batting .272 with eight homers, and Kelly Johnson, batting .275 with nine home runs. Outfield prospect Michael Conforto was called up to the majors.

On July 28, Syndergaard pitched eight shutout innings to beat the Padres. The 52-48 Mets were one game behind the first-place Nationals. The next night, reports circulated that Wilmer Flores and Zack Wheeler were being traded to the Brewers for Carlos Gomez. Aware of the rumor, Flores was crying at short during the game. "This is the craziest thing I have ever seen in a baseball game," Collins said. The trade fell through and Flores remained a Met. The fact that Lucas Duda hit three home runs in the loss was overshadowed.

Just minutes before the trade deadline, Alderson pulled off a deal for Detroit slugger Yoenis Cespedes, with two minor league pitchers going to the Tigers. "I think [Cespedes] is going to create a lot of energy in our clubhouse," Collins said. "All of a sudden you're looking around that clubhouse and there's some nice offensive pieces that are there."

The Nationals came to Queens leading the Mets by three games. In the first game, Flores, a new fan favorite, won it in the 12th inning with a home run. Washington was playing tight and Bryce Harper was ejected in the 11th inning after striking out looking. The next night, Duda was the hero. He homered twice off Joe Ross to tie the game at two. In the bottom of the eighth, Cespedes was intentionally walked with a runner on second and Duda made the Nationals pay with a go-ahead double.

New York won 16 of the next 22, taking a 6.5 game lead. Cespedes was on fire, hitting eight home runs between August 12 and August 27, including a three home-run game in Colorado. The team won back-to-back 14-9 games against the Rockies. On August 24, Wright returned to the lineup and homered in his first at-bat. The Mets would hit eight home runs in a 16-7 win at Philadelphia, beginning a four-game sweep of the Phillies. The offense, so dormant for several months, had exploded. Granderson hit .282 with seven home runs and 22 RBI in August. Murphy hit .311 with four homers and 20 RBI. And the team acquired Addison Reed from Arizona to improve the already reliable pen. Familia had an ERA of 0.59 in August and Clippard's was 0.60.

Harvey, who was 12-7 with a 2.60 ERA, became the center of controversy when his agent, Scott Boras, said the pitcher couldn't go past his 180-innings limit, meaning he would be unavailable for the playoffs. Alderson said he wouldn't "roll over" for the agent. But Harvey eventually clarified he would pitch in the postseason.

TOP BATTERS

Pos	Name	G	AB	H	BA	HR	RBI	RS	SB	OPS
1B	Lucas Duda	135	471	115	.244	27	73	67	0	.838
2B	Daniel Murphy	130	499	140	.281	14	73	56	2	.770
SS	Wilmer Flores	137	483	127	.263	16	59	55	0	.703
RF	Curtis Granderson	157	580	150	.259	26	70	98	11	.821
OF	Yoenis Cespedes	57	230	66	.287	17	44	39	4	.942

TOP PITCHERS

Pos	Name	G	GS	W	L	SV	ERA	IP	SO	BB
SP	Bartolo Colon	33	31	14	13	0	4.16	194.2	136	24
SP	Jacob deGrom	30	30	14	8	0	2.54	191.0	205	38
SP	Matt Harvey	29	29	13	8	0	2.71	189.1	188	37
SP	Noah Syndergaard	24	24	9	7	0	3.24	150.0	166	31
CL	Jeurys Familia	76	0	2	2	43	1.85	78.0	86	19

FABULOUS: MATT HARVEY

After missing all of 2014, Matt Harvey returned to the rotation and went 13-8 with a 2.71 ERA and won the NL East clincher against the Reds. Harvey went 8-3 with a 2.23 ERA at Citi Field. Since 2015, Harvey's record is 26-40 and his ERA has never been below 4.50.

After losing three of five to begin September, the Mets, up by four games in the division, went to Washington for a three-game series against the Nationals. In the opener, the Mets hit three homers off Scherzer and beat the Nats bullpen in an 8-5 win. The next night, Harvey struggled, giving up seven runs in 5.1 innings. But the Mets erased a 7-1 deficit and Nieuwenhuis' homer gave the Mets an 8-7 win. "I am not sure I was involved in a bigger win than that," Collins said. With Washington looking to avoid a sweep, Stephen Strasburg took a 2-1 lead into the eighth inning before Johnson homered to tie it. Three batters later, Cespedes hit a two-run homer off Drew Storen and the Mets held on for the 4-2 win. It was the 14th home run for Cespedes in 36 games.

The Mets went to Atlanta and swept a four-game series, with Cespedes hitting two more homers. Then he went deep in a win against the Marlins. It was the eighth straight win for the Mets and gave Cespedes 17 home runs in 41 games.

New York finished the regular season 7-11, costing them home field in the NLDS against the Dodgers. The Mets were also no-hit again, this time by Scherzer on October 3.

Top 5 Highlights

1 Kirk Nieuwenhuis becomes the first Met to hit three home runs in a home game in a 5-3 win over the Diamondbacks on July 12. He hit a solo shot off Rubby De La Rosa in the second, a two-run shot off De La Rosa in the third and a solo homer off Randall Delgado in the fifth.

2 The Mets outlast the Cardinals in a 3-1, 18-inning win on July 19, lasting five hours and 55 minutes. Jon Niese pitched 7.2 shutout innings. Kevin Plawecki's 13th inning single gave the Mets a 1-0 lead but Kolten Wong homered off Jeurys Familia to extend the game. Ruben Tejada's sacrifice fly gave the Mets the lead in the 18th and New York added insurance on an Eric Campbell bunt.

3 Days after crying on the field after believing the Mets were going to trade him, Wilmer Flores beats the Nationals with a 12th inning home run off Felipe Rivero. The homer pulls the Mets to within two games of first.

4 Nieuwenhuis' pinch-hit homer in the eighth puts the Mets ahead in an 8-7 win over the Nationals on September 8. Michael Taylor's grand slam off Matt Harvey in the sixth gave the Nationals a 7-1 lead. In the seventh, the Mets scored six two-out runs to tie the game. The Mets fought back to tie the game in the seventh. Nieuwenhuis' homer to right-center off Jonathan Papelbon made it 8-7. Yunel Escobar grounded into a 5-4-3 double play to end the game.

5 Familia strikes out Jay Bruce as the Mets clinch the NL East with a 10-2 win over the Reds on September 26. Duda hits a grand slam off John Lamb in the first and Granderson hits a solo shot in the second. Matt Harvey gives up two runs in 6.2 innings. David Wright's three-run homer in the ninth is the exclamation point.

2015 NLDS

The Mets went to Los Angeles for the NLDS with deGrom and Kershaw dueling in Game 1. Murphy homered leading off the fourth. The Mets loaded the bases in the seventh and Don Mattingly called on Pedro Baez. Wright greeted him with a two-run single. DeGrom pitched seven shutout innings, striking out 13. The Dodgers got a run off Clippard in the eighth but Familia came in for a four-out save to give the Mets a 1-0 lead.

Zack Greinke, who had a 1.66 ERA in the regular season, was on the mound for Game 2. Cespedes and Conforto homered in the second inning. Andre Ethier's RBI double off Syndergaard made it 2-1 in the fourth. In the bottom of the seventh, Chase Utley's pinch-hit single put runners at the corners with one out. Colon came in to pitch to Howie Kendrick. Kendrick hit a 1-2 pitch to Murphy. Murphy's flip went to Tejada, covering second but he was taken out on a vicious slide by Utley as the tying run came in to score. It was also ruled that Tejada missed the base and everyone was safe, despite Utley never touching the bag. Tejada would be carted off and replaced by Flores. Utley was available and was also Public Enemy No. 1 at Citi Field.

After seeing Kershaw and Greinke, the Mets would face Brett Anderson in Game 3. LA took a 3-0 lead in the second on Yasmani Grandal's bases loaded single combined with an error. The Mets answered back with four in the bottom of the inning, with Granderson's three-run double putting the Mets ahead. D'Arnaud hit a two-run homer in the third and Cespedes' three-run blast off Alex Wood in the fourth gave the Mets a 10-3 lead on their way to a 13-7 victory.

Kershaw came back on three days' rest with LA facing elimination and he gave up one run on three hits over seven innings. Murphy's homer in the fourth was the only Met offense. The Dodgers scored three times in the third off Matz. There would be a deciding fifth game at Dodger Stadium.

Mets announcer Gary Cohen went on WFAN and said he had "no interest" in seeing the team re-sign Murphy. "He's a good hitter, he's a good hitter. He's a good sixth or seventh in a good lineup. That's what he is. And he hurts you so badly in the field and on the bases, and with all the craziness I think it's time to move on … Murph is a lovable guy but I think he's a net negative, and I've always felt that way."

In Game 5, Murphy gave the Mets a first inning lead with an RBI double off Greinke. DeGrom gave up four straight singles in the bottom of the inning as the Dodgers took a 2-1 lead. But deGrom limited the damage and settled down, working out of jams for several innings. Murphy's single started the fourth. With one out, Duda drew a walk. Murphy went to second and then, noticing nobody was near third because of the shift, he took third. He scored the tying run when d'Arnaud followed with a sacrifice fly. In the sixth, Murphy hit a homer, giving the Mets a 3-2 lead. DeGrom went six innings and then Collins called on Syndergaard to pitch the seventh. He struck out two batters in a scoreless inning. Familia got the final six outs to end the series.

2015 NLCS

Facing the Cubs in the 2015 NLCS Murphy homered off Jon Lester in the first inning of Game 1. Harvey retired the first 12 Cubs. Starlin Castro's RBI double tied the game in the fifth. Javier Baez singled to left but Cespedes threw Castro out at home to keep the game even. In the bottom of the fifth, Granderson's RBI single put the Mets ahead. D'Arnaud homered in the sixth and Granderson's sacrifice fly in the seventh made it 4-1. The Mets hung on for a 4-2 victory.

Jake Arrieta, who went 22-6 with a 1.77 ERA, took the ball for the Cubs in Game 2. Granderson led off with a single, Wright followed with an RBI double and Murphy hit a two-run home run. Arrieta faced three batters and the Mets had a 3-0 lead. In the top of the second, Granderson robbed Chris Coghlan of a home run. The Mets scored again in the third on a Cespedes single. Syndergaard cruised through five innings before getting in trouble in the sixth. Kris Bryant's RBI double made it 4-1. Niese came in and struck out Anthony Rizzo to end the inning. Reed, Clippard and Familia each pitched a scoreless inning and the Mets went to Wrigley Field with a 2-0 lead.

The Mets jumped on Kyle Hendricks with Cespedes' RBI double in the first. Schwarber tied it in the bottom of the inning with a homer off deGrom. Then Murphy went deep again, with a third inning blast to put the Mets up 2-1. Jorge Soler's homer in the fourth tied the game. The Mets took the lead in the sixth on a missed third strike and were one win away from the World Series.

New York quickly took any hope away from Chicago in Game 4. Duda hit a three-run homer off Jason Hammel and d'Arnaud followed with a blast to right-center. In the second, Duda doubled in two runs to make it 6-0. Leading 8-3, Famila struck out Dexter Fowler looking to end the series and the Mets were NL champions for the first time in 15 years.

Murphy hit .529 with four homers in the series and set a postseason record with home runs in six straight games.

2015 World Series

It was off to Kansas 2015 World Series City for the World Series. The Royals came up just short against the Giants the season before, losing at home in Game 7. On the first pitch Harvey threw, Alcides Escobar hit a fly ball to center. Cespedes attempted to backhand the ball and couldn't corral it as it bounced away and Escobar rounded the bases for an inside-the-park homer. The Mets built a 3-1 lead in the sixth and were two outs away from stealing the home-field when Alex Gordon homered off Familia to tie the game in the ninth. Neither team could break through. Wright fanned with two on to end the top of the 11th. Colon stranded the bases loaded in the bottom of the 12th. In the bottom of the 14th, Escobar reached on a Wright error. Ben Zobrist singled and Lorenzo Cain was intentionally walked. Hosmer's sacrifice fly to right ended the five-hour, nine-minute marathon.

Duda's single gave the Mets a 1-0 lead in the fourth inning of Game 2 but the Royals scored four times against deGrom in the fifth and added three runs in the eighth. Johnny Cueto pitched a complete game two-hitter with both hits from Duda.

Syndergaard sent a message in Game 3, with the first pitch near Escobar's head, sending the Kansas City shortstop to the ground. "If they have a problem with me throwing inside, then they can meet me 60-feet, six-inches away," Syndergaard said after the game. The Royals scored in the first but in the bottom of the frame, Wright hit a two-run homer off Yordano Ventura. The Mets broke it open with four runs in the sixth, including Wright's two-run single. Reed, Clippard and Familia each pitched 1-2-3 innings to finish it off.

Matz started Game 4 against former Met Chris Young, who won the first game out of the bullpen. Conforto homered in the third and Granderson's sacrifice fly made it 2-0. Gordon's RBI single in the fifth made it 2-1 but Conforto homered again in the fifth, this time off Danny Duffy, to make it 3-1. The Royals rallied, with a key hit going just under Murphy's glove, and they took a 5-3 lead. Royals manager Ned Yost went to Wade Davis for six outs. Davis pitched a 1-2-3 eighth. With one out in the ninth, Murphy and Cespedes singled, bringing up Duda. Duda hit a soft liner to third. Moustaksas caught it and threw to first, easily doubling off Cespedes.

Facing elimination, it was up to Harvey fanned nine in eight shutout innings. Granderson led off with a homer off Volquez and Duda's sacrifice fly in the sixth made it 2-0. But the Mets couldn't tack on any more. Cespedes would only hit .150 in the series with no extra-base hits and one RBI. Murphy hit .150 with no extra-base hits and no RBI. Still, the Mets were three outs away from sending the series back to Kansas City. Collins told Harvey he was done for the night. The star asked to stay in the game. "Obviously I let my heart get in the way of my gut," Collins said. Cain walked to begin the ninth and stole second. Hosmer doubled to left, making it 2-1. Familia came in and got Moustakas on a grounder to first, with Hosmer going to third. Perez grounded one to third. Wright threw to first for the second out and Hosmer broke for home. Duda's throw home was wide and the Royals tied the game. The Royals went ahead in the 12th against Reed. Davis struck out three Mets in the bottom of the inning, including Flores to end it.

2016

	W	L	GB	Pos
	87	75	8.0	2nd
RS/G	RA/G		**Manager**	
4.14	3.81		Terry Collins	

Cespedes Carries Offense to Wild Card

The Moves

Daniel Murphy signed a three-year deal with the division rival Nationals after turning down the Mets' qualifying offer of $15.8 million for one season. General Manager Sandy Alderson would later call not bringing the second baseman back his biggest regret on the job. New York had traded Jon Niese to the Pirates for Neil Walker and signed Asdrubal Cabrera. Both the Mets and Nationals had gone after Ben Zobrist, but he signed with the Cubs.

The team did bring back Yoenis Cespedes after it looked like he would be on the move. The Mets didn't seem interested in giving him a large contract but the market for him didn't heat up. When Washington offered $100 million for five years, the Mets jumped in, signing him to a three-year, $75 million deal with an opt-out after the 2016 season.

Other moves included the signings of lefty reliever Antonio Bastardo and outfielder Alejandro De Aza.

The Situation

Sports Illustrated predicted the Mets would win 95 games, 12 more than the Nationals. The biggest news for a confident team in spring training was Cespedes' car collection, as he showed up with several flashy cars. Matt Harvey,

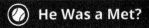

He Was a Met?

James Loney came to the Mets in May 2016 and played a lot of first base for them, in what would be the final year of Loney's career. Loney's failure to draw walks, poor speed, and limited power led to his driving in only 34 runs and scoring only 30 in 100 games and 343 at bats.

Yoenis Cespedis has continued the legacy of problem-filled free agent signings of left fielders, as numerous injuries have limited him to 308 games in his 5 years with the team. Cespedis was solid in 2016, his one close-to-full season with the team, hitting 31 home runs and driving in 86 in 132 games.

Jacob deGrom and Jeurys Familia were on the cover of *Sports Illustrated*, as the magazine released regional issues.

The Season

The Mets flew out of the gate with a 15-7 April. Walker hit nine home runs in April. Michael Conforto was batting .365 with four home runs and batted third in the lineup when Cespedes got off to a slow start. Cespedes recovered finished the month wtih seven home runs and 23 RBI. Familia saved eight games. The hot start came despite Harvey beginning the year 0-3 with a 5.71 ERA. "He's cruising along, and all of a sudden it just disappears fast," Terry Collins said. "That's on my mind a little bit ... I've seen it with guys, but not guys if his caliber."

On May 1, Collins kept Conforto in the starting lineup against San Francisco ace Madison Bumgarner. It was only Conforto's third career start against a lefty. He went 0-for-5 with three strikeouts. He would bat .130 from that day through late June and was sent to Triple-A. The Mets went 14-15 in May but injuries were starting to pile up. Travis d'Arnaud went on the DL in late April with a rotator cuff strain and was out until late June. Wilmer Flores missed two-and-a-half weeks in May with a strained left hamstring. Lucas Duda had a stress fracture in his back and was gone for four months. The team signed veteran James Loney to fill in at first base. Syndergaard was ejected along with Collins on May 28 when he threw behind Chase Utley. Utley would homer twice, including a grand slam. Harvey did have a throwback performance with seven scoreless innings on Memorial Day against the White Sox.

 Final Resting Ground

Two years removed from his Coor's field batting title, Michael Cuddyer signed with the Mets to provide some offense. Cuddyer had followed his .331 with a .332 for Colorado in part-time play, but he found the going much tougher at Citi Field and for the Mets. After putting up a slash line of .259/.309/.391 and 10 HR in nearly 400 at bats. Cuddyer retired after the 2016 season.

The Mets went 12-15 in June and fell six games behind Washington, getting swept by the Nationals late in the month. The offense was blanked four times and held to one run in four other losses. Wright was gone for the season after undergoing neck surgery. Juan Lagares went on the DL. Murphy was killing the Mets. To finish off the sweep in late June, he homered twice in a 4-2 win. He was batting .333 with four homers and 11 RBI against the Mets through June. De Aza was struggling, with a .158 batting average. Walker hit five home runs since his April outburst. The team did bring back Kelly Johnson from the Braves.

FUTILE: ALEJANDRO DE AZA

Alejandro De Aza hit .205 with 25 RBI in 130 games and was once called out by Terry Collins when he didn't run hard after popping up a bunt, resulting in a double play.

In an NLCS rematch, the Mets swept a four-game series against the Cubs at Citi Field. The Mets scored 32 runs in the four games. On July 4, they came back to beat the Marlins 8-6 for a fifth straight win. But it was Harvey's final game of the year. Harvey, 4-10 with a 4.86 ERA in 17 starts, was diagnosed with thoracic outlet syndrome, which causes pain in the shoulder, arm and neck and happens when the nerves or blood vessels are compressed. The ace underwent season-ending surgery.

Back in Queens was Jose Reyes, who signed with the Mets after being designated for assignment by the Rockies. He was arrested in October 2015 following a physical altercation with his wife. Domestic abuses were charged. Reyes was suspended by the league and was released after completing the suspension. It wasn't 2011, but Reyes would give the extremely slow-footed Mets a little speed and would play at third base.

Trailing the Nationals by four games, the Mets welcomed Washington to Citi Field for four games before the All-Star break. The Nationals took three of four from the Mets. In the final game before the break, Murphy hit a homer off Steven Matz. He had seven homers and 21 RBI against the Mets in 13 games, with six more still to go. The Mets were swept by the Rockies late in the month, scoring four runs in three games. The team signed outfielder Justin Ruggiano. Niese was brought back, with the struggling Bastardo going to the Pirates. And the Mets acquired Jay Bruce, who was hitting .265 with 25 homers and a league-leading 80 RBI. The Mets were batting .206 with runners in scoring position. Bruce

FABULOUS: YOENIS CESPEDES

Cespedes carried the offense when the season was on the brink in August, with three home runs in two games in San Francisco and a walk-off shot to beat the Marlins. He hit 31 homers during the season and totalled a team-leading 86 RBI. His 132 games played are more than he played the next 3 seasons total.

TOP BATTERS										
Pos	Name	G	AB	H	BA	HR	RBI	RS	SB	OPS
1B	James Loney	100	343	91	.265	9	34	30	0	.703
2B	Neil Walker	113	412	116	.282	23	55	57	3	.823
SS	Asdrubal Cabrera	141	521	146	.280	23	62	65	5	.810
CF	Yoenis Cespedes	132	479	134	.280	31	86	72	3	.884
RF	Curtis Granderson	150	545	129	.237	30	59	88	4	.799

TOP PITCHERS										
Pos	Name	G	GS	W	L	SV	ERA	IP	SO	BB
SP	Bartolo Colon	34	33	15	8	0	3.43	191.2	128	32
SP	Noah Syndergaard	31	30	14	9	0	2.60	183.2	218	43
SP	Jacob deGrom	24	24	7	8	0	3.04	148.0	143	36
CL	Jeurys Familia	78	0	3	4	51	2.55	77.2	84	31
RP	Addison Reed	80	0	4	2	1	1.97	77.2	91	13

was batting .360 with runners in scoring position. "Somebody like Jay Bruce can be a catalyst for more productive performance out of the other players that we have, especially hitting in the middle of our order," Alderson said. But Bruce would struggle, batting .219 with eight homers and 19 RBI.

Things got ugly in early August. Cabrera went on the DL with a knee injury. Cespedes went on the DL with a strained right quad. The team lost two of three, returned home and was swept by the Diamondbacks. In the finale, the lifeless Mets lost 9-0 on a Thursday afternoon. Niese gave up six runs in the sixth inning as the team fell to .500. "I don't care who is not here," an angry Collins said. "There are no excuses here. They are major league baseball players. I don't care where they came from. I don't care how they got here. The names on their back and on the front of their uniforms say they are a major league baseball player. It starts with them. When you come and when you owe what you do, you have a responsibility to the fans, our fan base, the organization and to yourself – the respect for this game to come out and grind it out."

The next night, Logan Verrett gave up eight runs in 2.2 innings as the Mets fell under .500. The next night, Familia gave up a homer with two outs in the ninth but Flores won it with a homer in the 11th. Matz took a no-hit bid into the eighth inning on August but it was his final start of 2016, as a left shoulder strain would put him on the DL.

Rumors were flying about Collins' job security when the Mets were out West. An 8-1 loss to the Giants on August 19 dropped the Mets to 60-62, 5.5 games out of the wild card but Cespedes was back. On August 20, he homered twice in a 9-5 win. The following day, he hit a two-run homer in a 2-0 win.

The Mets went to St. Louis for a critical three-game series, 4.5 games behind the Cardinals. In the first game, Niese had to leave in the first inning with a knee injury but Robert Gsellman pitched 3.2 shutout innings in his MLB debut and the Mets won 7-4. New York won two nights later with Seth Lugo earning his first major league win with five shutout innings. The Mets took two of three from the Phillies and then swept the Marlins. Cespedes' walk-off homer in the 10th won the first game against Miami.

A back injury would keep Walker out for the final month and deGrom's season ended early with discomfort in his forearm and elbow. After a loss to Washington on September 2, the Mets were 69-66, two games behind the Cardinals for the second wild card. It was Gsellman and Lugo who came to the rescue with consecutive wins. Gsellman gave up one run in six innings, Lugo one run in seven. "Those guys have really been exceptional," Collins said. "They've made a difference." T.J. Rivera filled in at second base and hit .333 after being called up in early August.

The Mets swept the Reds, then took two of three in Atlanta, though Flores was hurt in a home plate collision and gone for the season. The team lost two of three in Washington before returning home for 10 games. The Mets swept the Twins. Colon, the one Met starter to be healthy wire-to-wire pitched seven shutout innings and Familia saved his 49th game. Granderson was the hero the next night, tying the game with a homer in the 11th and winning it with a homer in the 12th. The Braves swept the Mets and New York fell to 80-72 with 10 games left. The Mets, Giants and Cardinals had identical records.

Cabrera's three-run homer gave the Mets a dramatic 9-8, 11-inning win in the first game against the Phillies. The offense scored 10 more runs the next night. Philadelphia won 10-8 in the third game, after the Mets almost erased a 10-0 deficit, and then the Mets won the home finale 17-0 with Cespedes hitting his 30th home run.

The Mets took two of three in Miami to close in on a playoff berth. Gsellman beat the Phillies on the final day of September. Gsellman was 3-1 with a 2.06 ERA in six September starts. Lugo won five straight decisions down the stretch. Bruce homered in three straight games, getting hot late in the year. On October 1, the Mets clinched a playoff berth with a 5-3 win over the Phillies. "It's great to see the team this year accomplish as much as it did with as many obstacles placed in its path," Alderson said. The team won 27 of 39 before losing on the final day of the regular season.

Top 5 Highlights

1 Bartolo Colon hits a two-run homer off James Shields in a 6-3 win over the Padres on May 7. Colon entered the game a career .089 hitter and the 42-year-old became the oldest player in league history to hit his first career home run. He's the second oldest Met to hit a home run, behind Julio Franco.

2 Noah Syndergaard hits two home runs off Kenta Maeda in a 4-2 win over the Dodgers on May 11. He leads off the third with a homer and then hits a three-run shot in the fifth. He becomes the second Met to homer twice in a game, after Walt Terrell, who turned 58 the night Syndergaard duplicated his feat.

3   Curtis Granderson hits a walk-off home run in the bottom of the ninth off Pedro Baez to beat the Dodgers 6-5 on May 27. The Mets blew a 5-1 lead in the top of the inning with Chase Utley tying the game with a three-run double. David Wright and Juan Lagares also homered for the Mets.

4   Asdrubal Cabrera's three-run homer off Edubray Ramos in the 11th gives the Mets a 9-8 win over the Phillies on September 22. The Mets trailed 6-4 in the ninth when Jose Reyes hit a two-run homer off Jeanmar Gomez to tie it.

5   Michael Conforto makes a sliding catch of an Aaron Altherr liner and the Mets clinch an NL Wild Card with a 5-3 win in Philadelphia on October 1. James Loney's two-run homer in the sixth off David Hernandez gives the Mets a 4-2 lead. Colon picks up his 15th win of the season, going five innings with five relievers finishing the job.

2016 Wild Card

Syndergaard matched up with World Series hero Madison Bumgarner as the Giants came to Queens for the Wild Card game. The San Francisco southpaw had pitched a shutout in the 2014 Wild Card game in Pittsburgh. Justin Ruggiano hit a grand slam off Bumgarner in August but had shoulder surgery in September and was out. Bumgarner was 5-0 with a 1.80 ERA six career starts against the Mets.

The pitching duel lived up to the billing. Syndergaard retired the first nine Giants. Bumgarner pitched to the minimum over the first three innings. Neither team had a runner in scoring position until the bottom of the fifth but Syndergaard fanned with two on to end the inning. In the top of the sixth, Dernard Span singled with two outs and stole second. Brandon Belt hit a fly ball to deep center but Granderson made a running catch before hitting the wall to preserve the scoreless tie. The Giants put two runners on in the seventh but Syndergaard kept them off the board. He was done after throwing 108 pitches, striking out 10 Giants.

In the top of the eighth, San Francisco loaded the bases against Addison Reed but Hunter Pence struck out to end the inning. Ty Kelly had a pinch-hit single in the bottom of the eighth and moved to second on a groundout but Cabrera lined back to Bumgarner to send the scoreless game to the ninth.

Brandon Crawford led off the ninth with a double. Joe Panik drew a one-out walk, prolonging the at-bat with a foul tip that almost struck him out. Bruce Bochy had a pinch-hitter ready for Bumgarner. Conor Gillaspie, the eight-hitter with six home runs all season, hit a three-run shot to right to stun the Mets. Bumgarner pitched a 1-2-3 ninth. "He's one of the game's great big-game pitchers," Collins said.

2017

OPENING DAY LINEUP

Jose Reyes, 3B
Asdrubal Cabrera, SS
Yoenis Cespedes, LF
Curtis Granderson, CF
Neil Walker, 2B
Jay Bruce, RF
Lucas Duda, 1B
Rene Rivera, C
Noah Syndergaard, P

	W	L	GB	Pos
	70	92	27.0	4th
RS/G	RA/G		Manager	
4.54	5.33		Terry Collins	

Pitching Collapses, Mets Limp to 70 Wins

The Moves

Yoenis Cespedes was locked down, given $110 million for four years. Otherwise, it was a quiet offseason for transactions. Bartolo Colon signed with the Braves. James Loney went to the Rangers. But for the most part, the Mets stayed quiet, convinced that they had the players in place to win if they stayed healthy.

The Situation

Good but not as good as the Nationals. That was the majority of predictions made, expecting a repeat of Washington first and New York second in the NL East. There were several Mets out with injuries. An oblique would keep Juan Lagares sidelined for the first two weeks. Elbow inflammation would keep Steven Matz and Seth Lugo on the shelf until June. Brandon Nimmo was out with a hamstring strain. And David Wright would miss the entire season as he dealt with ongoing back pain.

The Season

The Mets won seven of 10 to begin the season. Cespedes hit six homers in the first 10 games, including a three-homer performance in Philadelphia and a two-homer game in Miami. But then the team lost 10 of 11, including

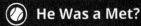 **He Was a Met?**

One of Japan's best players in the 2000s, Nori Aoki played 27 games in September, batting .284. He had four three-hit games in his one month as a player on the Mets.

Noah Syndergaard has struggled with arm troubles and an inability harness his gifts on the mound. After posting a very effective 13-4 in 25 starts in 2018, he slipped to 10-8/4.25 in 2019. Noah will miss the 2020 season due a ligament tear in his elbow.

a sweep by the Nationals at Citi Field. Daniel Murphy hit a grand slam off Zack Wheeler in the final game of the series. Wheeler entered the game with a .167 average, the highest of the 5-9 hitters in the lineup as Cespedes battled a hamstring issue and Travis d'Arnaud was out with a bruised hand. Lucas Duda went on the DL with back spasms. Wilmer Flores went on the DL with a knee infection.

"The concern is to get healthy, because once we get healthy and get our lineup back in there, I think things will turn around," Terry Collins said.

On April 27, Harvey lost his first game of the season after winning two decisions. He said he felt 'tight' after making an unexpected start due to Noah Syndergaard being scratched with a tired arm and sore biceps. More importantly, Cespedes had to be taken out after doubling in the fourth inning and aggravating his hamstring. The All-Star outfielder wouldn't return until June.

The Mets needed an escape and won the first two games of a series in Washington, beating Max Scherzer and Stephen Strasburg. Syndergaard got the ball in the final game of the series. Syndergaard had refused to take an MRI the week before. Sandy Alderson's reaction: "I can't tie him down and throw him in the tube."

It was sadly inevitable when he left in the second inning, after giving up five runs in the first, with a partial tear of his lat. He would be gone until late September. The Mets would lose 23-5, giving up seven home runs. Anthony Rendon went 6-6 with three homers and 10 RBI. Backup catcher Kevin Plawecki pitched the final two innings.

Jose Reyes, Curtis Granderson and Neil Walker were all batting under .200 but the team did open May

FABULOUS: JAY BRUCE

Jay Bruce led the team with 29 homers and 75 RBI despite only playing 103 games before being traded to the Indians. After the season, the Mets signed Bruce as a free agent, but he struggled mightily, though the Mets were able to make Bruce part of the package of players that brought Robinson Cano to the team from Seattle.

with four wins in five games. The team scored 16 runs in a laugher against Colon and the Braves. Then the team scored 19 runs in two wins over the Marlins. During the stretch, d'Arnaud was placed on the DL with a bruised right wrist.

On Sunday, May 7, Harvey was scheduled to take the mound as the Mets looked to sweep the Marlins. But he was a no-show on Saturday and he was suspended for three days. Adam Wilk was called up

FUTILE: RAFAEL MONTERO

Rafael Montero went 5-11 with a 5.52 ERA in 34 games. Low point for the right-handed came in early August when he lasted three innings against the Rangers and dropped to 1-8 with a 6.06 ERA. Despite showing a lot of promise, Montero's career record now stands at 8-16/5.00.

from Triple-A to make a spot start. In the top of the first, Giancarlo Stanton came up with runners on second and third with one out. Collins didn't order an intentional walk and Stanton creamed a three-run homer. In the third, he hit another homer. The Mets would lose 7-0. Rene Rivera's single to start the bottom of the sixth was the only hit for the Mets. It turned out Harvey was playing golf Saturday morning and got a headache.

Wilk was let go and soft-throwing southpaw Tommy Milone was signed. The Mets took two straight from the Giants to even the record at 16-16 but it would be the last time they would be at .500 for the year. Milone made his first start on May 10 and was in line for the win as the Mets took a 3-2 lead into the ninth. But Jeurys Familia, who was used in a five-run game the night before, gave up four runs in the top of the ninth. The Mets would lose 6-5. Familia, who had been suspended for the first 15 games of the season regarding domestic violence incident, went on the DL with an arterial clot in his pitching shoulder. He would be gone for three-and-a-half months.

The Mets then went on the road and lost six straight, getting swept by the Brewers and Diamondbacks. Harvey gave up five runs in five innings in his return, his ERA increasing to 5.62. Asdrubal Cabrera went on the DL with a strained thumb. The Mets gave up 11 runs in back-to-back losses in Milwaukee. Robert Gsellman's ERA was north of seven. On May 14, the Mets had a 7-1 lead with Jacob deGrom on the mound but the Brewers fought back and Manny Pina's three-run homer off Addison Reed in the bottom of the eighth beat the Mets 11-9.

Arizona finished off its sweep of the Mets with an 11th inning homer from Chris Herrmann off Rafael Montero, whose ERA went up to 9.69. The Mets returned home and took two from the Angels. Milone got the start with the Mets going for a sweep but gave up eight runs (seven earned) in 1.1 innings. Then he went on the DL with a knee sprain, not to be seen again until mid-August.

The last place Padres took two of three from the Mets at Citi Field. Worried about rain, the Mets pushed back deGrom a day and started Rafael Montero on May 25. There was no rainout and Montero needed 87 pitches to get through three innings in a 4-3 loss.

TOP BATTERS										
Pos	Name	G	AB	H	BA	HR	RBI	RS	SB	OPS
SS	Jose Reyes	145	501	123	.246	15	58	75	24	.728
LF	Yoenis Cespedes	81	291	85	.292	17	42	46	0	.892
RF	Jay Bruce	103	406	104	.256	29	75	61	0	.841
IF	Asdrubal Cabrera	135	479	134	.280	14	59	66	3	.785
OF	Michael Conforto	109	373	104	.279	27	68	72	2	.939

TOP PITCHERS										
Pos	Name	G	GS	W	L	SV	ERA	IP	SO	BB
SP	Jacob deGrom	31	31	15	10	0	3.53	201.1	239	59
SP	Robert Gsellman	25	22	8	7	0	5.19	119.2	82	42
SP	Seth Lugo	19	18	7	5	0	4.71	101.1	85	25
CL	Addison Reed	48	0	1	2	19	2.57	49.0	48	6
RP	Jerry Blevins	75	0	6	0	1	2.94	49.0	69	24

Even Mr. Met wasn't spared by the chaotic season as a video captured the mascot flipping off a fan. On the field, the Mets pitching was faltering. Paul Sewald gave up five runs in one-third of an inning against the Pirates. The Mets lost 11-1 to the Pirates on June 4. Neil Ramirez and Josh Smoker both had ERAs over seven out of the bullpen. On June 6, deGrom gave up eight runs on 10 hits in four innings in a 10-8 loss to the Rangers. The Mets did bounce back, winning five of six.

Then the injuries piled up some more. Cabrera went back on the DL with a sprained thumb. Smoker was lost for more than a month with a shoulder strain. Harvey pitched four innings against the Cubs and wouldn't pitch again until September, sidelined with a stress fracture in his scapula. Walker was gone for a month-and-a-half with a partial tear of his hamstring. Lagares went on the DL with a thumb fracture. Wheeler, who gave up 15 runs in 3.2 innings over two starts, and went on the DL with biceps tendinitis. Gsellman strained his hamstring trying to beat out a grounder and would miss a month-and-a-half.

Unable to take it anymore, SNY broadcaster Ron Darling let loose during the broadcast. "If baseball at some point doesn't get these newbie trainers ... we get them in a room with some of the old trainers and people that took care of baseball players and how to keep them healthy and get them in a room and try to tap into some of their knowledge on how you train baseball players," he said. "Not weightlifters, not six-pack wearers, baseball players. They're doing a disservice to their million-dollar athletes that they're paying. It's a joke to watch this happen each and every night."

The Mets were swept by the Dodgers in LA, falling to 31-41. The beleaguered pitching staff gave up 15 home runs in four games. New York did win seven of eight. But the team ended the first half losing five of six. On July 3, Granderson saved the day with a game-tying two-run homer with two outs in the ninth but in the bottom of the inning Ryan Raburn singled to left to end the game with Cespedes unable to make a sliding catch and limping off the field. Conforto was out for a week with a wrist injury.

New York won the first two games back from the break but again the Sunday afternoon home game was a downer with Matz giving up seven runs and recording three outs in a 13-4 loss. On July 17, the Mets trailed 6-3 with Cespedes coming to the plate in the ninth as the tying run. Collins gave his slugger the green light on 3-0 and Cespedes grounded into a game-ending double play. Wheeler made his final start on July 22 against Oakland. A stress reaction in his arm would keep him out the rest of the season. T.J. Rivera was batting .290 but was also gone for the year a partial tear of his elbow.

Then the selloff began. Duda was traded to the Rays for minor league reliever Drew Smith. The team did trade for Marlins reliever AJ Ramos, just to have a viable option in a horrifying bullpen. Reed was traded to the Red Sox for three prospects. The team lost nine of 11 from late July through early August. Jay Bruce, who hit 29 homers with 75 RBI in 103 games, was traded to the Indians. Walker was traded to the Brewers. The Cubs claimed Rivera. Granderson was traded to the Dodgers. The team lost eight of nine in the middle of August.

One player who wasn't traded was Cabrera, who asked to be traded after not seeing time at shortstop in favor of Reyes, who was batting under .200.

The Mets saw Chris Flexen become the first starting pitcher since Mike Pelfrey to be called up from Double-A. Shortstop Amed Rosario made his highly-anticipated debut and Dominic Smith came up a week later. Reyes went on the DL with an oblique strain. Cespedes was gone for the year with an injured hamstring. Matz, who was 2-7 with a 6.08 ERA, missed the final month-and-a-half of the season with elbow irritation. On August 24, Conforto, who hit 27 home runs, swung and missed at a pitch and collapsed to the ground. He dislocated his shoulder and suffered a tear during the swing and would miss the rest of the season.

"It turns your stomach," Collins said after Conforto's injury. "A player was having a tremendous year and really making a name for himself. To go down like that and that kind of injury is tough to watch."

Harvey returned in September. He gave up seven runs in two innings against the Astros. After pitching five innings and defeating the Reds, he gave up five runs in 3.1 innings in a 17-5 loss to the Cubs. Then he gave up seven runs on 12 hits in four innings in a 13-1 loss to the Marlins.

"It's kind of hard to take too many positives out of the last two years for me," he said after the Chicago shellacking. "It's extremely frustrating. It's hard going out there and not doing what I can to help this team win. All in all, it's extremely frustrating. That's really all you can say."

The Mets reached the 90-loss mark for the first time since 2009. The team set a record with 224 home runs but the pitching staff had a 5.01 ERA.

A Newsday report in the final days of the season drew attention to organizational unhappiness with Collins. One example was his bullpen management. "Once he falls in love with you, he abuses you," one official said. "He has run players into the ground. He has no idea about resting players. Even when you tell him, he doesn't listen."

A player added, "He has always been difficult to communicate with. It would be a surprise if he said 'hey' to you when you passed each other in the hallway if your name wasn't Harvey or Cespedes. It's always been those couple things along with some of the in-game decisions he makes."

The season came to an appropriate end with an 11-0 loss in Philadelphia. Collins, whose contract was up, announced he would not be returning as manager but would move into the front office.

Top 5 Highlights

1 Jay Bruce's 12th inning single off Wily Peralta gives the Mets a 5-4 win over the Brewers on May 30. Josh Smoker pitches three innings of shutout relief for the win.

2 Rene Rivera hits two homers and Rafael Montero picks up his first win of the season in an 8-2 win over the Giants to complete a sweep of San Francisco on June 25. Rivera homers twice off southpaw Matt Moore.

3 In the first game after the All-Star break, the Mets pound out 14 runs on 19 hits in a 14-2 laugher over the Rockies. Cespedes has four hits and Reyes adds three. T.J. Rivera and Michael Conforto homer. DeGrom pitches eight innings in the win.

4 Wilmer Flores' homer in the bottom of the ninth of Simon Castro gives the Mets a 6-5 win over the A's on July 22. The Mets trailed 4-0 after one and 5-0 after three. New York scored four in the sixth and tied it on Lucas Duda's single in the eighth.

5 Travis Taijeron's single in the ninth beats the Braves 4-3 on September 26. His single to left off A.J. Minter scores Juan Lagares with the winning run in a game the Mets trailed 3-0 entering the seventh.

2018

OPENING DAY LINEUP

Brandon Nimmo, CF
Yoenis Cespedes, LF
Jay Bruce, RF
Asdrubal Cabrera, 2B
Todd Frazier, 3B
Adrian Gonzalez, 1B
Kevin Plawecki, C
Noah Syndergaard, P
Amed Rosario, SS

	W	L	GB	Pos
	77	85	13.0	4th
RS/G	RA/G	Manager		
4.17	4.36	Mickey Callaway		

Mets' Limp Bats Let Down Great Arms

The Moves

After seven years of Terry Collins in the dugout, the Mets hired Indians pitching coach Mickey Callaway. The new manager spoke about how he would care for his players when he was introduced.

"We're going to care more about the players than anyone ever has before, and let them know they're human beings and individuals," he said. "This is going to be a group that feels that every day they come to the clubhouse. And that's going to be our main concern – is to show them that we know this game is difficult and we're going to care about you as a player, a human being and in your personal life."

The 42-year-old helped Cleveland's pitching staff and helped Corey Kluber develop into a Cy Young winner. It would be up to Callaway to restore the talented Mets rotation.

The team signed reliever Anthony Swarzak, who posted a 2.33 ERA with the White Sox and Brewers in 2017. Jay Bruce returned, signing a three year, $39 million deal. He hit 36 homers with 101 RBI with the Mets and Indians in 2017. Veteran first baseman Adrian Gonzalez, a five-time All-Star, was signed as protection for young Dom Smith at first.

Todd Frazier went from the Yankees to the Mets, signing a two year, $17 million deal. He hit .213 with 27 homers with the White Sox and Yankees in 2017. He was a two-time All-Star with the Reds and hit 40 homers in 2016

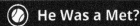 He Was a Met?

A six-time All-Star with the Blue Jays, the Mets acquired Jose Bautista though he hit .143 in 12 games with the Braves. He batted .204 with nine home runs in 37 games before being traded to the Phillies in late August.

In his first six seasons, Jacob deGrom won two Cy Young awards, was 2014 Rookie of the Year and a three-time All-Star. In 2018, he led the league with a 1.70 ERA and in 2019 he led the league with 255 strikeouts and a remarkable 0.4 HR/9IP. (Flickr photo)

with the White Sox. Jason Vargas returned to the Mets, signing a two-year deal. The southpaw led the AL with 18 wins in 2017 and made the All-Star team.

The Situation

The Mets would begin the season with a rotation of Noah Syndergaard, Jacob deGrom, Steven Matz, Matt Harvey and Seth Lugo. Vargas, considered an innings eater, was on the DL to begin the season, suffering a fracture of the hamate bone in his right hand. It looked like Zack Wheeler would be in the rotation but he was sent to Triple-A after struggling with an 8.10 ERA in spring training. Lugo secured the fifth starter spot, with a 2.87 ERA in 15.2 innings.

But early in the season bad weather meant skipping a Harvey start and Lugo was moved to the bullpen with Wheeler returning. Encouraged by Harvey's spring was new pitching coach Dave Eiland. "Matt Harvey was nails from Day One. Focused, working diligent, and just progressing right the way we hoped he would."

Could the Mets pitching bounce back? *Sports Illustrated*'s Tom Verducci and Ben Reiter both picked the Mets to make the postseason as a wild card.

The Season

Under Callaway, the Mets got off to the best start in team history, winning 11 of the first 12, including a nine-game winning streak. The stretch included sweeps of the Phillies, Nationals and Marlins. Every move Callaway was making was working. Trailing 1-0 in the eighth inning to the Marlins on April 11, he sent up Gonzalez to face lefty Chris O'Grady and Gonzalez responded with a go-ahead two-run single.

"In my six years in the major leagues, this is the best team I've ever been on," Cespedes said. "We've been showing it, and we will keep proving it."

Ray Ramirez was gone as trainer though the injuries would return. Swarzak strained his left oblique and would be gone for two months. Travis d'Arnaud was

 Final Resting Ground

Adrian Gonzalez's sweet swing had turned sour by the time he landed with the Mets. Gonzalez hit just 6 homers in 54 games and batted .237 before being released. Pete Alonso belting 36 homers and 119 in the minors, made the Mets' interest in Gonzalez that much more bizarre.

lost for the season with a partially torn ulnar collateral ligament in his right elbow. Kevin Plawecki was gone for a month and a half with a broken left hand.

When Wilmer Flores homered in the bottom of the ninth to beat the Brewers 3-2, it improved the Mets to 12-2. The next night the Mets had deGrom on the mound and a 6-1 lead against the Nationals in the eighth inning. DeGrom left with two on and one out. Jerry Blevins, AJ Ramos and Jeurys Familia combined to blow the lead. Hansel Robles gave up a homer in the ninth to make it 8-6. Michael Conforto came up as the tying run in the bottom of the ninth but Asdrubal Cabrera was inexplicably thrown out trying to get to third on a ball that bounced away from the catcher.

Harvey was struggling, falling to 0-2 with an ERA of six after giving up six runs in six innings in a loss to the Braves. He was demoted to the bullpen. "On a scale of 1 to 10, I'm obviously a 10 of being pissed off," Harvey said. "But my performance hasn't been there. I just have to do whatever I have to do to get back in the starting rotation, and that's right now to go to the bullpen and work on some things."

New York suffered more late heartbreaks. DeGrom pitched seven shutout innings in Atlanta on April 21 and the Mets scored three times in the eighth to take the lead. Blevins gave up a two-run double in the eighth and Familia gave up two runs in the bottom of the ninth. On the 26th, the Mets were one out away from an 11-inning win in St. Louis when Familia blew the lead. Paul Sewald gave up the game-ending single in the 13th. It was three blown saves in five chances for the closer. Still, the Mets were in first.

Vargas made his first start of the season, giving up nine runs in 3.2 innings. The Mets did end the month with a 14-2 laugher over the Padres. Harvey pitched a scoreless ninth. It was reported that he had been seen partying in Los Angeles the night before an appearance in San Diego.

Alderson was asked if he was upset. "Usually, I get upset if the report is unexpected," the general manager said. "I guess the short answer is no."

May began with the Mets getting swept at home by the Braves with the offense being blanked in two straight games. On May 3, Vargas gave up six runs on 11 hits in 4.2 innings. Then Harvey entered. He gave up five runs in two innings. A three-run homer off the bat off Ozzie Albies was the big blow. Ronald Acuna followed with a single and Callaway came out to get Harvey.

"This is just a little blip in the road ... again," Callaway said. "He's got a ways to go. What we can't do is give up on anybody." The team wanted to send Harvey Triple-A. Harvey refused. The Mets designated him for assignment.

FABULOUS: JACOB DEGROM

Suffering from historically bad run support, DeGrom won only 10 games on the season, but his ERA of 1.70 led the league, and he allowed only 10 HR in 217 IP while fanning 269. deGrom won the first of 2 consecutive Cy Young Awards.

Meanwhile, the Mets were swept by Colorado and then went on the road to Cincinnati. On May 8, Harvey was traded to the Reds for catcher Devin Mesoraco. Mesoraco was an All-Star in 2014 but his career was sidetracked by injuries. Still, he was an upgrade over Jose Lobaton and Tomas Nido, who were batting .154 and .135, respectively. It was the end of an era. Harvey, once considered the cornerstone of the franchise, had gone 34-37 as a Met.

While in Cincinnati, Frazier had to go on the DL with a strained hamstring and would be gone for a month. Things got weird on May 9, when Cabrera doubled with two outs in the first and Bruce came to the plate. Reds manager Jim Riggleman noticed that the lineup card had Cabrera batting second and Flores third but they hit out of order. Bruce was charged with an out to end the inning. The Mets lost 2-1 in the 10th when Adam Duvall homered off Ramos. "It's frustrating," Callaway said of the lineup blunder. "It probably cost us the game." And Robles went on the DL with a strained right knee.

The offense was struggling, scoring two runs or fewer in seven of nine games. Cabrera was hitting .319 but the rest of the offense was slumping. Conforto was batting .191. Rosario and Cespedes were under .250. Bruce was hitting .233 and Flores was hitting .221. Reyes was batting .122.

Cespedes, who hit eight homers, was placed on the DL with a strained right hip after playing through pain for more than a week. During a 12-1 loss to the Blue Jays, Lagares hurt his toe when he ran into the wall to make a catch. Lagares, who was batting .300, was done for the season.

New York won four straight to improve to 24-19. The Marlins, always seemingly a thorn in the Mets side, beat New York 5-1 on May 22. The next night, Familia blew another save and the Mets lost 2-1. The team went to Milwaukee and lost three of four. One loss ended with Ramos walking Travis Shaw with the bases loaded. The Mets gave up 17 runs in another loss, with Vargas, Jacob Rhame, Ramos and Chris Flexen all getting hit hard. An 8-7 loss ended the series. And the injuries continued. Syndergaard was on the DL with a strained ligament in his right index finger and would be out for a month-and-a-half. Ramos tore his labrum and was done for the season. Flores went on the DL with lower back soreness. Struggling for offense, the team signed 37-year-old slugger Jose Bautista, who had been released by the Braes after batting .143 in 12 games.

The Mets split a four-game series in Atlanta but lost two games on walk-offs. On May 28, deGrom left with a 2-1 lead but Lugo, who had pitched 17 straight scoreless innings, allowed the tying run to score. Mesoraco's homer in the ninth gave the Mets a 3-2 lead but Lugo gave up a two-run homer to Charlie

Culberson in the bottom of the ninth with Familia watching from the bullpen. The Mets were a .500 team for the first time. "Right now, the way things have been going, I feel OK that we're 25-25, tell you the truth," Callaway said. "That is how bad it's been going."

FUTILE: JOSE REYES

Reyes inexplicably made it into 110 games despite batting .189 and having limited range in the field. He drove in 16 runs, scored a mere 30, and stole only 5 bases.

On May 29, the Met led 6-2 in the seventh and 6-3 in the eighth but Rhame blew the lead and Gerson Bautista gave up a walk-off home run to Johan Camargo in the bottom of the ninth. The month ended with a home loss to the Cubs and the Mets ended May 27-27.

The Mets dropped the first three games of the month to the Cubs. Met pitching struck out Cubs batters 24 times in a Saturday night game but the Cubs won 7-1 in 14 innings, beating Buddy Baumann and Bautista in the final inning. The next day, the Mets lost 2-0 in a game that saw Javier Baez steal home when Matz stepped off and threw to first.

It looked like the Mets at least caught a break when the 17-41 Orioles came to town. Instead Baltimore won both games, 2-1 and 1-0. It was Familia who gave up the losing run in the second game. Struggles at the plate were team-wide, including an 0-for-18 stretch by Frazier and 0-for-16 skid by Cabrera. Gonzalez was soon let go after batting .237 with six homers in 54 games.

The Yankees came to Queens and won the first two games, extending the Mets losing streak to eight games. The Mets gave up an early 3-0 lead on June 9 and Aaron Judge hit a go-ahead homer off Swarzak, in his second game back off the DL. Behind Lugo, the Mets beat the Yankees on Sunday night. But then the Mets lost four straight.

DeGrom was a hard-luck loser in Atlanta, giving up one run in seven innings in a 2-0 loss. The ace was 4-2 with a 1.55 ERA on the season. Somehow, he had an ERA of 0.87 over his last 10 starts and the Mets had lost eight of them. He became the first pitcher since Randy Johnson in 1999 to make five straight starts of at least seven innings and giving up two earned runs or less only to see his team lose each one.

The Mets did win deGrom's next start, a 12-2 beatdown of the Rockies in Colorado to push a winning streak to three games. Bruce dealt with a hip strain, sat for three days and then played before being scratched from the lineup and put on the DL. The the team lost seven in a row.

Back in Queens, the Dodgers swept a weekend series. In the final game, Jerry Blevins made an emergency start and gave up homers to the first two batters he faced. Plawecki tied the game with a three-run homer in the eighth but Flexen gave up an 11th inning homer to Justin Turner. It was the seventh home run of the day for Los Angeles and the Mets fell 8-7. Alderson announced he was taking a leave of absence to address a recurrence of cancer.

TOP BATTERS										
Pos	Name	G	AB	H	BA	HR	RBI	RS	SB	OPS
1B	Wilmer Flores	126	386	103	.267	11	51	43	0	.736
2B	Asdrubal Cabrera	98	375	104	.277	18	58	48	0	.817
SS	Amed Rosario	154	554	142	.256	9	51	76	24	.676
LF	Michael Conforto	153	543	132	.243	28	82	78	3	.797
OF	Brandon Nimmo	140	433	114	.263	17	47	77	9	.886

TOP PITCHERS										
Pos	Name	G	GS	W	L	SV	ERA	IP	SO	BB
SP	Jacob deGrom	32	32	10	9	0	1.70	217.0	269	46
SP	Zack Wheeler	29	29	12	7	0	3.31	182.1	179	55
SP	Noah Syndergaard	25	25	13	4	0	3.03	154.1	155	39
RP	Seth Lugo	54	5	3	4	3	2.66	101.1	103	28
RP	Robert Gsellman	68	0	6	3	13	4.28	80.0	70	28

The Mets lost two of three to the Pirates. In the rubber game, Wheeler pitched seven shutout innings but was removed after 105 pitches. Robert Gsellman gave up a run in the eighth but the Mets still entered the ninth up 3-1. Familia pitched to four batters, retired none and left with the lead cut to 3-2 and the bases loaded. Swarzak came in and allowed all three inherited runners to score. Callaway was annoyed with a reporter who asked why Swarzak wasn't warming up sooner. "How it works in baseball in the ninth inning, or in any inning, you get a guy going and they call down when they're ready," he said. "So we know that they're ready when they go in."

The month ended with a pair of losses in Miami. Corey Oswalt couldn't make it out of the third inning, giving up six runs. DeGrom lost the next day, falling to 5-4 with a 1.84 ERA. Both times it was against a Marlin making his first start in the majors. The Mets finished the month 5-21, the worst June in team history. They went from 10 games over .500 to 15 under at an earlier date than any team in history.

With half the schedule still remaining, the season was virtually over. The team would play better, going 12-12 in July and 15-15 in August. There were still puzzling moves. Amed Rosario was improving at the plate but the team benched him instead of having him face Max Scherzer despite being six for his last 13 with two doubles and two triples. For some reason, the team kept giving Reyes starts despite batting under .170.

Cespedes returned to the lineup on July 20 and homered in a win at Yankee Stadium. But it was his final game of the season as he dropped a bombshell, saying he needed to have surgery on both heels. Callaway was asked by SNY's Steve Gelbs about Cespedes' comments that he had duel heel calcifications, with an expected eight- to ten-month recovery period. "I didn't get to read any of the stuff he said or hear it," Callaway said. "I'm not quite exactly sure what he said." A Mets official later said Callaway misspoke.

The team traded Familia to the A's and Cabrera to the Phillies.

Reyes would get to pitch in a game on July 31 as the Mets trailed 19-1 heading into the bottom of the eighth in Washington, in a game Matz failed to record three outs. Matz would go on the DL with a strain in his left forearm. Reyes gave up six runs as the Mets fell behind 25-1 before scoring three in the ninth.

DeGrom was still getting no help from the offense. He drove in the only run in a 2-1 loss to the Braves on august 3, falling to 5-7 with a 1.85 ERA. The Mets scored eight runs in the last 51 innings he pitched in his last seven starts. He was 0-5 during the stretch with a 2.47 ERA.

The Mets would score 40 runs in two games. On August 15, they beat the Orioles 16-5. The next day, in the first game of a doubleheader, the Mets won 24-4. No team had scored 24 runs and allowed 24 in a game in the same season since 1894. The 24 runs and 25 hits set franchise records. DeGrom even won three straight starts, improving to 8-7 and lowering his ERA to 1.71.

McNeil was off to a hot start after being called up and Austin Jackson provided a stable bat in the outfield. The struggling offense even saw Frazier leading off.

The Mets won 10 of 13 to begin September, which included Syndergaard winning three straight starts. The Mets also won 10 of 13 to end the month. DeGrom finished his dominating season winning his final two starts to improve to 10-9. Eight shutout innings against the Braves in his final start lowered his ERA to 1.70. However, the Mets went 14-18 in his starts.

David Wright, who hadn't played since May 27, 2016, announced his retirement effective at the end of the season after trying to fight through neck and shoulder pain.

On September 28, he pinch-hit in a loss to the Marlins, grounding out to third against Jose Urena. The next night, he played third base for the final time and went 0-1 with a walk before being taken out in the top of the fifth to a standing ovation.

Top 5 Highlights

1 Jose Bautista's grand slam in the bottom of the ninth off Chaz Roe gives the Mets a 5-1 win over Tampa Bay on June 6. With two outs and runners on second and third, the Rays intentionally walked Brandon Nimmo to get to Bautista.

2 After replay shows he wasn't hit by a pitch, Wilmer Flores hits a 10th inning homer of Victor Arano to beat the Phillies 4-3 on July 9. The blast gives him a franchise-best 10 walk-off RBI and his four game-ending homers tie Mike Piazza, Cleon Jones, Chris Jones and Kevin McReynolds for the club record.

3 Brandon Nimmo hits a pinch-hit, three-run home run off Mark Leiter Jr. in the bottom of the 11th to give the Mets a 3-0 win on July 11. DeGrom pitched eight shutout innings to lower his ERA to 1.68.

4 The Mets score a team-record 24 wins in a 24-4 thumping of the Phillies on August 16. Bautista, who didn't start the game, still goes 3-4 with seven RBI, including a fifth inning grand slam off Leiter Jr. Amed Rosario goes 4-7 with three RBI, including a leadoff homer. Jerry Blevins even singled for the first hit in the 12th season of his career. New York scored 16 runs the night before in a win in Baltimore.

5 Michael Conforto and Todd Frazier hit back-to-back home runs to stun the Marlins in a 4-3 win on September 13. Down 3-2 with two outs Conforto ties the game with a blast to right off Kyle Barraclough. Frazier then homered off left-center to end the game.

2019

	W	L	GB	Pos
	86	76	11.0	3rd
RS/G	RA/G		Manager	
4.88	4.55		Mickey Callaway	

Alonso and McNeill Shine, Pen Implodes

The Moves

The Mets had a new general manager. In a surprise hire it was Brodie Van Wagenen, who never worked in a front office but did have plenty of negotiating experience as a player agent for nearly two decades. In fact, he was Jacob deGrom's agent. The co-head of the baseball division at Creative Artists Agency, he had accused MLB owners of collusion and later said the Mets should sign deGrom to a long-term contract or trade him. Now he was in the front office. Just days before the start of the regular season, deGrom signed a five-year, $137.5 million contract extension.

Van Wagenen made a splash, sending Jay Bruce and prospects to the Mariners for closer Edwin Diaz and second baseman Robinson Cano. Diaz closed 57 games in 2018. Cano was an eight-time All-Star, including five times with the Yankees, but only played 80 games in 2018 because of a suspension due to PED use. "This trade should be a signal to our players and our fans that words alone will not define this franchise," Van Wagenen said.

Jeurys Familia returned, signing a three-year, $30 million deal to be a set-up man for Diaz. Lefty reliever Justin Wilson was also signed. The team signed All-Star catcher Wilson Ramos to a two-year deal. Ramos hit .306 with 15 home runs with the Rays and Phillies in 2018. J.D. Davis was acquired from Houston. The move didn't receive a lot of attention but Davis would turn into one of the big contributors. Van Wagenen signed Jed Lowrie a former All-Star and client to a two-year deal, though it created somewhat of a logjam in the infield.

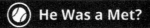

He Was a Met?

St. John's product Joe Panik returned to Queens, batting .277 with two homers in 39 games. Panik signed with Blue Jays for the 2020 season.

Pete Alonso set a rookie record with 53 home runs in 2019. The first baseman shattered the previous Met record of 41 homers in a season. Alonso his 36 and drove in 119 in the minors the year before, but the Mets chose to go with a washed-up Adrian Gonzalez and struggling Dominic Smith at first base instead. (Flickr photo)

The Situation

First baseman Pete Alonso hit .352 with four home runs in spring training and the Mets put him on the Opening Day roster instead of putting him in the minors at the start of the season in order to get an extra year of team control.

The Mets picked Travis d'Arnaud to back up Ramos behind the plate. Devin Mesoraco, a favorite of deGrom's, was reassigned to minor league camp. He asked for the team to release him and threatened retirement instead. Lowrie suffered a knee sprain and went on the Injured List. He would go hitless in seven September at-bats.

New York looked improved but was in a tough division. The Braves were defending NL East champs. Washington had young talent and veteran pitching. Philadelphia added Bryce Harper, Andrew McCutchen, Jean Segura, J.T. Realmuto and David Robertson.

The Season

New York took two of three in Washington and then swept the Marlins to open the season 5-1. It would be an up-and-down month. There was an extra-inning win in Philadelphia followed by Steven Matz giving up eight runs without recording an out the next night. But Matz beat the Phillies in his next start and the Brewers in the start after that. Zack Wheeler gave up seven runs in 4.2 innings in one start and pitched seven shutout innings in another. After winning his first two starts, deGrom lost three in a row and saw his ERA rise to 4.85. McNeil was batting .370 and Alonso hit nine home runs. But d'Arnaud was batting .087 and was designated for assignment with Tomas Nido being called up. D'Arnaud would go to Tampa Bay and thrive, especially in July when he hit .342 with eight home runs and 25 RBI.

Diaz had eight saves and an 0.84 ERA in his first 12 outings. On April29, he entered in a tie game and gave up a ninth inning homer in a loss to the Reds. The same thing happened two days later. The Mets were swept in Milwaukee, including an 18-inning loss with Chris Flexen giving up a pair of runs after the Mets finally took the lead in the 18th. The team lost two of three in San Diego, with the Mets again giving deGrom no run support.

FABULOUS: PETE ALONSO

Alonso broke the record for most home runs in a season by a Met and then set the major league rookie record, surpassing the inflated Mark McGwire, finishing with a whopping 53, many of which were tape measure blasts. He went deep 11 times in September.

At 17-20, rumors were already spreading about Mickey Callaway's job security. Jeff Wilpon had a 90-minute meeting with Callaway and Van Wagenen. The Mets won three straight but then lost a pair of games in Washington. On May 16, Michael Conforto hit his ninth homer and then had to leave the game with a concussion suffered in a collision with Cano. Down 7-6 with two outs in the ninth, Keon Broxton, who replaced Conforto, came up with two outs and the bases loaded. He struck out. Broxton had also struck out to end a game with the bases loaded weeks earlier in Philadelphia. After the loss in Washington, Broxton, who was batting .143, questioned why he wasn't getting more playing time. He was designated for assignment the next day.

The Mets traveled to Miami to take on the 10-31 Marlins. The Mets were swept, getting blanked in two straight games. McNeil's leadoff double was the only hit in a 2-0 loss. The next day, the team was two-hit. The team also announced Yoenis Cespedes fractured his right ankle on his ranch, ending his hopes of playing in 2019.

A struggling Cano was under the microscope, especially after failing to hustle twice against the Marlins. "He understands that it's not acceptable to not run balls out," Callaway said, benching Cano in the first game of a series against Washington. Back in the lineup, Cano ran out a routine grounder to short, injured his quad and went on the IL. New York did sweep the Nationals in four straight at Citi Field. There were unlikely heroes. Rajai Davis hit a three-run homer. Carlos Gomez hit his first homer with the Mets since 2007, a go-ahead three-run shot to put the Mets up 6-4 in the final game of the sweep. The Mets took two of three from Detroit. Adeiny Hechavarria, who was called up with Dom Smith surprisingly demoted, hit three homers in four games.

Looking to get back over .500, the 27-27 Mets held an 8-3 lead against the Dodgers, with Alonso hitting two homers, giving him 19. Diaz entered with an 8-5 lead but gave up four runs in the ninth. Three games later, the Mets blew a 5-1 eighth inning lead in Arizona and lost in extras. It was the ninth blown lead by the bullpen in 13 games. Familia's ERA was over 6.50. Looking to get back to .500, the Diaz blew a two-run lead against the Cardinals on June 13 and lost in the 10th.

A loss in Atlanta dropped the fourth-place Mets to 35-39. Pitching coach Dave Eiland and bullpen coach Chuck Hernandez were fired. The staff had a 4.67 ERA and 16 blown saves. Familia was on the IL with a shoulder problem. Syndergaard's ERA was 4.55. Matz would briefly be sent to the bullpen. Phil Regan, 82, was the new pitching coach.

TOP BATTERS

Pos	Name	G	AB	H	BA	HR	RBI	RS	SB	OPS
C	Wilson Ramos	141	473	136	.288	14	73	52	1	.768
1B	Pete Alonso	161	597	155	.260	53	120	103	1	.941
LF	J. D. Davis	140	410	126	.307	22	57	65	3	.895
RF	Michael Conforto	151	549	141	.257	33	92	90	7	.856
UT	Jeff McNeil	133	510	162	.318	23	75	83	5	.916

TOP PITCHERS

Pos	Name	G	GS	W	L	SV	ERA	IP	SO	BB
SP	Jacob deGrom	32	32	11	8	0	2.43	204.0	255	44
SP	Noah Syndergaard	32	32	10	8	0	4.28	197.2	202	50
SP	Zack Wheeler	31	31	11	8	0	3.96	195.1	195	50
SP	Steven Matz	32	30	11	10	0	4.21	160.1	153	52
RP	Seth Lugo	61	0	7	4	6	2.70	80.0	104	16

On June 23, Seth Lugo gave up a go-ahead three-run homer in the eighth to Chicago's Javier Baez in a 5-3 loss. After the game, Callaway and Jason Vargas had words with a Newsday reporter, who said, "See you tomorrow, Mickey," with the manager replying "Don't be a smart-ass." Vargas threatened to knock out the reporter.

The Mets went to Philadelphia and lost four straight. Jay Bruce delivered a walk-off hit after the Mets blew a 4-0 lead. In the finale, the Mets trailed 1-0 entering the ninth but Todd Frazier hit a two-run homer and New York added an insurance run. In the bottom of the ninth, Diaz gave up a game-tying homer to Maikel Franco and then a three-run homer to Jean Segura. The Mets' bullpen ERA in June was just under eight. The Mets went into the All-Star break with a 40-50 record. Alonso had 30 home runs at the break and won the Home Run Derby. McNeil was batting .349. DeGrom made the All-Star team with a 4-7 record.

A series in San Francisco saw the Giants win three games on walk-offs, including one in 16 innings. Cano hit three homers in a win over San Diego but a loss at home the next day to the Padres dropped the Mets to 46-55, tied for the second-worst record in the National League. Then the Mets, seemingly out of nowhere, won 15 of 16. It was the best stretch for the team since 1990. The team swept the Pirates and White Sox. Vargas was traded to the Phillies and the team acquired All-Star starter Marcus Stroman from the Blue Jays. Stroman only won one of his first seven starts. Van Wagenen didn't part with Syndergaard, Wheeler or Todd Frazier. The Mets were in a playoff race. Ramos had four hits and six RBI in a win against the Pirates.

FUTILE: Edwin Diaz, Jeurys Familia

Diaz and Famila both appeared in 66 games. Familia had a 5.70 ERA. Diaz was slightly better, with a 5.59 ERA, but Diaz allowed a mind-boggling 15 home runs and he blew 7 saves as the bullpen cost the Mets a playoff berth.

The Mets got back over .500 with a 5-4 win over the Marlins on August 5. Davis, Conforto and Alonso homered in the seventh inning of the win, the second of a four-game sweep. The Nationals came to town and the Mets delivered late-inning heroics. Conforto's hit won a game after Frazier tied it with a three-run homer. Luis Guillorme, with a career .192 average, tied the next night's game with an eighth inning homer, the first of his career, and the Mets went on to win 4-3. The team was only a half-game out of a playoff spot. New York couldn't finish a sweep as the Nationals beat deGrom in the finale.

On August 14, Matz threw 79 pitches in six innings and singled in the top of the seventh. However, Callaway brought in Lugo to start the seventh and Atlanta scored five runs. "I'll make that move 100 times out of 100, that's the right move in my mind," Callaway said. A five-game winning streak, including a sweep of the Indians, put the Mets at 67-60, 1.5 games out of a playoff spot with the Braves and Cubs coming to Citi Field for crucial series.

In the first game against Atlanta, deGrom, who won four straight decisions, fanned 13 Braves and even homered but that was all the offense the Mets would get. The Braves won in 14. Then Atlanta won the next two to complete a sweep. The Cubs also swept the Mets. Syndergaard gave up 10 runs (nine earned) in three innings of a 10-7 loss. The only positive of the week was that Alonso tied and set the team record for homers in a single season. But the Mets were 67-66 with the season slipping away. "Things have snowballed," Callaway said. "Six in a row, that's a big snowball."

New York won three of four and had deGrom on the mound in Washington on September 3. DeGrom pitched seven innings and Lugo pitched a scoreless eighth as the Mets entered the bottom of the ninth with a 10-4 lead. It was 10-6 when Paul Sewald was taken out. Luis Avilan gave up a single to the one batter he faced as Callaway called on Diaz. Ryan Zimmerman's double made it 10-8. Kurt Suzuki's three-run homer gave the Nationals an 11-10 win. "Definitely hard to wrap your head around," Brandon Nimmo said. "Coming back from [six] runs down in the bottom of the ninth against guys throwing 99 mph, I don't have words for that." Teams leading by six or more entering the bottom of the ninth had been 274-0. "You have a six-run lead, major league pitchers have got to be able to hold that," Callaway said.

Syndergaard was voicing his displeasure with Ramos being behind the plate for his starts. He reportedly confronted Callaway and had a sit-down with Van Wagenen over the situation. Syndergaard had thrown seven shutout innings to Rene Rivera but found himself working with Ramos. Ramos' 26-game hitting streak kept him in the lineup. "You can't make everybody happy and it's not about making guys happy," Callaway said. "It's about winning at this point."

The team didn't go away quietly, sweeping four straight from Arizona to hang around the playoff race. A three-run double by Davis beat the Dodgers. But on September 15, the Dodgers dealt a blow to the Mets' wild card chances. Wheeler, who had a 1.85 ERA in September, gave up one run in seven innings. LA tied the game against Wilson in the eighth and scored off Lugo in the ninth. The Mets dropped four games out of the second wild card with 13 left to play.

The team won nine of 13 to end the season but didn't get enough help from other contenders to make the postseason. The good news was deGrom padded his resume, winning his second straight Cy Young and Alonso broke Aaron Judge's rookie home run record, hitting 53.

Callaway was fired and the Mets hired Carlos Beltran. Zack Wheeler signed a $118 million deal with the division rival Phillies. The Mets signed veteran pitchers Michael Wacha and Rick Porcello. And the Mets signed four-time Yankee All-Star Dellin Betances to improve the pen.

When Beltran's connection to the Astros sign-stealing scandal in 2017 was revealed, the Mets ousted him and hired Luis Rojas. Rojas, a son of Felipe Alou, spent more than a decade in the team's system and was on the major league staff in 2019.

Top 5 Highlights

1. Jacob deGrom pitches six shutout innings in a 2-0 Opening Day win over Max Scherzer and the Nationals. Robinson Cano homers in his first at-bat and later adds an RBI single off Matt Grace.

2. Tomas Nido's 13th inning homer off Buck Farmer gives the Mets a 5-4 win over the Tigers on May 25. Wilson Ramos went 3-4 with two homers and four RBI.

3. Michael Conforto's walk-off single off Sean Doolittle beats the Nationals 7-6 on August 9 for the Mets' seventh straight win. Todd Frazier's three-run homer tied the game earlier in the inning. The Mets trailed 3-0 in the fourth before Pete Alonso and J.D. Davis hit back-to-back homers off Stephen Strasburg to tie the game.

4. Pete Alonso breaks the rookie home run record, hitting his 53rd of the season off Atlanta's Mike Foltnewicz in the third inning of New York's 3-0 win on September 28.

5. Dom Smith ends the season with a three-run home run with two outs in the bottom of the 11th to beat the Braves 7-6. Joe Panik's eighth-inning homer gave the Mets a 4-3 lead but Hechavarria tied the game in the ninth with a homer. In the top of the 11th, Hechavarria and Adam Duvall hit back-to-back homers to put Atlanta on top.

Mets Quiz Answers

Mets All Time

1. Ed Kranepool, who also appeared in the most games by far, 1853, which is 278 more than runner up David Wright in that category. Only 10 players in the team's history have played in 1000 games or more.
2. Mike Piazza, with 6. Piazza also hit 8 for the Dodgers, giving him 14 in his career, including 3 for LA in one month in 1998.
3. John Olerud hit a scalding .354 for the Mets in 1998, his second year with the team. Olerud's OBA was .447 that season, also a team single-season record.
4. Casey Stengel, Yogi Berra, Joe Torre, and Dallas Green. All four had losing records at the helm of the Mets, though Berra came close to .500 at 292-296 (.497).
5. Gary Sheffield played his final season in the big leagues with the Mets in 2009, connecting on 10 home runs in 268 at bats. His first homer of the season was #500.
6. True. The single-season high in innings pitched for a Mets hurler is 290.2, by Tom Seaver in 1970.
7. Jerry Grote, with 1176.
8. Bobby Jones's masterpiece in Game 4 of the NLDS against the San Francisco put the Mets into the NLCS. Jones made one start in both the NLCS and World Series and allowed a total of 9 runs in 9 IP.
9. R. A. Dickey defeated the Rays 9-1 and Orioles 5-0 during his 2012 Cy Young Award season.
10. Lee Mazzilli hit a game-tying, pinch-hit home run in the 8th inning of the 1979 All-Star Game off reliever Jim Kern. The NL put up another run in the 9th to win 7-6.
11. Bobby Valentine was manager for both the 1999 and 2000 Mets.
12. Darryl Strawberry, 252; David Wright, 242; Mike Piazza, 220; Howard Johnson, 192. Dave Kingman is a distant fifth with 154.
13. Carlos Beltran achieved this feat between 2006 and 2008, with 116, 112, 112.
14. Tom Seaver set the team record for strikeouts in 1971 with 289, a mark that still stands nearly 50 years and numerous fireballing pitchers later.
15. Mike Piazza compiled the incredible streak between June 14, 2000 and July 2, 2000.
16. Roger McDowell went 14-9 in 1986 and added 22 saves, appearing in 75 games and totaling 128 IP.

17. David Cone, who went 20-3 for the Mets in 1988 and 10 years later 20-7 for the Yankees.
18. The Mets have reached the playoffs 9 times—one Wild Card defeat, three losses in the NLCS, and five appearances in the World Series, of which they won two.

1960s

1. Gil Hodges, in the 4th inning of the Mets' first game.
2. Jim Hickman on 9/3/65 vs the St Louis Cardinals. Hickman was also the first Mets player to hit for cycle, on 8/7/63, also vs the Cards.
3. Ed Kranepool was 17. He grounded out to second.
4. Stengel said Coleman was "the fastest catcher in the National League chasing passed balls."
5. Don Zimmer. Stengel broke the news to Zimmer this way. "One of us is going to Cincinnati."
6. Pete Rose, also a second baseman at the time, who collected 170 hits and scored 101 runs.
7. Carlton Willey who went 9-14, but had a fine ERA of 3.10.
8. Roy McMillan, who played in more than 2000 games in his career and compiled an excellent career defensive WAR of 21.7.
9. In 1960, Fisher gave up Ted Williams' home run in the Splinter's final major league at bat and the next year Roger Maris's 60th home run to tie Maris with Babe Ruth's single-season record.
10. Ron Hunt, who started at second base and went 1-for-3, with a single in his first at bat.
11. Goossen was a body double for Gene Hackman for many of Hackman's films of the 1980s and 1990s, and also had minor roles in a number of the films.
12. The Mets, with their 66 wins, finished 9.5 games ahead of the Chicago Cubs.
13. The Atlanta Braves signed Seaver after the college baseball season had begun, which was not allowed. Three teams were willing to equal Atlanta's signing bonus of $50,000, and the Mets' name was drawn randomly.
14. Jim McAndrew.
15. The Houston Astros defeated the Mets in 10 of their 12 match-ups, including wins in all six games played at the Astrodome.
16. Bud Harrelson, who played shortstop in 1969 and was third base coach in 1986.

1970s

1. Joe Foy, who had a sparkling rookie season in 1966 (15 HR, 97 RS), played on the Impossible Dream Red Sox in 1967, and a strong year for the expansion Kansas City Royals in 1969. To get Foy, the Mets traded the unproven Amos Otis, who proved to be one of the better players in the American League throughout the next decade.

2. Tom Seaver, Jerry Koosman, Nolan Ryan, Ray Sadecki, Dean Chance.
3. Tug McGraw, who also went 8-6, 1.70, 106 IP for the Mets in 1976 and achieved even greater fame later with the Philadelphia Phillies.
4. Willie Mays, who became a more selective batter as his hitting skills declined, came to the plate nearly 250 times for the Mets in 1972 and batted .262 with 43 BB, good for a .402 OBA.
5. Bob Apodaca, whose best year of his 5-year career came in 1975 when he had a microscopic ERA of 1.49 in 84.2 IP.
6. Don Hahn, who went 7-for-29 in the series with a double, triple, and 2 RBI. After playing somewhat regularly for the Mets in 1974, Hahn appeared in only 50 more games in 1975 for two other teams and was out of baseball.
7. George "The Stork" Theodore.
8. Randy Tate. Tate drew only one BB in his 47 plate appearance, but reaching first base must have made him giddy as he also has a caught stealing on his ledger.
9. Joe Frazier, who never managed again in the major leagues.
10. Rusty Staub, who drove in 105 and scored 93 for the 1975 Mets.
11. Mickey Lolich, who was obtained in a trade with the Tigers for Rusty Staub. After 1976, Lolich pitched only 84 more innings in his career (for the Padres), while Staub had 2 100+ RBI seasons in Detroit and made his way back to the Mets where he spent the last 5 years as part-time player and pinch hitter extraordinaire.
12. Koosman went 21-10 in 1976 and followed that up with an 8-20 in '77. After an extremely tough-luck 3-15 for New York in 1978, he was dealt to Minnesota where he bounced back with another 20-win season.
13. Lenny Randle swiped 33 bags for the Mets in 1977 and teammate Lee Mazzilli had 22 steals, but he was caught 15 times, another very poor ratio.
14. Craig Swan, who had another strong season in 1978, winning a career-high 14 games and posting a solid ERA of 3.29 in more than 250 IP.
15. Elliott Maddox played for 5 American League teams over 8 seasons before winding up his career with 3 seasons with the Mets.
16. Mike Scott, who the Mets gave up on after 4 seasons and traded him to Houston straight up for Danny Heep. Scott won 15 games in his his first two years with the Astros (giving him 29 in 6 big league seasons) before blossoming and winning 86 in the next 5.

1980s

1. Frank Taveras, who the Mets allowed to bat nearly 1400 times between 1979 and 1980. Taveras also had error totals at shortstop of 25, 25, and 24 (in 79 games), putting him well below average among shortstops in fielding percentage, runs saved, and range factor.
2. Hubie Brooks, who hit .307 in strike-shortened 1981, after batting .309 in 24 games and 81 at bats the season before.

3. Mike Marshall (1974 LAD), Randy Jones (1976 SDP), Mike Scott (1986 HOU).
4. Dave Kingman, who belted 37. Kingman's batting average was, incredibly, .204 for the season, and he hit just 9 doubles. In 1979 Kingman led the NL with 48 dingers for the Chicago Cubs, batting .288 with a league-leading SA of .613.
5. Bruce Bochy, who led the Padres to the postseason four times and did the same with the Giants, who won three World Series with Bochy at the helm.
6. Jesse Orosco, who was obtained by New York in the deal that involved Jerry Koosman.
7. The Milwaukee Brewers.
8. Frank Howard, who was interim manager after Bamberger was let go in 1983 after a 16-30 start.
9. Mike Torrez, who went 10-17 that year and was a disastrous 11-22 in his 1+ season with the Mets.
10. Calvin Schiraldi. Schiraldi was fantastic for the Red Sox during the 1986 season in limited action (1.41 ERA, 25 App, 50 IP), but melted down on the biggest stage, taking two losses in the World Series with an ERA of 13.50.
11. Kelvin Chapman.
12. Jesse Orosco, who also saved two games in the World Series that followed.
13. Marty Barrett was 13-for-30 in the Series (.433), though somehow he scored only one run. Barrett was also 11-for-30 that year in the ALCS against the Angels, which also led both teams and earned him MVP of that series.
14. Ron Darling, who allowed 4 runs in 5 innings in his only start in the NLCS.
15. Gary Carter, who drove in 9, and also collected 8 hits, including 2 doubles and 2 homers.
16. John Gibbons, who never played again in the majors after 1986, and after 4 years in the minors, began coaching for the Mets organization and then others until his first managerial stint in 2005.
17. Gary Carter, in 1985. Carter had 2 seasons of 30+ HR, two more with 29, and a total of four 100+ RBI seasons, included 3 in a row from 1984-1986.
18. Terry Leach, who after leaving the Mets pitched for 3 AL teams before retiring after 1993 at age 39.
19. Kevin McReynolds, whose only 3 seasons with double-digit steals came between 1987-1989 for the Mets.

1990s

1. The Montreal Expos. Darling started 3 games for the Expos, going 0-2, with an ERA of 7.41.
2. Todd Hundley went deep on Opening in 1994, 1995, 1996, and 1997.
3. Wally Backman.

4. David Cone, who didn't get the 20th strikeout to tie the all-time record, but his 19 put him in a tie with Roger Clemens for the major league lead for the season.
5. Dwight Gooden (1985), David Cone (1994), and Bret Saberhagen (1985, 1989).
6. Kevin McReynolds, who hit a so-so .256 in the final year of his career, with only 4 home runs in 180 at bats.
7. Jeff Torborg was a catcher who finished with a career BA of .215 and an OPS+ of 57, while Dallas Green was a pitcher who finished 20-22 with a 4.26 ERA and an ERA+ of 88.
8. The San Francisco Giants, for whom he played for 3 seasons, before finishing up in 2006 with a handful of games with the Angels and Blue Jays.
9. Brian Bohanon.
10. Brian McRae, whose 21 HR and 79 RBI were career highs, as were his 80 BB and .822 OPS. Father Hal batted .290 in a long career, primarily as a DH, having his finest season at age 36 when he led the AL with 133 RBI and 46 2B and finished fourth in the MVP voting.
11. Preston Wilson, whose trade to the Marlins brought Mike Piazza to New York.
12. A.J. Burnett, who would go on to win 164 games in his career.
13. Lance Johnson, whose 227 in 1996 is still the team record.
14. Gooden played for 3 teams in 1996, the last of which was the New York Yankees, for whom he threw the only no-hitter of his career, against the powerful Seattle Mariners.
15. Greg McMichael, who lost one and saved one for Los Angeles during his brief stay.

2000s

1. Derek Bell, who hit 18 HR and had 69 RBI and 87 RS for the Mets – decent numbers, though only about average for the run-crazy environment of the 2000 season.
2. Glendon Rusch, Rick Reed, and Bobby Jones.
3. A walk-off home run by Benny Agbayani off Aaron Fultz.
4. John Franco, who pitched a scoreless top of the 8th before the Mets put across two in the bottom half.
5. Todd Zeile, though he only drove in one run and scored one run.
6. Robin Ventura and David Justice, though a week later Justice was traded by the Mets to Oakland for Mark Guthrie and Tyler Yates.
7. Zeile homered in the last at bat of his major league career. Zeile also played catcher that game—the position he broke into the majors playing—but until 2004 had not caught in a big league game since 1990.
8. Mike Cameron, who surpassed 20 HR seven other times in his career, but reached 30 only that one time.
9. Willie Randolph, who managed the Mets from 2005-2008, had a winning percentage of .544 (302-253).

10. The Philadelphia Phillies, who were swept in 3 games by the Colorado Rockies in the NLDS.
11. Marco Scutaro, who spent 5 seasons at the AAA level, the last two with the Mets, in which he hit .319 and .311, but got minimal playing time with the big club before they let him go.
12. Greg Maddux, who got a no-decision in the game, but compiled a record of 11-14 in the postseason, including 3-9 from the 1997 NLCS to the end of his career.
13. A 2-run home run by Yadier Molina in the top of the 9th off Aaron Heilman.
14. John Maine and Oliver Perez. The following year, they both won 10 games for the Mets.
15. Carlos Delgado drove home 9 in the first game of a Subway Series double header in which the Mets pummeled the Yankees 15-6. Delgado got all his RBI (a 2-run double, grand slam, and 3-run home run) from the fifth inning on.
16. The Baltimore Orioles, who had acquired Turner from Cincinnati. The Mets then picked up Turner on waivers before the 2010 season, but after he failed to excel over the next 3 seasons, was allowed to leave, signing a free agent contract with the Dodgers. Turner hit .340 in first year in LA and a star was born.

2010s

1. Pedro Feliciano, with 92 in 2010 (and 62.2 IP), the third consecutive year he led the NL in appearances.
2. Hisanori Takahashi, who came to the major leagues at age 35.
3. Edgardo Alfonzo, in 1999, and Wllmer Flores in 2016.
4. Jordany Valdespin, who as a rookie in 2012, hit 5 PH home runs in 42 at bats.
5. Brandon Nimmo was taken as the 13th selection in the 2011 draft and Michael Conforto went 10th overall in the 2014 draft.
6. Armando Benitez 2000, 2001; Billy Wagner, 2006; Jeurys Familia, 2015 and 2016.
7. John Buck.
8. Jacob DeGrom, who fanned 20 in 13 IP in winning Games 1 and 5.
9. Matt Harvey, Jacob DeGrom, Noah Syndergaard, Bartolo Colon.
10. Alex Gordon. It was one of only two home runs hit by Kansas City in the Series.
11. Curtis Granderson went deep 3 times in the series, in Games 1, 3, and 5.
12. Lucas Duda hit 27, one more than Curtis Granderson.
13. DeGrom was a shortstop for Stetson University in Florida, then a reliever, then becoming one of the team's best starters. He was drafted in the 9th round by the Mets.
14. Addison Reed.

15. Brandon Nimmo, with 22 in 2018. Hit-by-pitch artist Ron Hunt took 41 for the team in his 4 years with the Mets, not hitting his stride until two years removed from New York when he led the NL 7 years in a row, with nearly 200 HBPs during that stretch.
16. In a homer-happy season, Michael Conforto hit 33, Jeff McNeil hit 23, J. D. Davis hit 22, and Todd Frazier hit 21. McNeil hit 3 in 2018 and Davis hit 1.